Understanding Children's Spirituality

Understanding Children's Spirituality
Theology, Research, and Practice

edited by
Kevin E. Lawson

CASCADE *Books* · Eugene, Oregon

UNDERSTANDING CHILDREN'S SPIRITUALITY
Theology, Research, and Practice

Cascade Books
An Imprint of Wipf and Stock Publishers
199 W. 8th Ave., Suite 3
Eugene, OR 97401

www.wipfandstock.com

ISBN 13: 978-1-61097-525-4

Cataloging-in-Publication data:

Understanding children's spirituality : theology, research, and practice /
edited by Kevin E. Lawson.

xvi +438 p. ; 23 cm. —Includes bibliographical references.

ISBN 13: 978-1-61097-525-4

1. Children—Religious life. 2. Christian education of children. 3. Church
work with children. I. Lawson, Kevin E. II. Title.

BV 4571.3 .U55 2012

Manufactured in the U.S.A.

Contents

Contents

Acknowledgments

All publications, especially edited books, involve the efforts and contributions of many people. We would like to briefly acknowledge the various people who have helped shape this book and make it possible for it to come into your hands.

- The Board of the Society for Children's Spirituality: Christian Perspectives, for having the vision and being willing to work hard to put on the conference in 2009 where the papers and presentations that serve as the basis for the chapters of this book were first shared.

- Chris Boyatzis, a member of that Board, who first took the lead in identifying potential chapters for this book and recruiting several of the authors.

- Various members of the Board who assisted us with reviewing the chapters as they came in: Holly Allen, Chris Boyatzis, Lisa Long, Scottie May, and William Summey.

- Each of the authors who worked hard to craft their chapters, and responded graciously and patiently to the request for revisions that came from the review process.

- Nathan Lawson, for careful and thorough editing of the final submitted chapters.

- Christian Amondson, and the staff at Wipf & Stock, for their efforts to prepare, publish, and distribute this work.

- And, our families and friends, who have supported us in our writing efforts, believing that this was a worthy stewardship of our time and effort for the sake of God's church and its ministry with children.

Kevin E. Lawson, Editor

Introduction

How important is childhood in the spiritual formation of a person? How do children experience God in the context of their lives as they grow? What does God do in the lives of children to draw them to himself and help them grow into a vital relationship with him? How can adults who care about children better support their spiritual growth and direct it toward relationship with God through Jesus Christ? These are critical questions that church leaders face as they consider how best to nurture the faith of the children God brings into our lives.

Welcome to the third volume of conference papers from the triennial "Children's Spirituality Conference: Christian Perspectives" conferences. This ongoing publication project is a way for us to share our research in a variety of fields related to the spiritual life and nurture of children. We hope you will find these chapters informative, challenging, and encouraging. They represent the efforts of many who wrestle with the questions above and who hope to better understand how to help parents and the church with their ministry efforts with children.

About the Society of Children's Spirituality: Christian Perspectives

Interest in the spiritual life of children, and the church's ministry of nurturing that spiritual life with God, has been growing in the North American context over the last few decades. Books, conferences, and journal publications addressing these important issues have increased. Many writers and conference presenters approach the spiritual life of children in a broad, non-religious sense. Others approach these issues from a particular denominational perspective. While these are both beneficial in many ways, we have felt that it was important for Christians of different denominational backgrounds who are concerned about and involved with children to have a venue for discussion of these issues. The conferences of the Society of Children's Spirituality: Christian Perspectives, and the three books that have come from those conferences, approach the spiritual life of children from a specifically Christian perspective, but representing different denominational traditions within the faith. We take as our focus the following working definition of children's spirituality:

> *Children's spirituality is the child's development of a conscious relationship with God, in Jesus Christ, through the Holy Spirit, within the context of a community of believers that fosters that relationship, as well as the child's understanding of—and response to—that relationship"* (adapted from Sheldrake, 2000, p. 40, and Morgenthaler, 1999, p. 6).

The mission of the Society for Children's Spirituality: Christian Perspectives is to foster research and examine theory related to children's spiritual characteristics, growth, and experiences. Presenters and those who attend represent a wide variety of theological and denominational backgrounds. We dialogue with one another, discuss theory, and share research related to children's spiritual development. Goals of the conference include:

1. Networking Christians who are currently conducting research and who are writing on children's spiritual development and spiritual formation.

2. Providing a forum for the integration of biblical, theological, and social science perspectives on children's spiritual experiences, development, and formation.

3. Exploring innovative approaches to children's ministry and providing encouragement to those in this important area of ministry.

The Society has sponsored three conferences so far. These triennial events (2003, 2006, 2009) have been held at Concordia University, River Forest, Illinois. The next conference will be held at the same site in 2012. Each conference has resulted in the publication of an edited volume of presentations and papers. We are pleased to be able to share this current volume, the third in the series, with you.

About This Book: *Children's Spirituality: Theology, Research, and Practice*

This edited volume contains chapters by a range of researchers and writers across the Christian faith tradition. Most of the chapters are based on plenary sessions or papers presented at the conference in 2009. Others were developed as a follow up on issues raised and discussed at the conference. The volume is organized into two main sections.

Section One: Theological, Historical, and Social Science Research Perspectives

This first section focuses on theological, historical, and social science research on the spiritual life of children and the church's ministry response. Some of the chapters, like William Brown's chapter on Proverbs, and Sharon Short's chapter on the metanarrative of Scripture, are studies of important biblical texts relevant to our understanding of the spiritual life of children and how we might nurture that life and faith toward God. Other chapters, like Marcia Bunge's chapter on biblical and theological perspectives and best practices for faith formation, and Dean Blevins' chapter on childhood depravity, address controversial issues regarding the theology of childhood and sin and how they impact how we should approach life and ministry with children within the family and the church community.

Three of the chapters in this section address historical issues regarding the spiritual life and nurture of children. Jennifer Mosher focuses on the views of Irenaeus regarding childlike belief and God as teacher. Elizabeth Dodd looks at the thought of Thomas Traherne, a seventeenth-century rector in the Anglican Church, and his views of childhood revealed in his poetry from a "sacramental" perspective. An historical overview of changing theological perspectives and practices surrounding baptism and their impact on the spiritual nurture of children within the family and church are the focus of Kevin Lawson's chapter in this section.

The final two chapters shift attention from the biblical and theological perspective to contemporary social science research that has important implications for understanding the spiritual life and thinking of children and adolescents today. Gene Roehlkepartain reports on the results of a major international study of how adolescents understand and experience spiritual development within various religious and faith traditions. Jim Estep tackles the implications of recent Neo-Piagetian theories of cognitive development for understanding the cognitive aspects of children's spiritual formation. Both of these chapters have great potential to help us think more clearly about how to encourage spiritual growth and the nurture of Christian faith.

Section Two: Contexts of Children's Spirituality: Family, Church, and Community

The main part of the book is a collection of twelve chapters on both the results of various research efforts regarding the spiritual life and nurture of children and various approaches to faith formation with children—within the contexts of family, church, and the broader community.

Spiritual and faith formation in families and the church is a focus for several articles, including Holly Allen's qualitative research with some of her students on how parents nurture the spiritual development of their children, and Scottie May's research with her students on how "new forms" of churches are doing ministry with children and their families. Karen Marie Yust offers a chapter on ways churches can develop their ministries with children and their families to encourage children's faith formation, with a particular focus on intergenerational aspects of church and family life.

Two chapters in this section look at children's literature as a formative influence in the spiritual life of children. Cathy Posey focuses on children's online discussion of fantasy literature and what it reveals of their spiritual life and longings, and Ann Trousdale analyzes how religion and gender issues are portrayed and related in contemporary children's literature. Many of us can recall the impact of our own reading as children, so these chapters will help us think more deeply about the kind of literature we encourage our children to read and ways of interacting with it.

Four of the chapters address different kinds of challenges and trauma that some children experience, how children respond to those experiences, and ministry opportunities that these can lead to. Melodie Bissell addresses the spiritual impact of child abuse and how churches can help children and their families recover and grow through these traumatic experiences. La Verne Tolbert tackles important issues of how foster care impacts African American children and how churches can be more involved in ministry both with these children and their foster families. Duane Bidwell and Don Batisky report the results of their research on the role of hope in the experience of children with end-stage renal disease. Jenny Korneck discusses the issue of theodicy and how reading, teaching and discussing the book of Job with children can help them better understand and interpret the hard things that sometimes happen in their lives and how God is still there in the midst of their struggles.

Other chapters in this section address a wide range of issues and practices that impact the spiritual lives of children. For example, the formative influence of Christian naming ceremonies is explored by David Cainos, and Jennifer Beste discusses what has been learned through research with second grade children as they go through their first experience of the Sacrament of Reconciliation within the Catholic Church. Kelly Flanagan and Rebecca Loveall examine the importance of helping children learn the "craft of forgiveness" for fostering a healthy spirituality in childhood. They provide both a theological and a psychological perspective on this issue, and discuss ways to facilitate forgiveness, both affectively and behaviorally.

We hope that you will find these chapters a stimulus to your own thinking, commitment, and active service on behalf of children. As Christians, we understand that children are precious to God, and he challenges us to love and care for them as much as he does. In so doing, we have an opportunity to learn much about our own relationship with God. After all, it was Jesus who said, "Let the children come to me, and do not hinder them; for to such belongs the kingdom of God. Truly, I say to you, whoever does not receive the kingdom of God like a child shall not enter it" (Luke 18:16-17).

Kevin E. Lawson, Editor

Section 1

Theological, Historical, and Social Science Research Perspectives

1

Biblical and Theological Perspectives and Best Practices for Faith Formation[1]

Marcia J. Bunge

Introduction

The Children's Spirituality: Christian Perspectives conference gathers together a unique group of people. We come from different parts of the country and the world as well as from various disciplines. We are also engaged in diverse professions: psychology, sociology, social work, ministries for children and families, health care, pediatrics, education, theology, child advocacy, and international work for children at risk. Although we come from different countries, fields, backgrounds, and professions, we all share a deep interest and passion for children. All of us care about children and have learned a lot from them.

My Background

My own academic background is in the area of historical theology, and I am a Professor at Christ College—the Honors College of Valparaiso University. Over the past eight years, I have become deeply interested in a host of issues regarding children and religious

1. This chapter is taken from Marcia Bunge's plenary session presentation at the 2009 conference and builds on several previously published works (cited below). The editors wish to express their gratitude to Mimi Larson, who transcribed Bunge's session.

3

understandings of who children are and what we owe them. This interest has grown for several reasons, of which I will mention three. First, we have two children, one adopted and one biological, and having children has raised many questions for me about priorities in life, values, and faith formation.

Second, as a professor at a church-related college (Valparaiso University is an independent Lutheran university), my colleagues and I are concerned not only about intellectual formation but also about moral and spiritual formation. I teach undergraduates who are eighteen to twenty-two years old, and while approximately 95 percent of my students are confessing Christians, I am surprised at how little most of them know about their faith tradition. Like the American teenagers represented in the study called *Soul Searching*, many of them do not know how to connect what they believe with their daily lives (Smith and Lundquist, 2005). Teaching undergraduates has raised questions for me about what goes on in those eighteen years before they come to college and what is going on in the United States and around the world in terms of faith formation for young people in the church.

Third, I am also an historical theologian, and I have noticed in the fields of theology and ethics there is little serious theological reflection directly on children or parenting. Many theologians and ethicists have treated the subject of children as "beneath" the serious theologian and as a subject only for religious educators or youth pastors. Few contemporary theologians and ethicists have devoted their attention to child-related issues, even though many Christians have children and think about children, and even though many children are suffering around the world.

These kinds of questions and concerns from my experiences as a mother, professor, and historical theologian sparked my passion in exploring religious understandings of children and childhood, and I have now edited three books on the subject: 1) *The Child in Christian Thought* (2001a), a collection of essays about various historical theologians, including Augustine, Luther, Aquinas, and their conceptions of children; 2) *The Child in the Bible* (2008), a collection of essays by biblical scholars; and 3) *Children and Childhood in World Religions: Primary Sources and Texts* (2009), with primary texts on children from six world religions.

Treatment of Children: A Mixed Record in Church and Society

As a mother, professor, and theologian deeply interested in child-related issues, I have been both impressed and disturbed by our conceptions and treatment of children today and in the past. Although I see many wonderful programs, resources, and initiatives for children, I also see a mixed record in the church, in my own country, and in countries around the world regarding our attitudes toward children. Both in Church and society, children are too often treated as the very "least of these."

Here are a few examples from the United States of how children are neglected or suffer injustices. Every person over sixty-five can have medical insurance; yet approximately nine million children are without health care or medical insurance. Most affluent children have access to a good education; yet, as Jonathan Kozol and others have revealed, many poor children attend inadequate or even dangerous schools (Kozol, 1992). Furthermore, many children, regardless of their economic situation, suffer neglect or abuse and struggle with drug addictions, suicide, and depression.

Around the world, we also see examples of children treated as the "least of these." Many children die from hunger or preventable diseases each and every day. Poor children are being used as cheap laborers or soldiers. More than a million children per year are forced into prostitution. In a global economy, rich and poor children alike are bombarded with brand names and market pressures.

In the church, we find a similar mixed record in our attitudes toward and treatment of children. Perhaps most alarming have been the child abuse scandals, not just in the Catholic Church but in other churches as well, where the reputations of pastors or bishops have had priority over child safety. But children are neglected or treated unjustly in far more subtle ways in many congregations and homes. Many churches do not adequately support programs for children and youth. Child and family ministries are underfunded, and leaders are difficult to recruit and maintain. Furthermore, there is little coordinated effort between the church and the home regarding faith formation.

Two Key Insights from My Research
and Experience

As I have thought about these challenges in Church and society, and as I have worked on various research projects and books on religious views of children, I have discovered two foundational insights that I would like to share with you today. These two insights are mined from the Christian tradition and have been helpful for me as I work with children and young people in my home, my church, and my university. Perhaps you will also find these two insights helpful in your own various personal and professional contexts.

First, although Christian understandings of children and adults' obligations to them have varied (and will continue to vary), they could all be strengthened by incorporating a range of resources from tradition and developing theological conceptions of children that acknowledge: their strengths and gifts as well as their vulnerabilities and needs; their full humanity as well as their need for guidance; and their spiritual wisdom as well as their growing moral capacities. The Bible and the Christian tradition express complex and multi-faceted views of children that incorporate multiple dimensions of their strengths and vulnerabilities, and therefore, also multiple dimensions of our obligations to children.

A second insight is that the more we can keep in mind and hold in tension the many paradoxical strengths and vulnerabilities of children expressed in the Bible and the Christian tradition, the more likely we are to learn from children, to carry out our many obligations to them, and to enrich our understanding of children and of child-adult relationships. In other words, any solid model of parenting, child-adult relationships, religious education, children's ministries, youth and family ministries, or child advocacy must incorporate a complex theological view of children that attends to the many dimensions of who children are and what we owe them.

These two foundational insights might seem rather simple, but they address a serious problem: today and in the past we have commonly held narrow and simplistic views of children and thereby narrow and simplistic views of child-adult relationships. This problem is widespread. We find narrow views of children in religious communities, contemporary cultures, and international and national debates about children. For example, many Christians today and in the past have viewed children as sinful and defiant. Given this view of children, they emphasize that adults should primarily be teaching, punishing, and disciplining children, yet they say little about enjoying or learning from children. Other Christians today and in the past have tended to view children as gifts of God. Given this view of children, they emphasize that adults should primarily enjoy children, yet they say little about helping guide and teach children.

Simplistic views of children can also be found in public debates or discussions of children in contemporary culture. For example, in issues regarding reproductive technology, adoption, or foster care, we tend to speak of children as commodities and products. The goal in reproductive technology is a *quality product*. Millions of dollars are spent on reproductive technology and ethical debates about "designer babies," but children in foster care are often overlooked. One of my Jewish colleagues, ethicist Laurie Zoloth, contrasts "designer babies" with children in foster care, who Zoloth calls "the Walmart babies." They are the cheap versions of children; the cheapest option; the ones you might consider if you do not have the money to pursue costly fertility treatments in the hopes of having a biological child. This idea of children as commodities is also seen in adoptions. White babies cost more than black babies to adopt. Chinese girls are easier to adopt than boys from other countries. There is, indeed, a market sensibility even in the system of adoption.

In our culture, we also speak of children as consumers and economic burdens. Children are the objects of intense marketing campaigns and viewed as consumers who buy products and influence the choices of their parents. At the same time, we sometimes speak of them as economic burdens. One hears, "If you have a child, then it will cost you $150,000." We think about children in terms of cost-benefit analysis.

Even in national and international debates about children's rights and responsibilities, we can find narrow conceptions of children. Some speak about the rights of children, describing them primarily as victims. Others emphasize the responsibilities of children, describing them primarily as participants and social agents.

These and many other kinds of simplistic views of children that can be found in both church and society reflect narrow understandings of children and our obligations to them.

My Aim Today: Exploring Biblical and Theological Perspectives on Children

As a way to deepen and broaden our understanding of children and child-adult relationships, I would like to explore with you selected resources from the Bible and the Christian tradition for developing robust Christian understandings of children that acknowledge both their vulnerabilities and strengths and that can strengthen the church's commitment to and appreciation of children themselves. The approach I would like to take for introducing you to these resources is to focus on the duties and responsibilities of both adults and children. By mining the resources in this way, we deepen our understanding not only of the needs of children and our responsibilities to them but also of the gifts and strengths they offer to communities.

The duties and responsibilities I will outline are not exhaustive, but they do exemplify how the Bible and the Christian tradition offer us several rich and varied perspectives on children and our obligations to them. Furthermore, as you will see, by holding these various biblical and theological perspectives in tension instead of in isolation from one another, we gain a richer understanding of children and child-adult relationships. There are many other ways to speak about the strengths and vulnerabilities of children. However, exploring even a few duties and responsibilities provides a springboard for discovering further resources in the Bible and the Christian tradition for reflecting more deeply on who children are and what our relationship to children should be.

Six Duties and Responsibilities of Parents and Adults

The Bible and the Christian tradition mention several duties and responsibilities of parents and adults and corresponding convictions about children. Here are six of them.

(1) One of the first obligations of adults to children in the biblical and Christian theological tradition is that adults are to treat children with dignity and respect. From a Christian perspective, children are whole and complete human beings who are made in the image of God. They are worthy of dignity and respect from the beginning of their lives.

The basis for this claim is Genesis 1:27, which states that God made humankind, male and female, in God's image. It follows that children, like adults, possess the fullness of humanity and are fully human from the start. While this may seem obvious, Christian theologians in the past and today have spoken about children as "beasts," "pre-rational," "pre-adults," "almost human," "not quite human," or "on their way to being human." However, there are several theologians who emphasized that a child is fully human from the beginning and not growing up to be one. For example, Cyprian, a third-century theologian, depicts infants as complete human beings. He states that *all* people, regardless of age, are made in the image of God. For him, everyone shares a divine and spiritual equity that is there from the beginning (*Epistle 58: To Fidus, on the baptism of infants*). Similarly, twentieth-century theologian Karl Rahner asserts that children have value and dignity in their own right and are fully human from the beginning (Rahner, 1971; and Hinsdale, 2001).

(2) A second duty of parents that we find in the theological tradition is that adults should protect children, provide them with their basic needs, and seek justice not merely for their own children but for *all* children. Although children are fully human from the start, they are also dependent and vulnerable. They are orphans, neighbors, victims, and strangers in need of compassion and justice. Many biblical passages explicitly command adults to help widows and orphans, the most vulnerable persons in society (cf. Exod 22:22–24; Deut 10:17–18; 14:38–29). The Bible depicts many ways in which children suffer and are the victims of war, disease, or injustice. In the New Testament, Jesus touched, blessed, and healed children. These and many other passages clearly show us that all children, like all adults, are our "neighbors," and caring for them is an aspect of seeking justice and loving the neighbor. Walter Brueggemann's chapter in *The Child in the Bible* (2001) highlights this point, underscoring many passages that speak of our obligation to care for all children in need—not just our own.

There are many examples of Christians today and in the past who have sought justice for children by creating orphanages, schools, or pediatric hospitals. We see care for children, for example, in the early church's rejection of the practice of child abandonment, in the orphanages and schools established by Francke or John Wesley in the eighteenth century, and in the work of faith based organizations that help children at risk today.

(3) Third, the Bible emphasizes that adults are to enjoy children and be grateful for them. Children are not just dependent beings or victims. They are also gifts of God and sources of joy and pleasure. Many biblical passages speak of children as gifts of God, as signs of God's blessing or sources of joy. Sarah rejoiced at the birth of her son, Isaac (Gen 21:6–7). Even in his terror and anguish, Jeremiah recalls the story that news of his own birth once made his father, Hilkiah, "very glad" (Jer 20:15). An angel promises Zechariah and Elizabeth that their child will bring them "joy and gladness" (Luke 1:14). In the gospel of John, Jesus says, "When a woman is in labor, she has pain, because her hour has come. But when her child is born, she no longer remembers the anguish because of the joy of having brought a human being into the world" (John 16:20–21).

The innovative seventeenth-century Moravian educator and theologian, Johannes Amos Comenius, wrote a short yet beautiful essay in one of his books about children as gifts. He states that they are more precious than gifts of gold, silver, pearls, and gems. John Calvin, who is sometimes thought to have said little about children, emphasized that we should be grateful for children. For him, being grateful for children and remembering they are gifts can bring you through many struggles and difficult times.

(4) A fourth duty and significant responsibility of adults emphasized in the Bible is to teach children to love and serve God and the neighbor. Although children are fully human and made in the image of God, they are also developing beings in need of instruction and guidance. Adults need to help nurture their faith. Several biblical passages in the Hebrew Scriptures speak about these responsibilities. For example, Christians, like Jews, refer to the famous lines from Deuteronomy 6:5–7: "You shall love the Lord your God with all your heart, and with all your soul, and with all your might. Keep these words that I am commanding you today in your heart. Recite them to your children and talk about them when you are at home and when you are away, when

you lie down and when you rise." Adults are to "train children in the right way" (Prov 22:6) and to tell children about God's faithfulness (Isa 38:19) and "the glorious deeds of the Lord" (Ps 78:4b). They are to teach children the words of the law (Deut 11:18–19; 31:12–13) and what is right, just, and fair (Gen 18:19; Prov 2:9). Other New Testament texts often cited by Christians regarding the teaching of children use the terms "discipline" and "obedience": adults are commanded to bring up children "in the discipline and instruction of the Lord" (Eph 6:4) and children are commanded to "obey" their parents (Eph 6:1 and Col 3:20).

There are many examples in the Christian tradition of theologians who took seriously the spiritual formation and education of children, and Christians speak about this duty in various ways. Some Christians say that parents should bring up children in "godliness." Others emphasize that we should help children become "disciples." While theologians from various contexts today and in the past use different concepts, they all emphasize the importance of nurturing and passing on the faith to the next generation.

(5) A fifth responsibility is to listen to and learn from children. The Bible, the Christian tradition, and common experience reveal that children are not just students of adults. They can also be moral witnesses, models of faith for adults, sources or vehicles of revelation and inspiration, and representatives of Jesus. They can nurture, deepen, and challenge the faith of adults. Several biblical passages depict children in striking and even radical ways as moral witnesses, prophets, models of faith for adults, sources or vehicles of revelation, and representatives of Jesus. The Hebrew Bible includes stories of children and young people, such as Samuel, who are called to be prophets or messengers of God (1 Sam 3–4). Several Gospel passages challenge the common assumptions held in Jesus' time and our own: that children are to be seen but not heard and that the primary role of children is to learn from and obey adults. In contrast, these New Testament passages remind us that children can teach and challenge adults. They can prophesy and praise God. They can be vehicles of revelation and even paradigms for entering the reign of God. Jesus identifies himself with children and equates welcoming a little child in his name to welcoming himself and the one who

sent him. In the Gospel of Matthew, Jesus "called a child, whom he put among [his disciples]" and warns them, "Truly I tell you, unless you change and become like children, you will never enter the kingdom of heaven. Whoever becomes humble like this child is the greatest in the kingdom of heaven. Whoever welcomes one such child in my name welcomes me" (Matt 18:2–5; cf. Mark 9:33–37; Luke 9:46–48).

Like the notion that children are fully human and made in the image of God, the idea that children can be teachers, bearers of revelation, or models of entering the kingdom has sometimes been neglected in the Christian tradition and among Christians today. However, throughout the tradition and today, we do find theologians who have grappled seriously with these New Testament passages, forcing them to rethink their assumptions about children and "childlike faith" and challenging adults to be receptive to the lessons and wisdom that children offer them, to honor children's questions and insights, and to recognize that children can positively influence the community and the moral and spiritual lives of adults. For example, German theologian Friedrich Schleiermacher (1768–1834) emphasized that adults who want to enter the kingdom of God need to recover a childlike spirit. For him, this childlike spirit has many components that we can learn from children, such as "living fully in the present moment," being able to forgive others, and being flexible (cited in DeVries, 2001). Christian theologians have linked many other qualities to a "childlike" faith, such as dependence, purity, humility, trust, acceptance, innocence, openness, wonder, tenderness, the ability to forgive, and playfulness, and reflected on how adults might not only "become as little children" but also learn from children themselves. Comenius, the Moravian educator mentioned earlier, commented that infants are given to us as a mirror in which we may behold humility, gentleness, goodness, harmony, and other Christian virtues. For this reason he called infants and children "preceptors."

These and other biblical and theological texts remind us that we need to be receptive to the lessons and wisdom that children offer. We should honor their questions and insights, and recognize that children can influence the community in positive ways, as well as affect the moral and spiritual lives of adults.

(6) A sixth duty of adults emphasized in the tradition is taking up a Christ-centered approach to discipline and parental authority, recognizing that both children and adults are sinful creatures and moral agents who need forgiveness and whose final loyalty should be to God. Although some Christians today equate disciplining children with physically punishing them, discipline in its fullest sense has much more to do with instructing them in wisdom, as Bill Brown, a prominent biblical scholar and speaker at this conference, has discussed in his work on Proverbs (Brown, 2001). For Christians, discipline has more to do with becoming disciples of Christ and growing in wisdom than with physical punishment.

Furthermore, although most Christian theologians claim that parents have authority over their children, they also recognize that this authority is never absolute. Parental authority must never become an excuse for treating children unjustly or unkindly. Parental and adult authority is always limited because parents and adults are sometimes sinful, unjust, or inept. The final authority for both children and parents is always God.

Theologians also recognize that as children grow, their moral capacities and responsibilities also develop. Children, like adults, are moral agents and sinful creatures. They make mistakes. They can harm others and themselves. At times they must be prepared to ask for forgiveness. They also must be prepared to name injustices and to challenge the injustices of parents or other adults.

Eight Best Practices for Nurturing the Moral and Spiritual Lives of Children

Throughout the Christian tradition, theologians have discussed ways that parents can best fulfill these central duties. Today, I would like to mention eight best practices for accomplishing these duties and responsibilities of parents and other adults. Of course, there are many more. This is not an exhaustive list. However, these eight practices are often mentioned in the Christian tradition as ways to strengthen a child's moral and spiritual development.

(1) Reading and Discussing the Bible and Interpretations with Children

Chrysostom, Luther, Calvin, Schleiermacher, Bushnell, and many other Christian theologians have emphasized the importance of reading and discussing the Bible with children. Regardless of their view of biblical authority or biblical interpretation, so-called conservative and liberal Protestant Christians today would all agree that the Bible is the central text for the Christian Church and contains truths and stories that parents or caring adults need to tell and to teach children. Adults will read different Bible stories to children in different ways, but no matter what their approach, they should cultivate in children the practice of what Paul Griffiths calls "religious reading" (in contrast to "consumerist reading"). "Religious reading" involves reading and re-reading the texts, "digesting" them, and viewing the Bible as a vast and abundant gold mine of wisdom that can never be fully excavated (Griffiths, 1999).

(2) Participating in Community Worship, Family Rituals, and Traditions of Worship and Prayer

Theologians have also emphasized that parents should worship regularly with their children. They should "remember the Sabbath and keep it holy" and participate in corporate worship. Parents should underscore the importance of the sacraments and related practices of the church. Rituals of worship and prayer at home are also important. Many theologians have emphasized praying daily with children, and they have written special prayers that can be said before and after meals and at bedtime. They have also carried out particular rituals and family traditions during seasons of the liturgical year, such as Lent and Advent. Prayer frames the day for a child, and rituals highlight the events of the church calendar.

(3) Introducing Children to Good Examples and Mentors

Christian theologians have recognized the importance of good examples in the lives of children. In general, being a good example means that parents or care-givers are believers themselves and strive to live out their faith in their everyday lives. Other important examples for children are often teachers, coaches, or other adults who have cared for children and taken an interest in them. We can also introduce children to examples by reading or telling stories of people of faith who have served others in various situations.

(4) Participating in Service Projects with Parents or other Caring Adults and Teaching Financial Responsibility

Christian theologians have also encouraged parents to serve others in the community with their children and to reach out to those in need. The family is not understood as an isolated, self-satisfied, or enclosed entity; it is not a fortress but rather a community that reaches out to those in need. Many theologians have emphasized the notion that the family should serve others in need by speaking about it as a "little church." Parents and other caring adults teach children much about their faith and values when they find ways to help the poor or to carry out service projects together with children. The value of this kind of mutual service was underscored in a survey that found that "involvement in service proved to be a better predictor of faith maturity than participation in Sunday School, Bible study, or worship services" (Strommen and Hardel, 2000). Introducing community service at an early age helps children become compassionate and service-oriented adults.

Because service is related to financial responsibility, and because people do live in a consumer culture, it is important for parents to speak to their children about money and financial responsibility. In the United States today, a country in which children are daily bombarded with commercials, there are more shopping malls than schools, the favorite activity of 95 percent of high school girls is shopping, and the number one reason that students must drop out of college is credit card debt. Parents must realize that financial responsibility—knowing how to spend money wisely and to use it to help others—goes along with service to and love of others.

(5) Singing Together and Exposing Children to the Spiritual Gifts of Music and the Arts

The arts, especially music, have always been an important vehicle of moral and spiritual formation in the Protestant tradition. Martin Luther, for example, believed that music was not simply an ornament for worship service but rather a vital element of human existence, an instrument of the Holy Spirit, and a powerful vehicle for spreading the gospel. He emphasizes the value of music in these bold words, "Next to the Word of God, music deserves the highest praise." Because of the vital role of music and the arts in spiritual life, he specifically encourages Christians to sing with children and to train them in music and the arts. In one passage Luther claims, for example, "I would like to see all the arts, especially music, used in the service of Him who gave and made them. I therefore pray that every pious Christian would be pleased with this [the use of music in the service of the gospel] and lend his help if God has given him like or greater gifts. As it is, the world is too lax and indifferent about teaching and training the young for us to abet this trend."[2] Practicing music and the arts helps children grow closer to God and to others.

(6) Appreciating the Natural World and Cultivating a Reverence for Creation

There are many examples within the Christian tradition, other religious traditions, and in our own experience of how close contact with the natural world has been a source of spiritual growth and inspiration. Many biblical passages emphasize the beauty and goodness of creation and the importance of going to the wilderness for spiritual renewal, cleansing, or insight. Early in the Christian tradition, monks retreated to the wilderness to meditate and wrote eloquently about the insights they gained about God's creation and their place in it. The important relationship between the spiritual life and the natural world is also found in the works of Celtic Christians, medieval mystics, St. Francis, and many contemporary Christian writers today, such as Leonardo Boff or Wendell Berry. Many young Christians today attend Bible camps or wilderness retreats, and such experiences not only help cultivate a love of others but also a love and respect for the natural world.

(7) Educating Children and Helping Them Discern Their Vocations

Many Protestant theologians, such as Luther and Francke, would add that parents nurture faith in children by helping them discern their gifts and talents and by providing them with a good liberal arts education so that they can better use their gifts to love and to serve others. Both believe a strong liberal arts program will help children develop

---

2. See "Preface to the Wittenberg Hymnal" (1524) in *Luther's Works* 53:316.

their God-given gifts and talents, enabling them to serve both Church and society. Parents and caring adults are to help children find their vocation: not just help them see what is fulfilling or makes the most money, but how they can best use their talents to make a difference in the world and to contribute to the common good. In a letter to the councilmen of a German city, Luther underscores the importance of education by saying:

> Now the welfare of a city does not consist solely in accumu-lating vast treasure, building mighty walls and magnificent buildings and producing a goodly supply of guns and armor. Indeed, where such things are plentiful, and reckless fools get control of them, it is so much the worse and the city suffers even greater loss. A city's best and greatest welfare, safety, and strength consist rather in its having many able, learned, wise, honorable, and well-educated citizens.[3]

Given their views of education and vocation, both Luther in the sixteenth century and Francke in the eighteenth, in contrast to many in their time, were advocates of excellent schools and education for all children (including girls and the poor). They prompted real edu-cational reforms that continue to influence German schools today. As Luther stated, "We must spare no diligence, time, or cost in teaching and educating our children" to serve God and the world (Luther, *The Large Catechism*). In the Jewish tradition, too, one of the major re-sponsibilities of parents is to provide their children with an education that prepares them for a trade or a profession. Thus, many theologians and religious leaders in both the Jewish and Christian traditions have started or supported schools and colleges, fought for educational re-form, and demanded that all children be given an excellent education.

(8) Fostering Life-Giving Attitudes toward the Body, Sexuality, and Marriage

Although the Christian tradition has a somewhat ambivalent legacy regarding the body, the Jewish and Christian traditions both affirm the goodness of the body and sexuality and the goodness of the natu-ral world in general. Because of this conviction, and because even very

---

3. Martin Luther, "To the Councilmen of All Cities in Germany That They Establish and Maintain Christian Schools," in *Martin Luther's Basic Theological Writings*, edited by Timothy F. Lull (Minneapolis: Fortress, 1989), 712–13.

young children today are bombarded with messages about sex in the news, TV, and other forms of technology, parents and other caring adults should therefore help children understand from an early age that taking care of their bodies is part of honoring God and God's gifts to us. They should also help children understand the proper context for the expression of sexuality and speak to them about Christian understandings and expectations of marriage and sexual activity.

Christian theologians in the past have also typically encouraged parents to do more to help children think about a future mate. Luther considered this to be one of the central duties of parents. Jews today also consider this to be one of the primary duties of parents (Dorff, 2003). Today, Christian theologians do not tend to speak about this as a parental duty, since they want children to choose their own mates, but helping children find a mate is not the same as promoting forced marriages. It is simply saying that just as one "makes sure" children have good friends or a good education or music lessons, parents need to "make sure" that they talk to their children about sex and marriage, help them learn from both parental mistakes and positive experiences in relationships, and later ensure that when and if they become engaged, they take advantage of strong premarital programs offered in the Church today.

Summary of Parental Duties and Best Practices

If you only hold onto one or two of these six different duties and attitudes towards children, or if you follow just one or two of the eight best practices, then your relationship to children could be very narrow. However, if you affirm the six duties and attitudes, and work towards incorporating more of these best practices as a way of life, then you can truly enrich your understanding of and relationships to children.

Six Duties and Responsibilities of Children

In addition to addressing these kinds of practices and the responsibilities of parents and other caring adults to children, the Bible and the Christian tradition also mention several duties and responsibilities of children. Here are six of them.

(1) Children should honor their father and mother. Throughout the

Christian tradition, one of the most commonly cited duties of children is to honor and respect their parents. The fifth commandment is "Honor your father and mother so that your days may be long in the land that the LORD your God has given you" (Exod 20:12; Deut 5:16).

Children should honor their parents, theologians have said, because parents have done so much for them. Luther states, for example, that God commands children to honor their parents because parents have nurtured and nourished them. They owe their parents body and life and "every good." Even if parents sometimes seem unjust, he says, children should still honor their parents because of what parents have done to sustain their lives. Without parents a child would have, as Luther says so delicately in his *Large Catechism*, "perished a hundred times in his own filth." He believes that even young children can honor their parents by being grateful for the love and protection of their parents or guardians.

However, the commandment to honor and respect parents does not stop with the end of childhood. Christians, like Jews, believe that this command continues through adult life, since as long as one's parents are alive, one still has an obligation to honor and respect them. Adult children of elderly parents have an obligation to provide food and clothing for them and honor them by caring for them as they grow old.

(2) Another duty of children often cited in the Christian tradition is that children are to obey their parents. "Children, obey your parents in everything, for this is your acceptable duty in the Lord" (Col 3:20). Children are to obey their parents "in the Lord, for this is right" (Eph 6:1).

Many Christian theologians have emphasized that children should honor and obey their parents to such a degree that they are seen as God's representatives. Karl Barth, the twentieth-century theologian, for example, spoke of parents as "God's representatives." For Barth, parents are "elders" in their relationship to their children. Thus, children are to heed and obey them. This does not mean, however, Barth clarified, that children are the parents' property, subjects, servants, or even pupils. Rather, children are their parents' "apprentices who are entrusted and subordinated to them in order that they might lead them into the way of life. The children must be content to accept this leading from their parents. In general outline, this is what the command of God requires of them" (cited in Werpehowski, 2001).

(3) Although almost all theologians emphasize children should honor and obey their parents, the biblical tradition also claims that children have a responsibility and duty *not* to obey their parents, if their parents or other adult authorities cause them to sin or to carry out acts of injustice. Although children should honor and obey their parents, their ultimate loyalty is to God.

Several examples in the Bible illustrate that parents are sometimes unjust and unfaithful and that children must follow God's law above the commands of parents when the two conflict. Ezekiel, for example, commands children, "Do not follow the statues of your parents, nor observe their ordinances, nor defile yourselves with their idols. I the LORD am your God; follow my statues, and be careful to observe my ordinances, and hallow my sabbaths" (Ezek 20:18–19). In the New Testament, Jesus also points out potential conflicts between parents and children, when one is called to follow him. Speaking to his disciples, he says "You will be betrayed even by parents and brothers, by relatives and friends; and they will put some of you to death. You will be hated by all because of my name" (Luke 21:16–17).

Building on such passages, Christian theologians generally qualify a child's absolute obedience to parents. Barth, for example, qualifies absolute obedience to parents when he states that "no human father, but God alone, is properly, truly and primarily Father. No human father is the creator of a child, the controller of its destiny, or its savior from sin, guilt and death" (cited in Werpehowski, 2001). Parents and other caring adults, therefore, have a duty to recognize that they are certainly not gods on earth, and they should not demand blind obedience from their children.

(4) Consistent with children's responsibility to evaluate adult demands and to disobey unjust authority is the call to fear and love the Lord. Although parents are to be honored and obeyed, God alone is to be feared and held in reverence. Again and again, the biblical texts emphasize that everyone, including children, is called to "fear the Lord" (Deut 4:10; 6:1–2; 14:23; 17:19, 31:12–13). "The fear of the LORD is the beginning of knowledge; fools

scorn wisdom and instruction" (Prov 1:7; cf. 9:10). As the biblical scholar, William Brown, notes, in Proverbs the "fear of God is eminently edifying and life-enhancing" (Brown 2001; building on Proverbs 10:27; 14:27; 19:23). Here is where true security for both children and parents has its root: "In the fear of the LORD there is strong confidence, and one's children will have a refuge" (Prov 14:26).

(5) The tradition often emphasizes a fifth duty or responsibility of children: to go to school, to study diligently, and to cultivate their unique skills, gifts, and talents so that they can love and serve others and contribute to the common good in the future. This duty is tied to the idea of vocation and built on the notion that children are uniquely created with diverse gifts and talents that enable to them to serve others, thereby offering families and communities hope for the future. Indeed, many people today and in the past speak about children as our future or as our hope. This duty of children is related to the responsibility of parents to educate their children and help them cultivate their skills, gifts, and talents so that they can love and serve others in both church and society.

(6) Finally, children have a responsibility to love and serve others in the present. While cultivating gifts and talents for the future, they can still love others now. Rather than asking a child, "What are you going to do when you grow up?" perhaps we should ask "What are you going to do now to love and serve others?" They can certainly do much to help grandparents, parents, and people in the community. The Bible provides many examples of children helping others or naming injustices, such as young David or Naaman's servant girl. We can give many examples from our own experiences of children who have actively loved and cared for others or who have been strong social agents for change. Consider the story of Ruby Bridges and the amazing power of forgiveness.[4] We can all think of other examples from our own experience.

---

4. This story is told in a particularly poignant manner by Robert Coles (1995/2007) in the PBS video "Listening to Children" – ed.

Children of all ages already strengthen and enliven families and communities simply by being who they are. Children's playfulness, their sense of awe, and their ability to laugh and be in the present are positive social roles that children play. We all recognize that children often have a sense of awe and wonder that delights and refreshes us. They are also often far more forgiving than adults and can often bring humor to difficult situations. As some contemporary philosophers have recognized, children also offer us fresh perspectives. They often ask fundamental questions about life that open our eyes to new possibilities in our thinking. They are like the new employees in a company who can ask, "Why do you do things like this?" Their questions force us to reevaluate our priorities and to reexamine "business as usual."

Furthermore, the notion of children at play is tied to visions of restoration and peace and to the notion of divine wisdom itself. For example, the prophet, Zechariah, included the image of children at play in his vision of a restored Zion. At a future time, when Jerusalem is restored as a faithful city, "the streets of the city shall be full of boys and girls playing in its streets" (Zech 8:5). In Proverbs, divine wisdom, often portrayed solely as a woman, is also depicted as a child who is playing, delighting, and growing (Brown, 2001):

> When [God] established the heavens, I [Wisdom] was there,
>   When he circumscribed the surface of the deep,
> When he secured the skies above,
>   When he stabilized the spring of the deep,
> When he assigned the sea its limit,
>   Lest the waters transgress his command,
> When he cared out the foundations of the earth,
>   I was beside him growing up.
> And I was his delight day by day,
>   Playing before him always,
> Playing in his inhabited world,
>   And delighting in the human race. (Prov 8:27–31)

As Brown notes, such imagery highlights the "primacy of play when it comes to the sapiential way of life. The authority that wisdom embodies is not 'grave' but creative, and playfully so" (Brown, 2001).

Implications for Home, Church, and Public Policy

What are some of the implications of exploring more fully and holding in tension (rather than in isolation) the many duties of children and parents and the many strengths and vulnerabilities of children outlined today? A sound theological understanding of the duties of children and parents has many positive implications in all spheres of our interaction with children, whether at home, at church, or in public life.

For example, the six duties of adults and six duties of children remind us of the complexity of child-parent relationships. Yes, children are fully human, yet they are also developing. Yes, they are made in the image of God, but we also need to teach and train them. Yes, they have a duty to obey parents, but they also should point out parental injustices. If you keep these various dimensions of child and adult duties in mind, then you can build a stronger sense that children and parents are on a mutual journey of faith. They are striving together to fear God, to love the neighbor, and care for creation. A complex view of child-parent relationships reminds us that adults and children both have an important role to play in helping one another continually examine and assess values and priorities in their families and communities and to serve others. Would it not empower the family if attended to these varied duties of children and adults and asked questions such as: How can we worship together as a family? How can we pray together as a family? How can we learn from one another? And how can we serve other people together?

Taking to heart and holding in tension (rather than isolation) these various duties of children and parents also has tremendous implications for congregational life. Having a clear idea of children's strengths and vulnerabilities can enliven our work in many areas of the Church, such as religious education, children's ministries, child advocacy, or faith-based organizations that work with children at risk.

Finally, in public policy—both nationally and internationally— attending to these varied duties of children and adults could also encourage the church to be a strong national and international advocate for child well-being in areas such as health care, education, and children's rights. The church would have a rich language for speaking about children's need for protection and excellent schools as well as their strengths and contributions to communities. Church leaders would stress the need for parents and communities to provide not only for the needs of one's own children but for the needs of all children.

Conclusion

In this presentation I have described resources from the theological and historical church tradition regarding the duties of children and adults. This brief overview illustrates that any strong view of the obligations to and of children can be built only by cultivating a vibrant and complex understanding of children themselves—an understanding that includes attention not just to their vulnerabilities but also to their gifts and strengths. Christian perspectives on the duties and responsibilities of both children and adults also challenge all of us— regardless of our religious and philosophical convictions—to think more seriously about our assumptions of children and our obligations not just to our own children but to all children in need.

References

Brown, W. (2001). To discipline without destruction: The multifaceted profile of the child in Proverbs. In M. Bunge (Ed.), *The child in the Bible* (pp. 63–81). Grand Rapids: Eerdmans.

———. (2001b). Education and the child in eighteenth-century German Pietism: Perspectives from the work of A. H. Francke." In M. Bunge (Ed.), *The child in Christian thought* (pp. 247–78). Grand Rapids: Eerdmans.

———. (2008). Biblical and theological perspectives on children, parents, and "best practices" for faith formation: Resources for child, youth, and family ministry today, in *Dialog* 47 (Winter 2008): 348–60.

———. (2008). The vocation of the child: Theological perspectives on the particular and paradoxical roles and responsibilities of children, in *The Vocation of the Child*, edited by Patrick McKinley Brennan (Grand Rapids: Eerdmans, 2008), 31–52.

———. (2007). The vocation of parenting: A biblically and theologically informed perspective. In *Understanding God's heart for children: Toward a biblical framework*, edited by Douglas McConnell, Jennifer Orona, Paul Stockley (pp. 53–65). World Vision.

———. (2007). Beyond children as agents or victims: Reexamining children's paradoxical strengths and vulnerabilities with resources from Christian theologies of childhood and child theologies. In *The given child: The religions' contribution to children's citizenship*, edited by Trygve Wyller and Usha S. Nayar (pp. 27–50). Göttingen: Vandenhoeck & Ruprecht.

———. (2006). The child, religion, and the academy: Developing robust theological and religious understandings of children and childhood. In the *Journal of Religion* 86.4 (October 2006): 549–78.

————. (Ed.). (2001a). *The child in Christian thought*. Grand Rapids: Eerdmans.

————. (Ed.). (2008). *The child in the Bible*. Grand Rapids: Eerdmans.

Bunge, M., and Browning, D. (Eds.). (2009). *Children and childhood in world religions*. Grand Rapids: Eerdmans.

Brueggemann, W. (2008). Vulnerable children, divine passion, and human obligation. In M. Bunge (Ed.), *The child in the Bible* (pp. 399–422). Grand Rapids: Eerdmans.

Chrysostom, J. (1986). *On marriage and family life*. Translated by Catherine P. Roth and David Anderson. New York: St. Vladimir's Seminary Press.

Comenius, J. A. (1956). *School of infancy*. Edited and introduced by E. M. Eller. Chapel Hill, NC: University of North Carolina Press.

Cyprian. *Epistle 58: To Fidus, on the baptism of infants*. Christian Classics Ethereal Library. Accessed 8/6/11 from http://www.ccel.org/ccel/schaff/anf05.toc.html

DeVries, D. (2001). "Be converted and become as little children": Friedrich Schleiermacher on the Religious Significance of Childhood. In M. Bunge (Ed.), *The child in Christian thought* (pp. 329–49). Grand Rapids: Eerdmans.

Dorff, E.N. (2003). *Love your neighbor and yourself: A Jewish approach to modern personal ethics*. Philadelphia: The Jewish Publication Society.

Griffiths, P. (1999). *Religious reading: The place of reading in the practice of religion*. Oxford: Oxford University Press.

Guroian, V. (2001). The ecclesial family: John Chrysostom on parenthood and children. In M. Bunge (Ed.), *The child in Christian thought* (pp. 61–77). Grand Rapids: Eerdmans.

Hamilton, C., and R. Denniss. (2006). *Affluenza: When too much is never enough*. Crows Nest, New South Wales, Australia: Allen & Unwin.

Hardel, R. and M. Strommen. (2000). *Passing on the Faith: A Radical New Model for Youth and Family Ministry*. Winona: St. Mary's Press.

Hinsdale, M. A. (2001). "Infinite openness to the infinite": Karl Rahner's contribution to modern Catholic thought on the child. In M. Bunge (Ed.), *The child in christian thought* (pp. 406–45). Grand Rapids: Eerdmans.

Kozol, J. (1992). *Savage inequalities: Children in America's schools*. New York: Harper Perennial.

Luther, M. (1978). *Luther's large catechism*. Edited by F. Samuel Janzow. St. Louis: Concordia.

Moltmann, J. (1993). *Theology of hope*. Minneapolis: Fortress.

Rahner, K. (1971). Ideas for a theology of childhood. In *Theological investigations*. Vol. 8: 33–50. Translated by David Bourke. New York: Seabury.

Werpehowski, W. (2001). Reading Karl Barth on children. In M. Bunge (Ed.), *The child in Christian thought* (pp. 386–405). Grand Rapids: Eerdmans.

2

Wisdom and Child's Play
Proverbs and Paideia

William P. Brown

As I began to ponder examine the topic of children's spirituality, I recalled a childhood epiphany that occurred, of all places, in a science museum in Seattle. Set off in a far corner was a small video screen with a button waiting to be pushed by a curious child. I happily obliged, and a serene scene unfolded of a young couple lounging on a picnic blanket in a Chicago park. Before my eyes could linger, the screen took me out above the park, then above the city, then Lake Michigan, the continent, and the globe. Vast stretches of outer space quickly came into view, until the solar system resembled something of an atom. Next came other stars, the swirling Milky Way, and finally empty space dotted with thousands of galaxies. Then, in a matter of seconds, I found myself once again suspended over the lounging couple, pausing only briefly before closing in on a patch of skin and proceeding all the way to the cellular, molecular, atomic, and quark-scale levels. I was mesmerized by this dizzying ride through the cosmos and the micro-cosmos. I saw things I thought were privy only to God.[1] The sum effect on me was nothing short of transcendent. From then on, I was caught up, like the author of Psalm 8 (see vv. 3–5), in

---

1. That presentation, I discovered years later, was *Powers of Ten*, the ingenious creation of Charles and Ray Eames. See the discussion book by Philip Morrison and Phylis Morrison and The Office of Charles and Ray Eames, *Powers of Ten: About the Relative Size of Things in the Universe* (New York: Scientific American Library, 1982).

wonder about the God who holds and beholds us from every possible scale and angle, from the unimaginably vast to the inscrutably tiny.

The wonder *of* it all prompts one—whether child or adult—to wonder *about* it all. Bioanthropologist Melvin Konner regards the capacity to wonder as "the hallmark of our species and the central feature of the human spirit" (2002, p. 488). Although our self-designated taxonomic label *Homo sapiens* ("wise human") may be too self-congratulatory, there is no doubt that we are *Homo admirans*, the "wondering human." Wonder is what unites the psalmist and the scientist, the biblical sage and the postmodern seeker (Konner, 202, p. 486). And it begins in childhood. I am no developmental psychologist, but I would wager that the capacity to wonder is one of the most critically important things we adults carry forth from our childhood, though it can easily become lost, suppressed, or even deconstructed. And I would claim this capacity as a deeply spiritual gift. To borrow from Genesis 1, I believe the capacity to wonder is part and parcel of being made in God's image (vv. 26–27).

Wonder takes me back to Proverbs. For her volume *The Child in the Bible*, Marcia Bunge asked me to write an essay on the child in the book of Proverbs (Brown, 2008, pp. 63–81). I must admit that I took on that task grudgingly, because I knew that Proverbs was filled with harsh admonitions about disciplining children. Take two examples:

> Do not withhold discipline from a boy;[2]
>   if you strike him with a rod, he will not die.
> If you strike him with the rod,
>   you will save his life from Sheol. 23:13–14

> He who withholds the rod hates his son,
>   but he who loves him seeks earnestly to discipline him. 13:24

But I knew there was something more about children in Proverbs than just the "virtues" of physical discipline. And that "something more" finally struck me when I came across a remarkable discovery in chapter eight that changed everything for me. It, too, was an epiphany of sorts, a spiritual discovery.

One of the most exquisitely crafted poems in all of Scripture lies in this chapter, a singularly evocative passage that has captivated

---

2. The Hebrew *na'ar* can designate a boy from infancy to upper teenage years (e.g., Exod. 2:6; Gen. 37:2).

readers for centuries, from ancient sages and church fathers (as well as church heretics) to feminists and ecologists. The text has been fought over in the Christological disputes of the past and the theological controversies of the present. Through no fault of its own, the text bears a bruised legacy, and we may do well to drop at least some of the interpretive baggage, weighty as it is, that the text has gathered over the centuries, and to walk about a little less encumbered and a little more open-minded and open-hearted within the text's strange world with eyes wide open, come what may.

To begin our sojourn, I propose a way of reading and engaging the text that I consider playful yet fully in keeping with the spirit of the text. Below is my literal translation of the Hebrew.

> 22YHWH created[3] me (as) the beginning of his way,
>   the earliest of his primordial works.
> 23Of old I was woven,[4] from the very beginning,
>   before the earth itself.
>
> 24When the deeps were not existent, I was engendered.
>   when the wellsprings were not yet laden with water,
> 25when the mountains were not yet anchored,
>   before the hills themselves, I was birthed.[5]
>
> 26Before YHWH made the earth abroad,
>   and the first clods of soil,
> 27when he established the heavens, I was there.
>   When he circumscribed the surface of the deep,
> 28when he secured the skies,
>   and stabilized the springs of the deep,
> 29when he assigned the sea its limit
>   (lest the waters transgress his decree),
> when he inscribed the foundations of the earth,
>
> 30I was beside him growing up.[6]

3. The verb can mean "create" or "acquire." The context suggests a procreative sense, namely, Wisdom's conception (see vv. 24, 25).

4. The verb is best derived from the root *skk*, offering a suggestive parallel to Ps 139:13, which is set in the context of gestation.

5. Same verb as in v. 24a ("engendered").

6. A much disputed line that hangs on the meaning of one word (*āmôn*). Contrary to many English translations (e.g., NRSV "master worker," NIV "craftsman"), the grammatical form of the word appears to be verbal, specifically infinitival (see the same verb with similar meaning in Esther 2:20b). The larger context, moreover, tips the scale semantically. Given the lack of reference to creative activity on Wisdom's

I was his delight day by day,
> playing before him every moment,
31playing with his inhabited[7] world,
> delighting in the offspring of Adam.

To engage children (and adults) with Scripture, I sometimes have them repeat after me certain variations of the text that I say out loud.[8] No knowledge of reading is required, for anyone can repeat and recite. Reciting, in fact, was the standard practice of reading Scripture in antiquity. In ancient times, reading was always performative; it was never silent. Below is an example at "reading" responsively Proverbs 8:22–31 with children:

In the beginning God created me.
> God created me.
>> Me!
>>> ME!

I was woven from the very beginning,
> woven,
>> woven in the womb.

Before the Big Bang, I was birthed.
> Before Earth and all stars,
>> before the hills were anchored in place,
>>> I was brought forth.

Before the moon kindled the darkness,
> before the wind kindled the fire,
>> before the rain filled every ocean,
>>> before the sun burst forth from its wedding canopy,

I was there.
> There I was!
>> And there, and there, and there!

I was beside God growing up,
> growing and developing,
>> nurtured and loved,
>>> growing in God's ways.

---

part anywhere else in the poem and the repeated reference to play at the end, the image of Wisdom as a growing child fits the context best. For detailed argumentation, see Michael V. Fox, "*Āmôn* Again," *Journal of Biblical Literature* 115 (1996): 699–702; idem, *Proverbs 1–9*, 286–87.

7. Hebrew *tēbēl*, which can mean "mainland" or "cultivable" part of the earth (*ʾeres*).

8. I am indebted to Christian Educator Paul Osborne for demonstrating this in worship.

I was God's delight day by day,
 day by day,
  ♪day by day♫.

I was delight of the world,
 playing and dancing,
  dancing and delighting,

Playing in God's wondrous world,
 in God's world of wonders!

Delighting in Adam's offspring,
 playing with the children of Adam and Eve.

Let us play.
 Amen!

This passage from Proverbs is truly a unique creation account of the Bible, and one reason for its uniqueness is that it is told not by a third-person narrator, as in the creation stories of Genesis and elsewhere, but by one speaking unabashedly in the first person. Creation's "I"-witness is Wisdom. Proverbs 8 is Wisdom's grand soliloquy; it is her hymn of self-praise.[9] As Wisdom herself seems to say in her own playful, self-absorbed way, "It's all about me." Proverbs 8 is all about Wisdom. But her self-praise has a distinctly edifying purpose. With this poem, Wisdom seeks to lift her voice above the fray of conflicting voices that resound throughout Proverbs 1–9, all of them vying for the reader's attention (e.g., Prov 1:11–14; 7:14–20; 9:13–18), and to persuade the reader—you and me—of her inestimable worth and authority.[10] Personified as feminine, Wisdom seeks no less than to charm, indeed to woo, her audience. By claiming an intimate association with both the creator and the creation, Wisdom hopes to capture our allegiance and captivate our imagination.

---

9. Wisdom's discourse resembles the impassioned aretalogies of the Egyptian goddess Isis. For texts and discussion, see Michael V. Fox, *Proverbs 1–9* (AB 18A; New York: Doubleday, 2000), pp. 336–38.

10. Rhetorically, the first nine chapters of Proverbs place the reader into the subject position of the listening child who is addressed by both Wisdom and the speaking parents. Carol Newsom suggests that this figure of the silent child (literally "son") serves rhetorically as the "interpellated" subject of the reader. See Carol A. Newsom, "Woman and the Discourse of Patriarchal Wisdom: A Study of Proverbs 1–9," in *Gender and Difference in Ancient Israel*, ed. Peggy L. Day (Minneapolis: Fortress, 1989), p. 143.

What makes this account unique is it depicts two categorically different modes of creation by God: the creation of Wisdom and the creation of the world, that is, birth and building. According to her testimony, Wisdom was birthed prior to the construction of creation, thereby assuming unrivaled status in all creation. She is conceived in v. 22, gestated ("woven") in v. 23, birthed in vv. 24–25, present before creation in v. 27, and actively "playing" in creation in vv. 30–31. Creation is told strictly from the standpoint of Wisdom's "genetic" primacy, and such primacy is asserted from a *child's* point of view.

Wisdom as Child

Verse 30 is the interpretive crux of the poem. Most translations cast Wisdom as the "master worker" or "artisan" in this verse, which even on the face of it seems a bit out of place. In the Hebrew text, it all comes down to one single word in Hebrew: *'āmôn*, and if you left that word untranslated, the meaning I think would still be clear:

> I was beside [God] *'āmôn*,
>> I was his delight day by day,
>>> playing before him every moment,
>> playing in his inhabited world,
>>> delighting in Adam's offspring.

However one translates and interprets this mystery word, it must have some connection with the image of a playing child. The context certainly suggests that, as does the Hebrew etymology of the word as it stands. In recounting God's creation, Wisdom also recounts herself as a child playing, delighting, learning, and growing. Wisdom, in short, is created in the *imago nati*, in the image of the child.

But what of these other translations? Many scholars see in this one word an Akkadian cognate, *ummānu*, which denotes Mesopotamian semi-divine sages responsible for bringing culture into the world. But in Proverbs 8, Wisdom never takes on such a role in creation (Yoder, 2009, pp. 96–97). She is simply there beside God, playing and delighting in God and in what God creates. Nevertheless, most translations and commentaries continue to associate Wisdom with the arduous work of creation by translating *'āmôn* as "artisan" or "master worker." Clearly, more than simply etymology is at stake here. For many interpreters, the alternative translation, the one featured in my translation, does not cohere with their impression of Wisdom's profile throughout Proverbs 8. One commentator, R. B. Y. Scott, is representative:

> The fact is that the thought of Wisdom as a child playing is not really congruous with the total context in Prov. viii, and this suggestion, based on the metaphors of birth and play, is superficial. The first part of the chapter and the peroration in verses 32–36 appeal to men to listen to Wisdom because of her *primacy* in creation, which is expressed as *priority* in sequence. For this high claim to grave authority *the imagery of a gay, thoughtless childhood is inappropriate.* (1960, pp. 218–19)

But, I ask, is a "gay childhood" a "thoughtless" one? Are the metaphors of birth and play so superficial as to be meaningless in Proverbs 8? To the contrary, Wisdom's self-identity as child in this passage is designed to heighten, not lessen, her appeal. Scott and others overlook that the reader of Proverbs is also addressed as a "child." "Here, my child, your father's instruction" (1:7a); "My child, if you accept my words and treasure up my commandments within you" (2:1) (See also 3:1, 11; 4:1 [plural], 10, 20; 5:1; 6:1, 20; 7:1, 24 [plural]; 9:32 [plural]). Wisdom was once a child, but in Wisdom's case, she was a child and play partner of God no less. Therein lies her authority and appeal. Are Wisdom's "primacy" and "playing" so mutually exclusive, as Scott thinks?

Perhaps it comes down to this: Many biblical interpreters have a hard time associating any educative value to play, play in relation to *paideia*, the education and formation of the whole person. But then we biblical scholars tend to bury ourselves in ancient texts and history, and barely come up for air to read Jean Piaget and Joe Frost, let alone Maria Montessori. But the children educators and ministers among us know all about the power of play, of how play heals and builds community, of how play leads to creativity and learning. And I suspect the sages of ancient Israel had some inkling of this, too, otherwise, why would they cast Wisdom in the form of a playing child at all? Wisdom cast in the *imago nati* underscores the primacy of play in the sapiential way of life, the way of wisdom. Wisdom's authority is not "grave"—to borrow a word from Scott—but creative, enlivening, and formative as much as it is normative. The image of playful child Wisdom cannot be dismissed or minimized in this passage, for she clearly revels in describing herself playing and delighting before God and in creation as she "grows up" beside God. In Wisdom, "child's play" takes on entirely cosmic, if not biblical, proportions.

According to her testimony, Wisdom's play is everywhere and at every time in creation. She is no passive spectator: every step of God's creating is graced by Wisdom's playful presence. But, again, she does not join God in the arduous task of cosmic construction. No child laborer is she. Instead, she is a child player, and her play serves double duty. Her activity engages both God and the world in the mutuality of play, holding creator and creation together through the common bond of delight. As God's partner in play, she is "beside" the creator of all as much as she is beside herself in joy. As a child, Wisdom is "delight" of the world, the delight that enlightens the world.

The poem that Wisdom gives in Proverbs 8 is itself tangible testimony to her continued delight in creation; it is her ode to joy. God has given her birth and nurtured her growth to take delight in her cosmic home. Wisdom is no mere instrument of God's creative abilities; she is more than an attribute, divine or otherwise (cf. 3:19). According to the sages, she is fully alive, interdependent, and interactive with God and the world. Wisdom is God's full partner in play, and all creation is hers to enjoy. The world was made for her, for her flourishing and delight, and it is her delight that embraces the world. The world is important to Wisdom. As Terence Fretheim aptly notes, "*wisdom needs a world to be truly wisdom*" (2005, p. 206). But I would add to Professor Fretheim's insightful remark: in order to be truly wise, Wisdom first needs a world to be truly playful.

Wisdom's World

And what kind of a world does Wisdom require for her play? From this ancient text it seems that Wisdom requires a world that is made safe and secure, but a world that is also richly manifold and thoroughly engaging: a world secured for the purpose of play. In other words, God creates a world that is both "childproof" and child-friendly, safe and enriching. Wisdom recounts God at work in carving, anchoring, stabilizing, establishing, circumscribing, securing, and setting boundaries. The mountains serve as weight-bearing pillars that hold up the heavens to prevent cosmic collapse. As divine architect, God sets the cosmic infrastructures and boundaries firmly in place, all to maintain the world's stability. The universe is a cosmic construction zone in which God builds an eminently secure place. It is a world carefully designed for habitation – but whose?

Strikingly absent is any specific reference to the creation of life, human or otherwise, except for a glancing reference in the final verse. The cosmos is all bricks and mortar, with life only a lingering by-product – but not quite. The poem acknowledges something vibrantly alive in and beyond the world: Wisdom. By her play, Wisdom marks herself as life *in principium*. She embodies, moreover, life at God's very side, and does so as a child. To her, God is not just the creator of the cosmos; the deity of design is also a doting parent. And as far as Wisdom is concerned, God is both parent and architect. The world is her playhouse.

In Wisdom's world, there is no chaos lurking around the corner, or under the bed; creation does not hang by a thread. It is a world in which fear is banished and joy reigns. As a child grows in wisdom by engaging her environment with wide-eyed abandon, so Wisdom actively engages creation in her wanton delight. From the text it is easy to imagine Wisdom's joy stemming from her discovery of the creation's wondrous complexities, from quarks to quasars, but what seems to rivet her attention the most are creation's marvelous inhabitants: the offspring of Adam. Wisdom's world is more relational than referential.

E. O. Wilson, perhaps the greatest living biologist today, has pointed out that a much better alternative to the policy "No Child Left Behind" is "No Child Left Inside." Children in the U.S. spend an inordinate amount of their time indoors and have yet to discover what lies even beyond their back door. They need to go into the woods, into the wild, to discover the blooming, buzzing world that lies beyond flat panel TVs and computer screens. Children in the USA suffer from NDD: Nature Deficit Disorder. To an extent we all do. But Wisdom is not a child left inside. She does not suffer creation deficit disorder. To the contrary, God lets her go to play, and her play embraces all creation. Playing in creation is an indispensable part of Wisdom's curriculum, her education, her *paideia*.

Wisdom's Maternal Side

So when and how does Wisdom's education begin, when and how does her play commence? A clue can be found in just a few short verses that follow her creation poem, where Wisdom's childlike delight shifts to

maternal love as she addresses her "children" with the lessons of life
(8:32–34).

> And now, my children, listen to me:
>> happy are those who keep my ways.
> Hear instruction and be wise,
>> and do not neglect it.
> Happy is the one who listens to me. . . .

The transition from playing child to teaching mother in Proverbs 8,
though abrupt, is deliberate. Wisdom has a maternal side, even if tak-
en metaphorically, for she, the text claims, fills a critically important
maternal role in human development. When it comes to the evolution
of learning, anthropologists have shown that it is the mother, rather
than the father, who takes the lead.

In fact, the maternal role of teaching is practically universal
among mammals, and it comes from the simple fact that the young
must be nursed for its survival. Up until the time of weaning, mother
and infant form an intimate bond that, at least among primates, involves a period of "voluntary isolation" (Avital & Jablonka, 2000, p.
344). While such isolation, primatologists point out, affords protection from "cannibalism, predation and disturbance," it also "enhances
the mother's impact as a 'teacher' at a time when the capacity of her
offspring to learn is at its peak" (p. 344). Because females are the primary caregivers and because they constitute the "stable nucleus" of the
group among primates, biologists conclude that the "maternal trans-
mission of behaviors may have driven the evolution of intelligence in
primates" (p. 347).

Identifying another evolutionary feature of the maternal bond,
Ellen Dissanayake locates the human origins of art in the special
"rhythms and modes" that characterize the social interactions between mother and infant (Dissanayake, 2000, p. xi). The evolutionary
development of artistic creativity, she claims, began with the inborn
capacity and need for "mutuality" between mother and infant, whose
bonding sets the stage for intimacy and learning. Because human infants are helpless for a much longer time after birth than those of other
species, they require much longer attention and care (p. 14). This evolutionary distinction has occasioned greater mutual interaction between human mother and child, thereby providing the foundation for

various capacities, including "belongingness," "finding and making meaning," and "elaborating these meanings and competencies" (p. 8).

Such acquired capacities are what Dissanayake call the "legacies of mutuality" between mother and child (pp. 49–50), and it is the last capacity, "elaborating," that according to her gives rise to the arts. Elaborating is "making special," a characteristic of human nature that extends well beyond the aim of survival (p. 134). In her words, the arts of "chant, song, poetry, dance, and dramatic performance . . . [are] multi-media *elaborations* of rhythmic-modal capacities" (p. 145, italics added) that began in the mutual bonding between mother and child. In short, what is commonly referred to as "baby talk" between mothers and infants is much more than meets the eye or the ear. The communication that transpires uniquely between mother and child is rendered both bodily and verbally. It is "exquisitely" aesthetic (p. 15). Its rhythmic, "patterned sequences" are mutually sustained by the facial, verbal dance between infant and mother. In other words, it is fundamentally play.

Dissanayake's profound thesis lends added significance to Wisdom's relation to the God who gave her birth and to Wisdom's relationship with her "children." The intimate, playful bond between God and Wisdom, like that of mother and child, is what enables Wisdom's growth. And specifically as a mother, Wisdom is also an artist, indeed, a poet, as we have come to know in her great poem. Not only does Wisdom's mythic preexistence before creation place her as the teacher above all teachers. Her maternal side confirms her central pedagogical position, and her child-ness forges a natural, intimate bond with us all, children of God that we are. Far from "grave," Wisdom's authority is intimate and nurturing, and that is the stuff of "primacy"!

Wisdom's Play

Now that we have roamed around a bit within and beyond the strange world of Proverbs 8, it is only fitting to conclude with the question: What is it like to live in Wisdom's world today? That only you can answer, but for me to live in Wisdom's world is to experience the joy of discovery, the delight of discernment, and the thrill of edifying play. To live in Wisdom's world, the biblical sages say elsewhere, is to walk the path she forges, the path of "righteousness, justice, and equity" (1:3), a path that "is like the light of dawn, shining brighter and brighter until full day" for all who desire wisdom (4:18). And what is a path but the passage of many feet? A path is always communal. And on the path of wisdom, to quote a prophet, "a little child shall lead them" (Isa 11:6). Wisdom's path is the playful journey of discernment in which what is discovered and what is revealed become nearly one and the same.

Admittedly, the "full day" that ushers in all knowledge and insight never arrives within any given lifetime. God's world will always be more than what we know. The aged, according to Proverbs, still have much to learn (1:5). As Wisdom's growth begins in joy, may the wide-eyed delight of children never be lost on the wise. For in Wisdom's eyes there really are no grownups. And in Jesus' eyes, only as children do we enter God's kingdom (Matt 18:3–4). The playful quest for wisdom is ever ongoing, and progress on the path will always be marked with baby steps.

> An argument arose among them as to which one of them was the greatest. But Jesus, aware of their inner thoughts, took a little child and put it by his side, and said to them, "Whoever welcomes this child in my name welcomes me, and whoever welcomes me welcomes the one who sent me; for the least among all of you is the greatest."
>
> Luke 9:46–48 (NRSV)

I can only imagine that as the disciples were deliberating among themselves about the import of their Lord's shocking pronouncement, Jesus and the child beside him, like God and Wisdom, were playing.

References

Avital, E., and Jablonka, E. (2000). *Animal traditions: Behavioural inheritance in evolution.* Cambridge: Cambridge University Press.

Brown, W. P. (2008). To discipline without destruction: The multifaceted profile of the child in Proverbs, in M. J. Bunge (Ed.), *The child in the Bible* (pp. 63–81). Grand Rapids: Eerdmans.

Dissanayake, E. (2000). *Art and intimacy: How the arts began.* Seattle: University of Washington Press.

Fox, M. V. (1996). 'Āmôn Again. *Journal of Biblical Literature, 115,* 699–702.

———. (2000). *Proverbs 1–9.* (Anchor Bible, Vol. 18A). New York: Doubleday.

Fretheim, Terence E. (2005). *God and world in the Old Testament: A relational theology of creation.* Nashville: Abingdon.

Konner, M. (2002). *The tangled wing: Biological constraints on the human spirit* (2nd ed.). New York: Henry Holt.

Morrison, Philip, Morrison, Phyllis, and Office of Charles and Ray Eames. (1982). *Powers of ten: About the relative size of things in the universe.* New York: Scientific American Library.

Newsom, C. A. (1989). Woman and the discourse of patriarchal wisdom: A study of Proverbs 1–9, in P. L. Day (Ed.), *Gender and difference in ancient Israel* (pp. 142–60). Minneapolis, MN: Fortress Press.

Scott, R. B. Y. (1960). Wisdom in creation: The *'Āmôn* of Proverbs VIII 30. *Vetus Testamentum, 10,* 218–19.

Yoder, C. R. (2009). *Proverbs.* (Abingdon Old Testament Commentaries). Nashville: Abingdon.

3

The Story That Grew
The Metanarrative of Scripture as Recounted by Storytellers in the Bible

Sharon Warkentin Short

The Question

Over the course of more than four decades of ministry with children, I have found one overriding assumption about why we tell Bible stories to children. This prevailing and generally unexamined premise is that we teach Bible stories to children in order to provide them with examples that they should either emulate or avoid. Children's Bible learning curricula typically specify one or more "behavioral-response aims" that children are expected to exhibit as evidence that the Bible lessons have been effectively taught and learned. Bible stories are assumed to provide illustrations of propositions to believe, attitudes to imitate, or behaviors to perform.

How biblical is this taken-for-granted approach to children's Bible education? Does Scripture itself suggest clues for the appropriate use of biblical narratives in spiritual formation? In my research I examined ways in which stories are used *in* the Bible for evidence about how stories *from* the Bible might be used profitably in Christian preaching and teaching today. Specifically, I analyzed narratives in the Bible in which individuals are telling stories to others.

Stories-Within-Stories in the Bible

Some of the stories that are recounted by characters in the Bible are relevant only within the immediate contexts in which the stories occur. They may be stories of *personal experiences*, such as Peter's report to the Jewish Christians in Jerusalem describing his extraordinary visit in the home of the Gentile Cornelius (Acts 11:5–17). Alternatively, these stories-within-stories may be *imaginative tales* told to make a point, such as the prophet Nathan's poignant tale to David about the poor man and his little ewe lamb (2 Sam 12:1–4).

In addition to the various personal and imaginative stories that are told by individuals in the Bible, Scripture records numerous episodes in which narrators relate stories about what God has done in the past. The stories that are told on these occasions are reviews of historical events that have continuing significance for their hearers. Furthermore, these special stories-within-stories are often recitals of events that have been reported previously in the Bible. These narrations by individuals in Scripture about past experiences with God were of special interest for my research, because these stories that are retold by people in the Bible are *precisely the same Bible stories* that we teach in Christian education today. They are reiterations of prior events in which God has acted and spoken. By carefully observing how these historical stories are used by storytellers in the Bible, we might gain some understanding about how these same stories could be used appropriately in our educational ministries today.

The Story That Grew

Nature of the Story

What quickly becomes evident as one examines these historical retrospectives that are rehearsed periodically throughout the Bible, is that they are always a *cumulative reiteration of the same story*. Although the story continually expands as new episodes are added to it, the preceding installments of the story do not change. Thus the Bible is a historical record that contains within itself numerous partial retellings of its own complete story. These occasional retellings of the comprehensive story of Scripture as it emerges could be regarded as "mini-narratives" of the Bible's metanarrative. I called it The Story That Grew (Table 1)

Table 1

The Story That Grew

Reference and Form	Storyteller and Audience	Location and Turning Point	New Story Elements	Open End
Genesis 24 Personal conversation	Abraham to Chief Servant	*Canaan.* Abraham commissions his servant to find a wife for Isaac from among Abraham's relatives.	God's promise to give the land to Abraham's descendants	Will Isaac remain in Canaan and produce offspring to inherit the land?
Genesis 28 Personal conversation	Isaac to Jacob	*Canaan.* Isaac sends Jacob to Rachel's relatives to escape Esau's threatened revenge.	Isaac's transfer of God's promise to Jacob	Will Jacob return to claim the land and produce heirs?
Genesis 48 Last words and blessings	Jacob to Joseph	*Egypt.* Jacob is near death and gives final instructions and blessings to his sons and grandsons.	Jacob's transfer of God's promise to Joseph	Will Jacob's clan return to Canaan to claim the promise?
Exodus 3–4; 6 Report of God's words	Moses to Israel	*Egypt.* End of slavery. Moses persuades the Israelites that God will deliver them.	God's concern about Israel's suffering in Egypt and his plan rescue them	Will the Israelites believe Moses and accept his leadership?
Deuteronomy 1–3 Farewell address	Moses to Israel	*Moab, east of Jordan.* End of wilderness wanderings. Moses prepares the Israelites to enter the Promised Land without him.	Events of 40 years in the wilderness	Will the Israelites enter and claim the land, and live there according to God's commands?
Joshua 24 Farewell address	Joshua to Israel	*Shechem.* End of conquest. Joshua prepares the Israelites for life in Canaan without him.	Events of 50 years of conquest in Canaan	Will Israel remain faithful to God in Canaan?

Table 1 (*continued*)

Reference and Form	Storyteller and Audience	Location and Turning Point	New Story Elements	Open End
1 Samuel 12 Farewell address	Samuel to Israel	*Israel.* End of judges era and beginning of monarchy. Samuel prepares the Israelites for life under a king.	Events of failure, punishment, and deliverance during the era of the judges, and demand for a king	Will Israel serve God faithfully under a king?
Jeremiah 2 Prophetic oracle	Jeremiah to Judah	*Judah.* After fall of Israel; before and after fall of Jerusalem. Jeremiah warns the people of impending judgment.	Assyrian conquest of Israel and threat of conquest of Judah	Will Judah repent and avert judgment?
Nehemiah 9 Public prayer	Nehemiah (?) to Returned Exiles	*Jerusalem.* After the exile. Worshippers express repentance and recommitment.	Exile and return to the land	How will God's promise to Abraham be fulfilled under foreign domination?
Acts 7 Trial defense	Stephen to Sanhedrin	*Jerusalem.* Beginning of the church. Stephen defends the Gospel to the Jewish leaders.	Betrayal and murder of the Righteous One	Will the Jewish leaders recognize Jesus as their Messiah?
Acts 13 Synagogue sermon	Paul to Jews and Gentiles in Pisidian Antioch	*Antioch of Pisidia.* First missionary journey. Paul preaches the Gospel to Jews and Gentiles.	Jesus the promised Messiah has come. Facts of the life, death, and resurrection of Jesus	Will the Jews acknowledge Jesus as the promised Savior? Will the Gentiles find a place in the story?

Observations About the Story

In my study I examined a number of situations reported in the Bible in which The Story That Grew was retold to a particular audience. The passages that I selected for consideration were identified through my own survey of Scripture and confirmed in similar lists found in other sources (Middleton and Walsh, 1995; House, 2005).

Careful inspection of the context, content, purpose, and outcomes of these retellings of the Bible's story in specific episodes in Scripture reveals several significant observations. First, these historical reviews were told at important turning points in the Bible's overall story, such as the inauguration of Israel's exodus from Egypt, the crossing of the Jordan River into Canaan, the coronation of Israel's first king, the reconstruction of Jewish life in Jerusalem after the exile, and the missionary efforts of the apostle Paul. Second, the evolving story that was told on these occasions always implied purposeful progress toward an anticipated future. It was a story with a consistent forward trajectory—a story that both teller and hearers believed was going somewhere (Beecher, 1905/1975). Third, although the story was told with the expectation that it would continue to move forward, and that God intended it to move forward in a specific direction, the ending always remained open. The story was brought up to date for its contemporary audience, but it remained unfinished and its outcome remained uncertain (Kaiser, 1978, 2008). Finally, and most importantly, the story was told in order to influence the future decisions and actions of the hearers, because they were the ones who would have to continue it. They would determine how the next installment of the story would be told (Beecher, 1905/1975).

Examples of Narrations of the Story

I illustrate these observations with details from the following selected storytelling situations in the Bible.

Old Testament Reiterations

The patriarchs. The first explicit mention of one person telling the grand story of the Bible to another occurs in Genesis 24. On this occasion Abraham commissioned the chief servant of his household to travel to Abraham's home country and the relatives remaining there, to find a wife for Abraham's son Isaac. To assure his servant that God would help him carry out this challenging task, Abraham retold the core story of the Bible up to that point in these words:

> "The Lord, the God of heaven, who brought me out of my father's household and my native land and who spoke to me and promised me on oath, saying, 'To your offspring I will give this

land'—he will send his angel before you so that you can get a
wife for my son from there." (Gen 24:7)

The essential elements of the plot so far included Abraham leaving his home country and receiving from God the promises of descendants and a new homeland. Whether these promises would be
fulfilled—and the direction in which the story would move forward—
now depended on this servant's faithfulness in carrying out Abraham's
instructions, on his success in finding a potential bride (Gen 24:12–
14), and on the woman's willingness to travel back to Canaan with him
(Gen 24:58).

In turn Abraham's son Isaac relayed the story to his son Jacob
upon Jacob's departure for Haran (Gen 28:3–4). Many years later,
Jacob repeated the story of God's promises to his son Joseph and his
grandsons Manasseh and Ephraim in Egypt (Gen 48:3–4).

Moses to the Israelites. Four hundred years were to elapse in Egypt
before the descendants of Abraham began the long journey home to
the land that God had promised their ancestors. Somehow the story
that began with Abraham, Isaac, and Jacob was kept alive in collective
memory from generation to generation of Jacob's descendants during
that long and grueling tenure in Egypt. When Moses was born four
centuries later and eventually summoned by God to lead the liberation
of the Israelites, God introduced Himself as "the God of your father,
the God of Abraham, the God of Isaac and the God of Jacob" (Exod
3:6). Then God explained His plan "to rescue [the Israelites] from the
hand of the Egyptians and to bring them out of that land into a good
and spacious land, a land flowing with milk and honey. . . ." (Exod 3:8).
Although Moses had plenty of objections to being put in charge of this
venture (Exod 3:11—4:17), he did not seem surprised by or opposed
to the mission itself. Thus Moses became (very unwillingly at first) a
teller of the story for his generation.

The liberation of Israel that Moses initiated at God's command
ultimately consumed the next forty years of Moses' life. Finally the
Israelites stood poised to enter the land that God had promised to give
to their ancestors. Moses, knowing that both his leadership and his life
were nearing their conclusion, and that he would not be crossing the
Jordan River into Canaan with the Israelites, prepared them for the
momentous changes ahead by reviewing their experiences under his
leadership.

The story that Moses narrated at this critical juncture in Israel's national life included many new episodes that had occurred since the time they had left Egypt. In this much-enlarged story, which is summarized in Deuteronomy 1–3, Moses recalled events that had transpired from the time the Israelites left Sinai until the present moment when they stood on the threshold of the promised land, including: (a) the command to leave Horeb (Deut 1:6–8), (b) the appointment of leaders (Deut 1:9–18), (c) the sending out of the spies (Deut 1:19–25), (d) the rebellion against the Lord (Deut 1:26–46), (e) the journey from Kadesh to Kedemoth (Deut 2:1–25), (f) the conquest of Transjordan (Deut 2:26—3:20); and (g) God's refusal to allow Moses to cross the Jordan (Deut 3:21–29) (Kalland, 1992). With this final reminiscence, Moses brought the story up to date right to the moment when he was addressing the congregation of Israel there on the plains of Moab (Deut 1:5).

How the story continued from that point on depended on them. Would they claim as their own God's ancient promises made to Abraham, and would they live in the new land in a manner consistent with the intent of those promises?

Joshua to the nation of Israel. Moses carefully prepared the Israelites for the transition of leadership to his trusted colleague Joshua (Deut 31:1–8), and Joshua faithfully took up the mantle (Josh 1:1–5). From the miraculous crossing of the Jordan River, to the dramatic victory at Jericho, and through many subsequent battles, Joshua led the charge to claim for Israel the land that God had pledged to give to their ancestors (Josh 1–12). Then Joshua presided over the allotment of the conquered territories to the various tribes of Israel (Josh 13–21) and released the two and one-half tribes to return to the land they had requested to occupy on the other side of the Jordan (Josh 22). In his old age this venerable leader addressed the newly established nation of Israel a final time in order to prepare them for his impending death and their subsequent life in Canaan without him (Joshua 23–24).

Approximately half a century had elapsed since Moses' reiteration of the story on the plains of Moab, and much had transpired. In this context, Joshua brought the great story of the Bible up to date for his generation (Josh 24) (Hess, 1996). Joshua concluded his story with a summary of new events that had occurred since Moses' time, recalling how the Lord had delivered first the residents of Jericho, then the

Amorites, Perizzites, Canaanites, Hittites, Girgashites, Hivites, and Jebusites over to Israel (Josh 24:11).

In the remainder of this final address to the Israelites, Joshua urgently exhorted them, in light of all that God done for them, to abandon all idolatry and to firmly resolve to worship and serve the Lord alone (Josh 24:14–15). Once again, the continuation of the story was not guaranteed. Despite their fervent declaration of loyalty to the Lord (Josh 24:24), the Israelites always retained the potential for apostasy. How the story would be carried forward in subsequent generations was in their hands.

Samuel to the nation of Israel.   After Joshua's death, Israel was governed by judges for the next four hundred years (Hill & Walton, 2000), culminating in Samuel's lifelong leadership of the nation (1 Sam 7:15; 12:1–5). In Samuel's old age, the people rejected Samuel's attempt to install his sons as judges, and demanded that he anoint a king instead (1 Sam 8).

As recorded in 1 Samuel 12, Samuel conceded leadership of Israel to the newly installed king (Arnold, 2003), and in his farewell address he rehearsed the great story for the congregation. In this retelling, Samuel again brought the story up to date for his listeners. He opened his review of the story with greatly compressed references to the patriarchs, the sojourn in Egypt, and the exodus (1 Sam 12:6–8). Then he elaborated on the more recent past—the period of the judges during which their forefathers repeatedly "forgot the Lord their God" (1 Sam 12:9), alluding to Deborah and Barak; Gideon (also known as Jerub-Baal); Jephthah; and possibly Ehud, who led the revolt against the king of Moab (Youngblood, 1992). Samuel rounded out his historical review by naming himself as the most recent—and now last—judge to rule Israel (1 Sam 12:9–11).

Although Samuel had persistently opposed the transition to a monarchy, he was now determined to teach the people of Israel how to make the best of it. The essential conditions of their relationship with Yahweh had not changed: as long as they *and their king* served and obeyed the Lord, He would bless them; but if they disobeyed and rebelled, the Lord's hand would be against them just as it had been against their forefathers (1 Sam 12:24–15) (Arnold, 2003; Evans, 2000). Samuel thus invited the current generation of Israelites to recognize that they represented the continuation of the story that God had begun with Abraham. How the story went on from there was—as always—up to them (Youngblood, 1992).

Jeremiah to the southern kingdom. Israel was ultimately no more faithful to God under the rule of kings than she had been under the judges. The monarchy split, and both kingdoms slid inexorably toward judgment and disaster (1 & 2 Kings) (Pate, Duvall, Hays, Richards, Tucker, & Vang, 2004). In this grim milieu the prophets of God rose to prominence. Their essential mission was to speak to the people on God's behalf, exhorting them to repent, and warning them of impending judgment if they failed to change their ways. In doing so the prophets frequently appealed to the story of Israel's past to persuade the Israelites to turn from the path of self-destruction that they had chosen (Pate et al, 2004).

Jeremiah 2:1–19 is a representative passage of prophetic use of Israel's story. In this narrative Jeremiah alluded to Israel's exodus from Egypt and the early months in the wilderness (Jer 2:2), God's special care for His people (Jer 2:3) (Harrison, 1973; Thompson, 1980), and their long history of idolatry (Jer 2: 5–13) (Feinberg, 1986). He continued his story with references to the more recent past, including the very real danger of becoming enslaved again (Jer 2:14) (Davidson, 1983) in light of the devastating Assyrian conquest of the ten northern tribes in 722–721 B.C., as well as trouble in Judah at the hands of both Assyria and Egypt (Jer 2:15–17) (Feinberg, 1986; Thompson, 1980). Jeremiah brought Israel's story up to the present moment, at an extremely crucial turning point. Would his listeners act decisively to reverse the disastrous direction in which the story was certainly heading? What would become of the promises that God had made to Abraham long ago?

Nehemiah to Israel after the exile. In spite of the impassioned pleas of the prophets, both kingdoms were vanquished by foreign powers and their populations deported. However, God never forgot or abandoned His chosen people. Seventy years later, a remnant of the exiles returned to their homeland and began the struggle to reconstruct their national identity (Fensham, 1982; Yamauchi, 1988). The next one hundred or so years of Israel's history are covered in the biblical books of Ezra and Nehemiah (Kidner, 1979). Under the godly leadership of both Ezra and Nehemiah, the evolving story of Israel was retold on two separate occasions that are reported in Scripture, both times in the form of a public prayer (Ezra 9, Neh 9).

Nehemiah 9:5–38 is the longest prayer recorded in the Bible (Luck, 1961) and is one of the most comprehensive surveys of the great story of the Bible up to this point in Scripture. Key events include: (a) creation (Neh 9:6); (b) the patriarchs, represented by God's covenant with Abraham (Neh 9:7–8) (Fensham, 1982); (c) Egypt and the exodus (Neh 9:9–12); (d) provision in the desert (Neh 9:13–15); (e) rebellion in the desert (Neh 9:16–18); (f) wanderings in the desert (Neh 9:19–21); (g) conquest of Canaan (Neh 9:22–25); (h) disobedience in Canaan (Neh 9:26–28); (i) monarchy and exile (Neh 9:29–31); and (j) the present situation (Neh 9:32–38).

The story retold in this devout prayer would inevitably move forward, and its future episodes would, as always, be plotted by its current hearers. It was a precarious juncture in Israel's history. These heirs of God's promises to Abraham were once again residing in the land, but it was no longer *their* land (Neh 9:36). The temple had been reconstructed, but it was a pale reflection of the former glorious sanctuary (Hag 2:3). Many of the Israelites had chosen not to come back at all, and would in the coming decades and centuries be scattered far and wide among the other nations (Bartholomew & Goheen, 2004). In other words, "life in the land now [did] not resemble at all the description of the good life in the land promised in Deuteronomy" (Pate et al, 2004, p. 68). Where could the story possibly go from here?

New Testament Reiterations

In the best stories, the climax reveals an outcome that is startling, surprising, and utterly unexpected—and at the same time perfectly consistent with the narrative that has led up to it. Even though the climax is unanticipated, the reader or hearer can look back to the events that built up to it and realize that, of course, that is precisely where the story was headed all along. So too it is with the story of the Bible. Jesus came, the climax of the great story, and He was everything God's people had hoped for and nothing like they had imagined.

In the Scripture text, the evolving story of the Bible is not narrated in detail again until the preaching of the apostles in the decades following the life, death, and resurrection of Jesus Christ. It was the same old story, and yet it was astonishingly new (Vang & Carter, 2006).

Stephen to the Sanhedrin. One of the most dynamic leaders of the early Christian movement was Stephen, a Hellenistic Jewish Christian (Longenecker, 1981) and a gifted apologist for the gospel (Williams, 1990). His aggressive proclamation of the revolutionary implications of Jesus' message (Neil, 1973) drew fierce opposition from the Hellenistic Jews in Jerusalem, although "they could not stand up against his wisdom or the Spirit by whom he spoke" (Acts 6:10). Defeated in public debate over these issues, some of these men resorted to treachery in order to silence Stephen's powerful arguments, and so Stephen ended up before the Sanhedrin to defend himself against fabricated charges leveled by false witnesses (Acts 6:11–14). In this perilous situation, Stephen retold the great story of Israel.

By reviewing for the Sanhedrin the broad sweep of Israel's history beginning, with the call of Abraham and continuing right up to the present moment, Stephen was employing a preaching pattern that was very familiar to his Jewish audience (Longenecker, 1981). What was not immediately obvious was how Stephen expected this historical retrospective to acquit him of the serious charges for which he was on trial. By the end of his long and impassioned speech, however, it became clear that Stephen was not defending himself at all; he was defending the truth and integrity of the gospel of the Lord Jesus (Neil, 1973) without regard for the costly personal consequences. By the conclusion of his long narrative, his essential purpose became clear: "to show that the present conduct of the Jews was all of a piece with that of their ancestors and at the same time that God was still working in the same way as he had done in the past" (Marshall, 1980, p. 134).

Stephen's story-sermon consisted of a simple three-part structure (Bruce, 1954): (a) the patriarchal period (7:2–16), (b) Moses and the law (7:17–43), and (c) the tabernacle and the temple (7:44–50). He concluded with a sudden and fierce attack directed toward his Jewish listeners: "You stiff-necked people, with uncircumcised hearts and ears! *You are just like your fathers* [emphasis added]: You always resist the Holy Spirit!" (Acts 7:51). He reminded them that their forefathers had consistently persecuted the prophets and had killed those who had predicted the coming of the "Righteous One" (Acts 7:52). Then in a final disastrous act of rebellion, *they themselves* had "betrayed and murdered" this very One (Acts 7:52) who had lived in their midst! Thus Stephen used his recital of Israel's story to rebuke his Jewish contemporaries for the same rebellious spirit that had characterized their ancestors throughout their history (Bruce, 1954).

As it had been so many times in Israel's past, their story was re-told to these Jews at a crucial turning point in their life as a people. The story had been brought up to date for the Sanhedrin—the authoritative body of Jewish leaders in Jerusalem—and now they were responsible for how it would be carried forward. They could continue their habitual pattern of resisting the representatives sent by God, or they could embrace and celebrate this latest installment of their on-going story and be forever changed by it. We know from the remaining verses in Acts 7 which choice the Sanhedrin made that terrible day. In teeth-gnashing fury, they stoned Stephen to death (Acts 7:54–60).

Paul to the congregation in Pisidian Antioch. Even though the Sanhedrin as a body refused to take up the story and live it out in the direction demanded by Stephen's telling of it, at least one person present that day eventually made that story his own. "A young man named Saul" who witnessed (Acts 7:58) and approved of Stephen's martyrdom (Acts 8:1), and who then made it his mission to "destroy the church" (Acts 8:3), was dramatically intercepted by the Lord Jesus Himself (Acts 9) and turned into a vigorous defender of the story he had once condemned. This Saul, also called Paul (Acts 13:9), devoted the rest of his life to telling this story all over the known world in places where it had not been heard before (Rom 15:20). We have a record of one such telling on a Sabbath day in a synagogue in the city of Pisidian Antioch, during Paul's first missionary journey with his companion Barnabas (Acts 13), before a mixed congregation of Jews and Gentiles (Fernando, 1998; Williams, 1990).

In his story, Paul succinctly summarized God's choice of the patriarchs, the sojourn in Egypt, the exodus, the forty years of wilderness wanderings, and the conquest of Canaan (Acts 13:17–19). Next he briefly mentioned the period of the judges that culminated in the ministry of Samuel; the disappointing reign of their first king, Saul; and the accession of King David (Acts 13:20–22). Paul used these compressed allusions to major episodes in Israel's history to situate the *new* episodes of the story that he was about to reveal into their appropriate narrative context (Bruce, 1954).

Paul certainly knew—as his hearers also knew—that a thousand more years of Israelite history lay between the kingdom under David and their present day, but for Paul's message it was important to break off his telling of the story at that point. Leaping over the intervening millennium, skipping entirely the period from Solomon to Nehemiah and Malachi (Morgan, 1924), Paul connected that pivotal event in Israel's history directly to the stunning news that he and Barnabas had come to proclaim: "From this man's descendants God has brought to Israel the Savior Jesus, *as he promised* [emphasis added]" (Acts 13:23).

Then Paul deftly narrated the rest of the story. He commenced with John the Baptist (Acts 13:24–25) and then outlined the essential facts of Jesus' earthly life: (a) Jesus was crucified (Acts 13:28); (b) Jesus was laid in a tomb (Acts 13:29); (c) God raised Jesus from the dead (Acts 13:30); and (d) after Jesus' resurrection, He was seen for many days by those who knew Him (Acts 13:31) (Longenecker, 1981). To sum up the story as it had unfolded right up to that present moment, Paul concluded, "We tell you the good news: What God promised our fathers he has fulfilled for us, their children, by raising up Jesus" (Acts 13:32–33).

It was a momentous story. It was a story that demanded a response. How would the story move forward now? That was the question with which Paul left the congregation that day.

The Story for the Church

The synopses of sermons that are recorded in the book of Acts demonstrate how the message that the apostles proclaimed was consistently grounded in the story of Israel. In the epistles to churches and individuals that are preserved in the New Testament, this relationship of the Christian gospel to the history of Israel is explicated further. As the church matured and her doctrines were refined throughout the early decades of the Christian movement, it became clear, as evidenced in these documents, that the history of Israel constituted the back story not only for Jewish believers but for Gentile Christians as well. The story of Israel became the story of the entire church—for Jewish and Gentile converts alike. One passage in which this new relationship of Gentile Christians to the comprehensive story recorded the Old Testament is convincingly developed is Ephesians 2:11—3:6.

Twice in this segment of verses Paul stated clearly that he was specifically addressing Gentile converts (Eph 2:11; 3:1). In every segment of his discussion, Paul connected the experiences of these Gentile Christians in some way to the Jewish story.

Paul opened his argument by listing five deprivations that had characterized these Gentiles outside of Christ (Eph 2:12), and he related each of these disadvantages to the story of Israel (Hoehner, 2002). These unsaved Gentiles had had (a) no expectation of Israel's Messiah (Wood, 1978), (b) no membership among the people of Israel (Barth, 1974; Foulkes, 1963), (c) no benefit from God's covenants with Israel (Wood, 1978), (d) no hope in the plan that God was putting into effect through Israel (Foulkes, 1963; Hoehner, 2002), and (e) no knowledge of Israel's God (Stott, 1979).

Paul went on to describe four dramatic changes that had occurred when these Gentiles became Christians, in each case contrasting their former condition with their new status in relation to converted Jews (Eph 2:13–18). He showed how these Christian Gentiles had entered into a new relationship not only with the story of Israel, but also with the Christian Jews whose story it was. In Christ, (a) the barrier separating Jews and Gentiles had been eradicated (Bruce, 1984; Patzia, 1990), (b) both together had joined a new corporate entity (Barclay, 1958; Snodgrass, 1996), (c) both together had been reconciled to God (Robinson, 1904/1979), and (d) both together experienced ongoing access to the Father (Hoehner, 2002).

Next, Paul elaborated three significant consequences for the Gentiles who had come to faith, by employing three images drawn from Israel's story (Eph 2:19–22). He explained that Gentiles in Christ were no longer outsiders to God's dealings with Israel, but were fellow citizens with the people of God (Wood, 1978), full members in God's family (Robinson, 1904/1979), and integral components of the intangible temple that was indwelt by God's Spirit (Hoehner, 2002).

Paul summarized his case for the unrestricted inclusion of the Gentiles in the plan of God with three wonderful compound words (Eph 3:6) that each begin with the prefix *syn-*, meaning "co-" or "with" (Wood, 1978). Each word highlights an aspect of the new partnership that Gentiles had with Jews in Christ (Stott, 1979). These Gentiles were (a) "co-heirs" (*synkleronoma*) of the kingdom (Wood, 1978); (b) "con-corporate" (*syssoma*)—that is, "of the same body" (Foulkes, 1963) with the Jews; and (c) "co-sharers" (*symmetocha*) in the promises that God made to Abraham (Bruce, 1984).

In short, Paul claimed that by their faith in Jesus these Gentile Christians of Asia Minor had merged into the grand ancient story of Israel—a tale that had been in the telling for several thousand years. The bright promises to which the Israelites continually looked forward had become the dazzling hope for the future of the Gentile believers as well.

The Story We Live By

My stated goal at the beginning of this chapter was to examine ways in which stories are used *in* the Bible to discover how stories *from* the Bible might be used effectively in Christian education today. I selected for analysis a number of instances in which stories from Israel's history were retold to a contemporary audience, and I found that in each of these storytelling occasions essentially the same progressively evolving story was retold in order to bring the story up to date for the current audience and then challenge them to carry it forward. The actions of the audience in each case would determine the direction that the story took in the future.

If, as Paul argues in Ephesians and other passages, the story of Israel became the story of the church, then The Story That Grew is also the story of every Christian living today. And if that is the case, then Christians today stand in precisely the same relationship to the overarching story of Scripture as did the believers who heard the it from Moses, Samuel, Paul, and the rest. We too must listen to the story and decide how we will live in light of it.

Improvising the Story

For me, the most illuminating model of what it means to live within the trajectory of the Bible's story is offered by Bartholomew and Goheen (2004) in their book *The Drama of Scripture*. Building upon the imaginative illustration suggested by N. T. Wright (1992), they compare the Christian experience in the present day to the discovery of an incomplete Shakespearean play. Suppose, they suggest, that a six-act play by the great playwright was found, but most of the fifth act was missing. The play is given to experienced Shakespearean actors who are asked to work out the missing section.

> They immerse themselves in the culture and language of
> Shakespeare and in the partial script that has been recovered.
> Then they improvise the unscripted parts of the fifth act, al-
> lowing their performance to be shaped by the trajectory, the
> *thrust*, of Shakespeare's story as they have come to understand
> it. In this way they bring the play toward the conclusion that
> its author has provided in the script's final act. (Bartholomew
> & Goheen, 2004, p. 197)

Christians today stand in a comparable relation to the great story
of the Bible. The first four acts of the biblical drama (Creation, Fall,
God's Choice of Israel, the Coming of Jesus) have already been written, as has the sixth and final act (Jesus' Return). Of the fifth act (The
Church in the World) we have only a few scenes described in the
Acts of the Apostles and the New Testament epistles (Bartholomew
& Goheen, n.d.). Followers of Jesus today are "improvising" the part
of God's great story that is not told between the apostolic era and
the book of Revelation. In order to play their parts as the Author
intended, Christians need to know the rest of the book very, very
well. And they need to know the whole story, the broad sweep of
the plot, so that the parts they contribute will flow logically from the
story that has already been revealed and correspond accurately to
the ending that is already known.

The one grand story narrated in the Bible is still unfinished
and is still moving unswervingly toward the dénouement that God
has always planned (Eph 1:9–10). God's people in every age have the
privilege of participating in the advancement of this story toward the
culmination that God desires, and in doing so they enjoy his generous blessings in their present lives. The story is meant to be lived *in*
and lived *out*. The story becomes the background of every believer as
well as the current environment in which he resides. It provides explanations for her experiences and motivations for her decisions. The
Bible's story, in short, gives meaning to the day-to-day occurrences of
a believer's life.

I opened this chapter by asking why we tell Bible stories to
children. How do we expect Bible stories to function in the spiritual
formation of children (or of anyone)? On the basis of my analysis of
the way Bible stories are used in the Bible, I have come to the conclusion that the purpose for telling Bible stories is to give people the
one, true, fundamental story by which to live. Far beyond providing

exemplary models for human behavior, far beyond providing explicit instructions for appropriate actions, the Bible teaches us the right way to think about who we are and what we are doing on planet earth. We are here to join the story that God inaugurated with Abraham and will finish when Jesus returns. If we participate in the Bible's story in a way that is consistent with its trajectory, our lives will be joyful and satisfying.

Fragmenting the Story

However, teaching the Bible as a metanarrative to indwell has not been the typical approach to church education in the past half century or so, especially with children. Much more common has been a psychological-educational perspective that uses isolated Bible episodes as examples of what students should know, feel, or do in response to the lesson. Bible teaching from such a behaviorist orientation can produce several inadvertent and regrettable results.

Losing the Whole Story

One unintended consequence is that the overarching, comprehensive story of Scripture frequently gets lost as smaller subplots within it are isolated and highlighted to promote specific behavioral outcomes. Story episodes are pulled out of their chronological context and re-assembled into "units" organized around conceptual themes. Lesson planners might decide, for example, to create a teaching unit about "honesty," and in it juxtapose the stories of Rebekah and Jacob, Achan, and Ananias and Sapphira. When Bible stories are grouped on the basis of their expected value to prove a point, hearers may never discover that the Bible as a whole tells one coherent, amazing tale (Beckwith, 2004). "We carve up the Bible into 'Bible stories,' so that few children even suspect that the story of God's people—our story—is not a collection of object lessons or heartwarming anecdotes, but a long story of unbearable loss—and unbearable hope" (Pritchard, 1992, p. 4).

A Different Controlling Narrative

Another potential hazard of organizing Bible teaching around behavioral-response aims is that Scripture may cease to be the real foundational or controlling story. The lesson aims that the stories are supposed to instill may actually represent a different metanarrative, and the lesson may end up not being true Bible teaching at all.

Some years ago, I participated in a workshop at a national children's ministry conference about writing Bible curriculum for children. We were assigned to small groups and tasked with producing a children's Bible lesson. As my group launched enthusiastically into the project, some of the participants declared that the first thing we had to do was choose a lesson aim, and then we could find a Bible story that supported the aim. I protested that we ought to choose the Bible story first and then discover what aim the narrative legitimately taught. One woman tried to mediate by asking in complete sincerity, "It doesn't make any difference, does it?" At the time I felt that it did indeed make a difference, but I could not have articulated the reason.

Now I recognize that what bothered me about choosing a lesson objective prior to choosing a Bible text is that this practice runs the risk of making the Bible's story subservient to some other story. Lessons exhorting children to be mannerly, industrious, thrifty, goal-oriented, and punctual, for example, might reflect an American personal success metanarrative rather than Scripture (see Bendroth, 2002). Even when examples of such conduct can be found in the Bible, the stories were probably not preserved for that purpose. Every alert Christian educator has run across Bible lessons that manipulate the text in a similar way to make a predetermined point. At the same conference cited above, another participant asked the group if we knew of any Bible stories that taught children to clean up their rooms—a theme that they wanted to emphasize in their program. Of what metanarrative would that particular value be a part?

Focus on the Human Characters

In a behaviorally oriented approach to Bible stories, the focus is typically on individual characters as exemplars to imitate or to avoid, producing a third difficulty. Giving primary attention to the human actors in the stories and highlighting *their* actions and attitudes shifts the focus away from the true main character of the great story: "God is the center of the story! Yes, we are to be kind, but the point is that it is God who wants us to be kind; God wants us to learn how to do this through the Holy Spirit" (May, Posterski, Stonehouse, & Cannell, 2005, p. 278).

Using Bible stories to inculcate desirable behaviors in individuals on the basis of what people in the Bible did or did not do robs listeners of both the motivation and the power they need to perform those actions. The stories in the Bible describe what God did in the lives of people—weak, fallible people just like us. Exhorting people to personify forgiveness like Joseph, loyalty like Ruth, friendship like Jonathan, courage like Esther, or perseverance like Paul places upon them the impossible burden of trying to imitate people who seem super-human. These Bible "heroes" were heroic only because of the power of God in their lives; they are not offered to us as models of what we too could accomplish if only we try hard enough (Hill & Walton, 2000; Walton, 2001; Enns, 2000; Woudstra, 1981).

Reclaiming the Story

It was not until the early 2000s that I began to hear voices who protested the received behavior-modification approach to presenting the Bible to children. In new books and articles about children's ministry, I suddenly began to encounter scholars and authors who insisted that Bible stories should be presented to children and then *left alone* (Beckwith, 2004; May et al, 2005; Pritchard, 1992; Stonehouse, 1998). These children's ministry experts insisted that the meanings of Bible stories should *not* be prescribed for children, and that Bible stories should *not* be "Aesop's fableized" (Beckwith, 2004).

Why do we tell Bible stories to children? I believe that the short answer to that question is to help children understand who they are and who they are becoming within the ongoing story that starts in the book of Genesis and that is yet to be finished in the book of Revelation. We tell children Bible stories to help them take their place in that great story, the true story about the world.

References

Arnold, B. T. (2003). *The NIV application commentary: 1 and 2 Samuel: The NIV application commentary series*. Grand Rapids: Zondervan.

Barclay, W. (1958). *The letters to the Galatians and Ephesians* (2nd ed.). Philadelphia: Westminster.

Barth, M. (1974). *Ephesians: Introduction, translation, and commentary on chapters 1–3: The anchor Bible*. Garden City, NY: Doubleday.

Bartholomew, C., & Goheen, M. (n. d.) *The story-line of the Bible*. Retrieved December 3, 2008 from http://www.biblicaltheology.ca/bluearticles.htm.

————. (2004). *The drama of scripture: Finding our place in the biblical story.* Grand Rapids: Baker.

Beckwith, I. (2004). *Postmodern children's ministry: Ministry to children in the 21st century.* Grand Rapids: Zondervan.

Beecher, W. J. (1975). *The prophets and the promise.* Grand Rapids: Baker (Original work published 1905).

Bendroth, M. L. (2002). *Growing up Protestant: Parents, children, and mainline churches.* New Brunswick, NJ: Rutgers University Press.

Bruce, F. F. (1954). *The book of Acts: The new international commentary on the New Testament.* Grand Rapids: Eerdmans.

————. (1984). *The epistles to the Colossians, to Philemon, and to the Ephesians: The new international commentary on the New Testament.* Grand Rapids: Eerdmans.

Davidson, R. (1983). *Jeremiah volume 1: The daily study Bible (Old Testament).* Philadelphia: Westminster.

Enns, P. (2000). *The NIV application commentary: Exodus: The NIV application commentary series.* Grand Rapids: Zondervan.

Evans, M. J. (2000). *1 and 2 Samuel: Vol. 6. New international biblical commentary.* Peabody, MA: Hendrickson.

Feinberg, C. L. (1986). Jeremiah. In F. E. Gaebelein (General Ed.), *The expositor's Bible commentary with the New International Version: Vol. 6, Isaiah, Jeremiah, Lamentations, Ezekiel* (pp. 355–691). Grand Rapids: Zondervan.

Fensham, F. C. (1982). *The books of Ezra and Nehemiah: The new international commentary on the Old Testament.* Grand Rapids: Eerdmans.

Fernando, A. (1998). *The NIV application commentary: Acts: The NIV application commentary series.* Grand Rapids: Zondervan.

Foulkes, F. (1963). *The epistle of Paul to the Ephesians: An introduction and commentary: The Tyndale New Testament commentaries.* Grand Rapids: Eerdmans.

Harrison, R. K. (1973). *Jeremiah and Lamentations: An introduction and commentary: The Tyndale Old Testament commentaries.* Downers Grove, IL: InterVarsity.

Hess, R. S. (1996). *Joshua: An introduction and commentary: The Tyndale Old Testament commentaries.* Downers Grove, IL: InterVarsity.

Hill, A. E., & Walton, J. H. (2000). *A survey of the Old Testament* (2nd ed.). Grand Rapids: Zondervan.

Hoehner, H. W. (2002). *Ephesians: An exegetical commentary.* Grand Rapids: Baker.

House, P. R. (2005). Examining the narratives of Old Testament narrative: An exploration in biblical theology. *Westminster Theological Journal, 67,* 229–45.

Kaiser, W. C., Jr. (1978). *Toward an Old Testament theology.* Grand Rapids: Zondervan.

————. (2008). *The promise-plan of God: A biblical theology of the Old and New Testaments.* Grand Rapids: Zondervan.

Kalland, E. S. (1992). Deuteronomy. In F. E. Gaebelein (General Ed.), *The expositor's Bible commentary with the New International Version of the Holy Bible: Vol. 3. Deuteronomy–2 Samuel* (pp. 1–235). Grand Rapids: Zondervan.

Kidner, D. (1979). *Ezra and Nehemiah: An introduction and commentary: The Tyndale Old Testament commentaries.* Downers Grove, IL: InterVarsity.

Longenecker, R. N. (1981). Acts. In F. E. Gaebelein (General Ed.), *The expositor's Bible commentary with the New International Version of the Holy Bible: Vol. 9. John–Acts* (pp. 205–573). Grand Rapids: Zondervan.

Luck, G. C. (1961). *Ezra and Nehemiah.* Chicago: Moody.

Marshall, I. H. (1980). *The acts of the apostles: An introduction and commentary: The Tyndale New Testament commentaries.* Grand Rapids: Eerdmans.

May, S., Posterski, B., Stonehouse, C., & Cannell, L. (2005). *Children matter: Celebrating their place in the church, family, and community.* Grand Rapids: Eerdmans.

Middleton, J. R., & Walsh, B. J. (1995). *Truth is stranger than it used to be: Biblical faith in a postmodern age.* Downers Grove, IL: InterVarsity.

Morgan, G. C. (1924). *The acts of the apostles.* Old Tappan, NJ: Fleming H. Revell.

Neil, W. (1973). *The acts of the apostles: New century Bible commentary.* Grand Rapids: Eerdmans.

Pate, C. M., Duvall, J. S., Hays, J. D., Richards, E. R., Tucker, W. D., Jr., & Vang, P. (2004). *The story of Israel: A biblical theology.* Downers Grove, IL: InterVarsity.

Patzia, A. G. (1990). *Ephesians, Colossians, Philemon: New international biblical commentary.* Peabody, MA: Hendrickson.

Pritchard, G. W. (1992). *Offering the gospel to children.* Cambridge, MA: Cowley.

Robinson, J. A. (1979). *Commentary on Ephesians.* Grand Rapids: Kregel. (Original work published 1904).

Snodgrass, K. (1996). *The NIV application commentary: Ephesians: The NIV application commentary series.* Grand Rapids: Zondervan.

Stonehouse, C. (1998). *Joining children on the spiritual journey: Nurturing a life of faith.* Grand Rapids: Baker.

Stott, J. R. W. (1979). *The message of Ephesians: God's new society: The Bible speaks today.* Downers Grove, IL: InterVarsity.

Thompson, J. A. (1980). *The book of Jeremiah: The new international commentary on the Old Testament.* Grand Rapids: Eerdmans.

Vang, P., & Carter, T. (2006). *Telling God's story: The biblical narrative from beginning to end.* Nashville: Broadman & Holman.

Walton, J. H. (2001). *The NIV application commentary: Genesis: The NIV application commentary series.* Grand Rapids: Zondervan.

Williams, D. J. (1990). *Acts: New international biblical commentary, New Testament series.* Peabody, MA: Hendrickson.

Wood, A. S. (1978). Ephesians. In F. E. Gaebelein (General Ed.), *The expositor's Bible commentary with the New International Version of the Holy Bible: Vol. 11. Ephesians-Philemon* (pp. 1–92). Grand Rapids: Zondervan.

Woudstra, M. H. (1981). *The book of Joshua: The new international commentary on the Old Testament.* Grand Rapids: Eerdmans.

Wright, N. T. (1992). *The New Testament and the people of God.* Minneapolis: Fortress.

Yamauchi, E. (1988). Ezra–Nehemiah. In F. E. Gaebelein (General Ed.), *The expositor's Bible commentary with the New International Version of the Holy Bible: Vol. 4. 1 Kings–Job* (pp. 565–771). Grand Rapids: Zondervan.

Youngblood, R. F. (1992). 1, 2 Samuel. In F. E. Gaebelein (General Ed.), *The expositor's Bible commentary with the New International Version of the Holy Bible: Vol. 3. Deuteronomy–2 Samuel* (pp. 551–1104). Grand Rapids: Zondervan.

4

What "Has" Happened to Sin?
Reconceptualizing Childhood Depravity

Dean G. Blevins

Ministers are often confronted by Karl Menninger's (1973) fateful question, "whatever became of sin?" as they deal with the theological conundrum of both supporting children and addressing the nature of child depravity. Menninger wrote the book to help ministers, and to some degree psychotherapists, reassert their role by raising the moral issues undergirding human misdeeds. Menninger recognized society's tendency to replace moral definitions with legal and medical classifications, limiting any theological definition of sin. The noted psychologist hoped to overcome the adult "morality gap" in America during his day (pp. 225–30). Unfortunately children's ministers today also feel the need to bridge the "gap" between the promise of childhood and views of sin in childhood. Ministers need to recognize a diverse range of theological and developmental assumptions within their definition of childhood depravity. In addition, new research in neuroscience challenges traditional versions of personhood, questioning assumptions about the *Imago Dei*, spiritual awareness, moral choice, and depravity.

Ministers must do more than merely assert the presence—or absence—of child depravity. They need a robust, nuanced, view that sharpens their theological view of people and incorporates their understanding of child spirituality and psychology. Wesleyan theology may offer some suggestions often overlooked with approaches to sin indebted to St. Augustine. Wesley offers a relational and therapeutic view of depravity different from traditional Augustinianism, Cartesian dualism, and representations of sin as spiritual impairment. Contrary to Augustine, but consistent with scripture and the early church, ministers may view children as innocent, moral, agents but subject to environmental influences (sinful and Christian) that shape their development even at their synaptic level. However this view of sin resists any sense of permanent impairment, recognizing by God's grace, and through the means of grace, children may overcome their environment and live vibrant Christian lives. The following writing provides a Biblical and historical overview of child depravity which demonstrates that most current approaches rely heavily on Augustinian assumptions. The writing surveys how contemporary neuroscience troubles this view. Finally the article explores Wesley's approach to children, providing "clues" that might reframe the issue of depravity and open doors for greater engagement with contemporary psychology.

Historical Roots for Child Depravity

Local church advocates for a strong view of child depravity point to scripture, but often do not recognize how their theology and historical location guide their interpretations. Traditional views of child depravity remain rooted within a deeply Augustinian perspective. Even within this perspective, views of salvation, including baptism and faith commitments, often guide people to embrace particular methods of child rearing.

Scripture and Depravity

Often ministers provide scriptures to support their view of original sin. However, pastors rarely reconcile the scriptural view of sin with the Bible's overall depiction of childhood. Obviously biblical communities felt called to provide spiritual formation and oversight for children and young people. However, the oversight of children often corresponds with the promise children offered the community within the biblical narrative (Bunge, 2008, xxii–xxvi). Children often find themselves at the center of God's covenant relationship with God's people, as in the person of Isaac (Gen 15–22) in establishing Abraham's hope and faith before God. Biblically a number of passages indicate an adult responsibility to nurture children into the faith such as Deuteronomy 6:4–9 and Proverbs 22:5–6. In addition, passages such as Deuteronomy 11 or other selections from Proverbs (2:9–11; 3:1, 5–6, 11–12; 4:10; 6:20, 23) indicate the Old Testament concern to raise, form, and shape children into the religious life as well as cultivate their appreciation of God and the world. Ultimately the simple act of Jesus placing a child in the midst of the disciples and announcing the kingdom of God belongs to children challenges adults to welcome children as they would welcome Christ (Matt 18:2–5, Luke 9:47–48, Mark 10:13–16). Children often signal the presence of God's covenant love and the power of the Kingdom based not on the inherent goodness of a child but upon their marginality; as people desperately in need of grace. Jesus admonition to receive children, replicated in three of the gospels, reveals a startling fact that the role of children includes revealing the nature of the Kingdom of God (Gundry-Volf, 2001, pp. 45–52).

In contrast to this positive role of children, actual scriptural depictions of childhood depravity remain amazingly slim. This view does not diminish the reality of sin in scripture, but it does raise the questions concerning beliefs concerning childhood depravity. Traditionally the roots of child depravity take specific textual references, for instance Psalm 51:5 (Sisemore, 2004, p. 221), or rely extensively on general definitions of sin (Issler 2004, p. 61; Sisemore, 2008, pp. 97–98) often taking clues from Pauline definitions read back into childhood (Gaventa, 2008, pp. 240–43). However, the issue of childhood depravity proves more complicated than often assumed. For instance, the translation of Psalm 51 raises interesting questions on the source of the sin, whether biological or experiential.

> 51:5 (KJV) Behold, I was shapen in iniquity; and in sin did my mother conceive me.

> 51:5 (ESV) Behold, I was brought forth in iniquity, and in sin did my mother conceive me.

> 51:5 (NRSV) Indeed I was born guilty, a sinner when my mother conceived me.

While the NRSV represents the strongest representation of childhood depravity, the very nature of the text raises a key question. Were children born "with" sin or born "into" a sinful world where influence remains pervasive? When dealing with childhood depravity, answering this issue proves crucial. J. Clinton McCann (1993), a leading scholar in Psalms, favors the latter. He writes:

> Sin and its consequences are pervasive. The climatic verse 5 has traditionally been cited in discussions of 'original sin,' and rightfully so. While it is not intended to suggest that sin is transmitted biologically, verse 5 does suggest the human fallibility is inevitable. In each human life, in the human situation, sin is pervasive; we are born into it (p. 103).

Hebrew prepositions have the same range of possible meanings and nuances as do English terms. The Hebrew term "in"—the same preposition used both places in this verse—exists as one of the first three prepositions Hebrew students learn. The preposition occurs as a single letter (*bet*; essentially the same letter as the English "b"), and always attaches itself as a prefix to the noun, participle, etc., with which it makes up the prepositional phrase. The original meanings students learn for this term includes English prepositions: "in," "with," or "by." In addition, a number of other translations may be required here and there, based on context. At no time does the preposition by itself support conclusively inbred or inherent depravity (Coleson, 2008).

Of course ministers must also balance such "sin" passages with other passages such as Psalm 22:9–10 (NRSV) which affirm God's direct intervention with children even at birth.

> Yet it was you who took me from the womb;
> you kept me safe on my mother's breast.
> On you I was cast from my birth, and since my mother bore
> me you have been my God.

To reiterate, while children face the inevitability of sin, the "etiology" of childhood depravity remains unclear at best. The key concern may well be asking how adult lives cultivate sinful behavior rather than advocating the "natural" (or "unnatural") sinfulness of children.

Historical/Theological Perspectives

The power of children to reveal the Kingdom versus child depravity apparently continued through the early church. However, issues soon surfaced that created real theological differences over ministerial approaches toward children. O.M. Bakke (2005) and James Estep (2008) assert early church fathers viewed children as innocent, or at least morally neutral, until the fifth century when a larger battle with Pelagianism forced a doctrine of original sin that portrayed children as sinful and deserving of judgment (Bakke, p. 105). To be sure the early church did acknowledge children proved capable as moral subjects who bore some responsibility for their actions. However a child's capacity for moral action might actually culminate in Christian virtue rather than sinful action, though possibilities continue as the child grows older (pp. 106–107). Augustine's vision however, cast children as bearers of original sin and thus recipients of a judgment of eternal damnation unless baptized (Storz, 2001, pp. 78–102). To be sure, infant baptism influenced much of this discussion prior to Augustine, though the motivation with many of the early church fathers did not rest specifically with child depravity (Lawson, 2011, pp 133–35). However, as Kevin Lawson notes, the fourth century marked not only a growing acceptance of infant baptism but a change of perspective on the part of the church. Lawson writes,

> A theology of original sin supplanted the view of the innocence of children held by many earlier church leaders. For church leaders like Augustine, the concerns over original sin and infant mortality led to an insistence on the baptism of newborn infants as a means to safeguard them from eternal damnation.

This view, though a perceived act of redemption, included a very specific view of childhood depravity that shaped future generations.

This tension between children as neutral but capable moral agents, versus children as necessarily evil, even in the womb, influenced the church's teaching from the fifth century forward in Western Christianity. Eastern Orthodox theologians, and other non-western Christians, avoided much of the tension with a different view. They acknowledged human mortality as the primary consequence of the fall rather than persuasive sinful action (Gurorian, 2001, p. 67). Nevertheless the Augustinian view prevailed in the West, not only with Augustinian Catholics, but also particularly through the Reformers and Puritan child rearing principles (Sisemore, 2004, pp. 222–26).

Shifts toward revivalism and a strong emphasis on personal faith statements tended to generate other issues, both as a consequence and as a reaction to the Augustinian view. The first concern revolved around the emphasis placed on the child's responsibility—and ability —to make a faith statement at a particular age of accountability (Issler,

2003, pp. 54–55). Historically this tension manifested itself in differ-ent understandings of infant baptism. Under the Augustinian model, baptism deteriorated into serving either a perfunctory role of insur-ing salvation (Stookey, 1982, pp. 119–23), or a superficial but public role of lending testament to an "adult" faith decision. Many churches rejected infant baptism because of their struggle with individual ac-countability. Ministers posited a type of "intermediate" state where children remained within God's common grace until they were mor-ally culpable for their sin unless they responded to God. Anchored in primarily cognitive concerns, identifying this age fluctuates with different theorists and often proves problematic as younger children make faith decisions (Sparkman, 1983).

Augustine's "gift" to the church included a particular definition of sin as a "willful misdirection of the love that is fundamental to the soul" (James Wetzel, 1999, p. 800). While ministers cling to Augustinian notions of the source of sin, they often shy from secondary presup-positions, such as "God used affliction of various kinds, psychologi-cal as well as physical, to chasten pride, punish malevolence, and in general contain corruption with pain" (p. 800). Deeply indebted to his Manichean dualistic perspective, Augustine's perspective did harden over the years through his engagement with Pelagians who disliked Augustine's views; ultimately to the point of seeing sin as a willfulness that sprang from the inheritance of a mother and father (p. 802).

The heavy emphasis on will, what Menninger deemed volun-tarism (1973, pp. 75–80), proves important in maintaining a balance between dismissing sin as a symptom of blind behaviorism or disease (something Menninger himself resisted). However one may have a "will" yet acknowledge human experience and learning (something Menninger did acknowledge) in order to have a credible understand-ing of human activity. While the psychological world of Menninger has moved beyond his writing, relating will (and therefore sin) to hu-man biology continues—particularly in the field of neuroscience.

Shifts in Neuroscience

The discovery of the brain as the seat of knowledge actually surfaced as late as the seventeenth century and the advent of neurology and what Carl Zimmer (2004) calls the neurocentric age (pp. 3–55). Today, new insights from neuroscience result in theorists rewriting the entire framework for understanding human cognition and action, from the smallest level of synaptic exchange to the largest level of social neuroscience. In addition, researchers in popular literature (Gladwell, 2005; Goleman, 2006) also address how conscious or "interior" human action really manifests itself prior to conscious thought (Gladwell, pp. 197–214). With the rise of neuroscience new insights surfaced that challenged traditional views on the nature of persons (Clayton, 2004/2006; Green, 2004; Green and Palmer, 2005; Murphy, 2006; Murphy and Brown, 2007). These views challenge sinful innateness since such a perspective corresponds neither to the basics of synaptic development, nor to aspects of agency that take biology and social environments seriously.

Synaptic Self and Emergent Influence

Joseph LeDoux's (2002) overview of neuroscience provides a basic introduction not only to the various functions of different portions of the brain, but also the smallest processes of neurological processing at the cell level. LeDoux's views prove important since he asserts that core descriptions of various neurological processes must include the most basic physical processes, not just larger supervisory actions in the brain. As Ledoux notes "Synapses are the spaces between brain cells and the means by which most of what the brain does is accomplished" (p. ix). LeDoux's painstaking overview offers a number of early insights including the fact that learning (as learned behavior based on experience) occurs at the synaptic level (pp. 134–73). The genetic makeup of neurons starts them toward specific regions of the brain, but ultimately experience creates chemical interactions that also shape their final function (p. 63). This pruning method of both selection and instruction indicates the epigenetic relationship between genes and their environment (p. 82). The overall influences of these experiences shape both our understanding of the past, and perhaps more importantly, guides our approach to the future (Hogue, 2003).

LeDoux's observations lead to an understanding that our total neurological framework shapes our personhood. Rather than isolating specific brain regions for certain functions, LeDoux and other neurologists discover that various neural pathways form "circuitry" that guides human memory and response. LeDoux writes, "The essence of who you are is stored as synaptic interactions in and between the various systems of your brain" (p. 173). This "whole system" view helps child theorists recognize just how complex and varied human development might become. While a cursory review might lead Christian educators to suspect a new form of behaviorism, LeDoux argues one must move past simple notions of nature and nurture and recognize "people don't come preassembled, but are glued together by life" (p. 3) based both on different gene distributions but also different life experiences. While humans may possess a common genetic heritage (separating us from dogs and fishes); the influences of "nature" and "nurture" process through the synapses, resulting in mind and behavior (pp. 3–5). The deep interplay between experience and agency cannot be ignored by those advocating depravity, or free will for that matter.

Many neuroscientists and materialist philosophers of the mind resist notions of finding free will, the "self" or the "soul," beyond basic biological factors since most dualistic views lack any real explanation how purely non-material influences actually change physical activity (Flanagan, 2002; Green and Palmer, 2005). Refusing to give into a purely materialist view of humanity, Nancey Murphy (2006, 2007) and Warren Brown (2007), offer an anthropology that resists a purely dualistic view of humanity (body/mind, body/soul, or material/immaterial views) yet opposes materialistic reductionism by stating the "mind" exists as a supervening quality that cannot be reduced to particular biological functions. The authors argue for an emergent monism that asserts consciousness, and free will, which "emerges" from complex mental circuitry that guides responses. This view proves important both for allowing the direct interplay between biological and cognitive factors. What gives the concept of emergence particular strength is its ability to describe a host of biological phenomena where new levels of complexity and self-organization demonstrate an agency that cannot be reduced to their parts (Clayton, 2004/2006; Morowitz, 2002). As an explanatory concept, emergence reveals what theorists often see as "family resemblances" among a number of phenomena at almost every stage of life, particularly in biology (Clayton, p. 93). Emergence appears to be a concept that fulfills this descriptive framework complementing earlier treatments of agency; one that provides an understanding of how the mind, a biological organism, can exert "top down" influence, using system's theory that guides various neurological circuitry and elicits human action including free will (Juarrero, 1999; Murphy and Brown, 2007, pp. 73–104). However, this view leaves little room for depravity as an enduring biological reality at birth, and also rejects a dualism where depravity exerts influence from "within" the child as a separate spiritual quality. However, emergence does offer a separate interpretation of causal influence from beyond the child.

Emergence, Agency, and Social Factors

Philip Clayton notes "emergence theories sometimes go beyond the task of describing common features across scientific fields; they sometimes attempt to explain why these patterns should exist" (2004/2006, p. 41). Theorists working with the concept of emergence incorporate several approaches that might be characterized in two primary approaches, weak emergence and strong emergence. Weak emergence posits the presence of new phenomena but acknowledges that these new patterns remain dependent upon prior causes. Weak emergence represents new, yet unknown, complex patterns of activity; however these phenomena do not account for new forces in life (p. 30).

In contrast, "strong" emergence theory posits that new properties surface out of ongoing complexity that, by definition, actually exert "top-down" causal agency upon previous levels of life. Clayton (2004/2006) believes that the new, emergent, property includes an ability to exercise downward causation which he defines as "*the process whereby some whole has an active, non-additive causal influence on the parts*" (p. 49). This new phenomena actually changes the nature of the very elements that brought the new emergent property into being. For example, the human mind might prove to be an emergent property based on the mind's ability to effect change upon the whole biological system (so we make choices rather than capitulate to primary drives). Clayton insists on a form of causation consistent with the level of complexity, one that directly affects, "downward," the organism (pp. 139–149). Clayton, however, believes consciousness does not merely rest within the "brain." Instead, Clayton notes:

> We need multiple layers of explanatory accounts because the human person is a physical, biological, psychological, and (I believe also) spiritual reality, and because these aspects of its reality though interdependent, are not mutually reducible (p. 148).

When tied to multiple levels of complexity shaped by sociological and ecological concerns, the "person as a whole" includes not only biological but also social, historical, cultural and religious contexts (pp.195–97). Clayton associates this state of emergence with a sense of "meaningfulness," a state more complex than simple mental "causes" shaped by hormones and neurotransmitters. Instead personhood incorporates the complex processes that emerge through complex levels that go beyond physicalism, or dualism, but includes multiple realities, including the influence of the divine (pp. 205–6). Clayton believes this view preserves the role of physical science but raises the question whether there exists other forms of scientific exploration to be conducted based on the social fabric of reality, that social networks have potential to exert additional causal influence. This view may provide an explanatory framework for helping us to understand the nature of child depravity, as well as moments of transformation, when considering this larger, holistic, social framework.

Ministers must recognize the challenges raised to any Augustinian view of depravity by scripture, church history, and neuroscience theory. In response ministers may need a different theological perspective that might serve as a resource in responding to both theological and neurological issues. This new perspective, anchored in the thought of John Wesley, is a theological move beyond an Augustinianism, a move that surfaced in part in Wesley's own context and flows more freely within contemporary Wesleyan perspectives on neuroscience.

Wesleyan Perspectives on Sin and Neuroscience

To be certain, John Wesley embodied many of the Augustinian assumptions of his day. He believed in the fall of the human race from birth, including its youngest members. According to Wesley, both young and old remain lacking in God's natural and moral image, and that sin dislodged the image of God in all humanity and brought alienation from God. Traditionally children's ministers struggle to reconcile contemporary interpretations of John Wesley's approach to child rearing practices in light of John's writings. Methodist historian Richard Heitzenrater (2001) articulates this concern well when he writes:

> Wesley's attitude toward children is often caricatured simply
> as a harsh reflection of his mother's dictum: "In order to form
> the minds of children, the first thing to be done is to conquer
> their will." It is true that he did say, "Break their will that you
> may save their souls," and the daily regimen for the students at
> Kingswood School seems harsh these days. Nevertheless, his
> views were very much in keeping with the prevailing English
> perspectives of the day. And his interactions with and con-
> cerns for children indicated a much more compassionate view
> that one might expect, given his writings on original sin and
> his strict regulations for Methodist schools (p. 279).

Wesley centered on the salvation of children. John believed one
of the primary means to this end occurs through Christian formation. In his sermon "On the Education of Children," Defining sin as a
disease, Wesley states,

> Now, if these are the general diseases of human nature, is it not
> the grand end of education to cure them? And is it not the part
> of all those to whom God has entrusted the education of chil-
> dren, to take all possible care, first, not to increase, not to feed,
> any of these diseases; (as the generality of parents constantly
> do). (Wesley, 1872, 7:90)

To this end Wesley spent much of his ministry educating children.
His method incorporated both sacramental and formational processes
that represent his era yet opened the door to an alternative approach
than those shaped by the same Augustinian assumptions.

Depravity and Steps to Childhood Redemption

Wesley believed that the first step in the redemption of the child was
baptism (Wesley, 1872, 10:188). Adults obtained the new birth, the
beginning of spiritual transformation, through baptism, only on the
condition that they repent and believe the gospel. However baptism,
as an outward sign, also indicated children reached the spiritual life
without this condition, for they can neither repent nor believe (Wesley,
1872, 5:38). True, for Wesley, infants begin in a state of original sin,
and they cannot be saved unless washed by baptism. Baptism initiates
grace, justifies and gives infants the privileges of the Christian religion.

Baptism, for Wesley, represented not only a proper, but also a
sacred duty (Wesley, 1872, 6:16). Rob Staples (1991) provides a summary of Wesley's rationale of infant baptism: (1) The benefit of baptism

is the washing away of the guilt of original sin; (2) Baptism was proper for children because of the continuity of the covenant of grace God made with Abraham; (3) Small children should be brought to Christ, and admitted into the Church, based on Matthew 19:13–14 and Luke 18:15; and (4) Wesley found support for infant baptism in the practice of the Church "in all ages and in all places" (pp. 167–72). Wesley saw infant baptism as an important step in the spiritual development of the infant and entrance into the faith community.

Wesley taught that through baptism, "a principle grace is infused" (Wesley, 1872, 6:15) and the "work accomplished is so far effectual, that if infants die before they commit sin, they will be eternally safe" (Wesley, 1872, 6:16). Most people ask how the transformation Wesley describes occurs in an infant who, so the argument goes, lacks the cognitive abilities necessary for this experience. Wesley replies "neither can we comprehend how it is wrought in a person of riper years" (Wesley, 1872, 6:74). Thus, if the child lives, he/she never passes again through the door of repentance to faith, unless he/she does actually commit sin. Based on Wesley's observations many evangelical educators deduced Wesley believed it natural for children to commit sin, for the principle of nature is still working in the child (Towns, 1975, p. 320). Yet Wesley seemed to include a systemic influence, one that proved equally pervasive. The only way to conserve the innocence of children (in baptism) would be to guard them completely against contamination during their helpless years and at the same time build character. As a result, children may resist evil by their own strength when they become of age. Wesleyan educators also note how education serves this role (Prince, 1926, p. 95).

However, Wesley also saw traditional conversion as a possible next step in the Christian formation of children. Wesley believed that anyone who had sinned after baptism denied that rite of baptism and, therefore, must have recourse to a new birth for salvation. Wesley felt conversion to be necessary for children as well as for adults (Prince, 1926, p. 96). For Wesley this formation took place in the home, in the schools, and in the societies to make children Christians, inwardly and outwardly (Naglee, 1987, pp. 228–37). Exactly what John meant by curing disease surfaces in the next section.

Rethinking Wesley

The portrayal of Wesley's approach to childhood reveals deep connections to an Augustinian perspective, replete with authoritarian child rearing methods and an ultimate emphasis on "adult" faith decisions (Greven, 1977). However, such a portrayal may prove incomplete when one takes seriously several factors: the role of baptism as a graceful framework for children, the nature of disease and the "cure" of salvation within a therapeutic view, and a Trinitarian ontology that incorporates children for the sake of the larger Methodist people.

Baptism and Prevenient Grace

Wesley, who often began with Augustinian assumptions, nevertheless overturned this view with his deep confidence in prevenient grace and the power of the Holy Spirit to work in and through children (Stonehouse, 2004, pp. 135–40). Anchored in Wesleyan sensibilities, infant baptism reflects covenantal language that expresses God's prevenient grace through the church and the elevation of children as a vital part of the community of faith (Staples, 1991, pp. 161–200). In this approach, infant baptism remains a "means of grace" by relationally binding the church, the family, and the child, under a bond of God's grace so that all benefit through this sacramental act that anticipates personal commitment and God's justifying grace (Stookey, pp. 44–50). Many churches still seek to publicly "dedicate" children to God and acknowledge their own responsibility as congregations and families to raise children "in the nurture and admonition of the Lord" (Eph 6:4). While lacking the theological strength of baptism, infant dedication may still serve as a means of grace in many settings (Staples, pp. 199–200).

Therapeutic Salvation

Returning to Wesley's depiction of sin in his sermon "On The Education of Children" in the critical edition of Wesley's Sermons (1986–1995), one notes that John discusses several "diseases of nature:" (3:350) atheism, willfulness, pride, love of the world, anger, avoiding truth (either in direct lying or skillful disguise), lacking mercy, and lacking love (3: 350–53). In each case Wesley seems to echo Augustine since these diseases reflect humanity's and therefore children's "nature." However, two clues exist that raise specific questions concerning the lasting quality of the malformations. The first lies within the sermon when Wesley contends these "diseases" are "rational" in nature and can therefore be cured by loving yet strict educational discipline including inculcating virtues like abstinence, humility, sobriety and devotion. Drawing from *William Law's Serious Call to a Devout Life*, Wesley believes (with God's help) Law's dictum "it is as reasonable to expect and require all this benefit from a Christian education as to require that physic should strengthen all that is right in our nature and remove all our diseases" (3:349). Law's dictum actually shapes the sermon, Wesley recognizes that Christian families cannot guarantee children will grow up well (3:347–48) but he does emphasize that the diseases of sin, rather than permanent malformations of the soul, may be cured!

While primarily the work of God, John assumes our participation in this therapeutic exercise; Wesley writes,

> Let it be carefully remembered that all this time that God, not man, is the Physician of soul; that it is he and none else, who giveth medicine to heal our natural sickness. That all 'the help which is done on earth, he doeth himself;' that none of all the children of men is able to 'bring a clean thing out of an unclean;' in a word that 'it is God who worketh in us, both to will and to do of his good pleasure.' But it is generally his pleasure to work by his creatures; to help man by man. He honors men to be, in this sense, 'workers together with him.' By this means the reward is ours, while the glory redounds to him. (3:349)

Wesley's appropriation of Law's metaphor reveals his desire to combine both a therapeutic and holistic approach to sin, reminiscent of early church traditions that normally inform eastern orthodoxy (Maddox, 1994, pp. 23, 91).

Wesley's employment of the term "physic[k]" represents an eighteenth century appreciation of medical knowledge alongside a theological perspective that incorporates therapeutic healing as one metaphor for salvation. Wesley remained deeply conversant with contemporary medicine of his day, as did many minsters who served as bi-vocational healers (Maddox, 2007). Wesley's holistic idea of health, that incorporated physical, emotional and spiritual well-being, undergirded his understanding of "dis-ease." In short, for Wesley, the concept of sin as disease invoked the idea of something that might be cured. Rather than a permanent infirmity, a longstanding impairment one carried throughout life, Wesley believed that people, including children, might well be cured through the formative practices of caring parents and other Christian educators. To be certain final restoration rested with God by grace, yet that grace might occur through the "means of grace" embodied in Christian parenting.

Wesley may have begun with Augustinian assumptions about the nature of child depravity, but the child did not live within just the pervasiveness of sinful life. Even beginning with an Augustinian view of life Wesley could trust both sacramental and therapeutic perspectives to guide our approach with children. Children marked by the prevenient grace of God even at birth, find themselves on a spiritual journey. True, the pervasiveness of sin might well overcome the effects of baptism, but God's grace serves as God's first word on the subject. Childhood depravity did not have to have the last word, even if Augustine seemed correct. The challenge rested with adults to begin to apply both, physic and medicine, to prescribe practices of good health and restoration, early and often in childhood.

Trinitarian Relationships

One additional reason for resisting a "high view" of sin in childhood also rested with John's Trinitarian ontology (Anderson, 1999; Wainwright, 1995). Wesley (1780/1986) systematically elaborates on the presence of the "Three-One" God (his preferred term) in 1 John 5 during his sermon on "Spiritual Worship." (3:88–97) Wesley writes that the original purpose for writing 1 John is not faith or holiness, "but of the foundation of all, the happy and holy communion which the faithful have with God the Father, Son and Holy Ghost" (3:89–90).

Wesleyan theology affirms that the primary characteristic of the triune God is holy love. God is the Creator of all that is, and remains lovingly related to it. God offers a particular love for humanity and desires communion with us. God's "being" incorporates holiness and relationality simultaneously, expressing holy love toward one another. This love manifests itself not merely in therapeutic terms but primarily in moral terms like complete truth and justice. God's moral purity is not something God must "exert" but stems out of the relationships shared within the Triune God-head. This means that God's relational love toward humanity extends out of the very "being" of the Trinity. While the Trinity describes the essence of God, already aspects of the triune God-head give insight into the nature of God's character and to the very nature of reality as relationship.

This perspective places children "within" a matrix of relationships where sin and salvation is understood both through individual and social terms. A relational ontology, undergirded by the triune relationship in God, provides the basis for a Wesleyan understanding of humanity. Sin defines primarily a broken relationship instead of either a natural inclination or permanent condition. Perhaps the closest Wesleyans might come to Augustine would be to regard sin as a misdirected desire, a broken relationship, just as holiness describes perfect "love" toward God and humanity. Children and adults live in a world filled with broken, sinful, relationships that influence their lives as well. Sin remains a pervasive reality through the myriad human relationships children experience. Rather than something "natural" to human living, sin defines a tendency to privilege one person to the detriment of another, something often evident in family systems theory but unheard of in the triune relationship of God (Thatcher, 2007). As humans return to God, re-establish relationship through God's grace, and participate fully in the triune life of God, the healing and restoration of relationships occur. Children, born in a world where they are desperately reliant on adult relationships, encounter either relational health or "dis-ease" early. Broken, sinful, relationships seem inevitable; however, for Wesley, they need not manifest themselves with equal intensity if people choose to model John's emphasis on holiness of heart and life, a possibility enabled through God's good relationship with humanity. Indeed Wesley often used the transformative experiences of children as a source of spiritual encouragement for adults, reflecting the deeply relational nature of God working through children as well as for children (Blevins, 2008).

The three theological frameworks of prevenient grace, therapeutic healing, and relationality provide a rich theological resource that problematizes several Augustinian assumptions. True, Wesley was a man of his time and embedded in Augustinian language at times. However, the overall theological perspective provides ministers with a different framework to move past the inevitability of sin as initial and ongoing impairment in children. Moving forward, Wesleyan theologians have also discovered intersections between theology and neuroscience that offer an alternative perspective that reframes sin and transformation in a new light.

Wesleyan Transformation and Neuroscience

Recent research lends new insight into the nature of child depravity and child salvation by raising key issues about the nature of spiritual transformation. Paul Markham (2007) provides a much needed introduction to a range of ideas in his recent book. Focusing on the nature of conversion, Markham's key thesis is as follows:

(1) Christian conversion is a process involving normal human biological capacities. (2) It is characterized by a change in socio-moral attitude and behavior, and (3) is best understood as the acquisition of virtues intrinsic to the Christian faith. Such acquisitions are facilitated through social interaction and participation in practices inherent to the Christian community. (4) Furthermore, the conversion process should be viewed as the co-operant result of Divine grace and human participation (pp. 131–32).

Markham's builds his thesis upon three major assumptions. First, following the work of Randy Maddox (2004), Markham develops a Wesleyan theological anthropology based on a holistic, relational, framework where God's grace transforms persons as their affections are shaped into moral tempers (enduring dispositions) like love and holiness (pp. 37–72, 130). Markham stresses the continual nature of this change, allowing for significant moral transformation, yet stressing that conversion or sanctification (one and the same for Markham) describes an ongoing process within a social context rather than mere private experience (pp. 68–72).

Second, following the work of Nancey Murphy and Warren Brown, Markham develops a neurobiological anthropology mentioned earlier. Markham embraces emergent properties that might warrant top-down causation (pp. 110–23). Markham offers this view to demonstrate how both changes within the biology of persons ("bottom-up") interact with complex forms of human relational interaction (intrapersonal and interpersonal) to bring about change (p. 126).

Markham's third primary emphasis rests on the need for goal-directed practice, not just a cognitive assent, in the midst of human communities that both shape and encourage practices that serve as means of grace (p. 152). Drawing from Alasdair MacIntyre, Markham calls for practices that shape virtues that result in moral transformation (pp. 154–67). Practitioners learn these virtuous practices within communities that engender and encourage certain formative practices Wesley titled "means of grace" (pp. 185–206). Markham bases this need on the fact that divine action, following Murphy, occurs primarily at the quantum level to trigger conversion but then allows community to "structure" the quality of conversion. Indeed, Markham believes that "it is necessary for an individual to be within the context of community to undergo the process of religious conversion." (p. 186).

The three-fold approach to a Wesleyan theology of moral transformation generates a holistic discipleship through Christian practices as "means of grace." His view also provides the clearest approach that resists mind/body dualism, providing a new way to affirm the insights of Wesleyan theology and neuroscience (pp. 206–10).

Nuancing Childhood Depravity

The lengthy descriptions offered above serve to provide an overview of the various perspectives that may well provide a larger, more nuanced, understanding of sin than previously addressed in many studies of childhood depravity. As noted, scriptural warrants for sin seem evident, but less so for childhood depravity based either on specific Bible passages or the early church understanding of children prior to Augustine. Such a view raises particular concerns for later reformed traditions directly indebted to an Augustinian view (Sisemore, 2008, pp. 93–94). One possible strategy would be to posit "sin" as a spiritual reality rather than a physical manifestation. Historically Cartesian dualists offer such a view. To claim a "three tiered" created order with a distinct ontology of physical, spiritual, and God's realm or being, may allow for this approach if one understands God creates a "spiritual" realm distinct from the physical but also distinct from God. However, such a view can be quite problematic both in neuroscience (as noted earlier) and in theology since this view can denigrate the physical for the spiritual (and open up Gnosticism) and often disrupts the unity of God's creation (Gunton, 2002, pp. 15–19). If the "spiritual" is consigned as the realm of God (i.e. part of God's distinct being), it also proves problematic based on two perspectives: First, sin, so consigned, would have to be part of the realm of God, allowing evil an ontological standing beyond the created order, one on par with God—a peculiar trait reminiscent of the Zoroastrian roots of Manichean dualism Augustine rejected (McDonald, 1988, pp. 410–11) and an issue that pushes beyond the scope of this paper. The second problem rests with divine (and in this case malevolent) activity upon physical properties. As noted, neuroscience research troubles this view either at a synaptic level or with larger models of agency and freewill. The work of Murphy and Brown, as well as Clayton, offer a form of emergent activity that refuses to separate the material from the immaterial. Their view leaves ample space for top-down causation, yet remains related to the created order. Such a view does not reduce God to the created order, but it also refuses to allow sin any ontic status with God—a problem already presented.

If sin proves to be inevitable, yet may not be "in-bred," how might one understand childhood depravity either through contemporary neuroscience or in conversation with another theological tradition? First, following LeDoux, one might note that our whole bodies shape and form memory from birth beginning at the core synaptic processes of our being. Sin begins to affect children as they experience the sinful acts and responses of caregivers, often shaping implicit as well as explicit memory and pathways. The "embeddedness" of this level of experience at the core of our biological construction reveals one reason why sin may prove such a dominant force in a person's life. Just how those experiential events interact with certain genetic proclivities (for instance genetic dispositions toward alcoholism or other addictive behaviors) vary from one person to the next (Webb and Drury, 2009, pp. 3–4). Yet children find themselves deeply influenced in a systemic environment that incorporates a number of such sinful experiences. They remain a systemic influence in the world around children.

Looking for specific "sin" experiences (like trying to determine a sin gene or the "seat" of sin in the brain) proves fruitless in a holistic understanding of what LeDoux (2002) calls the mental trilogy of cognition, emotion, and motivation (pp. 174–80). People with genetic proclivities may be at risk, though those genetic tendencies may not be deterministic. Genetics may cause quicker responses to certain sinful behaviors, behaviors may lead to certain forms of "synaptic sickness"

(LeDoux, pp. 260–300), yet the outcomes of these experiences may be defined as moral sin, not just symptoms of illness (Menninger, 1973, pp. 74–93). What determines their moral nature rests with the power of emergent consciousness as described by Murphy and Brown (2007). Humans ultimately do possess the ability to make conscious decisions, and constrain pathways, though often the very nature of those decisions remain deeply affected by the synaptic experiences one possesses. This influence is pervasive, providing one reason why God's grace is so desperately needed. Decisions, i.e. faith, remains possible and transformation offers a deeper possibility due to the ongoing levels of emergent, top-down, causation. Children, whose overall cognitive and emotional capacities remain in development, prove particularly susceptible. No wonder, following Markham, and even Wesley, formation remains so crucial in shaping children toward an alternative community.

If one includes Clayton's speculative ideas of a form of social emergence, a higher level of social top-down causation, one might posit that the very nature of the social fabric around children (whether malevolent or redemptive) might have potential influence. This view, though debatable, does help ministers understand how certain social sins (e.g., Nazism, racism, ethnic cleansing) sometimes seem to have a "life" or "spirit" of their own in their influence of children, but still retains sin's pervasiveness within the created order. To be sure, moral sin, even if not "in-bred," proves quite inevitable and pervasive even within a neuroscience model.

Beginning with Wesleyan theology, ministers might begin to wonder if childhood depravity proves to be an abstraction. In some sense humanity in its original "form" of the *imago Dei* remains an abstraction due to the inevitability of sin, particularly from an Augustinian point of view. Wesley appears to concede with Augustine, whatever our original design in the image of God might have been, sin changed that reality (Collins, 2007, pp. 70–73). Yet, for Wesley, whatever we were intended to be as sinful creatures also proves an abstraction, due to the prevenient grace of God (Collins, pp. 73–82). One reason Wesley held such a high view of infant baptism, yet resisted an Augustinian belief of its final soteriological impact, rested with his belief God retains the "first word" of grace over sin even at birth. That first word may not be the final word, particularly since God's triune relationality invites participation with God, and even rejection of relationship due to the later influence of sin (i.e., sinning away the grace of baptism).

Nevertheless, children find themselves born into a world of grace as well as a world of sin. Graceful experiences may shape their lives just as profoundly as sinful experiences. While children need not be blank slates (the false view of behaviorism) they remain experiencing beings. Following Markham (2007), God's grace frames those experiences through certain practices and life experiences as "means of grace" providing a means of ongoing participation within the triune life of God through formation in communities of holiness and love. Indeed, if Clayton's speculation proves true, those selfsame communities given to love and care may create the same level of "top-down" influence that manifests itself in the lives of children dramatically but not inevitably (Blevins, 2008).

Childhood depravity may be inevitable. As noted, sin seems to be pervasive within the systemic realities of the world. Childhood depravity need not be inherent, nor inherited. Yet, even if one concedes some form of inherent sinfulness, providing a metaphysical status to sin on par with God, grace must be seen as having the primary, and prior, influence or else one risks raising a new form of Manichean dualism. Whatever the inherent nature of depravity might be, if one attends to Wesley, sin need not determine that one's life remains malformed. This "dis-ease" may find its cure through different forms of "instruction" (implicit and explicit) or participation in the means of grace.

Conclusion

Children definitely face a world shaped by sin, thanks to sinful adults if nothing else. God, if we believe Wesley, would not release them into this world without prevenient grace and without the "means of grace" to guide and shape their lives and cure their moral diseases. Currently children's ministers must acknowledge that a primary challenge to nurturing and empowering children rest with adults. As Bonnie Miller-McLemore (2003) notes, the first concern to address when it comes to faithful discipleship rests with adult conceptions of children (p. xxv). To be sure, this does not place the sole responsibility on certain adults to insure a child's spiritual life. Wesley (1988–95) himself noted that sometimes things go wrong with children raised by good parents (pp. 347–48), the systemic influences of sin, including the varying genetic proclivities of children, result in a matrix far too complex to reduce to specific interventions in a vast and varied world.

An unreflective view of child depravity demeans children through an Augustinian lens without truly reflecting on the limits of that view from the perspective of theology, church history and neuroscience. This view risks encouraging adult practices that may well reflect more sinful activity than anything children might present themselves. Theorists have changed their view of children during large intellectual shifts within history. Early attempts to portray children within certain extremes that promoted children or restricted them now seem to give way to what Miller-McLemore observes as "a rich moral and religious complexity has returned along with the honesty and real ambiguity of children and parenting" (2003, pp. 21–22). A balanced view that projects neither an idyllic view of children as unblemished romantics, nor a demonic view as willful sinners, probably serves a Wesleyan perspective best. Like Miller-McLemore, adults might be better served to see children as a "labor of love" (pp. 105–36) that require attention yet also serve as a means of grace in their own right—to adults.

References

Anderson, Byron (1999). "Trinitarian grammar of the liturgy and the liturgical practice of the self," *Wesleyan Theological Journal* 34(2), 152–74.

Bakke, O. M. (2005). *When children became people: The birth of childhood in early Christianity.* Minneapolis: Fortress Press.

Blevins, Dean G. (Spring 2008). To be a means of grace: A Wesleyan perspective on Christian practices and the lives of children. *Wesleyan Theological Journal,* 43(2), 47–67.

Bunge, Marica J. (2008). Introduction. In M. J. Bunge (Ed.), *The child in the Bible* (pp. xiv–xxvi). Grand Rapids: Eerdmans.

Clayton, Philip (2004/2006). *Mind & emergence: From quantum to consciousness.* New York: Oxford University Press.

Coleson, Joseph. "Hebrew Prepositions" Personal Correspondence, Email, 06 June 2008.

Collins, Kenneth J. (2007). *The theology of John Wesley: Holy love and the shape of grace.* Nashville: Abingdon.

Estep, James Riley Jr. (2008). The Christian nurture of children in the second and third centuries. In Holly Catterton Allen (Ed.), *Nurturing children's spirituality: Christian perspectives and best practices* (pp. 61–77). Eugene, OR: Cascade.

Flanagan, Owen (2002). *The problem of the soul: Two visions of the mind and how to reconcile them.* New York: Basic.

Gaventa, Beverly Roberts (2008). Finding a place for children in the letters of Paul. In M. J. Bunge (Ed.), *The child in the Bible* (pp. 233–48). Grand Rapids: Eerdmans.

Gladwell, Malcolm (2005). *Blink: The power of thinking without thinking.* New York: Little, Brown.

Goleman, Ronald (2006). *Social intelligence: The new science of human relationships.* New York: Bantam.

Green, Joel B. (Ed.). (2004). *What about the soul? Neuroscience and Christian anthropology.* Nashville: Abingdon.

Green, Joel and Palmer, Stuart L. (2005). *In search of the soul: Four views of the mind-body problem.* Downers Grove, IL: InterVarsity.

Greven, Phillip (1977). *The Protestant temperament: Patterns of child-rearing, religious experience, and the self in early America.* Chicago: University of Chicago Press.

Gundry-Volf, Judith M. (2001). The least and the greatest: Children in the New Testament. In M. J. Bunge (Ed.), *The child in Christian thought* (pp. 29–60). Grand Rapids: Eerdmans.

Gunton, Colin E. (2002). *The Christian faith: An introduction to Christian dDoctrine.* Oxford: Blackwell.

Guroian, Vigen (2001). The ecclesial family: John Chrysostom on parenthood and children. In M. J. Bunge (Ed.), *The child in Christian thought* (pp. 61–77). Grand Rapids: Eerdmans.

Heitzenrater, Richard P. (2001). John Wesley and children. In M. J. Bunge (Ed.), *The child in Christian thought* (pp. 279–99). Grand Rapids: Eerdmans,

Hogue, David A. (2003). *Remembering the future, imagining the past: Story, ritual, and the human brain.* Cleveland: Pilgrim.

Issler, Klaus (2004). Biblical perspectives on developmental grace for nurturing children's spirituality. In D. Ratcliff (Ed.), *Children's spirituality: Christian perspectives, research and applications* (pp. 54–71). Eugene, OR: Cascade.

Juaerrero, Alicia (1999). *Dynamics in action: Intentional behavior as a complex system.* Cambridge: MIT Press.

Lawson, Kevin E. (2011). Baptismal theology and practices and the spiritual nurture of children part I: Early and medieval church. *Christian Education Journal, l Series 3, 8*(1), 130–45.

LeDoux, Joseph (2002). *The synaptic self: How our brains become who we are.* New York: Penguin.

McDonald, H.B. (1988). Manichaeism. In S. B. Ferguson, D. F. Wright and J. I. Packer (Eds.), *New dictionary of theology* (pp. 410–11).. Downers Grove, IL: InterVarsity.

Maddox, Randy L. (October 2007). John Wesley on holistic health and healing. *Methodist History 46*(1), 4–33.

———. (2004). Psychology and Wesleyan theology: Precedents and prospects for a renewed engagement. *Journal of Psychology and Christianity, 23*(2), 101–9.

———. (1994). *Responsible grace: John Wesley's practical theology.* Nashville: Kingswood.

Markham, Paul N. (2007). *Rewired: Exploring religious conversion.* Eugene, OR: Pickwick.

McCann, J. Clinton Jr. (1993). *A theological introduction to the book of Psalms.* Nashville: Abingdon.

Menninger, Karl (1973). *Whatever became of sin?* New York: Hawthorn.

Miller-McLemore, Bonnie (2003). *Let the children come: Reimagining childhood from a Christian perspective.* San Francisco: Jossey-Bass.

Morowitz, Harold J. (2002). *The emergence of everything: How the world became complex.* Oxford: Oxford University Press.

Murphy, Nancey (2006). *Bodies and souls, or spirited bodies?* Cambridge: Cambridge University Press.

Murphy, Nancey and Brown, Warren (2007). *Did my neurons make me do it: Philosophical and neurobiological perspectives on moral responsibility and free will.* Oxford: Oxford University Press.

Sisemore, Timothy A. (2004). From doctrine to practice: The influence of the doctrine of original sin on Puritan child-rearing. In D. Ratcliff (Ed.), *Children's spirituality: Christian perspectives, research and applications* (pp. 219–32). Eugene, OR: Cascade.

———. (2008). Theological perspectives on children in the church: Reformed and Presbyterian. In H. C. Allen (Ed.), *Nurturing children's spirituality: Christian perspectives and best practices* (pp. 93–109). Eugene, OR: Cascade.

Sparkman, G. Temp. (1983). *The salvation and nurture of the child of God: The story of Emma.* Valley Forge, PA: Judson.

Staples, Rob (1991). *Outward sign and inward grace: The place of the sacraments in Wesleyan spirituality.* Kansas City: Beacon Hill.

Stookey, Lawrence Hull (1982). *Baptism: Christ's act in the church.* Nashville: Abingdon.

Stonehouse, Catherine (1998). *Joining children on the spiritual journey.* Grand Rapids: Baker.

———. (2004). Children in Wesleyan thought. In D. Ratcliff (Ed.), *Children's spirituality: Christian perspectives, research and applications* (pp. 133–48). Eugene, OR: Cascade.

Stortz, Martha Elen. (2001). 'When or where was your servant innocent?': Augustine on childhood. In M. J. Bunge (Ed.), *The child in Christian thought* (pp. 78–99). Grand Rapids: Eerdmans.

Thatcher, Adrian (2007). *Theology and families.* London: Blackwell.

Wainwright, Geoffrey (1995). *Methodists in dialogue.* Nashville: Abingdon.

Webb, Burton and Drury, Keith (2009, June). "Possible influence of genetic factors on sin, sanctification, and theology." *Didache: Faithful teaching, 9*(1). Retrieved June 09, 2009, from http://didache.nts.edu/index.php

Wesley, John (1872). *The works of John Wesley* (Vols. 1–14, 3rd ed.). T. Jackson, (Ed.). London, UK: Wesleyan Methodist Book Room.

———. (1988–1995). On the education of children. In A. Outler (Ed.), *Sermons* (Vols. 1–4, Bicentennial Ed., pp. 347–60). Nashville: Abingdon.

Wetzell, James (1999). Sin. In A. D. Fitzgerald (Ed.), *Augustine through the ages: An encyclopedia* (pp. 800–802). Grand Rapids: Eerdmans., pp 800–802

Zimmer, Carl (2004). *The soul made flesh: The discovery of the brain—and how it changed the world.* New York: Free Press.

5

The Sacramental Image of the Child in the Thought of Thomas Traherne and Its Theological Significance

Elizabeth Dodd

Introduction

> An Antepast of Heaven sure!
> I on the Earth did reign.
>   Within, without me, all was pure.
> I must become a Child again.
> ("Innocence," ll. 57–60, Margoliouth II, 1958, pp. 14–15)

These extraordinary words in praise of childhood come from a poem by Thomas Traherne of Hereford (*c.* 1637–1674). Traherne, the rector of Credenhill and chaplain to the Keeper of the Seals, led an apparently unremarkable life, but his writings disclose a remarkable man, an exuberant yet erudite mystical poet, metaphysical philosopher, devotional and theological writer. Traherne was virtually unknown until the attribution by Bertram Dobell of two manuscripts discovered in a book barrow in 1896–1897, which contained the devotional work, *Centuries of Meditations* (hereafter CM), and a copy of Traherne's poems (see Dobell, 1903, pp. lxxxiv–xcii). Since then, further manuscripts have been discovered, including the *Church's Yearbook* (CY), a collection of prayers following the liturgical calendar from the resurrection to All Saints' Day, *Select Meditations* (SM), a work similar to the *Centuries* although probably of earlier composition, the *Commentaries of Heaven* (CH), a collection of commonplace book-style entries that aims to redefine all things "In the Light of GLORY" (CH, title page, Ross II, p. 3), and the Lambeth Manuscript, which contains several theological treatises (including *A Sober View of Doctor Twisse* (SV). See Osborn, 1964; Jordan, 1983; Inge & MacFarlane, 2000; the complete works are currently under publication by Ross, 2005–2017).

Traherne has primarily been the subject of literary studies, but recent work by Denise Inge, Edmund Newey, David Ford, and Mark McIntosh among others, has begun to bring Traherne into the theological sphere (Inge, 2004, 2008 & 2009; Newey, 2010; Ford, 1999 & 2007; McIntosh, 2004). Traherne's love of childhood has been a particularly prominent theme in Traherne studies. Critics often saw in this a connection with the Romantics of the nineteenth-century, or described it as a feature that distinguished Traherne in his own period (see Blevins, 2007, pp. ix–x; Hopkins, 1962, p. 118; Marcus, 1978; Sabine, 1980). Recent criticism has often downplayed or ignored this theme, but Newey's important article on Traherne's "iconic child" (2010), has demonstrated the continuing relevance of the theme of childhood for theological work on Traherne.

This paper will demonstrate that, as opposed to the biographical and poetic analyses that have hitherto dominated Traherne criticism, and in contrast to Newey's "iconic" interpretation, a sacramental reading is both appropriate for Traherne's child-image and uncovers unexamined aspects of its theological significance. Traherne's sacramental child draws together the outer and inner worlds of matter and spirit and bridges the gulf between the speculative realm of human nature, origins, possibility and potential, and the world of actual experience, while maintaining their distinction. The mediatory character of the sacramental image embodies a fusion of the biological and spiritual child that draws childlike attributes normally associated with the ideal spiritual world into the drama of human living. Participation in sacramental childlikeness through the performative character of the sacramental is one way of understanding the process of becoming a child again. This is all demonstrated through the lens of infant innocence, an important but recently neglected theme in Traherne's thought. This analysis not only transforms understandings of

Traherne's child-image, but also challenges more general conceptions of infant innocence influenced by the Romantic ideal of the child, by presenting innocence as a partial and complex attribute conformed to the human condition of finitude and mutability. Finally, this paper applies its conclusions to the field of child spirituality. It assesses the significance of a sacramental image of the child and of a transformed concept of infant innocence to modern theologies of childhood, considering Traherne in relation to the interaction between the biological and eternal child in Karl Rahner's work, and it suggests that Traherne's varied modes of writing about the child may correspond to different methodologies for theologies of childhood.

I: Methodologies

1: Biographical Approaches to the Child

There have hitherto been two primary approaches to the child-figure in Traherne's writings: biographical approaches that treat it as a representation of Traherne's actual experience, and poetic approaches that see it primarily as a symbolic metaphor (*cf.* Wöhrer, 1982, pp. 151–71). The biographical approach includes literal biography and accounts of a spiritual or psychological progress, many of which draw on insights from psychoanalysis and developmental theory. Gladys Wade's rather imaginative biography of Traherne is avowedly reliant upon a literal reading of the autobiographical sections of the *Centuries* and poems (Wade, 1944, pp. 27–37 (27)). Many critics since Wade have persisted in interpreting Traherne's descriptions of childhood as autobiographical, sometimes in similarly uncritical readings of the *Centuries* (*e.g.* Dowell, 1990, pp. 62–65), sometimes in more subtle forms. Keith Salter adapts Wade's description of the literal loss of infant bliss and fall into childish apostasy, into an account of Traherne's inner spiritual progress (Salter, 1964, pp. 22–38), while Franz Wöhrer describes it as the development of Traherne's "mystical consciousness" (Wöhrer, 1982, especially pp. 99–135).

The biographical approach is problematic for several reasons. It draws its evidence primarily from the autobiographical third century of the *Centuries of Meditations*, in which Traherne claims to teach from experience (CM III.1; meditations 1–35 cover the period from infancy until university; *cf.* SM III.27–30). There is no reason to doubt his honesty, but it is equally clear that these accounts are shaped by memory, education, projection, and authorial concerns. Similarities between the *Centuries* and *Select Meditations* may not reflect biographical accuracy, but rather Traherne's attempt to construct a coherent vision of felicity by repeating and reworking themes: such as the infant vision of the divine city (SM III.29; CM III.3), which falls into an earthly city full of "Roaring Boys" (SM III.30; "Eden," l. 24, Margoliouth II, p. 13). The evidence of the poems of childhood is no better, since the use of the first person may be stylistic, the accounts of birth and infancy in "The Preparative" and "The Salutation" must rely at least partially on imagination or projection (*cf.* Wöhrer, 1982, pp. 168–71), and the didactic message of poems such as "Shadows in the Water" overshadows the value of any biographical accuracy (Margoliouth II, pp. 127–30).

Evidential problems are compounded by the way in which the biographical approach obscures the theological sense and purpose of the texts. The studies by Wade, Salter, and Wöhrer interpret Traherne's autobiographical descriptions of childhood more as accounts of the making of a budding mystic, emphasizing his own precocious childlike spirituality, rather than as exhortations to the reader to wonder at God's grace extended to all children and to participate in the spiritual life of the child, which is Traherne's stated purpose (see CM III.5–6). Biographical approaches limit the recognition of theological elements in Traherne's thought. This can be seen in individual cases, as in Wade's interpretation of Traherne's infant lack of knowledge of poverty, sickness, and death as no more than ignorance (Wade, 1944, p. 30). It can also be seen in broader issues: for example, most critics until Newey have underplayed the recurrent and central Pauline themes of being child, son, and image of God.

Developmental theory has had a vast influence on interpretations of Traherne's child, as it has in the field of child spirituality. This is exemplified by the work of Robert Ellrodt, who is "incline[d] to think that Traherne's doctrine was genuinely based on the common structures of the child's consciousness," as set forth in the developmental theories of Jean Piaget and Pierre Bovet (Ellrodt, 2000, pp. 93–94, 97–98; *cf.* Ellrodt, 1960; Clements, 1964, pp 502, 504; Wöhrer, 1982, pp. 163–68). The advantage of this approach is that Traherne's descriptions of early infancy can simultaneously be "solipsistic illusion" or projection and also genuinely and accurately autobiographical (Ellrodt, 2000, p. 91): *i.e.* the imagined and actual child are one and the same. On the surface a developmental approach appears appropriate to Traherne, due to his extensive use of traditional ideas of the stages of life, which can be traced through the thought of Plato, Aristotle, Augustine, Aquinas and Calvin (see Pitkin in Bunge, 2001, pp. 164–65). Traherne's descriptions of a blessed infancy, followed by an apostate childhood that contains the seeds of a return to felicity, conforms roughly to common ideas of the stages of childhood: infancy until the advent of speech, childhood until the age of seven or eight, and youth until the age of fourteen. However, this is where the utility of developmental theory ends.

The weakness of applying developmental theory to Traherne lies in an over-reliance on modern and often secular understandings of children's psychological development that sit anachronistically alongside Traherne's theological thought and obscure the mature Christian spirituality contained in Traherne's descriptions of infancy. The animism of the Piagetian infant is not the Trahernian child who walks with God in Eden (Ellrodt, 2000, p. 95; cf. CM III.4, l. 7), and the egocentricity or solipsism of the Piagetian child obscures Traherne's concept of circulation between the knowledge of self and God, that sees knowledge of "I" in the context of relationship (Ellrodt, 2000, pp. 96–100; see Inge, 2009, pp. 201–20; Newey, 2010, pp. 239–40n4). Unfortunately, Traherne criticism has not yet appropriated the more critical approach to developmental theory that characterises recent work on child spirituality (see Hay & Nye, 1998, pp. 40–56; Bunge, 2001, p. 5n6; Wall, 2006, pp. 525–27; Dillen and Pollefeyt, 2010, p. 5; Miller-McLemore in Dillen and Pollefeyt, 2010, pp. 28–34, 41). From the perspective of child spirituality, a major weakness of developmental theory is that it "instrumentalizes" the child. By focussing on the teleological movement of maturation into adulthood, it forms a "Spirituality of the Final Stage" that devalues childlike qualities and detracts from the integrity and dignity of the child in itself (see Miller-McLemore, 2010, p. 28; cf. Rahner, 1971, pp. 33–34; Devries, 2001, p. 163). Traherne's writings do not stand up to the rigors of modern studies of child spirituality in terms of knowledge of and interest in actual children's experiences and well-being but, as will be demonstrated, the material character of the sacramental prevents the total instrumentalization of the child by preserving an interest in the distinctiveness of childlikeness.

2: Poetic Approaches to the Child

The metaphorical or symbolic interpretation of Traherne's "poetic child" is just as problematic as the biographical approach. Considering Traherne's contempt for ornamental language, the poetic approach is hardly appropriate, "For Metaphors conceal,/ And only Vapours prove" ("The Person," l. 25, Margoliouth II, p. 76). Although this methodology demonstrates the universal scope of Traherne's child-image and avoids problems of evaluating biographical authenticity, it reduces the child to a metaphor, myth, or allegory that gives no value to the child in itself (Clements, 1969, pp. 16, 18, 31; *cf.* Balakier, 1989, p. 239; Gilbert, 1947, p. 441). The child as symbol becomes a representation of other things: virtues such as innocence, humility, joy, or love, capacities such as sense, true sight, intuition or imagination, or a status of being in immediate relationship to the divine. The metaphorical child is not even a genuine speaking subject, let alone the active "Tutor, Teacher, [and] Guid" of Traherne's poetry ("The Approach," ll. 41–42, Margoliouth II, p. 40). In Stewart's work the child's voice merely represents half of a dialectical conversation between child and adult that is united, and thereby subsumed, "by including the adult truth with the sweetness of the child's mistake in a wider, more complete view" (Stewart, 1970, p. 212). A poetic methodology thus turns Traherne's urgent call to "become a Child again," in obedience to Christ's injunction, into hollow rhetoric (see CM III.5; Matt 18:3; Mark 10:15; Luke 18:17).

The final approach to be addressed is Newey's recent work on Traherne's "iconic child." Newey's significance lies mainly in his definition of the child as less a figure of a "lost innocence" than as an "icon of the whole human condition" (Newey, 2010, p. 228). This gives the child-figure a broader meaning that was, incidentally, anticipated by Clements and Sabine (Clements, 1969, pp. 16–17; Sabine, 1980, p. 22). The term, "iconic," drawn from the work of Russian theologian Sergius Bulgakov, admirably expresses the direct sensory character of infant communication and perception as a pre-lingual, pre-symbolic form of referencing (Newey, 2010, p. 240n7; see Berryman, 2005, p. 127). However, the child as icon, meaning "imaginative focus" or object of contemplation, remains abstracted from the actual experience of childhood (Newey, 2010, p. 240n7). Like other symbolic and metaphorical interpretations, it fails to delineate the relationship between the biological and eternal child.

Newey's impact also lies in demonstrating the theological basis of Traherne's reflections, but this aspect of Newey's work is incomplete because it does not do full justice to Traherne's concern with distinctive childlike qualities. Newey highlights the centrality of Pauline thought on sonship to Traherne's reflections on childhood (Newey, 2010, p. 231). While the terminology of sonship and inheritance recurs throughout Traherne's writings, the language of adoption, which Newey stresses most, is less common. Sonship and inheritance for Traherne may be more closely allied to the theme of what it means to be in the image of God, than they are to Traherne's reflections on the nature and qualities of childhood (see *Thanksgivings*, Ross IV, p. 411; Newey, 2010, pp. 234, 238). This is reflected in the fact that Newey's assessment of the themes of sonship, inheritance, and adoption leads him to define childhood primarily by descent rather than age. This filial interpretation of Traherne's child downplays the importance of distinctive childlike qualities and thereby overshadows the call to "become a Child again." Therefore, while Newey provides invaluable insights into the relational character of Traherne's biblical child and its centrality to important theological issues of theological anthropology, soteriology, and sanctification, this paper will return to the other recurrent biblical theme in Traherne's thought, the gospel call to become a child again, in order to re-examine Traherne's treatment of childlike qualities in the light of a sacramental reading of the child.

3: The Sacramental Approach to the Child

A sacramental methodology avoids both the overly-literalistic and overly-symbolic tendencies of the biographical and poetic approaches. Like Newey's "iconic" approach it highlights the theological nature of Traherne's thought, but it is more appropriate to Traherne's context and the character of his theology, and more conducive to an analysis of the integration of the material and spiritual child in Traherne's writings.

The term "sacramental" carries various connotations in different contexts. It is particularly appropriate to seventeenth-century British literary history, in which it evokes the controversy between Laudian and Calvinist theologies of the sacraments, often seen in terms of a dispute between public devotion and private spirituality (Whalen, 2001; *cf.* DiPasquale, 1999, pp. 6–11). The divergent views of Louis Martz and Barbara Lewalski on the metaphysical poets (including Herbert, Donne, Vaughan, and Traherne), as either belonging to an Anglo-Catholic "poetry of meditation" or a "Protestant poetics," has been surmounted by more recent studies, which have seen in them an internalized "sacramental poetry" that forms an irenic or individual combination of these two devotional streams (see Whalen, 2001, p. 1288; Whalen, 2002, pp. 168–77; DiPasquale, 1999, pp. 1–15; Schwartz, 2008, p. 120; *cf.* Lewalski, 1979; Martz, 1954). This resolution reflects the Church of England's settlement on the sacraments, which was an exercise in unity through ambiguity, defining the Eucharist as both a sign and means of grace: "not only a sign of the love that Christians ought to have among themselves, one to another, but rather it is [also] a sacrament of our redemption by Christ's death" (Article Twenty-Eight, Thirty-Nine Articles). The combination of public and private piety, Arminianism and Calvinism, in internal sacramental piety, may be seen as not only a compromise between two devotional modes, but as a unity of outer and inner worlds, of matter and spirit.

In poetics, "sacramental" is a term that is seldom clearly defined. It can signify, for example, the manifestation of meaning in the physical form of a poem as an outward sign of inner grace, the effectual conveyance of grace through proper audience reception, or the evocation of mystery through the surplus of meaning inherent in metaphorical language (Whitlock, 1986; DiPasquale, 1999, pp. 16–22; Schwartz, 2008, pp. 6–8, 117–21). When defining Traherne's sacramental language, the "sacramental" must be distinguished from the "symbolic," by a complexity and materiality that is expressed in particular and sensory language (see Ballinger, 2000, pp. 85–97, 239–40). Philip Ballinger's study of Gerard Manley Hopkins' sacramental poetry employs a Balthasarian distinction between symbol and sacrament that expresses this incarnational character of sacramental language:

> Poetic language, as "sacramental," "certainly contains within itself the power of 'symbol', while it goes far beyond it;" for "the form of the image is a likeness to the primordial form in that it has the 'stress' of the latter in itself: *sacramenta continent quae significant.*" (Balthasar, 1986, pp. 393–94, quoted in Ballinger, 2000, pp. 188–89; *cf.* readings of sacrament as symbol: Dillistone, 1955; Barth, 2001, p. 39; Schwartz, 2008, p. 7).

Traherne's child-image may be understood as sacramental, according to the particular style of his sacramental devotion. The sacramental nature of Traherne's piety has been asserted by A.M. Allchin,
who sees Traherne's notion of the "sacramental character" of creation
and redemption as an element of an Anglican spirituality shaped by
the Book of Common Prayer, and by Thomas Merton, who defines
Traherne's sacramental spirituality as a Eucharistic "theology of
praise" (Allchin *et.al*, 1989, pp. 26–28, 34; Merton, 1967, pp. 133–34).
This characterization may be reasonably applied to the child-image,
because Traherne's sacramental devotion extended far beyond fidel-
ity to the outward sacraments of Eucharist and baptism. One cannot deny the Eucharist's centrality to Traherne's spirituality, but it is
rarely explicitly invoked, and is most present in his persistent note of
praise (see "Goodnesse," ll. 49–70, Margoliouth II, p. 184). Similarly
the outward sacrament of baptism, while immensely important, was
considered incomplete without the spiritual observance of the oath
in the ongoing life of faith (SV, pp. 81–82). The sacramental character
of Traherne's child-image is associated with his broader expressions
of sacramentality: his use of quotidian images to replace traditional
sacramental symbols such as the Eucharist, and his sacramental vision
of the world (see Ponsford, 1983, pp. 1–3; Brown and Fuller, 1995, pp.
6–7; Allchin *et.al*, 1989, pp. 26–27; Kershaw, 2005, pp. 177–79).

Traherne's depiction of the child conforms to the general character of his sacramental devotion. A sacramental spirituality centered
on praise is reflected in Traherne's response to the child as "a surpriz-
ing Wonder great enough to astonish even Men of yeers," and in the
response of the child-figure to its own existence and to the world,
which is one of awe, "How like an Angel came I down!/ How Bright
are all Things here!" ("Babe," CH, Ross III, p. 438; "Wonder," ll. 1–2,
Margoliouth II, p. 6). A sacramental *mysterium* is evoked by deliberate ambiguity over metaphysical issues such as the pre-existence of
the soul. In the poems, "The Salutation," "The Preparative" and "My
Spirit," the mystery of the child is compounded by the lack of clarity over whether the subject is a newborn infant, a fetus, or the pre-
existing soul (on the debate over Traherne's doctrine of pre-existence
see Day, 1968). A sacramental reading of Traherne's child thus makes
it both a wonder and a mystery.

Traherne's child-image employs sacramental language. Particularity is not a word often associated with Traherne, but he generates emotive force with affective descriptions of apparently personal experience: in infancy "The Green Trees when I saw them first through one of the Gates Transported and Ravished me; their Sweetnes and unusual Beauty made my Heart to leap" (CM III.3). Materiality is expressed in an emphasis on the child's sensory relationship with the world. Traherne describes the infant's first impressions primarily in the Platonic language of vision: the "hevenly Sence" of the "Infant-Ey" sees the true value of the world in the context of eternity ("An Infant-Ey," l. 5, Margoliuth II, p. 86; see Ridlon, 1964). The materiality of the sacramental is also reflected in Traherne's interest in the infant body: "These little Limmes,/ These Eys and Hands which here I find,/ These rosie Cheeks wherwith my Life begins" ("The Salutation," ll. 1–3, Margoliouth II, p. 4, *cf.* "The Preparative" ll.1–10, Margoliouth II, p. 20). Sensory and particular language asserts the physical nature of the child-image, which may be seen as conducive to a spirituality that values the real experience of childhood alongside its theological associations.

Traherne's child-image performs a sacramental function, as both sign and means of grace, and mediator between matter and spirit. The child-figure as sign of grace becomes a sacramental object, meaning an object of wonder or meditation, as achieved through the emblematization of the "Babe" in the *Commentaries.* The child as a means of grace is a sacramental subject that conveys grace by encouraging participation in childlikeness, like the speaking subject of the poems that facilitates the transfiguration of reader into child by imaginative participation in memory. The recollections of childhood in the *Centuries* and *Select Meditations* combine these two functions, since they present infancy as an object of wonder that should also be appropriated by the reader:

> Will you see the Infancy of this sublime and celestial Greatness?
> Those Pure and Virgin Apprehensions I had from the Womb
> . . . Pray for them earnestly: for they will make you Angelical,
> and wholy Celestial (CM III.1).

The child-image's mediatory function appears in passages that merge the biological and spiritual child. Traherne's babe is:

> wrapt up in the Swaddling clothes of his own infirmities . . .
> as Great in his Hopes and Possibilities, as he is Small in the
> Appearance of his present Attainments. If we consult either
> his Body, or his Soul, he is but a Seed of his future Perfection
> ("Babe," CH, Ross III, p. 437).

This blurring of boundaries between the material and spiritual child forms a hermeneutical circle in which they mutually interpret one another. The interdependence of definitions between the two enables Traherne to maintain the priority of the spiritual with the integrity of the biological child, and demonstrates the inseparability of the real child from its theological significance.

The sacramental child-image may be understood simultaneously as a focus for devotion and a mediator of the worlds of spirit and matter. It forms part of a spirituality that is centred on praise and wonder, but equally concerned with the operations of the material world. This image may be favourably compared to Kuchar's thesis on Traherne's "sacramental subject," which he describes as a "being whose every gesture is a joyful act of sacrifice" (Kuchar in Blevins, 2007, p. 174). The child-image shares the sacramental subject's mediatory function, which, Kuchar asserts, reconciles medieval and modern cosmologies by participating in changing attitudes to body and world and responding to the desacralisation of emerging modern thought (Kuchar, 2005, pp. 181–218; cf. Schwartz, 2008, pp. 11–17).

Traherne's sacramental child-image should not be confused with the popular concept of the child as sacrament or representative of Christ, which appears in many modern theologies of childhood (Légasse, 1969, pp. 322–26; Maas, 2000, p. 458; Gundry-Volf, 2000, p. 477; Jensen, 2005, pp. 130–31; Bunge, 2006, pp. 570–72; Chris Jamber in Nye, 2009, p. 74). This theme is based on an Irenaean interpretation of the incarnation, or on readings of the Gospel narratives that interpret the child placed in the midst as the institution of a sacrament, or Christ's command to his disciples to receive little children as reflecting the reception of Christ himself (Matt 18:1–5; Mark 9:33–37; Luke 9:46–48). In Traherne studies, "sacramental" should be understood in the poetic and devotional sense: the language of Traherne's child-figure may form a site of encounter with the divine. Just as Henry More described the people of Israel as "but one living and moving Sacramental Image of Christ and his Body" (More, 1664, p. 221),

Traherne's child may be an imperfect and incomplete, but material and effective, sacramental image of the inner or essential nature of humanity in relation to God.

II: The Sacramental Child and Infant Innocence

The theme of infant innocence is a fitting subject to demonstrate the implications of a sacramental interpretation of Traherne's child-image, in the light of recent developments in scholarship. While Newey and Inge have not denied Traherne's notion of childlike innocence, they have diminished its importance, in a reaction against the persistent influence of the Romantic ideal of the child on Traherne studies (Inge, 2009, pp. 1–6; Newey, 2010, pp. 227–28). Thus, innocence is not listed among the childlike qualities that Inge identifies in Traherne's writings (Inge, 2009, pp. 63, 100, 150–51, 187–88, 193–94). This move away from innocence initially appears justified: considering the popularity of the theme in early Traherne criticism, it is surprising how little the word is specifically used in connection with childhood, outside of the triptych of poems, "Wonder," "Eden," "Innocence," that all describe the infant estate explicitly in terms of the Adamic innocence of Eden (*cf.* CM III.2; CY, Ross IV, p. 305 (deleted section to p. 234, l. 8)). The theme should not be neglected, however, since in Traherne's thought innocence is one aspect of childlikeness to which humanity has been called to return. Rather, innocence should be reinterpreted through a sacramental reading of Traherne's child-image. When this is attempted, a concept of innocence appears that is very unlike the lost bliss of Romantic idealism. This innocence is fully involved in the materiality of the world and the drama of experience, and subsists within the mediation of the mystery of the divine and the corporeal and sensory nature of human living. It is a partial innocence that reflects human finitude, often concealed under the accumulation of guilt or overshadowed by other attributes. It is a complex innocence that combines the strengths and weaknesses of sinlessness in the face of sin.

The mystery of infant innocence is enacted in the realm of experience. Traherne's ambiguity over the nature and extent of childhood innocence engenders doubt as to whether one can call children innocent at all, but on another level it elevates innocence to the status of a divine mystery. In his more systematic and theological works,

Traherne makes it clear that he does not consider infants to be objectively innocent. In the *Commentaries* and *Sober View* Traherne states that infants, like all humanity, are already drawn from nothing into glory, fallen into corruption, and "Sacramentally regenerated" by grace in baptism (SV, pp. 80–81, 84–85 (81); "Babe," CH, Ross III, pp. 437–38; *cf.* CY, Ross IV, p. 163 on John the Baptist's redemption in the womb). However, alongside this orthodox narrative persists a strong memory of infant innocence that leads Traherne to conjecture as to its potential origins and attributes, whether natural or divine, essential or fleeting. Ultimately, the intensity of feeling associated with this memory makes him conclude that the experience and its effects have priority over philosophical speculation, and do not require explanation:

> Whether it be that Nature is so pure,/ And Custom only vicious; or that sure/ God did by Miracle the Guilt remov . . . Or that 'twas one Day,/ Wher in this Happiness I found;/ Whose Strength and Brightness so do Ray,/ That still it seemeth to Surround./ What ere it is, it is a Light/ So Endless unto me/ That I a World of true Delight/ Did then and to this Day do see.
> ("Innocence," ll. 37–39, 41–48, Margoliouth II, p. 18)

The paradox between the doctrine of human fallenness and the experience of apparent innocence is never properly resolved, which has contributed to vastly divergent interpretations of Traherne's doctrine of original sin (see Salter, 1955; Marshall, 1958; Guffey, 1967; Grant, 1971; Poole, 2000, pp. 277–317). While these treatments are without exception more concerned with Traherne's hamartiology than with the complementary notion of innocence, the most convincing analyses are those which leave room for a relative innocence of the infant as "ten thousand times more prone to Good and Excellent Things, then evil" (CM III.8, *cf.* SV, p. 130). This may account for the enduring influence of Grant's Irenaean reading of Traherne, in which sin is gradually acquired by education rather than transmitted through procreation (Grant, 1974, pp. 170–97). Despite this partial success in unravelling Traherne's doctrine of original sin, Traherne's theological ambiguity maintains the priority of experience, creating a notion of innocence that has its origin and end in a eucharistic experience of praise and wonder. Regardless of the reality of infant innocence, this experience holds out the prospect of participation through sacramental performance, by presenting the possibility of a life lived "*As if* there were nor Sin, nor Miserie" (my italics, "The Preparative," l. 50, Margoliouth II, p. 22). Theoretical conjectures on innocence therefore can end, like the entry for 'Babe' in the *Commentaries*, with a poetic call for "the Light and the Simplicitie/ Of New Born Babes" ("Babe," CH, Ross III, p. 439).

Infant innocence is inseparable from Traherne's descriptions of Eden or the "Kingdom of Innocence" (SM IV.67) with which it is equated. Newey's description of Traherne's Eden as a "fixed state of reciprocal love" is typical of Traherne scholarship in making it an ideal but blank, static origin out of which human life emerges, as opposed to the "dynamic process of growth into the divine likeness" of the estate of grace (Newey, 2010, p. 238). It is this definition of Eden which leads him to declare that Traherne's "child is clearly very far from a purely innocent Edenic figure" (Newey, 2010, p. 234). On the contrary, Traherne's infant Eden forms part of the drama of grace. As opposed to the "Elizian feilds" of spiritual retirement (SM III.1), it is drawn into the mutability of human living through action and growth. Traherne's infant Eden is a theatre of action in which his soul walks, the world talks to him, the stars entertain him, and the works and glories of God are displayed to him ("Wonder," Margoliouth II, pp. 6, 8). In Eden the soul is employed in meditation, rejoicing, worship, love, and reigning over the world ("Innocence," ll. 13, 22, 26–27, 31, 58, Margoliouth II, pp. 16–18). Edenic growth forms part of a teleological narrative of natural development, exploration, and expansion. Somewhat like Milton's "untamed" Eden (Knott, 2005), Traherne's is a garden in which "A Native Health and Innocence/ Within my Bones did Grow" ("Wonder," ll. 17–18, Margoliouth II, p. 8). It is a process of discovery of the self, world, and God (see "The Salutation"), and the beginning of expansion into the world through possession of it (see SM III.99, ll. 1–8). The activity and growth encountered in the sacramental image of Traherne's infant Eden creates a correlation between pre- and post-fall human states that engages innocence in the mutability of history, thereby making it relevant to discussions of both original human nature, and the processes of spiritual life in the world.

A sacramental reinterpretation of Traherne's Eden displays an innocence that may be encountered in the reality and materiality of experience. Eden may be a memory and, moreover, "essentially a memory lost" (Inge, 2009, pp. 109, 163), but that does not mean that it is thereby abstracted from the world, since Traherne considered the inner life of memory and spiritual sense to have priority over the material world of outward experience: "The Inward Work is the Supreme: for all/ The other were occasiond by the Fall" ("Silence," ll. 3–4, Margoliouth II, p. 44). Particular and sensory language evokes a realism of interior spiritual experience and a reification of innocence. Personal exclamations describe the experience of innocence in particularist terms as "that which most I Wonder at, which most/ I did esteem my Bliss, which most I Boast/ And ever shall Enjoy" ("Innocence," ll. 1–3, Margoliouth II, p. 14). Sensory language creates the impression of materiality, making innocence both a sensory experience, a "Joyfull Sence and Purity," and an object of sense: Traherne claims to have had a "Sight of Innocence," and that it did "fill my Sence" ("Innocence," ll. 9, 4, 55, Margoliouth II, pp. 16, 18; "Wonder," ll. 30–32, Margoliouth II, p. 8). This embodiment of innocence in particular and sensory language subsists within the child-image's mediation of spiritual experience and theological significance, provoking an imagination of innocence as a divine mystery encountered in human life, and raising the possibility of the existence of a genuine childlike innocence.

The character of infant innocence, as drawn into the drama of history and situated within the multiplicity of the world through the incarnational quality of the sacramental child-image, is that of a partial and complex attribute. A partial innocence appears amidst various negative connotations of childhood which have hitherto been largely neglected by Traherne critics (*cf.* Newey, p. 232). The three sorts of childishness listed in Traherne's definition of a "Babe" demonstrate that negative associations are not confined in Traherne's imagination to the later stages of childhood, but also belong to an apparently innocent infancy. The childishness he refers to is equated with a lack of understanding, and covers aged and supposedly wise "Old Babes, that will never be men," "Weak and unskillfull men" who are set to rule over "Sinfull Nations," and "Raw Christians" who are not yet ready for the meat of acquaintance "with the Mysteries of all Ages" ("Babe," CH, Ross III, pp. 438–39). Other sorts of childishness appear elsewhere in Traherne's writings. Traherne's *Commonplace Book* quotes several sources in which the child is associated with folly, perverseness (unknown source, "Corruption," CB, ff. 28–29) and indiscretion (Jackson,

1625, quoted in "Retirement," CB, ff. 202–3). "Foolish Childishness" is a focus on the self rather than God; desiring power to do miracles and seeking after the "childish toys" of worldly treasures (*Thanksgivings*, Roth IV, p. 343; "The Apostacy," l. 43, Margoliouth II, p. 96). The childishness of ingratitude belongs to those who "will not know Him that Nourisheth them," "nor feel the Nature joy and Glory of His Image" (SM, I.84, III.25). A partial infant innocence appears both amid and in contrast to these negative connotations of childhood, much like the fragments of paradise, now lost and buried in ruins, which Traherne desires to recover and "Exhibit again to the Eys of Men" (CM IV.54). This implies that a notion of infant innocence need not be abandoned in the face of the reality of guilt, but rather deserves to be redefined in accordance with the limitations of the human condition.

A complex innocence appears within the juxtaposition of the strengths and weaknesses of the child, and of innocence and sin. Traherne's depiction of the double nature of the child is appropriate to a dual understanding of innocence as both weakness and strength. In Traherne's definition of a "Babe," the various weaknesses of the infant are inseparable from its glories: helplessness, nakedness, feebleness, infirmities, littleness, exposure to injuries, its origin in nothing, and fall into misery, sit alongside the "Spark of immortal fire, that can never be extinguished," the unexercised power of the man, the protection of parents and the favour of God, and the exaltation of its very existence. The ambiguity of the innocent infant state is aptly expressed in exclamations such as "My Naked Simple Life was I" ("My Spirit," l. 1, Margoliouth II, p. 50). The nakedness of the infant suggests its unmediated relationship to the divine, but also its vulnerability to the world. Its simplicity is a likeness to the divine attribute, but is also associated with ignorance. The supreme "I" denotes the glory of the individual in relation to God and world, but is also at risk of accusations of solipsism, as Traherne was well aware (SM III.65). The juxtaposition of innocence and sin is the result of the definition of innocence with reference to and in contrast with sin. In the poem, "Innocence," the bliss, purity, brightness, light, joy, summer, admiration, prizing, praise, love, humility (kneeling), contentment, and delight of innocence, is juxtaposed with a long list of terms associated with sin: stain, spot, darkness, guilt, night, avarice, pride, lust, strife, pollution, fraud, anger, malice, jealousy, and spite. A complex infant innocence thus appears within the inseparability of vulnerability and strength in the image of the child, and is defined in juxtaposition to the guilt of fallenness.

The incarnational, partial, and complex innocence that appears within Traherne's sacramental image of the child mediates between the mystery of humanity's nature and end, and the experience of guilt and finitude, drawing the two together and holding them in tension. This is a definition of innocence that may legitimately form part of the image of the child to which Christ calls us to return. Such a drastic redefinition overturns contemporary understandings of infant innocence as a lost ideal spiritual estate, which are inspired by the Romantic legacy, and may even help to rehabilitate the now oft-despised category of innocence to the field of child spirituality.

III: The Relevance of Traherne' Sacramental Image to Modern Theologies of Childhood

The theological significance of Traherne's sacramental image of the child is best seen through a comparison with Karl Rahner's "Ideas for a Theology of Childhood" (1971). The mediatory character of the sacramental, like Rahner's equation of the biological and eternal child, facilitates a simultaneously ontological and epistemological interpretation of childhood that recognizes the integrity and "unsurpassable," "unique and unrepeatable" value inherent in the biological child (Rahner, 1971, p. 33), while drawing it into an account of mature spirituality. Rather than a Schleiermacherian symbolic or emblematic "pure child" or a Moltmannian child as "metaphor of hope" (see Tice, 1967; Devries, 1989, pp. 173–75; Devries in Bunge, 2001, pp. 329–49; Moltmann, 2000), "it is rather the *reality* of childhood in the human sense that is 'transferred' into childhood in the divine sense" so that "the latter is always and right from the first contained in the former, and finds expression in it" (Rahner, 1971, pp. 48–49). Traherne's sacramental child-image forms a hermeneutical circle between the biological and eternal child and its material and spiritual significance (*cf.* Rahner, 1971, pp. 40, 43–44). Through this sacramentality the complexity, finitude and mutability of the drama of human childhood is not divinised or subsumed, but is inseparably linked to the immutable spiritual truths contained within the divine image of the eternal child.

The redefinition of innocence envisioned through a sacramental interpretation of Traherne's child-image may encourage a reconsideration of common rejections of a notion of infant innocence, which define it as an absolute ideal and associate it with "the erasure of childhood as a vital moral and religious phase of development" (Miller-McLemore, 2010, p. 21). A definition of innocence as partial, complex and incarnational, may complement recent moves away from the language of innocence to the language of grace in theologies of childhood (see Rahner, 1971, p. 40; Jensen, 2005; Berryman, 2009; Nye, 2009). Rather than a binary opposition between simplistic understandings of children as either wholly innocent or sinful, a complex innocence may contribute to narratives of a "double beginning" of guilt and grace, of "fallen angels," or "graced vulnerability" (Rahner, 1971, p. 39; Wall, 2004; Jensen, 2005, pp. 1–12; see also Miller-McLemore, 2003, pp. 22, 52, 143; Bunge, 2006, pp. 563–68).

On a methodological level, the different tones employed in Traherne's treatment of childhood can be equated with different approaches to the child in modern theology (see Bunge, 2006, pp. 569–79; Dillen and Pollefeyt, 2010, p. 6; Champagne in Dillen and Pollefeyt, pp. 373–96). The first-person voice of the child in the poems is appropriate to the methodology of child theology, which attempts to reassess theological issues from the child's perspective. The autobiographical passages of the *Centuries* and *Select Meditations* reflect the approach of child spirituality, which takes seriously the actual experiences of children. The more systematic approach exhibited in the *Commentaries* and *Sober View* echoes that of theologies of childhood, which attempt to draw out the theological significance of childhood. The combination of these voices in Traherne's writings demonstrates the value in all three methodologies, and could suggest ways in which they may interact and be mutually educative. A full understanding of Traherne's theology of childhood cannot exist without taking into account all three voices. Similarly, a successful theology of childhood should incorporate all three methodologies. The potential applications of Traherne's theology of childhood demonstrate that, far from being worthy of neglect, this is a subject that should be returned to with renewed enthusiasm. An exploration of Traherne's child-image through the lens of sacramentality and innocence could uncover new avenues of interpretation for what it means to "become a Child again."

References

Allchin, A. M., Ridler, A., & Smith, J. (Eds.). (1989). *Profitable wonders: Aspects of Thomas Traherne*. Oxford: Amate.

Balakier, J. J. (1989). Thomas Traherne's Dobell series and the Baconian model of experience. *English Studies, 70*, 233–47.

Ballinger, P.A. (2000). *The poem as sacrament: The theological aesthetic of Gerard Manley Hopkins*. Louvain, Belgium: Peeters.

Balthasar, H. U. Von. (1995). Jesus as child and his praise of the child. *Communio, 22*(4), 625–34.

———. (1986). *The glory of the Lord: A theological aesthetics* (Vol. 3). San Francisco: Ignatius.

Barth, J. R. (2001). *The symbolic imagination: Coleridge and the Romantic tradition*. New York: Fordham University Press.

Berryman, J. (2005). Children and mature spirituality. Retrieved from http://www.godlyplay.org/uploads/pages/downloads/Children__Mature_Spirituality.pdf

———. (2009). *Children and the theologians: Clearing the way for grace*. New York: Morehouse.

Blevins, J. (Ed.). (2007). *Re-reading Thomas Traherne: A collection of new critical essays*. Tempe, AZ: Arizona Center for Medieval and Renaissance Studies.

Brown, D. & Fuller, D. (1995). *Signs of grace: Sacraments in poetry and prose*. London: Cassell.

Bunge, M. J. (2006). The child, religion, and the academy: Developing robust theological and religious understandings of children and childhood. *Journal of Religion, 86*(4), 549–79.

———. (Ed.). (2001). *The child in Christian thought*. Grand Rapids: Eerdmans.

Bunge, M. J., Fretheim, T. E., & Gaventa, B. R. (Eds.). (2008). *The child in the Bible*. Grand Rapids: Eerdmans.

Clements, A. L. (1964). The mode and meaning of Traherne's mystical poetry. *Studies in Philology, 61*(3), 500–21.

Clements, A. L. (1969). *The mystical poetry of Thomas Traherne*. Cambridge: Harvard University Press.

Day, M. M. (1968). Traherne and the doctrine of pre-existence. *Studies in Philology, 65*, 81–97.

DeVries, D. (1989). Schleiermacher's "Christmas Eve Dialogue": Bourgeois ideology or feminist theology? *Journal of Religion, 69*(2), 169–83.

———. (2001). Toward a theology of childhood. *Interpretation, 55*(2), 161–173.

Dillen, A., & Pollefeyt, D. (Eds.). (2010). *Children's voices: Children's perspectives in ethics, theology and religious education*. Leuven, Belgium: Peeters.

Dillistone, F. W. (1955). *Christianity and symbolism*. London: Collins.

DiPasquale, T. M. (1999). *Literature and sacrament: The sacred and the secular in John Donne*. Pittsburgh: Duquesnes University Press.

Dobell, B. (1903). *The poetical works of Thomas Traherne, B.D., 1636?–1674: Now first published from the original manuscripts*. London: Author.

Dowell, G. (1990). *Enjoying the world: The rediscovery of Thomas Traherne*. London: Mowbray.

Ellrodt, R. (1960). *L'Inspiration personnelle et l'esprit du temps chez les poètes métaphysiques Anglais* (Vol. 1). Paris: Corti.

————. (2000). *Seven metaphysical poets: A structural study of the unchanging self.* Oxford: Oxford University Press.

Ford, D. (1999). *Self and salvation: Being transformed.* Cambridge: Cambridge University Press.

————. (2007). *Christian wisdom: Desiring God and learning in love.* Cambridge: Cambridge University Press.

Gilbert, A. H. (1947). Thomas Traherne as artist. *Modern Language Quarterly, 8,* 436–42.

Grant, P. (1971). Original sin and the fall of man in Thomas Traherne. *English Literary History, 38*(1), 40–61.

————. (1974). *The transformation of sin: Studies in Donne, Herbert, Vaughan, and Traherne.* Montreal: McGill-Queen's University Press.

Guffey, G. R. (1967). Thomas Traherne on original sin. *Notes & Queries, 14,* 98–100.

Gundry-Volf, J. (2000). "To such as these belongs the reign of God": Jesus and children. *Theology Today, 56*(4), 469–80.

Hay, D., & Nye, R. (1998). *The spirit of the child.* London: Fount.

Hopkins, K. (1962). *English poetry: A short history.* London: Phoenix House.

Inge, D., & MacFarlane, C. (2000, June 2). Seeds of eternity: A new Traherne manuscript. *Times Literary Supplement,* 14.

Inge, D. (2004). A poet comes home: Thomas Traherne, theologian in a new century. *Anglican Theological Review, 86*(2), 335–48.

————. (2008). *Happiness and holiness: Thomas Traherne and his writings.* Norwich, UK: Canterbury.

————. (2009). *Wanting like a god: Desire and freedom in the thought of Thomas Traherne.* London: SCM.

Jackson, T. (1625). *A treatise containing the originall of unbeliefe.* London: John Clarke.

Jensen, D. H. (2005). *Graced vulnerability: A theology of childhood.* Cleveland: Pilgrim.

Jordan, R. D. (1983). The new Traherne manuscript "Commentaries of Heaven" *Quadrant, 27,* 73–76.

Kershaw, A. (2005). The poetic of the cosmic Christ in Thomas Traherne's *The Kingdom of God* (Doctoral dissertation, University of Western Australia, 2005).

Knott, J. R. (2005). Milton's wild garden. *Studies in Philology, 102*(1), 66–82.

Kuchar, G. (2005). *Divine subjection: The rhetoric of sacramental devotion in early modern England.* Pittsburgh, PA: Duquesne University Press.

Légasse, S. (1969). *Jésus et l'enfant: "enfants", "petits" et "simples" dans la tradition synoptique.* Paris, Gabalda.

Marshall, W. H. (1958). Thomas Traherne and the doctrine of original sin. *Modern Language Notes, 73*(3), 161–65.

Maas, R. (2000). Christ as the Logos of childhood: Reflections on the meaning and mission of the child. *Theology Today, 56*(4), 456–68.

Marcus, L. S. (1978). *Childhood and cultural despair: A theme and variations in seventeenth-century literature.* Pittsburgh: University of Pittsburgh Press.

McIntosh, M. A. (2004). *Discernment and truth: The spirituality and theology of knowledge.* Edinburgh, Scotland: Alban.

Merton, T. (1967). *Mystics and Zen masters.* New York: Farrar, Straus and Giroux.

Miller-McLemore, B. J. (2003). *Let the children come: Reimagining childhood from a Christian perspective.* San Francisco: Jossey-Bass.

Moltmann, J. (2000). Child and childhood as metaphors of hope. *Theology Today, 56*(4), 592–603.

More, H. (1664). *A modest enquiry into the mystery of iniquity*. London: J. Flesher.

Newey, E. (2010). "God made man greater when He made him less": Traherne's iconic child. *Literature and Theology, 24*(3), 227–41.

Nye, R. (2009). *Children's spirituality: What it is and why it matters*. London: Church House Publishing.

Osborn, J. M. (1964, October 8). A new Traherne manuscript. *Times Literary Supplement*, 928.

Ponsford, M. (1983). The poetry of Thomas Traherne in relation to the thought and poetics of the period (Doctoral dissertation, University of Newcastle upon Tyne, 1983).

Poole, W. (2000). Frail originals: Theories of the fall in the age of Milton. (Doctoral dissertation, University of Oxford, 2000).

Rahner, K. (1971). Ideas for a theology of childhood. *Theological Investigations* (Vol. 8). London: Darton, Longman & Todd.

Ridlon, H. G. (1964). The function of the "Infant-Ey" in Traherne's poetry. *Studies in Philology, 61*(3), 627–39.

Sabine, M. (1980). "Stranger to the shining skies": Traherne's child and his changing attitudes to the world. *Ariel, 11*(4), 21–35.

Salter, K. W. (1955). Thomas Traherne and a Romantic heresy. *Notes & Queries, 200*, 153-156.

———. (1964). *Thomas Traherne: Mystic and poet*. London: Arnold.

Schwartz, R. M. (2008). *Sacramental poetics at the dawn of secularism: When God left the world*. Stanford: Stanford University Press.

Stewart, S. S. (1970). *The expanded voice: The art of Thomas Traherne*. San Marino, CA: Huntington Library.

Tice, T. N. (1967). Schleiermacher's interpretation of Christmas: "Christmas Eve," "The Christian Faith," and the Christmas sermons. *The Journal of Religion, 47*(2), 100–126.

Traherne, T. (nd), *Commonplace book*. Bodleian Library, Oxford. Bodl.MS.Eng. Poet.c.42.

———. (1958). Centuries of meditations (in Vol. 1), & Dobell poems (in Vol. 2). In H. M. Margoliouth (Ed.), *Thomas Traherne: Centuries, poems, and thanksgivings* (Vols. 1–2). Oxford: Clarendon.

———. Lambeth M.S. (in Vol. 1), *Commentaries of Heaven* (in Vols. 2–3), *Church's yearbook & thanksgivings* (in Vol. 4). In Ross, J. (Ed.). (2005–2017). *The works of Thomas Traherne* (Vols. 1–4, 2005–2009). Cambridge: Brewer.

———. (1997). *Select meditations*. In J. Smith (Ed.), *Thomas Traherne: Select meditations*. Manchester: Carcanet.

Wade, G. I. (1944). *Thomas Traherne: A critical biography. With a selected bibliography of criticism, by Robert Allerton Parker*. Princeton: Princeton University Press.

Wall, J. (2004). Fallen angels: A contemporary Christian ethical ontology of childhood. *International Journal of Practical Theology, 8*(2), 160–84.

———. (2006). Childhood studies, hermeneutics, and theological ethics. *Journal of Religion, 86*(4), 523–48.

Whalen, R. (2001). George Herbert's sacramental puritanism. *Renaissance Quarterly, 54*(4), 1273–1307.

———. (2002). *The poetry of immanence: Sacrament in Donne and Herbert*. Toronto: University of Toronto Press.

Whitlock, B. W. (1986). The sacramental poetry of George Herbert. *South Central Review, 3*(1), 37–49.

Wöhrer, F. K. (1982). *Thomas Traherne: The growth of a mystic's mind. A study of the evolution and the phenomenology of Traherne's mystical consciousness.* Salzburg University, Austria: Salzberg Studies in English Literature, Elizabethan and Renaissance Studies.

6

Irenaeus' Stages of Faith
Childlike Belief and the Divine Pedagogy

Jennifer Haddad Mosher

As they seek to lay a narrative foundation for an informed, expanding Christian perspective, the fields of children's spirituality and the theology of childhood have yet to mine patristic writings adequately for early Christian understandings of childhood; too few scholars move beyond explicit references to childrearing or the childhood of Jesus to sift patristic writings for the insights on childhood embedded in biblical and theological commentary. This in part reflects the reality that, despite increased accessibility of and a significant broadening of interest in its sources, the patristic world remains somewhat mysterious and of marginal relevance to the average researcher or theologian of the Western church. Yet in their persistent role as the nutritive ground of Eastern Christianity, the patristic sources continue to actively shape the theological understanding of children and children's spirituality within the Eastern Christian traditions, for millions of children worldwide. How they do so is often surprisingly divergent from Western theological norms; yet they dovetail remarkably with the fruits of Western developmental and psychological research. This chapter will examine a single example of this phenomenon found in the writings of Irenaeus of Lyons (second century CE–c. 202).

With the post-Augustine growth of a vision of the human person as a being whose value and Christian identity is primarily posited in having "understanding, will and memory" (Augustine, *Trin.* XV:3.5), early childhood is assigned ambiguous spiritual worth in many parts of the Western Christian tradition; yet Irenaeus of Lyons, a bishop in Gaul separated from John the Evangelist by only two generations, gives center stage to a young child—Adam—in his account of the creation of man in the Garden of Eden. One might be tempted to label this portrayal of Adam as a child a fantastical idiosyncrasy; but Irenaeus shares it with Theophilus of Antioch and Clement of Alexandria. By envisioning Adam created as a child, what theological and pedagogical significance is Irenaeus assigning early childhood in the life of man?

And how does his vision intersect with the increasing amount of research being done on the spiritual life of children? What is documented in that research is that no one is born as an adult in the life of faith. Stages of faith, begun in infancy, are a necessary reality of human religiosity. Human faith, like human sanity, is constructed, one piece and experience at a time. When placed alongside the fruits of this research, what might seem a random illustration by Irenaeus of the various ages of man proves a brilliant icon of religious development that not only sheds light on a particular tradition of understanding the Genesis accounts, but also the theological significance of childhood.

Let us begin by examining Irenaeus' treatment of understanding, or comprehension, which he defines for us in this key passage from the Preface to *On the Apostolic Preaching*, his formulation and summary of the key dogmas of Christianity.

> . . . belief comes before comprehension, what is real before faith. Therefore, lest we suffer any such thing, we must keep the rule of faith unswervingly, and perform the commandments of God, believing in God and fearing Him, for he is Lord, and loving Him, for He is Father. Action then, comes by faith, as "if you do not believe," Isaias says, "you will not understand"; and the truth brings about faith, for faith is established upon things truly real, that we may believe what really is, as it is, we may always keep our conviction of it firm. Since, then, the conserver of our salvation is faith, it is necessary to take great care of it, that we may have a true comprehension of what is. (Irenaeus, *Epid.* Preface, 3)

The first thing important to note about this passage is that comprehension, that which we attach such value to within the culture of religious education, the Church and wider society as a whole, is placed last in the list of what knowledge it is possible for us to attain. Instead "belief," which seems to be equated here with "what is real," is the starting point in Irenaeus' developmental progression; belief is followed by "faith" and thereafter, finally, "comprehension."

This progression appears to put Irenaeus at loggerheads with the extreme rationalist. The rationalist perspective puts the greatest emphasis on comprehension, requiring it as the logical starting place, the only foundation on which one should build faith and belief. To start with belief is to suggest that neither faith nor comprehension can exist without a foundation of what is, to the rationalist, the least objective, least trusted source of knowledge. Yet Irenaeus is clear—without belief and then faith, there is no hope of ever achieving true comprehension. Thus he opens the door to types of knowledge of God not grounded in rationality and substantive participation by the non-rational, including children, in the life of God.

So what is "belief," this non-rational knowledge that begins our journey with God? Irenaeus seems here to define belief as "what is real." Belief is the most basic building block of any knowledge, religious or no, and as such, it is the realm of the child, both literally and figuratively. It is the set of starting premises that we all construct about the world, beginning in the womb and the earliest days of infancy, and that vary according to our experiences. The unique chemical cocktail we swim in within our mother and the most elementary of sensory experiences begin it; this is then built upon by what we glean from communication with our environment and the other persons in it. Personalities begin to form in relation to such stimuli, whole cosmologies evolve in response to them. Such is belief and, as such, it is perhaps the most objective, scientific knowledge of all (if not particularly rational, *per se*). Man can live without comprehension. Man can live without faith. But a man without belief, without even a subconscious sense of his world's realities—it is hard to imagine how such a person would be alive. Even the most vegetative, sub-mental human person, and surely the young child, has belief, for all human beings interact and communicate with their environment on some level. In the words of Dr. Silvana Quattrocchi Montanaro (1991),

> Communication, in the wider sense of the word, is establishing a relationship. Human beings are always able to communicate with their environment and with themselves. . . . Communication should be viewed as a quality of life that is

present at any level and that makes life possible. To communicate is to live! (p. 68)

As we inevitably communicate with our environment, we enter into
what has been described by James Fowler as the first stage in the foundation of belief:

If we start with infancy—the time from birth to two years—
we have what we call undifferentiated faith. It's a time before
language and conceptual thought are possible. The infant is
forming a basic sense of trust, of being at home in the world.
The infant is also forming what I call pre-images of God or the
Holy, and of the kind of world we live in. On this foundation
of basic trust or mistrust is built all that comes later in terms of
faith. Future religious experience will either have to confirm or
reground that basic trust. (Straugh, 2002)

Therefore, if we, as infants, are exposed to and commune with the true
God, one of our most elemental, subconscious beliefs will be in his
existence, his person. Irenaeus is convinced that all of us, by virtue of
being human, have access to the reality of God. For while in describing belief above we referred primarily to the natural elements of the
world, we must remember that for Irenaeus, the presence of the Spirit
and the image of God are as elemental to the world and the human
being as light or air or genome. Irenaeus states

But He fashioned man with His own Hands, taking the purest,
the finest and the most delicate elements of the earth, mixing
with the earth, in due measure, His own power; and because
he sketched upon the handiwork his own form—in order that
what should be seen would be godlike, for man was placed
upon the earth fashioned in the image of God—and that he
might be alive, "He breathed into his face a breath of life"; so
that both according to the inspiration and according to the
formation, man was like God. (*Epid.* I:11)

The child, for Irenaeus, need not discover God—he cannot escape
him. God is built into his material being, it is by God's Spirit that he
lives. Necessarily then, the life of God will be an element, the prime
vivifying element of the substance of his beliefs, since it is only by the
life of God that the child lives at all.

To the element of himself, God adds all other elements and
makes them available for the nurture of the child towards a secure

foundation of belief, a later faith, and an eventual comprehension. Indeed, in Irenaeus' version of the Genesis accounts, the world and, more specifically, Paradise are created to be the prime supportive and instructive environment for the spiritual and physical maturation of the man-child Adam.

> Now having made the man lord of the earth, and of everything that is in it, He secretly appointed him as lord over those who were servants in it. But they, however, were in their [full-development], while the lord, that is, the man, was very little, since he was an infant, and it was necessary for him to reach full-development by growing in this way: and that his nourishment and growth might take place in luxury, a place was prepared for him, better than this earth—excelling in air, beauty, light, food, plants, fruit, waters, and every other thing needful [for life]—and its name was Paradise. And so beautiful and good was the Paradise, [that] the Word of God was always walking in it: He would walk and talk with the man, prefiguring the future, which would come to pass, that He would dwell with him and speak with him, and would be with mankind, teaching them righteousness. But the man was a young child, not yet having a perfect deliberation, and because of this he was easily deceived by the seducer. (*Epid.* I:12)

Herein Irenaeus describes a fascinating world. Paradise is a place completely designed, it would seem, to aid in a very intentional building of the foundation of belief. Its primary mechanisms in that building are sensory impression and the Word of God's presence. An atmosphere of incredible luxury and abundance is created for the child Adam, a place "better than this earth—excelling in air, beauty, food, plants, fruit, waters, and every other thing needful for life." This extravagant environment, deemed "necessary" in order for him to grow to his full development, is "so beautiful and good" that "the Word of God was always walking in it"—as if it is a place that God himself cannot resist. This is hardly the stereotypical character-building ascetical environment!

The child Adam is served by fully developed angels and an archangel, "secretly," as if, as part of a fully thought-out pedagogical model, they are careful to hide from him the fact that he is actually "a little lower" than they are. The original "prepared environment" (Montessori, 1966, p. 267), Paradise is staffed and guarded so that

Adam can safely explore and use it at will and thus cultivate the foundation of belief that he is, Irenaeus states, "free and master of himself, having been made by God in this way, in order that he should rule over everything upon earth" (*Epid.* I:11).

Christ walks and talks with Adam in the garden explicitly as a sign of the future incarnation, as a literal "pre-image of God or the Holy" (Straughn, 2002). Note that at this time, there seems to be no explicit teaching going on. Explicit modeling or "teaching them righteousness" will come later, with the Incarnation, after the belief of Abraham and the generations of faith of Israel, bear fruit in the Theotokos, Mary the Mother of God. Right now, the Word is in Paradise simply as a sign and a presence. This richness of sensory experience, this Paradise, this immanence of God—these things constitute Adam's first pedagogical environment, rather than didactic lessons.

There is a sense that, if allowed to continue unhindered, the progression to the Incarnation and immortal, righteous life with God, the full development of man, is natural and even inevitable. Man has always been intended for something more, something he had to learn to become, something that will begin and end with spiritual childhood. We certainly do not see portrayed here any idea of the Incarnation as somehow precipitated by man's sin. Indeed, sin seems to have a far less weighty and definite character than traditionally given in Western versions of the history of "The Fall." Irenaeus states

> But, in order that the man should not entertain thoughts of grandeur not be exalted, as if he had no Lord, [and], because of the authority given to him and the boldness towards God his Creator, sin, passing beyond his own measure, and adopt an attitude of self-conceited arrogance towards God, a law was given to him from God, that he might know that he had as lord the Lord of all. And He placed certain limits on him, so that, if he should keep the commandment of God, he would remain always as he was, that is, immortal; if however, he should not keep [it], he would become mortal, dissolving into the earth whence his frame was taken. And the commandment was this, "You may eat freely from every tree of the Paradise, but of that tree alone, whence is knowledge of good and evil, you shall not eat; on the day that you eat of it, you shall die the death." (*Epid.* I:16)

Irenaeus seems to portray sin almost as if it were an attitude problem, exactly like one a child might have, a "passing beyond his own measure," reaching for what it not yet developmentally his, a relational speed-bump that introduces disorder, rather than something with real cosmological consequences. The pedagogy of the Incarnation has been planned from the beginning. The threat of death seems just that—a threat, and an empty one. How could an immortal child (as Adam is here portrayed), living in the lap of such luxury, have any real understanding of death? Death at this point seems a bogey not of substance but of pedagogical intent, meant to instill a belief that God, as man's Lord, understands that while everything is allowed, not everything is good for him; therefore, trust in God's judgment should be part of Adam's foundation of belief. When Adam fails this first test, the educational blueprint that it is merely a piece of is not scrapped or radically changed. Its method, its economy, simply shifts because of new realities, but its goal remains the same—that the Word would come and "He would dwell with him and speak with him, and would be with mankind, teaching them righteousness."

However, because "the man was a young child, not yet having a perfect deliberation, . . . he was easily deceived by the seducer" (*Epid.* I:12). It is the presence of an alternative pedagogue introducing a conflicting belief that undermines Adam's development and impairs his ability to grow into faith. The angel takes advantage of the vulnerability inherent in Adam's progression, in Fowler's schema, to the next stage within the foundation of belief:

> The . . . stage we call intuitive/projective [belief]. It characterizes the child of two to six or seven. It's a changing and growing and dynamic faith. It's marked by the rise of imagination. The child doesn't have the kind of logic that makes possible or necessary the questioning of perceptions or fantasies. Therefore the child's mind is "religiously pregnant," one might say. It is striking how many times in our interviews we find that experiences and images that occur and take form before the child is six have powerful and long-lasting effects on the life of faith both positive and negative. (Straughn, 2002)

Faith, the second stage in Irenaeus' progression of knowledge of God, is the emerging dominance of a particular subset of premises that exist in the foundation of belief. With the arrival of the age of reason to an older child, choices are made as to how beliefs will be prioritized. If a belief in God exists, then a faith in God, and a reorganization of one's life relative to that faith, can emerge. Christian faith is the choice to organize belief within the structure of the truth found in the Nicene Creed. Only once that choice has been made, can we act according to faith, including acting out the Christian beliefs Irenaeus cites of fearing God as Lord and loving Him as Father (*Epid.* Preface:3), and thereby move into new realms of knowledge, those that only exist within the structure of faith. Irenaeus is very clear—faith is maintained only by choice. Faith must be kept "unswervingly," performed, established.

However, Adam misses his first real opportunity to make the transition from belief in God to faith in God by "being mislead by the angel" (*Epid.* I:16). The apostate angel introduces confusion at the level of Adam's belief by introducing mistrust of God. Therefore, as Adam did not have "perfect deliberation" yet because of his inexperience, which left him, "without comprehension or understanding of what is evil" (*Epid.* I:14), Adam made the wrong choice, essentially choosing not faith in God, but his own interpretation of his confused beliefs. For this, Irenaeus says, as if acknowledging Adam's disadvantage, God punishes the angel; "the angel becoming, by falsehood, the head and originator of sin, was himself struck, having offended God . . ." (*Epid.* I:16). Adam's fate of expulsion is portrayed not as a punishment, but as a logical consequence; something about the nature of Paradise means that it "does not receive sinners" so the man must leave.

According to Irenaeus, only once we have established faith can we hope to build understanding or comprehension. Comprehension is essentially a final, synthetic type of knowledge that teaches us how the knowledge gained by belief and faith about God and the knowledge gained by "what is real" about everything else inter-relate. It is only possible as a final step, and may not be arrived at by all. But in no way is it the necessary starting point of sanctity. That is retained for child-like belief. Indeed, Irenaeus has very little respect for knowledge per se and people who think outside of the context of proper faith. As he explains,

> This, beloved, is the preaching of the truth, and this is the character of our salvation, and this is the way of life, which the prophets announced and Christ confirmed and the apostles handed over and the Church, in the whole world, hands down to her children. This it is necessary to keep with all strictness, being [. . .] pleasing to God, by good works and a sound mind,

> not thinking that there is another God the Father besides our
> Creator, as the heretics think, who despise the God who Is, and
> make an idol of that which is not, and fashion for themselves
> a "father" much higher than our Creator, and think that they
> have found something greater than the truth; for they are all
> impious and blasphemers against their Creator and Father, as
> we have demonstrated [in] "Refutation and Overthrowal of
> Knowledge falsely so-called." (*Epid.* IV:98)

Indeed, according to Irenaeus, from Adam on, comprehension
has seemed largely out of reach for humanity, as the struggle to keep
faith has been an all-consuming one. All of the later stages of faith,
wrestled with in adolescence and adulthood, produce very few people
who actually achieve true comprehension. In this way the introduction of pure, angelic reason into the human experience, used in accord
with bad beliefs, brings, as sin did, suffering. With the near effortless,
pedagogical environment of Paradise lost, a less "natural" pedagogy
for helping man to maintain faith was introduced: the Law. Once outside of Paradise, man needed guidance in his choices—not because
he truly had more options, but because he was still operating from
an imperfect, immature faith. He needed to be told explicitly what
things offended God so that his choices had a chance of respecting
those realities. For generations the Law was the new pedagogical environment, taking over from Paradise, but only until that time when the
possibility of Paradise was restored in the Incarnation. "Therefore we
do not need the Law as a pedagogue. Behold we speak with the Father
and stand before Him, becoming as children in evil and becoming
strong in all righteousness and integrity" (*Epid.* IV:96).

And thus we are brought full circle, to a comprehension that
looks, not like the elaborately constructed "rational" schema of the
Gnostics, but to the child we began with—breathing the Spirit of the
Father, willing and loving as one with the Father, becoming, by adoption, a son.

It is in this re-approach to childhood and its own unique form
of comprehension that we find the possibility for sainthood, which
Fowler describes thus:

> Some few persons we find move into Stage Six, which we call
> universalizing faith. In a sense I think we can describe this
> stage as one in which persons begin radically to live as though
> what Christians and Jews call the "kingdom of God" were al-

ready a fact. I don't want to confine it to Christian and Jewish images of the kingdom. It's more than that. I'm saying these people experience a shift from the self as the center of experience. Now their center becomes a participation in God or ultimate reality. There's a reversal of figure and ground. They're at home with what I call a commonwealth of being. We experience these people on the one hand as being more lucid and simple than we are, and on the other hand as intensely liberating people, sometimes even subversive in their liberating qualities. . . . These are persons who in a sense have negated the self for the sake of affirming God. And yet in affirming God they became vibrant and powerful selves in our experience. They have a quality of what I call relevant irrelevance. (Straugh, 2002)

It is precisely this lack of concern for or commitment to an interior self that infants and young children are able to model for us. Their ground of being is found in whomever they love. When we have learned the lesson of love, we have learned the lesson of a more generic, natural childhood and live into the particularity of being spiritual sons. All that matters is the Father, with whom we want to be and conform ourselves to. Amazingly, it is God who first loves us, humbles himself, and conforms himself to our earthly existence. As Irenaeus notes in *Against the Heresies*:

> Being a Master, therefore, He also possessed the age of a Master, not despising or evading any condition of humanity, nor setting aside in Himself that law which He had appointed for the human race, but sanctifying every age, by that period corresponding to it which belonged to Himself. For he came to save all through means of Himself—all, I say, who through Him are born again to God—infants, and children, and boys, and youths, and old men. He [Jesus Christ] therefore passed through every age, becoming an infant for infants, thus sanctifying infants; a child for children, thus sanctifying those who are of this age, being at the same time made to them an example of piety, righteousness, and submission. (*Haer.* II:XXII, 4)

In light of these things, perhaps it makes sense to understand the few examples of scriptural details of Jesus' infancy and childhood that are in the Gospels not as unsupported afterthoughts, but as very carefully chosen examples with pedagogical intent. Just as here Irenaeus adds no embellishments to his assertion that Christ sanctified infants, the

Gospels give no further details about Christ's incarnation as an infant because an infant is, surely, the most universal configuration of humanity. Christ's simply being an infant is enough to sanctify infants who, for the most part, simply "be," all in the same way. The later addition of "being at the same time made to them an example of piety, righteousness and submission" (*Haer.* II:XXII, 4) takes into account the further development of children. These are obviously direct references to the stories of Jesus' boyhood: the incident in the temple and his subsequent return and submission to his earthly parents recorded in Luke—all intended as models of Jesus' submission to the Law, and the grand design of the Incarnation.

The eschatological end of all of this is made especially clear when we examine the passage—Galatians 3:23–29; 4:1–5—that was surely in large part the inspiration for Irenaeus' particular gloss on the Genesis accounts:

> Brethren, before faith came, we were confined under the law, kept under restraint until faith should be revealed. So that the law was our custodian until Christ came, that we might be justified by faith. But now that faith has come, we are no longer under a custodian; for in Christ Jesus you are all sons of God, through faith. For as many of you as were baptized into Christ have put on Christ. There is neither Jew nor Greek, there is neither slave nor free, there is neither male nor female; for you are all one in Christ Jesus. And if you are Christ's, then you are Abraham's offspring, heirs according to promise. I mean that the heir, as long as he is a child, is no better than a slave, though he is the owner of all the estate; but he is under guardians and trustees until the date set by the father. So with us; when we were children, we were slaves to the elemental spirits of the universe. But when the time had fully come, God sent forth his Son, to redeem those who were under the law, so that we might receive adoption as sons. (Gal 3:23–29; 4:1–5, *Revised Standard Version*)

In this passage we find all of the elements of Irenaeus' account—faith, the law, custodians, the children "under guardians and trustees," the angels ("elemental spirits of the universe"), the divine plan with "the date set by the father," and, finally, "sons." In a future begun for us in Paradise, built for us on the childlike belief of Abraham that stars and sand and fire spoke of God's presence and promises, articulated in the faith of the Church—there we see true comprehension emerge, in a synthesis of rational knowledge with the irrational, where we, in all of our differences, join together into the Son of God. There we find that foundational reality or belief with which Irenaeus began—that it is Christ who is the author and perfector of these things.

> Thus God, from the beginning, fashioned man for His munificence; and chose the patriarchs for the sake of their salvation; and formed in advance a people, teaching the uneducated to follow God; and prepared the prophets, accustoming man on the earth to bear His Spirit and to hold communion with God; He Himself, indeed, having need of nothing, but granting communion with Himself to those who stood in need of it. To those that pleased Him, He sketched out like an architect, the construction of salvation; and to those who did not see, in Egypt, He Himself gave guidance; and to those who were unruly, in the desert, He promulgated a very suitable Law; while to those who entered into the good land He bestowed the appropriate inheritance; finally, for those converted to the Father, He killed the fatted calf and presented them with the finest robe. Thus, in many ways, He harmonized the human race to the symphony of salvation. (*Haer.* IV:XIV, 2)

God has never required our understanding—and certainly not education or intellect, rationality, or composure—in order to commune with us. Our births and re-births as children of God and our consequent state of need precipitate his giving of every good and perfect gift—including that of Himself as a human child.

Irenaeus' vision of the child Adam levels the landscape of access to God so concretely and completely that it challenges all our interactions with children with several questions. Do we approach children—in our homes, our churches, our religious education programs—as beings in whom God already lives and constitutes "what is real"? Do we take seriously the responsibility of environment and pedagogy as midwives of faith? Do we live in the long night of that faith with humility, or do we artificially push children (and ourselves) towards the horizon of comprehension? These considerations are the fruits of but a brief tour through a single aspect of patristic thought; what else lies ready to inform Christian perspectives on children's spirituality?

References

Augustine. (1994). *On the Holy Trinity*. In P. Schaff (Ed.), *The Nicene & Post-Nicene fathers* (Vol. 3, pp.17–228). Grand Rapids: Eerdmans. [=*Trin.*]

Fowler, J. (1995). *Stages of faith: The psychology of human development*. San Francisco: HarperSanFrancisco.

Irenaeus of Lyons. (1994). *Against heresies*. In A. Roberts and J. Donaldson (Eds.), *The Ante-Nicene fathers* (Vol. 1, pp. 315–567). Grand Rapids: Eerdmans. [=*Haer.*]

———. (1997). *On the apostolic preaching*. Crestwood, NY: SVS. [=*Epid.*]

Montanaro, S.Q. (1991). *Understanding the human being: The importance of the first three years of life*. Mountain View, CA: Nienhuis Montessori USA.

Montessori, M. (1966). *The secret of childhood*. Notre Dame, IN: Fides.

Straughn, H.K. (2002). My interview with James W. Fowler on the stages of faith. Retrieved March 13, 2001, from http://jmm.aaa.net.au/articles/23318.htm. Originally posted at http://www.lifespirals.com/TheMindSpiral/Fowler/fowler. html. *[Note: Unfortunately, at the time of publication, this web-page is no longer accessible on the Internet.]*

7

Baptismal Practices and the Spiritual Nurture of Children[1]
An Historical Overview

Kevin E. Lawson

Introduction

From the earliest days of the church, baptism has been a rite marking those identified as Christians. As rites of initiation, baptism and other practices associated with it (e.g., exorcism, anointing, confirmation, eucharist), have been viewed as either creating or reflecting a new spiritual reality in the life of the one baptized. Because of the critical importance of this rite and what it was understood to mean, it became a driving force in the development of the church's teaching ministry. For example, in the early church, extensive instruction in the faith, both belief and behavior, normally preceded baptism. Later, as theological views of human nature and childhood developed in the Western church, the practice of infant baptism increased, with instruction in the faith coming later as the child grew. Today, on this side of the Reformation, there are many diverse understandings of the nature and purpose of baptism and who is viewed as eligible for it. As a result, there have developed many different approaches to the spiritual formation and nurture of people both before and after the

1. This essay was originally published in slightly different form in the *Christian Education Journal*, Series 3, Vol. 8, No. 1 (Spring 2011). The essay is republished here with permission of the *Christian Education Journal*.

rite. In particular, differing views on the baptism of children has led to very different understandings of their relationship with God and the church, resulting in different approaches to their spiritual instruction and nurture.

Church leaders today stand in both theological and educational traditions that shape what we expect of and do with our children. This chapter explores how historical changes in the theology and practice of baptism have impacted the church's ministry with children. By carefully reviewing this history, I hope to help church leaders in the present more faithfully design and carry out educational ministries with children that reflect their baptismal theology and practice.

This chapter begins with an historic overview of why and how baptismal practices changed, and examines the resulting impact on the church's educational efforts with children.[2] It then presents a brief case study of theological reflection on the meaning and impact of baptism by Horace Bushnell as he wrestled with what the "Christian nurture" of children should be like. Finally, issues are explored for those in the church today who are responsible for the development of their church's educational ministry and other spiritual formation efforts with children.

Historical Overview

Children and Baptism in the New Testament

Though hotly debated, it is unclear whether or not children in the church during the New Testament era were baptized. Examples shared in the Bible generally either focus on adult believers receiving baptism (e.g., Ethiopian eunuch, Acts 8:26–39) or on entire households following new adult believers in baptism (e.g., Philippian jailor, Acts 16: 29–33). Whether or not these households included young children or infants is not discussed in the biblical texts. This ambiguity has led to considerable debate throughout the history of the church, as theologians sought both to understand and justify current baptismal practices, and give new direction where they felt it was needed. The tendency has been for scholars to either find support for their own

2. Unless otherwise noted, the quotations from early church documents that appear in this chapter are taken from the excellent compilation that Paul Turner has published on CD-ROM as part of *Ages of initiation: The first two Christian millennia* (The Liturgical Press, 2000).

current practices or to leave it ambiguous. Some of the relevant biblical texts include the following[3] (emphasis added):

> A woman named Lydia, from the city of Thyatira, a seller of purple fabrics, a worship of God, was listening; and the Lord opened her heart to respond to the things spoken by Paul. *And when she and her household had been baptized*, she urged us, saying, "If you have judged me to be faithful to the Lord, come into my house and stay." And she prevailed upon us. (Acts 16:14–15)
>
> And he called for lights and rushed in, and trembling with fear he fell down before Paul and Silas, and after he brought them out, he said, "Sirs, what must I do to be saved?" They said, *"Believe in the Lord Jesus, and you will be saved, you and your household." And they spoke the word of the Lord to him together will all who were in his house.* And he took them that very hour of the night and washed their wounds, *and immediately he was baptized, he and all his household.* (Acts 16:29–33)
>
> *Crispus, the leader of the synagogue, believed in the Lord with all his household;* and many of the Corinthians when they heard were believing and being baptized. (Acts 18:8)
>
> *Now I did baptize also the household of Stephanas;* beyond that, I do not know whether I baptized any other. (I Cor. 1:16)

Both Turner (2000) and Bakke (2005) argue that although children are not specifically identified within these texts, what we know of children being included in the worship of the early church, early views that identified baptism with the practice of ritual circumcision in the Old Testament, and the collective nature of the family in both Jewish and Greek cultures, it seems more likely that children were included in household baptisms in the New Testament record. What is clear is that the biblical examples all have a time of instruction of the adult believer preceding the baptism of the person and his or her household. In some cases the instruction was specifically given to the entire household (Acts 16:29–34; possibly Acts 18:8). This ambiguous beginning led to divergent practices as the early church spread and grew.

What also seems clear from the New Testament records is that parents bore the primary responsibility for teaching and nurturing their children in the Christian faith. Passages like Ephesians 6:4 reveal the expectations parents in the church were to fulfill: "Fathers, do not

3. All Scripture quotations are taken from the *New American Standard Bible*, updated edition, 1995, the Lockman Foundation.

provoke your children to anger, but bring them up in the discipline and instruction of the Lord."

Children and Baptism in the Early Church

First through Third Centuries

Baptism continued to be an important rite of initiation in the early church, marking a person as a believer and follower of Jesus Christ (e.g., see the *Didache*, Milavec, 2003). The general pattern involved having a sponsor attest to the faith and moral life of the person, his or her enrollment in the catechumenate for a period of time, then baptism (including exorcism, anointing, and the eucharist). However, the practice of baptizing infants and children of adult believers varied and was vigorously debated by church leaders.

The first direct reference to the baptism of infants appears in Tertullian's writings as he wrestled with his understanding of the innocence of children and the dangerous consequences of serious sin following baptism. He ended up rejecting the necessity of their baptism. The prevalent view was that baptism provided forgiveness for sins up to that point in time. Serious sins committed after baptism were seen as potentially removing one's salvation. (Emphasis added.)

> Granted, the Lord said, "Do not stop the children from coming to me." But they may come while they are maturing, they may come while they are learning—while they are taught where they may come. *They will become Christians when they are able to know Christ. Why should this innocent age rush to the forgiveness of sins?* Will worldly affairs be approached more cautiously, so that one who is not entrusted with earthly matters is entrusted with divine ones? *Let them know how to ask for salvation so that you may seem to have given to someone seeking it. . . .* For no less reason the unmarried should also delay. Temptation has made plans for them—virgins because of their maturation and widows because of their instability—until they either marry or are strengthened for continence. *If people understand the importance of baptism, they will fear its execution more than its delay. A blameless faith is sure of salvation.* (Tertullian, *Baptism* 18:3–6)

Likewise, Origen wrestled with the practice of infant baptism, but ended up supporting it as a rite of purification that removed the "stain" of birth, not the guilt of personal or original sin (Origen, *Homilies on*

Luke 14:5). Irenaeus, on the other hand, specifically identifies infants and children as ones who have been reborn through Christ (Irenaus *Against the Heresies* 2:22, 4).

Macarius describes the change of practice from the baptism of adults after time in the catechumenate to the inclusion of infants in baptism.

> In the first generation infants were not baptized, but those who were of an appropriate age were called catechumens, and it was to those that baptism was preached and the Christian religion was taught for three years, and they were baptized. . . .
>
> In the end, the baptism of adults was rejected and it was given to infants, because they were born in the faith of Christ, children of the faithful. But it was a continual rite in the churches up to today. (Macarius, "Letter")

Cyprian writes of the decision of 66 bishops at the Synod of Carthage (AD 251–253) that infants should be baptized as soon as possible, not waiting until the eighth day as some were advocating who equated infant baptism with ritual circumcisions of male infants in the Old Testament.

> This was our opinion in the council, that we should keep no one from baptism and from the grace of God, who is merciful and kind and gentle to all. Since this must be observed and maintained about everyone, we think it should be even more observed about infants themselves and newborns. They deserve more from our help and from the divine mercy, since crying and weeping immediately from the very beginning of their birth, they do nothing other than pray. (Cyprian *Letter* 64:2,5f.)

Finally, in the *Apostolic Tradition* (21), the baptism of children is described, including those "who cannot speak for themselves." This later reference is taken by Bakke (2005) to refer not necessarily to infants, but to all children under the age of seven who were not viewed as being able to take responsibility for their own actions and verbal commitments.

In general, children were viewed as being under the authority and responsibility of parents for their spiritual instruction and nurture. Because of the disagreement regarding children, two scenarios developed during this time period: (1) Believing adults were to instruct their own children in the faith, bring them to participate in the worship of the church, and encourage their enrollment in the catechumenate at a young age so that they could profess their own faith and be baptized, and (2) Believing adults had their newborn infants and other children baptized and then instructed them in the faith and brought them to participate in worship in the church. These two competing traditions continued for several centuries.

Fourth through Seventh Centuries

Early in the fourth century, as Christianity changed from a persecuted or tolerated religion to one favored within the Roman Empire, it grew quickly. In some areas, it became common for parents to present their children to become catechumens at a young age so they could be taught prior to baptism. However, as the practice of infant baptism spread it undermined the catechumenate and put more responsibility on the parents for instructing their children following baptism instead of in preparation for it.

In this time period the two competing scenarios described above developed differing patterns of teaching. On the one hand, this era is called by some the "Golden Age" of the catechumenate. Many church leaders developed extensive catechetical lectures and the catechumenate was a lengthy time of instruction leading to baptism (e.g., Cyril of Jerusalem, *Procatechesis*; Gregory of Nyssa, *The Great Catechism*). Following baptism additional instruction was carried out (mystagogy) to explain the sacraments just experienced. A concern of leaders in this tradition was that some adults were delaying baptism out of fear of the consequences of serious sin following this sacrament. Penance for sin after baptism was a rigorous process that could only be done once, and marked a person for life with a stigma (Bakke, 2005). This led some to become perpetual catechumens, unwilling to be baptized until late in life or on their deathbed.

On the other hand, this period of time also saw a growing acceptance of infant baptism. A theology of original sin supplanted the view of the innocence of children held by many earlier church leaders. For church leaders like Augustine, the concerns over original sin and infant mortality led to an insistence on the baptism of newborn infants as a means to safeguard them from eternal damnation. In the late fifth and early sixth century, as a theology of repeatable penance developed, the fears of the consequences of dying unbaptized came to overshadow those of the consequences of sin after baptism. This growth of infant baptism led at first to parents going through the baptismal preparation activities on behalf of their children (Dujarier, 1979). Eventually this practice disappeared. The norm eventually became having newborn infants baptized, anointed or confirmed, and receive communion all in one ceremony.

The Apostolic Constitutions affirmed the appropriateness of both baptizing children and teaching them the Christian faith based on Jesus' own teaching and example.

> Baptize also your little children, and "teach them in the instruction and the law of the Lord." For he says, "Let the little children come to me, and do not hinder them." (*Apostolic Constitutions* 6:15,7)

Augustine defended the idea that children should participate in both of the sacraments of the church relevant for their age: baptism and communion. Though they could not exercise their own faith, the sacraments were seen as providing forgiveness of sin and making the child a believer.

> Whoever says, "An infant's age does not possess within it what Jesus saves," says nothing other than, "Christ the Lord is not Jesus for faithful infants," that is for infants baptized in Christ. . . . They are infants, but they become members of him. They are infants, but they receive his sacraments. They are infants, but they become partakers of his table, so that they may have life in them. (Augustine, *Sermon* 174:6,7)
>
> Therefore although there is not yet that faith which is in the will of believers, nevertheless the sacrament of that faith already makes the child a believer. (Augustine, *Letter* 98:10)

Chrysostom, a leader in the church in the East, defended infant baptism on other grounds than Augustine. In his view, though mortal, infants were themselves sinless, and baptism was a sign of inclusion in the church and the reception of the Holy Spirit. As Guroian (2001) explains, for Chrysostom,

> Baptism, above all else, is an acceptance by the church and entrance of the baptized person into the redeemed and sanctified body of Christ. Baptism is the beginning of a life spent in spiritual combat (*askesis*) and instruction in holiness and

godliness and on a deepening journey into the kingdom of heaven. Infants and children are especially needful of being incorporated and socialized into the church because they benefit from the care and discipline of adults experienced in the spiritual struggle. (p. 70)

Finally, for the Western church, the Council of Carthage in AD 418 affirmed the idea of original sin, seeing in the rite of baptism the opportunity for children, who are guilty because of another's sin, to receive forgiveness of sin by the actions of another. A quote from their conclusions, and a letter by John the Deacon around AD 500, explain this perspective.

> Furthermore, it pleases all the bishops that the following be condemned: those who deny that children should be baptized fresh from the womb of their mothers; or who say that they are indeed baptized for the forgiveness of sins, but that they contract nothing of original sin from Adam, which is atoned for by the bath of rebirth; for it follows that the form of baptism "for the forgiveness of sins" is understood falsely, not truly. For what the Apostle says must not be understood in any other way except the way the Catholic church spread throughout the world has always understood it: "Through one person sin entered into the world (and through sin, death), and thus it is passed on to all people, since all sinned in that person" (cf. Rom 5:12). For because of this principle of faith, even children who have not yet been able themselves to commit any sin, are therefore truly baptized for the forgiveness of sins, so that what they contracted by birth may be cleansed in them by rebirth. (Council of Carthage XV [418] 2)
>
> However let this not appear to be omitted before we mention it, that all these baptismal rituals should also apply to children, who understand nothing up to this point because of the earliness of their age. For this reason you ought to know that, since they are presented by parents or by some others, it is necessary that those who have been condemned by another's sin now be saved by another's faith. (John the Deacon, *Letter to Senarius*, 7)

Over time, the increasing acceptance of the legitimacy of baptizing infants set the stage for the decline of the catechumenate, and placed the burden of spiritual instruction and nurture on parents, with the purpose of teaching children how to live the faith they were baptized into. What had been "catechumenate" now became "mystagogy," instruction following baptism. John Chrysostom explained it thus:

> Let us bring them up in the discipline and instruction of the Lord. Great will be the reward in store for us, for if artists who make statues and paint portraits of kings are held in high esteem, will not God bless ten thousand times more those who reveal and beautify His royal image (for man is the image of God)? When we teach our children to be good, to be gentle, to be forgiving (all these are attributes of God), to be generous, to love their fellow men, to regard this present age as nothing, we instill virtue in their souls and reveal the image of God within them. (Chrysostom, *On Marriage and Family Life,* 44)

The responsibility of instructing their children in the faith (both belief and behavior) was a great one, with some church leaders seeing this as critical for the salvation of parents, drawing on the story of Eli the priest in the Old Testament for their example. Salvation was not viewed as an individual experience, but corporate in nature with the family as a critical unit of responsibility. Both Chrysostom, writing in the fourth century, and the *Didascalia* of a century earlier show this concern.

> After God had stated the charge against Eli, he added the punishment with great wrath: *For I have sworn,* he said, *to the house of Eli that the iniquity of Eli's house shall not be expiated by sacrifice or offering for ever* [I Sam. 3:14]. Do you see God's intense anger and merciless punishment? . . . Except for the man's negligence in regard to his children, however, God had no other charge to make against the elder at that time; in all other respects Eli was a marvelous man. (Chrysostom, *Comparison/Against the Opponents,* 128–29, cited in Guroian, 2001, pp. 72–73)
>
> Now, whether this [that is, the sons' falling into fornication] happen to them without their parents, their parents themselves will be accountable before God for the judgment of their souls; or whether again by your license they are undisciplined and sin, you their parents will likewise be guilty on their account before God. (*Didascalia,* cited in Bakke, 2005, p. 159)

Finally, with infant baptism came the growing practice of separating the post-baptismal anointing, or confirmation, from the baptismal rite. The anointing became identified with the receiving of the Holy Spirit, and was viewed as an apostolic function to be carried out by the bishops. Infant baptisms were carried out in local communities by local priests, or even midwives, but the bishop was often not available to carry out confirmation until a later date. Parents were urged to have their children confirmed as soon as possible, at least within the first year or so of the child's life (Johnson, 1999). What began as a matter of practicality was later to develop into an educational opportunity in the medieval church.

Children and Baptism in the Medieval Church

Eighth through Twelfth Centuries

The patterns of child baptism by priests, confirmation by bishops, and the responsibility for the instruction and spiritual nurture of children falling primarily to the parents instead of church leaders, continued into and through the medieval period. Though there was considerable continuity, there were some major changes in theology and practice that impacted how church leaders, parents, and other adults viewed the spiritual needs of children and responded to nurture them in the Christian faith.

Gelasian Sacramentary and the Scrutiny of Infants. By the eighth century, the "elect" who underwent scrutiny prior to baptism were primarily infants, with parents or other adults answering for them. Gatch (1981) sees this as a witness to the continuity of the initiation rites, with catechesis being the focus of Lent leading up to baptism and the eucharist celebrated at Easter. However, now parents or other adult sponsors responded to the catechetical scrutiny for the infants and carried out all the actions of the ceremony on their behalf (p. 85). Children were admitted as members of the church under the care of adults who had been examined in the faith in their place. By the nineth century parents could no longer serve as sponsors of their own children (Council of Mainz in AD 813, cited in Lynch, 1986). Other adults, "godparents," were selected to serve as sponsors of infants for their scrutiny and baptism. This practice continued throughout the medieval time period.

Delayed Confirmation and Opportunity for Instruction. Because confirmation (anointing with chrism, symbolic of the giving of the Holy Spirit) of infants was reserved for the bishop, it continued to be observed some time after baptism for most infants. When this ceremony ought to occur was the subject of considerable debate. Some church leaders still argued that it should happen within 1–3 years of baptism. Others felt that confirmation should wait until children reached an "age of discretion" where they could affirm their faith. This time gap between baptism and confirmation began to be viewed as a natural time for teaching the basics of the faith. The responsibility for this instruction fell to the parents, and increasingly to godparents (see below).

A Return to Teaching the Fundamentals of the Faith. During the time of Charlemagne (nineth century), the Carolingian church leaders decided that the laity needed a better understanding of the faith they were practicing. Because most people were baptized as infants, there was no pre-baptismal catechesis, and the instruction received after baptism varied widely. In studying the catechesis of the church in the past, particularly the work of Caesarius of Arles (AD 502–542), Carolingian church leaders focused on the Apostles' Creed and the Lord's Prayer as the content of the faith that needed to be learned. "These two prayers were seen as ideal models because the Lord's Prayer taught what to pray for and the Creed taught what to believe" (Lynch, 1986, pp. 312–13). All who were in positions of responsibility were to teach these to those they oversaw: priests their parishioners, parents their children, masters their servants, and godparents their godchildren. This brought significant changes to the responsibilities of the clergy, making preaching a new part of their work (this had been generally reserved to the bishop). In addition, it resulted in the translation and paraphrasing of the Apostles' Creed and Lord's Prayer into the vernacular (Lynch, 1986, p. 315).

Godparents' Roles in Baptism, Instruction, and Confirmation. Parents and godparents were expected to teach their children/godchildren the fundamentals of the faith, and godparents were responsible to present their godchildren to the bishop for confirmation. Adults who desired to serve as godparents were examined in their own knowledge of the "prayers," and could be turned down if they did not know them (Lynch, 1986, p. 305). "No one should receive anyone from the font unless he holds the Lord's Prayer and the Creed according to his own tongue and powers of comprehension" (Archbishop Herard of Tours,

AD 858, cited in Lynch, 1986, p. 317). Not only was knowledge of
these prayers required, but godparents were also to be moral examples
and guides to their spiritual children. This "spiritual kinship" relationship became one of great responsibility and honor, thus socially desirable. The church capitalized on this to make this an opportunity to
ensure that people knew the foundations of the faith. According to
Lynch (1986),

> To serve as a sponsor had long been an honor and a social
> necessity in Frankish society, a reality that was used by the
> church to create a checkpoint where many laymen could be
> tested on their religious knowledge. Furthermore, in sermons,
> during visitations, and in confession laymen were reminded of
> their duty to carry out the promise to guide and teach that they
> had made as sponsors. Thus the Carolingian church grafted
> onto the flourishing institutions of sponsorship and spiritual
> kinship a significant pedagogical component. (p. 332)

Delayed Communion and Opportunity for Instruction. Throughout the
early church era and up through the 11th –12th century of the medieval
time period, it had been common for infants and children who were
baptized to receive communion as part of that rite. They were then
also admitted to the celebration of communion when it was offered in
the life of the church. However, two theological issues began to change
this. First, as the theology of the Eucharist developed, the doctrine of
the real presence of the flesh and blood of Christ (transubstantiation)
became accepted. With this, concern grew that infants and children
would not handle the elements well, resulting in spilling or regurgitat-
ing the blood of Christ. Infant communion disappeared, and much
debate took place regarding when it would be appropriate for a child
to partake in communion. Second, as part of this discussion, there
was a concern that those who participated in communion should discern what was happening as the wine and bread became the blood
and flesh of Christ. When could children be expected to do this? The
same concern was raised over when a child should make confession
to a priest and whether a child on the verge of death should receive
extreme unction (Orme, 2001, p. 214). These debates continued into
the later middle ages as well. This delay in receiving communion, how
ever long it lasted (5–14 years) and the need to understand what was

happening in it, created another opportunity for godparents and parents to instruct children in the fundamentals of the faith.

Thirteenth through Early Sixteenth Centuries

In the later medieval period, as infant baptism continued, several developments had a great impact on the spiritual instruction and nurture that children received. The one with arguably the greatest impact was the Fourth Lateran Council in AD 1215 and the resulting Canons regarding the necessity of all Christians receiving communion at least once a year at Easter. This seemingly simple requirement had great implications for the teaching ministry of the church for all of the laity, including children.

> All the faithful of both sexes shall after they have reached the age of discretion [i.e., fourteen] faithfully confess all their sins at least once a year to their own [parish] priest and perform to the best of their ability the penance imposed, receiving reverently at least at Easter the sacrament of the eucharist, unless perchance at the advice of their own priest they may for a good reason abstain for a time from its reception; otherwise they shall be [barred from entering] the church during life and deprived of Christian burial in death. (*Canon 21*, cited in Shinners, 1997, p. 9).

Confession, Communion, and Instruction. To celebrate communion one must first make confession to the local parish priest. In order to make a good confession, one must know what God requires and also what He considers to be sin. To know these, one must be taught God's laws and the basics of the faith and how to confess. The decision of the Fourth Lateran Council to require annual communion also meant annual confession and led church leaders to take initiatives to strengthen and extend their teaching ministry with the laity. Throughout the thirteenth to the early sixteenth centuries Dominican and Franciscan friars and others developed various documents (*pastoralia*) to aid parish priests and lay people in learning the fundamentals of the faith and how to make a good confession in preparation for communion. While these were generally written for adults, there was an expectation that parents would then teach these things to their children. There are also indications that beginning in the thirteenth century, some diocese encouraged parish clergy to teach the children under their care (Orme, 2001, p. 200).

Development of Written Catechisms. Written documents for instruction had been fairly limited in scope in Europe prior to the thirteenth century. The Apostles' Creed and the Lord's Prayer were the major documents available in the vernacular for instructional purposes. With the educational impetus coming from the Fourth Lateran Council, new expanded catechisms were developed. An example is the "Lay Folk's Catechism" written by Archbishop Thoresby in 1357 in England. This work was modeled on both the Canons of the Fourth Lateran Council and the Canons of the Lambeth Council called by Archbishop John Peckham in 1281. Available in both Latin (for priests) and the vernacular (translated into a rough verse form for less educated clergy and lay use), this is the first written catechism in the English language. Others soon followed and were used by clergy to guide their preaching and teaching and by literate lay people in learning and teaching the basics of the faith. These early catechisms tended to include the Lord's Prayer, Ave Maria, Apostles' Creed, Ten Commandments, and in many cases also included the seven deadly sins, seven acts of mercy, seven sacraments of grace, and the seven chief virtues. These new documents gave a template for use in the church (According to Thoresby, they were to be taught four times a year) and in the home by parents who were to teach them to their children (Simmons and Nolloth, 1901).

Renewal of the Preaching Ministry. One outgrowth from the Fourth Lateran Council was the renewal of the preaching ministry by mendicant friars (primarily Franciscan and Dominican) who traveled from town to town. Pfander (1937) says that,

> The friars preached . . . In the street, in the market, in house or castle, in private chapels, in cemeteries at the preaching corss, in churches ranging from the meanest to the greatest. They preached to lay folk, clerks, prelates, knights, and kings. They preached to nuns and to Benedictine monks. They preached commonly at Mass 'either between the creed and offertory or else after the latter,' and also in procession. They preached very brief sermons devised to please the common people, they preached collations, long sermons on Sunday afternoon after dinner. They preached on Feast Days, or at funerals, or at the

dedication of churches, or on various occasions at the univer-
sities. (pp. 4–5).

Their sermons covered the Scriptures, the Creed, the Lord's Prayer,
and the Ten Commandments. They also taught on the vices and virtues of life, about the lives of saints and martyrs. The response to these
preaching friars was very positive, with people gathering to hear new
preachers as they came into town. Not only adults, but children as well
would come to hear them explain the faith and exhort the people to
faithful living (Pfander, 1937).

Confirmation and First Communion. As discussed above, with the debates over when children should be confirmed in the faith, and when
they should make confession for sins and receive communion, the
church found itself delaying these events and creating new opportunities for instructing children in the faith. William Pagula (early 1300s)
felt that both communion and confirmation in the faith should wait
until children reached the "years of discretion," or age twelve for girls
and age fourteen for boys. Others, like John Mirk (early 1400s), felt
that confirmation should occur within five years of baptism (Orme,
2001, p. 218–19). In some areas and times, confirmation (e.g., age 5)
preceded first communion (e.g., age seven or older). In other times
and places, first communion (e.g., seven or older) preceded confirmation (e.g., seven–twelve). These two rites became the impetus for
parents, godparents, and increasingly priests, teaching the faith to
children to ensure that they were prepared to understand what they
were undergoing in confession, communion, and confirmation. The
earliest requirement of catechesis before the reception of communion
at age seven occurs in Henry of Segusia's *Manual* (AD 1245, cited in
Turner, 2000).

Children and Baptism in the Reformation Traditions

In the sixteenth century, the Reformation movements across Europe
brought with them new understandings and practices regarding baptism, communion, and confirmation. These new views had direct
impact on how children were viewed in the life of the church, their
participation in the sacraments, and the kind of spiritual instruction
and nurture they received. This section provides a brief summary
of the new positions reached in a few of the major branches of the

Reformation.[4] A full history of their development is outside the scope and focus of this chapter.

Martin Luther and Martin Bucer: Lutheran Traditions

In the early sixteenth century in Germany, Martin Luther called into question the Roman Catholic Church's sacramental system (*The Babylonian Captivity of the Church*, 1520). For Luther, "Since salvation is a divine gift, not a human work, the sacraments are subject to the same order of salvation. They are signs and promises of what God does for humans and, like redemption, can only be received in faith" (Johnson, 1999, p. 235). Luther ended up reducing the sacraments to two, baptism and Eucharist. He continued the practice of baptizing infants, defending it on the basis of the inherited sinful nature of infants, the vicarious faith of the Church, and the freedom of the Holy Spirit to bestow faith. For Luther, the Holy Spirit gives the gift of faith in the sacrament of baptism. "That is, infant baptism testifies to the reality that faith and repentance are not prerequisites *for* baptism but, rather, life-long consequences *of* baptism" (Johnson, p. 239).

In the Lutheran tradition, baptism began the journey of faith and the Church was to provide instruction and nurture to encourage the growth and maturing of that faith given by God. Instruction in the faith was provided through the use of the catechisms that Luther developed for children (*Small Catechism*) and adults and clergy (*Large Catechism*). These provided instruction on the Ten Commandments, the Apostles' Creed, the Lord's Prayer, and the sacraments. The order was intentional, to help the learner understand the demands of the Law and how they were fulfilled through the Gospel of Jesus Christ.

Later work by Martin Bucer, in Strassburg, emphasized the importance of the role of godparents in baptism and the early instruction of the child in the faith. Godparents were to pledge that the child would be raised and instructed in the faith, either by the parents or themselves. For Bucer, having godparents who were prepared to do this became a precondition to baptism.

---

4. I rely heavily on the work of Maxwell Johnson (*The rites of Christian initiation: Their evolution and interpretation*, The Liturgical Press, 1999) for the summaries that appear in this section.

Ulrich Zwingli: Reformed Traditions

In Switzerland, Ulrich Zwingli rejected a "means of grace" under-standing of the sacraments of baptism and the Eucharist. For him, faith came through the work of the Holy Spirit in the soul of the person. Baptism was to be used as a sign of the internal reality that God had already accomplished. In light of this understanding, it is initially surprising that Zwingli supported infant baptism. However, his covenant theology understanding of the nature of the family provided the basis for this practice.

> ... birth to Christian parents within the 'covenant' community, for Zwingli, seemed to convey membership in that community automatically. That is, birth to Christian parents already constituted their divine 'election' to salvation and so their baptism was simply an external sign of what was true for them already. . . . as a sign of membership in the covenant community, infant baptism had its parallel with circumcision among the Jews. (Johnson, 1999, p. 244)

Baptism itself then did not justify or save a person, but was a witness to God's saving work through His covenant with His people. Baptism was a rite of initiation and infants were dedicated and pledged to future faith in God. Baptism made the infant a member of a community of Christians where they could grow in the faith (Wandel, 2004, p. 276). In the corporate gathering of the baptism ceremony, those present interceded for the infant that on the basis of future faith this child be incorporated into the life of the church and instructed and nurtured in the faith. Similar to Martin Bucer, Zwingli's approach made baptism a pledge "that the infant, who by birth to Christian parents is already part of God's elect and now solemnly dedicated, will be brought up in the Christian faith and so one day make his or her own faith response" (Johnson, 1999, p. 249). All expectation was that the child would indeed follow Christ as he or she was to be taught, making the teaching ministry of the church critical for fulfilling this rite. Central in the teaching ministry of the church was the proclamation or preaching of the Word and teaching children how to read it. Schools were to create an environment of prayer where the Word could be taught and children could learn to pray. This was done as an "aid to the work of the Holy Spirit" (Wandel, p. 286). "Education in Zürich was intended to enable right faith to discern more accurately and fully God's will for the conduct of one's life and the content of one's belief" (Wandel, p. 288).

John Calvin: Reformed Traditions

In Geneva, Switzerland, John Calvin led the growing "Reformed" movement through his writings and leadership in the church and city government. Holding to a similar covenant theology as Zwingli, he retained a higher view of the sacraments as a means of grace for the elect. For Zwingli, the sacraments were signs of the church's pledge toward God (in baptism) and commemorations of past events (in the Lord's Supper). Calvin focused more on God's work in these sacraments, seeing them as testimonies of God's grace exercised in the present and confirmed by outward signs (Johnson, 1999, p. 250). Although no one could know who were elect and who were not, infant baptism was seen as appropriate because of the nature of God's covenant with his people and the place of children within the family. Regarding baptism, Calvin wrote:

> Hence it follows, that the children of believers are not baptised, in order that though formerly aliens from the Church, they may then, for the first time, become children of God, but rather are received into the Church by a formal sign, because, in virtue of the promise, they previously belonged to the body of Christ. (1559/1972, Vol. II, Ch. 15, p. 526)

The sacraments were seen as "visible words" that do not bestow grace in themselves, but ratify what God has accomplished. For Calvin, like Luther and Zwingli, baptism became a corporate event for the church, not a private event for the infant and family. It served to remind the congregation of their own baptism and the grace of God in their own lives for salvation. Unlike Luther, however, Calvin did not view the Holy Spirit bound to the external sacraments as means of grace.

Like Luther, Calvin developed catechisms to be used in instructing children in the faith they were baptized into. So important was instruction in the catechism that it was not left to parents to do on their own. Calvin, and those who followed his lead, both affirmed the importance of fathers teaching their children and developed catechism classes taught by ministers each Sunday between the morning and afternoon worship services (Kingdon, 2004, p. 300–301). The catechisms covered instruction on the Apostles' Creed, the Ten

Commandments, the Lord's Prayer, and the sacraments. The catechism became so important in Geneva under Calvin that adults could not receive communion until they were able to recite them from memory. This instruction in the basics of the faith was reinforced in the worship services, where the Creed and the Lord's Prayer were recited as part of the service (Kingdon, p. 306).

Thomas Cranmer: Church of England

In England, Thomas Cranmer authored the *Book of Common Prayer* (1549, 1552), which gave instructions regarding the practice of baptism for the newly reformed Church. Heavily influenced by both Luther and Bucer, the rite called for baptism to be done at times of regular corporate worship. The baptismal rite followed the earlier *Sarum Rite* in many respects but godparents were to promise on behalf of the infant that they would "forsake the devil and all his works, and constantly believe God's holy word and obediently keep his commandments." The baptismal rite closes with a final exhortation to the godparents, reminding them that it was

> ... your parts and duty to see that these infants be taught, so soon as they shall be able to learn, what a solemn vow, promise, and profession they have made by you. And that they may know these things the better, ye shall call upon them to hear sermons, and chiefly you shall provide that they may learn the creed, the Lord's prayer and the ten commandments in the English tongue. (*Book of Common Prayer,* 1549)

And, this important addition reveals the new model of catechetical instruction that the church intended to carry out:

> ... the children be brought to the bishop to be confirmed of him, so soon as they can say in their vulgar tongue the articles of faith, the Lord's prayer and the ten commandments, *and be further instructed in the catechism, set forth for that purpose.* (*Book of Common Prayer, 1549 – emphasis added*)

Baptism then is carried out with the infant to identify him or her as one who is part of the Church. It is carried out by others on his or her behalf, "in token that hereafter he shall not be ashamed to confess the faith of Christ crucified, and manfully to fight under his banner against sin, the world and the devil, and to continue Christ's faithful soldier and servant unto life's end" (*Book of Common Prayer,* 1552).

This approach has some language that is compatible with a Lutheran understanding of baptism as a means of grace, and other language that fits with a Calvinist focus on the promises of God and confirmation of faith. This has led to the Anglican practices being understood and practiced in both ways in the Church. Whichever approach is taken, there is a heavy emphasis on the necessity of instruction in the faith and the need for personal confirmation of the faith as the child grows. This led to an explosion of writing and printing of catechisms in England and their use in homes, schools, and the church. Parents and godparents were expected to teach the catechism at home. Schoolteachers taught and prepared their students for reciting the catechism to their priests. Priests were required to have regular times of instructing and checking the knowledge of the catechism by children in their parishes.[5]

Menno Simons: Anabaptists

The Anabaptist traditions of the sixteenth century (e.g., Swiss Brethren, Moravian, Hutterite Brethren, Mennonites) rejected the idea and practice of infant baptism all together. Their emphasis on the church being formed of believing persons who have responded to the call of God led Anabaptists to practice believer's baptism. Baptism was seen as part of the economy of obedience, not salvation, and faith (conversion) must come prior to baptism, with baptism being an outer sign of an already accomplished inner spiritual reality. Infant baptism was replaced with rites of infant dedication, with baptism being postponed until persons could give an account of their faith (Johnson, 1999, p. 268).

Infant dedication (seen as an ordinance, not a sacrament) brought the entire congregation together as the parents, supported by the congregation, dedicated the child to God and promised to raise and instruct the child in the faith so that he or she could one day respond in faith to the gospel.

Menno Simons, a leader within the Anabaptist movement, understood children to have inherited a sin nature, but not to be held accountable for actual sins due to their young age. They are "innocent"

---

5. For an excellent study on the growth and use of catechisms in England during the sixteenth through eighteenth centuries, see Ian Green's work, *The Christian's ABC: Catechisms and catechizing in England c. 1530-1740* (Clarendon Press, Oxford, 1996).

because through the grace of Christ their sinful natures are covered, at least until they reach an "age of discretion."

> Our entire doctrine, belief, foundation and confession is that our innocent children, as long as they live in their innocence, are through the merits, death, and blood of Christ, in grace, and partakers of the promise. (Simons, *Reply to Gellius Faber*, cited in Miller, 2001, p. 202)

Children then were raised and taught by their parents to understand the faith and its importance so that when they were old enough they could respond in faith to the salvation offered in Christ and be baptized. This instruction was generally not from a prescribed catechism (though some groups developed them), but through learning the Scriptures and parental discipline and guidance in what it meant to have faith in Christ. Dramatic conversions were not expected, but personal embracing of the faith modeled by the family and church community was understood to be the norm (Miller, 2001, p. 210).

General practice was to allow baptism when a child reached an "age of reason" or "age of discretion," but when exactly this was reached was debated. In some cases this was seen as age twelve, but this practice was not yet universally settled. The minimum age for baptism was variously proposed as six, seven, ten, eleven, twelve, fourteen and even older (Miller, 2001, p. 206–7). Without this personal faith commitment and baptism the child was not viewed as a part of the church.

Confirmation Practices in the Reformation Churches

> One of the great ironies of the Protestant Reformation is that, in spite of the Reformers' almost unanimous deletion of confirmation from the list of sacraments in the Church, Lutheranism, Reformed Protestantism, and Anglicanism all ended up with some form of 'confirmation' as the preliminary rite leading to the reception of first communion. (Johnson, 1999, p. 270)

For those reform groups that practiced infant baptism, confirmation was initially rejected as a sacrament, but eventually embraced as a rite of initiation into full participation in the life and worship of the church. Catechetical instruction became a prerequisite to being confirmed in the faith, and communion became available to those who were confirmed. Confirmation, often carried out on the day before the principal feasts of the church calendar (i.e., Christmas, Easter, Pentecost) involved a public examination of the faith of the children by a pastor. The congregation offered prayer for them, and the pastor laid hands on them and prayed that the Holy Spirit would strengthen them in the faith. Once this was completed, the children were admitted to their first communion celebration. The following quotes from Martin Bucer and from the *Book of Common Prayer* illustrate these practices.

> Such children who through catechetical instruction are suf-
> ficiently advanced in Christian knowledge to be permitted to
> go to the Lord's table shall on a high festival such as Christmas,
> Easter and Pentecost, at the instance of the elders and preach-
> ers, be presented by their parents and sponsors to the pastors
> in the presence of the congregation in a place designated in the
> churches for that purpose. The elders and all other ministers of
> the word shall stand about the pastor, who shall then examine
> these children in the chief articles of the Christian faith. When
> they have answered the questions and publicly surrendered
> themselves to Christ the Lord and his churches, the pastor
> shall admonish the congregation to ask the Lord, in behalf
> of the children, for perseverance and an increase of the Holy
> Spirit, and conclude this prayer with a collect. . . . Finally, the
> pastor shall lay his hands upon the children, thus confirming
> them in the name of the Lord, and establish them in Christian
> fellowship. He shall thereupon also admit them to the table of
> the Lord, adding the admonition that they continue faithfully
> in the obedience of the gospel and readily receive and faith-
> fully heed Christian discipline and reproof, especially from the
> pastors. (Martin Bucer, *Ziegenhain Order of Church Discipline*)
>
> The curate of every parish, or some other at his appoint-
> ment, shall diligently upon Sundays and holy days half an hour
> before evensong, openly in the church instruct and examine
> as many children of his parish sent unto him as the time will
> serve, and as he shall think convenient, in some part of this
> catechism. . . . And all fathers, mothers, masters and dames
> shall cause their children, servants and apprentices who have
> not learned their catechism to come to the church at the time
> appointed, and obediently to hear and be ordered by the
> curate, until such time as they have learned all that is here
> appointed for them to learn. And whenever the bishop shall
> give knowledge for children to be brought before him to any
> convenient place for their confirmation, then shall the curate

of every parish either bring, or send in writing, the names of all those children of his parish who can say the articles of their faith, the Lord's Prayer and the Ten Commandments: and also how many of them can answer to the other questions contained in this catechism. . . . And there shall none be admitted to the Holy Communion, until such time as he or she can say the catechism and be confirmed. (*Prayer Book of the Church of England*, 1552)

This "rite of passage" into full participation in the life of the church made preparation for this event important, motivating parents and parish leaders to invest time in teaching the basics of the faith in formal ways. Confirmation then became a driving force for the instruction and spiritual nurture of children. As Johnson comments, "in spite of the (differences in) theological understanding, all were, in practice, fully initiating only 'responsible' and faith-professing 'adult' individuals whose intellect and will had been shaped by catechetical education" (1999, p. 289).

Children and Baptism Since the Reformation Era

Developments in Roman Catholic Practice

From the sixteenth through the eighteenth centuries, the Roman Catholic Church continued its practice of infant baptism, followed later by confirmation and first communion. Various councils set standards for the preparation of children for their first communion experience. Children were expected to participate in confession and also be able to recite the Lord's Prayer, Ave Maria, Ten Commandments, and the Apostles' Creed, in addition to some basic understanding of confession and the Eucharist. The recommended age for First Communion was generally held to be ten to fourteen, with confirmation preceding it at age seven. The delay of first communion was motivated by a desire to both ensure that children were capable of confessing sins, and that they could distinguish the Eucharist from ordinary food. The new goal of preparing children for First Communion created a strong motivation for teaching them the basics of the faith (Turner, 2000).

The Reformation churches quickly developed catechisms for use in instructing both adults and children in the reformed faith. While these kinds of resources were not new to the Roman Catholic Church, with the emphasis on preparing for First Communion, their development and use increased dramatically from the sixteen century on. Emphasis still remained on parents and godparents instructing their children, but priests were also expected to teach children of the parish about confession and the Eucharist. As time progressed, priests began to hold catechetical classes for groups of children at specified times, with Lent being commonly used for this purpose. The practice spread in the nineteenth and twentieth centuries, becoming the norm for congregational practice.

> Pastors should not permit children who have just reached the years of discretion to receive the sacrament of the Eucharist, even if they have confessed, unless the children know well the Lord's Prayer, the Hail Mary, the Apostles' Creed, and the Ten Commandments, and if they have been educated with the capacity of understanding about the mystery of this sacrament. Therefore parents should be frequently urged to take care of the instruction of their youth in this matter. (Synod of Ypres [Ieper], 1577, 14:3)
>
> Once each month on a day firmly established, pastors should call to the church children who have reached age nine, and instruct them individually in the right way of confessing. . . . At the beginning of Septuagesima week they should invite those who have reached age ten and individually instruct them and prepare them for the knowledge and worship of the most holy sacrament of the Eucharist, and teach them how humbly, religiously, and reverently they should come to receive it. (Council of Milan VI, 1582)
>
> We desire that every year and in all the parishes there be established, as we have said, a period for instruction of children and at the same time the day of first solemn Communion. The ceremony should be preceded by an examination in which the children will show proof of a sufficient instruction and of a preparation of three days in the parish. (Pius X, *Letter to the Cardinal Vicar*, 1905)

Beginning in 1910, amidst considerable debate, Church practice of First Communion changed, with age seven becoming a new standard. A child's ability to use reason was in some ways equated with the older concept of age of discretion. This also impacted the practice of confirmation. Turner (2000) explains,

> Throughout this period the preferred age of confirmation remained seven, but permissions proliferated to confirm

earlier in emergencies, and later for the sake of catechetical formation. Confirmation was interpreted both as a sacrament of initiation and as one of commitment. Efforts to defer the age of confirmation seemed to fill a void left by lowering the age of First Communion. (CD-ROM, Chapter 12, Section 6, Confirmation: Age and Meaning, ¶ 11)

Expansion of Reformed Traditions

In the centuries following the Reformation era, Protestant denominations that practice infant baptism have tended to develop confirmation classes for children around ages twelve to fourteen, when they felt children were able to take responsibility for their own faith profession. These led to the development of catechetical materials and ceremonies that have also been used as "rites of passage," similar to the bar mitzvah in Jewish practice, marking the transition from childhood to becoming a full adult member in the church. Richard Osmer (1996) has provided a helpful history and contemporary analysis of confirmation practices and theology, covering the Lutheran, Anglican, United Methodist, and Presbyterian traditions. Arthur Repp (1964) produced a similar work in the Lutheran tradition. Those interested in the development of confirmation since the Reformation will enjoy reading these works.

A Case Study in Theological Reflection: Horace Bushnell, Baptism, and Children

Having reviewed this historical perspective on the ways that theologies and practices of baptism influenced the church's views and ministry practices with children, I would like to turn to a case study of theological reflection. The circumstances described below illustrate how important it is to carefully work through the ministry implications of our theological positions. I hope you will find it helpful.

In the early nineteenth century, New England was experiencing the impact of the "Second Great Awakening." It was a time of religious revival with renewed emphasis on personal religious experience and conversion. Within the Presbyterian denomination, in which Horace Bushnell served as a pastor, those who embraced the revivals and emphasis on personal experience were known as "New Lights" or "New Side," while those who were uncomfortable with this insistence on a conscious personal conversion experience were known as "Old

Lights" or "Old Side." This controversy began with the "First Great Awakening" in the early eighteenth century but was reignited during the new revival movement of the early nineteenth century.

One of the issues that arose within this context was the spiritual status of children and the best way to raise them in the Christian faith. Old Lights emphasized the covenant relationship of a believer's family with God and instruction toward embracing the faith children were baptized into. While not viewed as baptismal regeneration, the expectation was that as parents taught and guided their children in the light of the gospel, they would confirm this faith as their own when they reached an age of discretion. New Lights emphasized the necessity of a more specific personal religious experience and the ability to give a testimony of conversion and faith in Christ. In their view, without this experience, the child was not in right relationship with God, and parents were to let them know this, and teach to promote a personal conversion experience. In essence, the theological emphases of both pietism and an Anabaptist perspective were influencing what was viewed as normative for children growing up within a denomination whose roots were influenced more by Calvin and Zwingli.

Horace Bushnell, now famous for his major work, *Christian Nurture* (1847a, revised in 1861, 1876, 1888, and 1916), was deeply concerned about how parents and church leaders were viewing the spiritual lives of children and the impact of those views on their ministry with them. He saw a deep inconsistency between the Reformed theology of baptism and how the New Light emphases on experience and conversion were being applied to children.

In an earlier work, *Discourses on Christian Nurture* (1847b), a publication by the Massachusetts Sabbath School Society which grew out of two public lectures he had given to a ministerial association, Bushnell presents a two-fold argument for his major thesis that the true idea of Christian education is that the child is to grow up a Christian, and never know himself as being otherwise (1847b, p. 6). The first part of his argument for a nurture approach with children is based on human experience, and the second on theological grounds. One that he develops most fully is rooted in a reformed theology of baptism. What follows are some extensive quotes from this argument. (Emphasis added)

Last argument, which is *drawn from infant or household baptism—a rite which supposes the fact of an organic connection of character between the parent and the child; a seal of faith in the parent, applied over to the child, on the ground of a presumption that his faith is wrapped up in the parent's faith; so that he is accounted a believer from the beginning.* . . . the Christian parent has, in his character, a germ, which has power, presumptively, to produce its like in his children, though by reason of some bad fault in itself, or possibly some outward hindrance in the Church, or some providence of death, it may fail to do so. *Thus it is that infant baptism becomes an appropriate rite. It sees the child in the parent, counts him presumptively a believer and a Christian, and, with the parent, baptizes him also.* Furthermore, you will perceive that it must be presumed, either that the child will grow up a believer, or that he will not. The Baptist presumes that he will not, and therefore declares the rite to be inappropriate. God presumes that he will, and therefore appoints it. The Baptist tells the child that nothing but sin can be expected of him; God tells him that for his parents' sakes, whose faith he is to follow, he has written his own name upon him, and expects him to grow up in all duty and piety. (Bushnell, 1847b, p. 42)

I have been thus full upon the rite of baptism, not because that is my subject, but because the rite involves, in all its grounds and reasons, the same view of Christian education which I am seeking to establish. One cannot be thoroughly understood and received without the other. . . . The regeneration is not actual, but only presumptive, and every thing depends upon the organic law of character pertaining between the parent and the child, the church and the child, thus upon duty and holy living and gracious example. *The child is too young to choose the rite for himself, but the parent, having him as it were in his own life, is allowed the confidence that his own faith and character will be reproduced in the child, and grow up in his growth, and that thus the propriety of the rite as a seal of faith will not be violated. In giving us this rite, on the grounds stated, God promises, in fact, on his part, to dispense that spiritual grace which is necessary to the fulfillment of its import.* . . . *Therefore we bring them into the school of Christ and the pale of his mercy with us, there to be trained up in the holy nurture of the Lord. And then the result is to be tested afterwards, or at an advanced period of life, by trying their character in the same way as the character of all Christians is tried;* . . . (Bushnell, 1847b, pp. 49–52)

Bushnell calls church leaders to consider carefully what the baptism of their children signifies, and in light of that understanding to approach the instruction and nurture of children with an expectation of God's grace in their lives to give spiritual life as they grow toward taking on responsibility for their own faith and walk with God. This fits his church's theological understanding better than what he saw practiced in many of their congregations as the revival movement of the time swept through New England. Whether or not you agree with his theological views or final conclusions, it is a helpful example of how our theology of baptism gives guidance on what we should expect of and do with the children in our midst.

Review and Discussion

Review. A brief recap of the major changes in baptismal theology and practice covered in this chapter may be helpful:

1. In the earliest church, instruction and the testimony of a sponsor were seen as critical to prepare for baptism because of their theology of baptism and penance after baptism. Some church fathers opposed the baptism of infants out of concern for how sin would be addressed after baptism. As Christianity grew, this led many to delay baptism.

2. When the concern for the souls of children grew (i.e., dying without benefits of baptism), baptism of infants took priority over their instruction and nurture, but parents and godparents were expected to teach children the basics of the faith they were baptized into.

3. When confirmation was separated from baptism, this opened an opportunity for instruction prior to the rite, confirming children in the faith they had been raised in and equipping them for the struggles of adulthood.

4. When communion was separated from baptism, this opened an opportunity for focused instruction to prepare children for confession, which involved knowing the commandments, Lord's Prayer, Apostles' Creed, etc.

5. In the Reformation:

   A. Where baptism was viewed as God's initiative in planting

the seed of faith in the child, instruction and nurture was
to help the child grow into the significance of the baptism
and lead up to their own confirmation of this faith. (Lutheran, Anglican)

B. Where baptism was viewed as a sign of the covenant of
God with His people, children were included under the
faith of their parents and raised and taught in expectation
of their own confirmation of faith in adolescence. (Reformed, Anglican)

C. Where baptism was viewed as a sign of the faith of the
individual, instruction of children focused on knowing the
Scriptures, hearing the gospel, and preparing the heart to
respond in faith at an "age of discretion." (Anabaptist)

6. In the Roman Catholic Church in the modern era, First Communion and confirmation have both become important events
marking the faith journey of children, leading to extensive catechetical efforts in preparation for their celebration.

7. In most denominations today, instructing children in the faith
is a precursor either to their confirmation of the faith they have
been baptized into or raised to embrace. For those who practice
infant baptism, instruction within the church has been added to
parental instruction to ensure children know the basics of the
faith and can affirm them at an age when they can take responsibility for their own faith commitments. For those who practice
believer's baptism, instruction is toward a personal faith experience and commitment.

Discussion: Instructional Practice in Light of Baptism Today. So,
what kind of instruction and spiritual nurture should we provide
children in our various denominational settings? While not providing the only guidance to answer this question, our understanding of
the nature and practice of baptism creates certain expectations and
priorities that influence what we feel is appropriate. In many ways, it
continues to be a driving force shaping our ministry with children,
both at home and in the congregation. Three general approaches

have emerged, and I close with some reflections for consideration by those within these traditions.[6]

Children Viewed as Insiders: (e.g., Catholic, Lutheran, some Anglican).

These groups view baptism as the beginning of faith for the infant. God, in His sovereignty, uses the sacrament of baptism to bestow spiritual life. The teaching ministry of the church is aimed at guiding children into a fuller knowledge of and obedience to that faith into which they were baptized. *Teaching is for those in the faith.* The teaching ministry of the church is designed to help children grow into an identity that is seen as already theirs, God's adopted children in Christ. For Lutherans, "remember your baptism" is a call to grow into the reality that God has brought about through the sovereign work of His Spirit in baptism. The story of the gospel needs to be made clear and repeated frequently so that children will come to understand what God has done for them in and through Jesus Christ, encouraging responses of gratitude, love, and obedience. Instruction in the basics of the faith (Apostles' Creed, Lord's Prayer, Ten Commandments, etc.) and the redemption story presented in Scripture provides a grounding for understanding what God has done and continues to do on their behalf, and also helps the child begin to understand what it means to be God's child and how to live within that identity. Confirmation becomes a time for taking one's place as a responsible believer within the faith community. Confirmation is only a beginning, and should not be seen as a "graduation from," but a "graduation to" a journey of faith that requires both a deepening knowledge of the faith and carrying out spiritual practices that foster a vital walk with God.

Children Assumed to Be/Become Insiders: (e.g., Reformed groups, some Wesleyan, some Anglican).

These groups view baptism as an expression of the corporate nature of faith and the grace of God that comes to those in covenant relationship with Him. Children in these groups are expected to grow spiritually as they are taught and eventually embrace the faith as their own. *Teaching is for personal confirmation of the faith of the*

---

6. I myself fall within the latter category (believers baptism), but have done my best to consider important issues for those within the other traditions as well.

covenant community. As Bushnell explained, in a covenant theology perspective, children are viewed as within the community, not strangers. Every expectation is that by God's grace, as children are raised by believing parents and participate within the church community, God will make Himself known to them and the faith they have been raised within will be confirmed as they take on responsibility for their own faith commitments.

It is critical then to not wait until a confirmation class in the middle school years to help the child know the gospel story or to understand what it means to be a Christian. Clear instruction in the faith, and active involvement in the faith community, is important both before confirmation and after. Prior to confirmation it helps ensure that the child is familiar with the faith, what it means to follow Christ, and desires to make a public declaration identifying Jesus Christ as Lord and Savior. Following confirmation, instruction in the faith helps the believer continue to grow in knowledge and practice of the faith. They have not graduated from being taught, but have taken responsibility for continuing to learn and grow in faith and faithfulness. The confirmation experience itself needs to make clear the nature of the gospel, not assuming that because children have grown up with some exposure to it in the home and church they comprehend it, or have responded to it in faith. It should help the child consider how God has been working in his or her life to draw the child to faith and into a vital relationship with Himself. Confirmation needs to be more clearly developed as the confirming of God's work of salvation in the life of the child, and the beginning of a growing life of love and obedience.

Children Invited to Become Insiders: (Anabaptist, Baptist, many Evangelical and Charismatic groups).

These groups view baptism as a visible sign of the new life that God has brought about in a person through grace and faith in Jesus Christ. The teaching ministry of the church is to help children understand the importance of sin and to know the love and grace of God through Christ that is available to all who will respond in faith. *Teaching is toward personal affirmation of the faith and eventual baptism.* Teaching both the fundamentals of the faith (Apostles' Creed, Ten Commandments, Lord's Prayer) and the gospel story of redemption in the Bible is critical so children can be attentive to the Holy Spirit's work of conviction of sin and the need for receiving the grace of God in Christ through faith. Teaching and spiritual nurture need to make the gospel story both plain and compelling, but the environment of instruction is equally important for helping a child understand the very nature of love and forgiveness.

Children should not be viewed as "strangers" or "outsiders" by the church, but perhaps more like foster children, invited to partake of the full hospitality of the house and family so that they will grow to desire to know the one who loves them, and to become His fully adopted children. Children need to have time to both learn and respond to the gospel message. While a faith response can come at most any age, it is important that adults not pressure children to respond before they are personally capable or ready. Patience and trust is needed as we wait for the Holy Spirit to move in the heart of the child to draw them to faith. When a child responds to the gospel in faith, a well-developed instruction time leading to baptism can ensure the child knows the foundations of the faith and how to walk with God in this new life as a believer.

References

Bakke, O. M. (2005). *When children became people: The birth of childhood in early Christianity.* Minneapolis, MN: Fortress.

Beadle, R., and King, P. M. (1984). *York mystery plays: A selection in modern spelling.* Oxford: Oxford University Press.

Bushnell, H. (1847a/1975). *Views of Christian nurture, and of subjects adjacent thereto.* Delmar, NY: Scholars' Facsimiles and Reprints.

———. (1847b). *Discourses on Christian nurture.* Boston: Massachusetts Sabbath School Society.

Calvin, John (1559/1972). *Institutes of the Christian Religion.* Translated by Henry Beveridge. Grand Rapids: Eerdmans.

Dujarier, M. (1979). *A history of the catechumenate: The first six centuries.* Translated by E. J. Hassl. New York: Sadlier.

Gatch, M. McC. (1981) Basic Christian education from the decline of the catechesis to the rise of the catechism. In Westerhoff, J. H. III, and Edwards, O. C. Jr. (Eds.), *A faithful church: Issues in the history of catechesis* (pp. 79–108). Wilton, CT: Morehouse-Barlow.

Guroian, V. (2001). The ecclesial family: John Chrysostom on parenthood and children. In Bunge, M. (Ed.), *The child in Christian thought* (pp. 61–77). Grand Rapids: Eerdmans.

Johnson, M. E. (1999). *The rites of Christian initiation: Their evolution and interpretation.* Collegeville, MN: Liturgical Press.

Johnston, A. F. (1975). The plays of the religious guilds of York: The Creed play and the Pater Noster play. *Speculum, 50* (1), 55–90.

Kingdon, R. M. (2004). Catechesis in Calvin's Geneva. In Van Engen, J. (Ed.), *Educating people of faith: Exploring the history of Jewish and Christian communities* (pp. 294–313). Grand Rapids: Eerdmans.

Lynch, J. H. (1986). *Godparents and kinship in early medieval Europe.* Princeton: Princeton University Press.

Milavec, A. (2003). *The Didache: Text, translation, analysis, and commentary.* Collegeville, MN: Liturgical Press.

Miller, K. B. (2001). Complex innocence, obligatory nurturance, and parental vigilance: "The child" in the work of Menno Simons. In Bunge, M. (Ed.), *The child in Christian thought* (pp. 194–226). Grand Rapids: Eerdmans.

Muir, L. R. (1995). *The biblical drama of medieval Europe.* Cambridge, UK: Cambridge University Press.

Orme, N. (2001). *Medieval children.* New Haven, CT: Yale University Press.

Osmer, R. (1996). *Confirmation: Presbyterian practices in ecumenical perspective.* Louisville, KY: Geneva.

Pfander, H. G. (1937). *The popular sermon of the medieval friar in England.* Ph.D. dissertation, New York University, 1937.

Repp, A. C. (1964). *Confirmation in the Lutheran church.* St. Louis, MO: Concordia.

Shinners, J., and Dohar, W. J. (Ed.). (1997). *Pastors and the care of souls in medieval England.* Notre Dame: University of Notre Dame.

Simmons, T. F., and Nolloth, H. E. (Ed.). (1901). *The lay folks' catechism, or the English and Latin versions of Archbishop Thoresby's instruction for the people; together with a Wycliffite adaptation of the same, and the corresponding canons of the Council of Lambeth.* London: Scribner & Co.

Turner, P. (2000). *Ages of initiation: The first two Christian millennia.* Collegeville, MN: Liturgical Press. *[Note: This book also contains an extensive CD-Rom of documentation.]*

Van Engen, J. (2004). Practice beyond the confines of the medieval parish. In Van Engen, J. (Ed.), *Educating people of faith: Exploring the history of Jewish and Christian communities* (pp. 150–77). Grand Rapids: Eerdmans.

Wandel, L. P. (2004). Zwingli and Reformed practice. In Van Engen, J. (Ed.), *Educating people of faith: Exploring the history of Jewish and Christian communities* (pp. 270–293). Grand Rapids: Eerdmans.

Westerhoff, J. H. III, and Edwards, O. C. Jr. (Eds.). (1981). *A faithful church: Issues in the history of catechesis.* Wilton, CT: Morehouse-Barlow.

8

"It's the Way You Look at Things"
How Young People Around the World Understand and Experience Spiritual Development

Eugene C. Roehlkepartain

You may remember the 1989 movie, *Dead Poets Society*. It starred Robin Williams as John Keating, an idealistic, outside-the-box teacher in a New England boy's prep school who made it his mission to shake up the stodgy school and instill in his students the idea of *carpe deum*—"seize the day." The whole movie revolves around helping these young men discover their true selves and find their own voice and identity.

There are many ways we can reflect on that movie, but one of the scenes that stands out most was when, early in his time at the school, John Keating had all the students jump on their desks and look around at the classroom. He asked them what they saw from up there that they hadn't noticed before. In the process, he urged his students to look at the world around them from a different perspective—a different angle.

This chapter asks you metaphorically to look at children's spirituality from a different angle or perspective. You won't have to jump up on a desk, but to look at the topic from what may not be your normal perspective as someone who works with children in a Christian context in a particular place, most likely the United States. Instead, I want to explore with you recent Search Institute research that looks at spiritual development among twelve to twenty-five year olds from many countries and religious traditions around the world. In addition, rather than thinking of spirituality in primarily Christian terms, I invite you to reflect on the idea of spiritual development as an integral, essential part of human development from a social science perspective. That is, I'd like us to consider together this question:

What is spiritual about being human?

Put another way, are there some things about how all of us grow and develop that we might think of as spiritual—no matter what we specifically believe about the divine, or the particular practices and traditions we uphold, or what part of the world we live in? And, if so, how might a better understanding of these processes affect how we minister with children?

These are important questions for those of us who seek to use the tools and approaches of social science to deepen our understanding of human beings and human development. Although some of the early pioneers in the social sciences in the late 1800s and early 1900s considered religion and spirituality as integral to their fields, this study was marginalized throughout much of the twentieth century (Benson, 2006).

Recent years, however, saw a marked growth in scholarship related to spirituality and spiritual development. Though the word *spirituality* did not even appear in the MedLine database until the 1980s, "in recent years, every major medical, psychiatric, and behavioral medicine journal has published on the topic" (Mills, 2002, p. 1), including a number of examinations of child and adolescent spiritual development (see Coles, 1990; King & Roeser, 2009; Oser, Scarlett, & Bucher, 2006; Roehlkepartain & Benson, in press; Roehlkepartain, King, Wagener, and Benson, 2006; and Yust, Johnson, Sasso, & Roehlkepartain, 2006). Each of these and other efforts have advanced the scientific study of child and adolescent spiritual development, making it more and more integral to how we understand human development.

But what is it? Social scientists (and theologians, by the way) struggle to define what we mean by spiritual development and spirituality, particularly in the lives of children and youth. For some, it is a set of practices that represent one dimension of a faith tradition or commitment. (Hence, many Christians think of spirituality as involving practices or "spiritual disciplines" such as prayer or fasting.) For others, it is an unseen, mysterious dimension of life or the universe that may or may not be accessible to humans. These are just two examples in an array of approaches.

The approach we have taken at Search Institute is slightly different. We have been exploring whether and how spiritual development might be understood as a core dimension of human development. If our hypothesis is that being spiritual is a core part of being human, then we ought to be able to find evidence of spiritual development across all cultures and traditions.

So, like the students in *Dead Poets Society,* we climbed on the desk to see what we might see when we looked at spiritual development from this different vantage point. Between 2006 and 2009, Search Institute engaged in a series of exploratory studies aimed at deepening our understanding of child and adolescent spiritual development in a global context. The John Templeton Foundation supported this work. We explored several questions, including these:

- Is it possible to reach a broad consensus on the underlying developmental processes and dimensions of spiritual development that may be expressed, experienced, and nurtured in many different ways across cultures and traditions around the world?

- Does claiming spiritual development as an integral part of human development help us understand child and adolescent development beyond the territory that is already claimed by cognitive, emotional, physical, moral, and other areas of development?

- And, finally, what factors within a young person and her or his environment—her family, community, school, religious community, broader culture, and natural world—enhance or thwart spiritual development?

We used four research methods to shed light on these questions. First, we engaged research partners in thirteen countries to conduct focus groups with youth, parents, and youth workers. These focused on uncovering participants' implicit understandings of spiritual development. Next, we engaged a group of 120 social scientists, philosophers, theologians, youth development experts from nineteen countries and various religious and philosophical traditions in a web-based consensus-building process, to develop a conceptual framework of spiritual development. We conducted interviews with thirty young people who were nominated by experts as "spiritual exemplars," or young people with a profound sense of spirituality in their everyday lives (King, Ramos, & Clardy, 2008). Finally, we engaged research partners in seven countries to conduct an exploratory survey of 7,600 youth ages twelve to twenty-five, based on the theoretical framework we developed from the focus groups and the consensus-build process with advisors (Benson & Roehlkepartain, 2008).

Taken as a whole, these efforts allowed us to explore spiritual development from a number of different angles using a variety of methods that begin to illuminate what we might mean when we think about spiritual development as a core dimension of human developmentity. In order to tell a bit of this story, I will first highlight findings from the focus groups and our surveys of young people, each of which focus on young people's own perspectives. Then I will introduce the framework spiritual development that evolved from the consensus-building process, and illustrate the dimensions of spiritual development with quotes from the spiritual exemplars.

Starting with Young People's Perspectives

One of the core values we brought to this research project was that we wanted to listen to how young people themselves think about spiritual development. A primary way we listened was through a series of focus groups we conducted through research partners in different parts of the world. In all, we engaged 171 diverse youth, ages twelve to nineteen, in twenty-seven focus groups in thirteen countries: Australia, Canada, China, India, Israel, Kenya, Malta, Nigeria, Peru, South Africa, Syria, the United Kingdom, and the United States. The participants self-identified with a broad range of religious traditions: Buddhism, Christianity (Roman Catholic, Orthodox, Protestant, and Reform), Hinduism, Judaism, Islam, Sikhism, and a few had no religious affiliation (Kimball, Mannes, & Hackel, 2010).

Perhaps most striking about these conversations with young people was how excited and engaged they became (after they got over their initial uneasiness and awkwardness with finding the words to express themselves). Time and again, they said something like, "This was really interesting. Even though I go to church, no one has ever asked me what I think about what it means to be spiritual. Usually people just tell me what I need to do or believe to be spiritual." Here are some other things they said about how they understand spirituality and spiritual development:

- A young woman from Nigeria remembered a person she considered to be particularly spiritual (which is how we began the conversation). She described a neighbor who is "very humble, very sincere, truthful—you can trust him. . . . He is very generous."

- A girl in South Africa said: "Spirituality is experienced in your own being. . . . Being spiritual means standing on a mountain with the wind blowing through your hair, and the feeling of being free."

- Another young person from South Africa said: "If you are not spiritual, then you don't ever struggle with things, you don't make a choice or ask, 'Why did this happen to me?' If you are not spiritual, you will never learn anything. . . . You have to reflect on what's happening to you."

- A young Canadian said: "Spirituality in my life gives me meaning. I'm not a religious person, but I need to feel like there's something else to my life, even if it's only to try to make my world a better place."

- Finally, a young man in Israel gave me the title of this presentation: "I think spirituality is the way you look at something: the way you look at pictures, the way you look at nature, the way you read books, what kind of movies you like to look at."

Grounded theory analysis of the focus group transcripts yielded several themes that informed other aspects of our research agenda moving forward:

- Young people believe that a capacity for spiritual development is natural and readily available to all young people, though many can identify impediments.

- Being actively spiritual is an individual choice.

- Active spirituality shapes a purposeful orientation to life.

- Spiritual development is not dependent upon age but is affected by other dimensions of human development.

These focus groups gave a clear sense that young people may not always have the words to describe their sense of the spiritual, or they may use traditional religious language to give meaning and structure to their spiritual experience. Yet, given encouragement to reflect and express their own experience, many became articulate and passionate about how they see and experience the spiritual dimension of their own lives. For me, it suggests a hunger, interest, or openness that we too easily overlook or dismiss, rather than engaging with it and guiding children and youth to find meaning and purpose from their own experiences.

Survey Highlights: How Young People Experience Spiritual Development

We also sought to get young people's perspectives about spiritual development through a 200-item survey, which we conducted with 6,725 youth ages twelve to twenty-five in eight countries. We did not seek representative samples in each country; rather, we tried to get a broad diversity of youth in each place. Local research partners in each country collaborated to collect the data. Table 1 describes the sample.

Table 1

Eight-country survey sample sizes, by religion and gender

Total Sample		6,725
Country	Australia	661
	Cameroon	848
	Canada	383
	India	1,896
	Thailand	1,027
	Ukraine	974
	United Kingdom	569
	United States	367
Religious Affiliation	Buddhist	139
	Christian	3,303
	Hindu	1,017
	Muslim	600
	Other religion[a]	135
	None[b]	1,192
	Missing	339

Table 1 (continued)

Age	12–14	1,803
	15–17	1,377
	18–21	1,840
	22–25	1,161
Gender	Female	3,496
	Male	3,156

a. Includes Judaism, Paganism, Sikhism, Native or Traditional Spirituality, and Other.

b. Combines atheism and agnosticism.

For our current purposes, we will highlight some of the descriptive findings from this study, focusing on how young people perceive spirituality and its role in their lives. Though this sample is not representative, it begins to suggest both commonalities and distinctives in how young people in different traditions and parts of the world understand and experience this dimension of life. Here are some key descriptive findings from the study (also see Roehlkepartain et al., 2008).

1. The vast majority of youth surveyed believe life has a spiritual dimension.

In most countries where surveys were conducted, an average of only 9 percent of youth said they didn't believe life has a spiritual dimension or they didn't know (Table 2). Thus, though young people have different understandings of the nature of spirituality, relatively few (under 5 percent in this sample) would argue that there is no spiritual dimension to life.

Table 2

Youth's views of "what it means to be spiritual," by religious affiliation*

	TOTAL	Buddhist	Christian	Hindu	Muslim	Other or None
Believing there is a purpose to life.	34%	30%	37%	31%	26%	31%
Being true to one's inner self.	26%	44%	21%	37%	12%	32%
Having a deep sense of inner peace or happiness.	23%	35%	22%	27%	8%	27%
Being a moral person.	21%	22%	25%	16%	14%	19%
Believing in God.**	35%	14%	39%	39%	65%	13%

Table 2 *(continued)*

	TOTAL	Buddhist	Christian	Hindu	Muslim	Other or None
Believing there is a dimension to the universe we cannot see.	9%	16%	9%	8%	4%	13%
Going to church, mosque, temple, etc.	6%	7%	7%	6%	10%	3%
I don't think there is a spiritual dimension to life.	4%	3%	2%	2%	1%	12%
I don't know.	5%	7%	4%	2%	2%	2%
Other.	6%	10%	1%	2%	2%	6%

*. This item reads: "Here are some ideas about what it means to be spiritual. Choose one or two that are most important to you." (Percentages sum to more than 100% because some adolescents made two choices.)

**. Prior to this item, the following definition was given: "Some questions in this survey ask about 'God.' To keep questions brief, we use 'God' to mean the many ways in which people around the world refer to Higher Power(s). 'God' includes Allah, Great Spirit, Krishna, and all the names for Higher Power(s)."

The Christian youth (in multiple countries) are most likely to view spirituality as involving a belief in God (39 percent) and having a sense of purpose in life (37 percent). For the Buddhist youth in this sample, spirituality is primarily about being true to one's inner self (44 percent) and having a deep sense of inner peace or happiness (35 percent). Muslim youth in this survey indicate that believing in God is the primary way they see spirituality (65 percent). So though the nature of beliefs and practices across traditions vary widely, it is noteworthy to see areas of both commonality and distinctiveness in how young people understand this dimension of life.

2. Youth see religion and spirituality as related, but different.

Like adults, many youth struggle with the relationship between religion and spirituality. Youth in this study are most likely to indicate that they are both spiritual and religious (36 percent), with 17 percent indicating that they are spiritual, but not religious. Fifteen percent of the youth surveyed indicated that they don't know.

We see a lot of differences in this item among youth in different countries. In the U.S. sample, 45 percent indicated that they are both spiritual and religious, with 27 percent indicating that they are spiritual but not religious. Only 8 percent said they are neither religious nor spiritual. In the United Kingdom and Australia, only 23 percent indicate that they are spiritual and religious, with 25 percent in each country indicating that they see themselves as neither spiritual nor religious.

3. Young people view both religion and spirituality positively.

A majority of youth in the survey thinks that both being religious (65 percent) and being spiritual (70 percent) as "usually" or "always" good, with just over one-fourth of respondents saying that being either is neither good nor bad.

4. Young people are most likely to report that their spirituality has increased.

We asked young people to indicate whether they believe their spirituality has increased, decreased, or remained the same over the past two or three years. More than half of the youth surveyed (53 percent) indicated that, overall, their spirituality had increased. Only 20 percent indicated that it had decreased a little or a lot. More specifically, the majority of youth surveyed reported that various aspects of their spirituality changed. For example, 68 percent say they have more of a sense that life has meaning or purpose. At the same time, 45 percent of youth said their doubts and questions about spiritual or religious matters had increased during this time.

5. Most young people say family and friends help them spiritually, but one in five say no one does.

When asked to identify who helps them most in their spiritual life, young people surveyed were most likely to point toward family, with 43 percent of youth survey selecting this option. Just 14 percent of youth indicated that their religious institution (church, synagogue, mosque, temple, or other religious or spiritual place) helps them the most. In addition, one in five youth surveyed (19 percent) say that no one helps them regarding their spiritual lives.

6. Everyday experiences and relationships seen as nourishing young people's spirit.

When asked how much various influences and experiences either made it easier or harder to be spiritual (to find meaning, peace, and joy), at least three-fourths of young people in the survey pointed to being outside or in nature, listening to music, serving others, and being alone (Table 3). They also noted that the influence of family and friends make it easier. They are less likely to point to spiritual mentors, religious activities, school, or the Internet as making it easier. Experiencing challenges in life is seen as making it more difficult by 45 percent of youth. However, many in youth focus groups also indicated that spirituality was a resource that helps them through the hardships of life and that they grew spiritually during difficult times.

Table 3
Youth perspectives on what nurtures their spirituality*

	Somewhat or much easier	No effect	Somewhat or much harder
Spending time outside or in nature.	79%	15%	6%
Listening to or playing music.	76%	17%	6%
Being alone in a quiet place.	72%	19%	10%
The influence of parents.	68%	19%	13%
Spending time helping other people or the community.	64%	26%	10%
The influence of other family members.	63%	25%	13%
The influence of friends.	61%	30%	15%
The influence of school.	56%	28%	17%
Participating in worship services, classes, or other religious rituals.	55%	30%	15%
Watching TV or videos, or spending time on the Internet.	55%	31%	15%
Being guided by a spiritual mentor, guide, teacher, or guru.	53%	33%	14%
Reading or studying sacred texts.	45%	37%	18%
Experiencing disappointment, grief, pain, or loss.	36%	20%	44%

* Based on responses to this question: How much does each of the following make it easier or harder for you to find meaning, peace, and joy?

> 7. *Youth most often nurture spiritual development alone or by helping others.*

When asked how often they engage in various activities that help them grow spiritually, young people were most likely to say they read books (46 percent), pray or meditate alone (43 percent), help others (43 percent), or attend religious worship or prayer services (39 percent). Three of the six most common activities involved acts of compassion, service, or generosity. Thus, for young people in this survey, spiritual growth is nurtured most often through individual practices or disciplines and acts of compassion and service.

Connecting Experience and Theory

To this point, the findings have focused on what young people themselves think and experience. That is an important starting point, but we want to go further in interpreting patterns and shaping new tools and frameworks for thinking about, discussing, and studying young people's spiritual development. In our work, we have taken three steps in that direction. First, we engaged our 120 international advisors in an online consensus-building process on the dimensions of spiritual development. Then we linked the findings from interviews with young spiritual exemplars with the findings. Finally, we have begun analyzing the data from our international survey to see whether and how in validates, reflects, or refines the conceptual framework that emerged from our advisors.

To tap the wisdom of experts in the field, we engaged our 120 advisors in a web-based consensus-building process (based on the Delphi Technique, see Andrews & Allen, 2002; Dunham, 1996; and Linstone & Toroff, 2002) around the definition and dimensions of spiritual development. The advisors included leaders and scholars from every continent, various disciplines (psychology, sociology, religious studies, anthropology, various practice-oriented fields, and others), and people with expertise in ten religious traditions (including people who are not religious).

First we presented the advisors with criteria for definitions for review and feedback, then began proposing a series of dimensions of spiritual development for consideration. These led to refined sets of criteria and dimensions. The advisors initially evaluated fifteen potential dimensions of spiritual development, based on current literature and research to date (including early analysis of focus group data). After three rounds of critique and feedback, three central processes of spiritual development emerged around which a strong majority of advisors from each of the different perspectives had reached agreement.

Through the feedback and interaction with advisors, we developed a theoretical framework in which spiritual development is the dynamic interplay between one's inward journey and one's outward journey. This involves at least three core developmental processes:

- Awareness or awakening—Being or becoming aware of or awakening to one's self, others, and the universe in ways that cultivate identity, meaning, and purpose. This process can be subdivided into two themes: (1) *self-awareness,* or awakening to one's inherent strength; and (2) *world-awareness,* or awakening to the beauty, majesty, and wonder of the universe, including the Divine.

- Interconnecting and belonging—Seeking, accepting, or experiencing significance in relationships to and interdependence with others, the world, or one's sense of the transcendent; and linking to narratives, beliefs, and traditions (including religious traditions and texts) that give meaning to human experience across time.

- Living an integrated life—Authentically expressing one's strengths, identity, passions, values, and creativity through relationships, activities, and/or practices that shape bonds with oneself, family, community, humanity, the world, and/or that which one believes to be transcendent or sacred.

These dimensions are embedded in and interact with an ecology of development that includes family, and community beliefs, values, and practices; culture and sociopolitical realities; traditions, sacred writings, and other interpretive frameworks; and significant life events, experiences, and changes. This framework is illustrated in the diagram shown in Figure 1.

Children and youth engage in theses processes and dynamics in many different ways with different emphases and levels of intensity (from highly engaged to passive). They also engage with them differently in different cultures and contexts, in different traditions, and at different developmental periods of life. Some quotes from the young spiritual exemplars illustrate some of the ways these three core processes are lived out in young people's lives:

Figure 1

A theoretical model of key dimensions and processes of
spiritual development

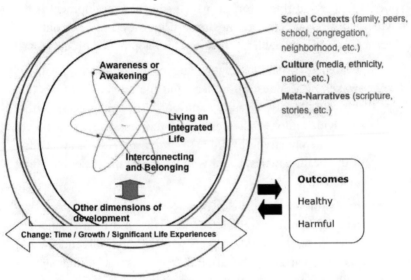

Awareness or awakening

The exemplars exhibited a heightened sense of awareness of both themselves and others (human or divine). In these interviews, they voiced a growing awareness of themselves—their weaknesses, their purpose in life, and their reason for acting. Sometimes they connect this to their spirituality; sometimes they do not. Here are examples:

- "I have to pay attention to everything around me, whether visible or invisible, tangible or not, thinking about the now and also about the future. I believe it is something I need in my life." (Christian, Peru)

- "I think you have to be conscious. I think that's the main thing. You have to be conscious that . . . you have to want to change. And, yeah, like I said, the more you spend time with God the more you *will* change." (Christian, Kenya)

- "But when I spend time with God I think the whole day goes better for me all day long, because I have his presence with me. The whole day I can feel his presence. So it's really important for me to spend time with him every day. I love to pray." (Catholic, India)

- "I went to Ecuador this summer and helped kids and really realized that all the world is one and that every single thing you do helps, no matter how small." (Poly-religious, USA)

Interconnecting and belonging

Spiritual development does not happen in isolation. The exemplars all articulated that their journey of spiritual development occurred in relationship; the exemplars were very aware of being a part of something greater than self. Although that sense of interconnection or belonging is to different things, the theme was present in almost all of the interviews. Here are some examples:

- "I feel really connected to something bigger, but I can't explain it any further than that really. I don't really know how to put it into words." (Christian, USA)

- "I think people are connected with God through their worship, through their connection with each other. . . . We are all connected in one way or another." (Muslim, Jordan)

- "Yeah, there's a sense of togetherness among family. And that's a very important thing. It's because of the ceremonies which are held, and it makes people come together . . . and then sometimes you get a connection with God, a special time with God." (Hindu, India)

Living an integrated life

Many of the exemplars suggest that a growing sense of awareness and connecting with something beyond the self that results in a conscious manner of living. Some of the exemplars describe an intent and commitment to living a righteous or holy life, worthy of God. Other exemplars talk about their commitments to leading a life characterized by compassion and caring. Here are some examples:

- "'Spirituality' means how well, to me, you can follow a set of morals that everyone pretty much has in common, and how well you can live up to I guess good standards for moral settings. So that would be kind of 'spirituality.' And how well you can connect with God." (Hindu, USA)

- "Being compassionate and sensitive with other people is very important. This is the basis of relationship between people. . . . We sat with them, we listened to them, we listened to their problems and circumstances. And we offered them solutions for their problems." (Muslim, Jordan)

- "My service was very important; getting involved helped my spiritual life because it was one more demand since I didn't only have to respond to God, but also to the people I was working with. I had to maintain my testimony especially for the kids who were watching me since I was their role model." (Christian, Peru)

- "I'm really, really passionate about justice. And I think when people look at me that's the one thing they see: I've just got loads of passion about sort of eradicating poverty . . . And I'm always challenging people about how they're living and how they're spending their money and things like that. That's motivated me. I think God's given me that passion." (Christian, UK)

Emerging Empirical Support

To this point, we have presented young people's own perspectives on spiritual development, then begun to integrate dimensions of spiritual development into a multi-dimensional framework. As of this writing, we continue to conduct analyses and empirically test the model, at least in a preliminary way. The early results are promising. We created scales that capture some of what is meant by four areas: The two sub-theme in awareness or awakening: (1) self-awareness and (2) world-awareness; (3) a sense of interconnectedness; and (4) living an integrated life. These brief scales appear to be adequately reliable in most of the countries (internal reliabilities correlations of .60 or higher), suggesting that these core processes may work in a wide range of cultural and religious contexts. In addition, these scales statistically correlate with some important social outcomes. For example, youth from diverse traditions and countries who score higher on these scales are more likely to volunteer. They also appear to be predictive of lower levels of high-risk behaviors.

In addition, those young people who are above the median on all four of these constructs (suggesting a level of integration across all four areas) appear to do better on a wide range of outcomes, including volunteering, concern for the environment, caring for their own health, and lower engagement in violent behavior. These relationships hold true even when we control for gender, age, and religious engagement. In addition, we found that youth who are high on the four processes are also more likely also to be religious. This would suggest that young people who are stronger in these four areas tend to be those young people who are actively engaged in a religious tradition. However (and this is important), a subset of youth—about 20 percent—score high on all four of these scales but are not actively engaged in religious activities and traditions.

If these preliminary analyses are confirmed, it will lend credence to the idea that there are aspects of spiritual development that are at work in a wide range of young people globally and in different traditions. In addition, these processes seem to be related to societal concerns and priorities, or outcomes. Finally, religious commitment appears to be an important resource for many, though not all, young people who are thriving spiritually.

Implications for Ministries with Children

We have been standing, metaphorically, on the desk for a while, getting a different perspective on spirituality among children and youth. From this vantage point, we have explored this dimension of life from a broad perspective of multiple countries, multiple faiths, and multiple cultures, looking for areas of commonality as well as distinctive differences. That is quite different from the daily work of ministering with children in a Christian church in the United States. The age range for the findings presented (primarily ages twelve to twenty-five) is also different than the focus of this book, which focuses on children from birth to early adolescence.

What insight might this broad, global exploration offer that could deepen understanding and strengthen work for people in ministry with children in Christian contexts? I propose that this developmental look at adolescents suggests the need to shift our thinking in six different areas (which are summarized in Table 4):

Table 4

Shifts in emphasis that are suggested by this global developmental research

	Shift from Emphasizing ...	Toward Emphasizing ...
Importance	Spiritual development is nice, but not necessary	Spiritual development is core to human development
Primary goal	"Pass on" tradition (development from the outside in)	Nurture young people's intrinsic spirit (development from the inside out)
View of children and youth	Recipients of programs and information	Active agents in their own development
Emphasis	Programs	Relationships
Responsibility	Religious institutions	All socializing systems in a community and society
Scope	Programmatic or institutional focus	Young people's whole world
Perspective	Program year	Ongoing growth and development

The importance of spiritual development

Too often, we see spiritual development as a "higher order" need that only needs to be addressed after "basic needs" are addressed. If we recognize that spiritual development is core to human development, then we must also challenge ourselves to take it as seriously as we take intellectual, physical, emotional, and social development. That means we should expect every textbook on child development to devote space to children's spiritual development. That means we must have leaders who are as well-equipped to nurture the spiritual lives of children as they are in providing a safe and stimulating environment where children can learn.

Rebalancing our primary goals

There is much talk in Christian circles about "passing on" the faith to children. This language presumes that children are "empty vessels" that we have to fill up with knowledge and beliefs. We call this development from the outside in, and it presumes that adults have what children need. If children have a spiritual life that involves their own experiences, gifts, perspectives, and hungers (as suggested by this research), then perhaps we need to think more about the ways we might nurture that intrinsic spirit—what we might call development from the inside out. Models such as Godly Play (Berryman, 2009) have a lot to teach us about what it means to nurture children's own spirit.

Recognizing children's voice and agency

If our primary perspective is that we have to pass on the faith to our children, then we are most likely to view them as the recipients of programs and activities that we design to meet their needs. The challenge is to find creative ways to capture and keep their attention so they will learn from us. In contrast, this research invites us to listen to children and recognize them as active agents in their own spiritual development. The challenge becomes to discern and celebrate how their story, experience, and commitments connect with and are shaped by the story of faith that has been passed down from generation to generation and that comes alive in new ways in each generation.

Reclaiming the centrality of relationships

Everyone seems to agree that relationships are central to ministry with children. Yet we continue to assume that getting "just the right" curriculum or program will be what makes our ministries strong. When the youth we surveyed were asked what helps them grow spiritually, they most often talked about the people, the relationships that nurtured them. I would propose that those relationships are much more likely to be life-shaping for children when the leaders are attentive to the other shifts outlined here.

Broadening responsibility for spiritual development

If spiritual development is core to children's development, and if it interacts with other areas of development, then we need to think beyond the church as having a stake in young people's spiritual life. To be sure, families (including extended families) play a central role, and the challenge for churches is how best to support and nurture all family members so that the home can be a crucible of spiritual development. In addition, we need to ask questions about what roles other institutions in society might play, positively or negatively, in children's spiritual development. If spiritual development is more than a sectarian issue that is important for all children, then we may be able to being new, mutually respectful conversations with other institutions in society about the ways they might attend to dimensions of spiritual development that are compatible with their mission and respectful of the children, families, and communities they serve.

Recognizing spiritual development in all areas of life

The research we conducted with young people confirmed what we all intuitively know: Young people are as likely to have spiritual experiences when they are in nature, engaged in service, participating in music or art, caring for a terminally ill grandparent, or dozens of other everyday activities that can take on spiritual significant. In this sense, the scope of spiritual development is children's whole world, not just their participation in explicitly religious or spiritual activities. The challenge and opportunity for people in ministry with children in Christian churches is how to help children integrate these experiences and connect them to their own faith story and the broader narrative of the Christian faith.

Maintaining a long-term focus

If your goal is to get a particular story or idea to "stick" with children, it can be fairly straightforward to design a scope-and-sequence of curricula that teaches what needs to be taught at particular times during the program year. I would suggest that spiritual development as we've conceived it is more complex and dynamic. It is unlikely to be contained within the confines of a program year; rather, it becomes an ongoing, lifelong process of growth, reflection, and discovery.

"It's the Way You Look at Things"

I chose for the title of this article a quote from a young man in Israel, who described spirituality as the lens through which he looked at the world, at nature, at books, at movies. He was describing a spiritual worldview that informs his perspective on the world. That perspective is one that many would embrace. How do we guide and mentor young people to view the world through the lens of faith? I would propose that truly attending to their spiritual development and trusting them with their own voice and experience would be good first steps.

I also selected the title to highlight the value of stepping outside our everyday ways we see children and their world in order to see them in a new light and from a new perspective. Often, the process of stepping outside of our own culture and comfort zone can give us a new perspective on life and the world. (Just ask anyone who has spent time in a culture other than their own.) My hope is that this excursion into the spiritual development of adolescents from around the world and from many traditions has had a similar effect. My hope is that it has helped you view children and their spiritual lives in a new way that informs and strengthens how you interact and minister with the children in your midst.

References

Andrews, C. G., & Allen, J. M. (2002). Utilization of technology-enhanced Delphi techniques. *Workforce Education Forum, 29*(1), 3–17.

Benson, P. L., (2006). The science of child and adolescent spiritual development: Definitional, theoretical, and field-building challenges. In E. C. Roehlkepartain, P. E. King, L. Wagener, & P. L. Benson (Eds.), *The handbook of spiritual development in childhood and adolescence* (pp. 484–99). Thousand Oaks, CA: Sage.

Benson, P. L., & Roehlkepartain, E. C. (2008). Spiritual development: A missing priority in youth development. In P. L. Benson, E. C. Roehlkepartain, & K. L. Hong (Eds.), *Spiritual development: New directions for youth development,* 118 (pp. 13–28). San Francisco: Jossey-Bass.

Berryman, J. W. (2009). *Teaching Godly Play: How to mentor the spiritual development of children.* New York: Morehouse.

Coles, R. (1990). *The spiritual life of children.* Boston: Houghton Mifflin.

Dunham, R. B. (1996). *The Delphi technique.* Downloaded April 2, 2005, from www.instruction.bus.wisc.edu/obdemo/readings/delphi.html

Kimball, E. M., Mannes, M., & Hackel, A. (2010). Voices of global youth on spirituality and spiritual development: Preliminary findings from a grounded theory study. In M. de Souza, L. J. Francis, J. O'Higgins-Norman, & D. Scott (Eds.), *International handbook of education for spirituality, care and wellbeing* (pp. 329–48). Dordrecht, Netherlands: Springer.

King, P. E., Ramos, J. S., & Clardy, C. E. (2008). Exemplars of spiritual thriving in adolescents: Findings from an exploratory study. Paper presented at the 20th Biennial International Society for the Study of Behavioural Development conference in Wurzburg, Germany on July 15, 2008.

King, P. E., & Roeser, R. (2009). Adolescent religious and spiritual development. In R. M. Lerner & L. Steinberg (Eds.), *Handbook of adolescent psychology* (3rd Ed., pp. 435–78). Hoboken, NJ: Wiley.

Linstone, H. A., & Toroff, M. (Eds.) (2002). *The Delphi method: Techniques and applications* [online book]. Downloaded April 2, 2005, from www.is.njit.edu/pubs/delphibook/.

172   Eugene C. Roehlkepartain

Mills, P. J. (2002). Spirituality, religiousness, and health: From research to clinical practice. *Annals of Behavioral Medicine, 24,* 1–2.

Oser, F. K., Scarlett, W. G., & Bucher, A. (2006). Religious and spiritual development throughout the lifespan. In W. Damon & R. M. Lerner (Series Eds.) & R.M. Lerner (Volume Ed.), *Handbook of child psychology: Theoretical models of human development* (6th ed., Vol. 1, pp. 942–98). Hoboken, NJ: Wiley.

Roehlkepartain, E. C., & Benson, P. L. (in press). Children, religion, and spiritual development: Reframing a research agenda. In A. Ben-Arieh, J. Cashmore, G. S. Goodman, J. Kampmann, & G. B. Melton (Eds.), *Handbook of child research* (pp. not available). London: Sage.

Roehlkepartain, E. C., Benson, P. L., Scales, P. C. (in press). Spiritual identity: Contextual perspectives. In S. J. Schwartz, K. Luyckx, & V. L. Vignoles (Eds.). *The handbook of identity theory and research: Domains and categories* (Vol. 2, pp. not available). New York: Springer.

Roehlkepartain, E. C., Benson, P. L., Scales, P. C., Kimball, L., & King, P. E. (2008). *With their own voices: A global exploration of how today's young people experience and think about spiritual development.* Minneapolis: Search Institute.

Roehlkepartain, E. C., King, P. E., Wagener, L. M., & Benson, P. L. (Eds.) (2006). *The handbook of spiritual development in childhood and adolescence.* Thousand Oaks, CA: Sage.

Yust, K. M., Johnson, A. N., Sasso, S. E., & Roehlkepartain, E. C. (Eds.) (2006). *Nurturing child and adolescent spirituality: Perspectives from the world's religious traditions.* Lanham, MD: Rowman and Littlefield.

9

The Implications of Neo-Piagetian Theories of Cognitive Development for Understanding the Cognitive Dimension of Childhood Spiritual Formation

James Riley Estep Jr.

The influence of developmental theories on Christian educators' understanding of childhood spiritual formation is readily apparent. The perspectives from educators such on faith and spiritual development of writers such as James Fowler (1989), Gabriel Moran (1983), Iris Cully (1984), Catherine Stonehouse (1998), Perry Downs (1994), and Estep and Kim (2010) all make use of insights from developmental theories to inform their theoretical and practical understanding of spirituality and formation, even in childhood.

One of the most influential developmental theorists was Jean Piaget (1896–1980). His theory of cognitive development, especially in childhood, has directly influenced the Church's approach to spiritual formation with children both practically and theoretically. However, Piaget's successors, the neo-Piagetians, have made significant revision to his original theory, partially in response to critics. Neo-Piagetian theory is not merely a restatement or refinement of Piaget's original theory, but a more holistic approach to cognitive development primarily through the integration of Piaget's theory with other developmental perspectives. However, the Christian education community has paid little (if any) attention to it, or its possible implications (cf. Buzzelli 1992 as one of the only references to neo-Piagetian theory in a Christian source).

This chapter will present the implications posed by neo-Piagetians' theories for understanding spiritual formation in childhood. Its aim is to better understand the process of spiritual formation in children through a better understanding of cognitive development from neo-Piagetian theories. It will address this subject in four sections: (1) Description of Piaget's impact on the Church's understanding of childhood spiritual formation, based on a survey of literature in Christian education and children's ministry that made use of Piaget's theory in addressing matters of childhood spiritual formation, (2) A summation of neo-Piagetian theory, particularly those of Robbie Case and Kurt B. Fischer, so as to provide us with a basic understanding of neo-Piagetian thinking, i.e. *What is Piagetian and what is "neo" about it?* (3) *In so far* that spiritual formation is connected to cognitive development, itemize neo-Piagetian theory's value and implications for understanding spiritual formation in childhood, i.e. *how would the process of spiritual formation of children be understood through a neo-Piagetian lens?*, and (4) a practical agenda for childhood education in the Church.

One cautionary note: It is impossible and erroneous to directly correlate or equate any developmental theory to the formation of spirituality in any stage of human development, and perhaps especially childhood. What this chapter asserts is that *in so far as* spiritual formation is associated with or influenced by a child's cognitive development, then neo-Piagetian theories of cognitive development can aid the Christian educator in better conceptualizing spiritual formation in childhood, and developing practices conducive to facilitating it in children.

Impact of Piaget and Developmentalism on Childhood Spirituality

Without belaboring the point, Piaget has indeed had profound impact on how Christian educators understand in part childhood spirituality. While no one would equate Piaget's theory of cognitive development, or any other developmental theory, with Christian spirituality; the relationship between them is indeed evident (Ratcliff, 1980). For example, British educator David Heywood (1986) wrote an article entitled, "Piaget and faith development: a true marriage of minds?" assessing the benefits and concerns of integrating Piaget into our understanding of faith. Sparkman's (1986) survey of the numerous treatments of religious development in childhood readily demonstrates a reliance on Piaget's developmental theory. All the previous Christian educators mentioned in the beginning of this chapter, likewise devote considerable attention to insights into childhood faith and spirituality gleaned from Piaget's theory.

Ronald Goldman studied at the Piaget Institute in Geneva in the early 1960s. He proceeded to adapt Piaget's model of child-interview to assess the religious understanding of children, i.e. did religious thought in children reflect Piaget's stages? Based on these interviews, which focused on a child's understanding of biblical narratives, he published two books: *Religious Thinking from Childhood to Adolescence* (1964) and *Readiness for Religion: A Basis for Developmental Religious Education* (1965). While not presenting an entire theory of child faith or spiritual formation, he did conclude that the growth of religious thinking from childhood to adolescence in fact reflected Piaget's developmental stages.

Later, David Elkind (1979), a student of Piaget, concluded that one could in fact gain insight into a child's religious conceptualization by using Piaget's developmental theories. From this, he began to draw conclusions and make affirmations regarding the nature of childhood faith in reference to religious identity and prayer. In fact, perhaps the most frequent application of Piaget's theory in recent times has been for the study of prayer in childhood (Ng, 1978; Finney and Maloney, 1985). Gottlieb (2006, p. 245) comments of Goldman and Elkind, "The main impact of Piagetian research on religious education was to impose restrictions on what was taught to young children," but then proceeds to express the benefits of integrating Piagetian insights in our understanding of how children process religious instruction and how it impacts their faith.

Stephen Fortosis (1990), though not addressing early childhood, does address in part the transition from childhood to adolescence, and how Piaget's idea of disequilibration can inform the process of nurturing faith. Jonathan Kim (2007; 2010) most recently explained the connection between cognition and faith formation, not only using

Piaget's theory, but also that of Vygotsky, for insights into how faith is in part formed through cognition. Piaget has been used by Christian educators as an interpretive lens so as to better comprehend the cognitive development of the child, and in turn the cognitive dimension of spiritual formation and faith at given ages and stages of cognitive development. But, what if the lens was not wholly accurate? What if the lens was not the right prescription?

A Summation of Neo-Piagetian Theories

There is indeed no *single* neo-Piagetian theory, but a plurality of theories comprising a spectrum of neo-Piagetian perspective. As such, it is indeed a task to isolate what makes something neo-Piagetian. Forty years of reformulation about Piaget's theory, some taking place even before his death, has even caused a leading neo-Piagetian to ask "still 'neo'?" and "why neo-?" (Morra, Gobbo, Marini, and Sheese, 2008, p. 1). For example, one of the earliest uses of the term neo-Piagetian was in an article by Pascaul-Leone and Smith (1969), at one of the peaks of Piaget's early popularity. So we are left with two basic questions: What makes it Piagetian? What makes it "neo-"?

What makes them Piagetian?

Basically neo-Piagetians often times will acknowledge some feature that originated with the theory of Jean Piaget, and are unwilling to compromise on it. Almost all neo-Piagetians share in common Piaget's constructivist approach to knowledge, rather than a static view (Popp and Portnow, 2001). They also tend to accept the general notion of developmental stages (Pascual-Leone and Smith, 1969; Halford, 1980; Case, 1984, Fischer and Canfield, 1986). In general, neo-Piagetians would accept three or four structures or levels, wherein higher structures include the lower ones, and that there is to an extent an age-range for development (Case, 1987). Case observes in this regard that,

> the various theories that have been proposed in the present issue share a great deal in common. To a considerable degree, these commonalities stem from the fact that all the theories arose from the same theoretical tradition, and were created in response to the same perceived dilemma: That of the preserving the strengths of Piaget's theory, while eliminating its weaknesses. (p. 787)

What makes them "neo-"?

Neo-Piagetian theory is integrative. It endeavors to integrate constructivist approaches to child development, e.g. Piaget, with sociocultural
approaches, e.g. Vygotsky (Mascolo, Kanner, and Griffin, 1998). It was
at one time fashioned Piaget vs. Vygotsky vs. Bruner vs. *ad infinitum.*
Neo-Piagetians are more inclined to be inclusive, more of a Piaget-
and-others; a both-and approach rather than the typical either-or. In
fact, when listening to a neo-Piagetian, you hear almost a simultaneous
double speak, e.g. stages *ala* Piaget along with contextual determinants
ala Vygotsky. Most neo-Piagetians affirm or imply that development is
indeed a series of cyclical recursions of sublevels within the stages of
development (Case, 1987, pp. 777–87).

   *Neo-Piagetians have certain core agreements between themselves,
but that disagree with Piaget.* They would also agree that cognition
transcends domains, inter and intra-individual cognitive development differences, and that the rate and content of structural growth is
domain specific. Similarly, neo-Piagetians do not agree with Piaget in
regard to the number or criteria for distinguishing major stages from
substage, as well as the inclusion of transitional or shared stages (cf.
Fischer 1983). For example, Piaget postulated four stages of cognitive development, each one sequential and distinct from the previous; whereas Fischer identifies a total of twelve stages, with two of the
twelve being shared as transitional stages, i.e. a stage signifying the
end of a level and beginning of the next level, counted in both, but are
in fact the same stage.

   *Neo-Piagetians are a diverse group of theorists that sometimes
disagree even with one another.* They do not agree with one another
in regard to the nature of basic structural units, e.g. schemes, skills,
conceptual frameworks, three-way structures of control, or component processes. But, they do agree that these are the pieces in play in
understanding the process of cognitive development.

Piaget v. Neo-Piagetians

Neo-Piagetian theory originates not only in its affirmation of some of
Piaget's fundamental notions on cognitive development, but also in
their critique and reformulation (Lewis and Ash, 1992, pp. 338–39).
(I must admit a bias toward the neo-piagetian theories of Kurt W.
Fischer and the late Robbie Case. Hence, most of my presentation will

engage them, but with other voices in the field likewise given attention.) *First, cognitive development is described as occurring as a smooth process vs. occurring in spurts of growth.* Neo-Piagetians contend that development does not progress as smoothly as theory indicates, i.e. Décalages or unpredicted gaps in developmental progression would be examples of these spurts of development (Morra *et. al.* 2008, pp. 14–15, 107–10). It is to some extent tied to neurological development and DNA (Mascolo, Kanner, and Griffin 1998, pp. 40–41). It is not a retreat to genetic epistemology, but cognitive development that goes beyond the physical structures of the brain (Morra *et. al.* 2008, pp. 18–22). Hence, neo-Piagetian theories allow for cognitive surges and rapid development.

Second, cognitive development is viewed as domain general vs. domain specific. The principle of generalizability maintains that cognitive maturation occurs concurrently across different knowledge domains, e.g. cognitive development should manifest itself in math, logic, physics or language at an equal sophistication. Figure 1 first depicts cognitive development from the Piagetian perspective, where math is used to assess the level of cognition across the developmental board, assuming uniformity in cognitive development; whereas in the second part the neo-Piagetian perspective is illustrated, wherein multiple means of measurement are used to assess cognition on various levels of development, assuming differences in developmental ability.

Figure 1.
Piagetian vs. Neo-Piagetian Developmental Models

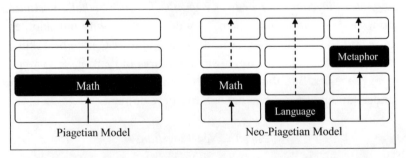

Piaget used math as the single measurement for *all* cognitive development. However, neo-Piagetians believe development is domain specific or modular, not spread across domains; development in one cognitive area does not equal that in another (McKeough, 1987;

Fischer and Silvern, 1985). Hence, development is tied to specific cognitive abilities, though not uniformly developed, and is not just the ability to do mathematical calculations (Lewis and Ash, 1992, pp. 228–29; Lin and Lesniak, 2006). This is represented by Fischer's metaphor of a web of development, discussed later in this chapter (Geert and Fischer, 2009, p. 330).

   Third, cognitive development measured by math vs. language et al. As previously mentioned, Piaget used a child's mathematical abilities to measure cognitive growth; however, Vygotsky used language acquisition. Neo-Piagetians tend to use more than just one measure, and more than math, as a cognitive development "litmus test," as depicted in Figure 1. Much research in neo-Piagetian theorists uses language or communication skills rather than mathematics, signaling a shift from Piaget's math toward Vygotsky's linguistic measurements approach (Seibert, 1980a; 1980b). This is why both Case and Fischer would utilize both as a means of measuring cognitive development. Can we not see cognition in the right side of the brain, rather than continually testing only the left?

   Fourth, cognitive development considered universally consistent vs. contextualized. Piaget regarded cognitive development to be contextually neutral, occurring almost independent of the individual's context. As such, cognitive development was thought to occur independently from the individual's interaction with society or culture. Conversely, neo-Piagetian theories can be characterized as context-centered or as ecological systems theories (cf. Bullock, 1983). Their advocates note studies where children in certain cultures consistently pick up ideas quicker than in other cultures due to activity. As Vygotsky notes, context matters, and cognitive development is not just biologically driven, but involves an interplay of biological and environmental factors (Suizzo, 2000, pp. 846–49; Morra *et. al.,* 2008, pp. 17–18; Mascolo, Kanner, and Griffin, 1998, pp. 42–43; Fortosis, 1990, pp. 635–36).

   Fifth, cognitive development's stages as static vs. dynamic. Neo-Piagetians favor individualistic or personal stages of cognitive development, as opposed to the rigidly defined, uniform stages or transitions Piaget identified (Mascolo, Kanner, and Griffin, 1998, pp. 42; Wollman, 1977). Morra *et. al.* (2008) and Lewis (1994) speak of children exhibiting competencies out of sequence with Piagatian stages of development as anomalies in the development of childhood reasoning abilities. Neo-Piagetian developmental theories do not tend to place capstones or ceilings on cognitive development in childhood; nor regard child performance outside the Piagetian norms as unexpected.

Finally, the theories of cognitive development theories are represented by metaphoric differences: ladders, staircases, and webs, demonstrating their distinctive assumptions and presentation of cognitive development. The distinctions between the various theories of cognitive development are reflected in the divergence of metaphors used to demonstrate and express them. For example, Piaget's theory of development can readily be described as a ladder, linear and unidirectional. Case's approach to cognitive development is best described as a staircase, with increasing orders of relationship occurring within each step, producing a cumulative result of new cognitive abilities (as will be described later); whereas Fischer presents his theory of cognitive development as a web, non-linear and multidirectional, with various possible cognitive finishes (Bidell and Fischer, 1992, p. 13 and Case, 1992d, p. 346)

Figure 2

Piaget, Case and Fischer Metaphors of Development (modified from Bidell and Fischer, 1992, p. 13 and Case, 1992d, p. 346)

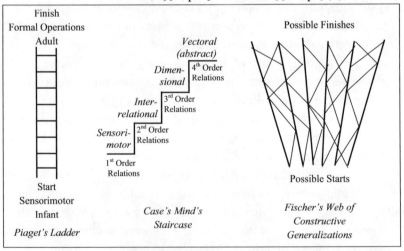

Hence, neo-Piagetian theories are not simply restatements or expansions of Piaget's original theory of cognitive development, rather they are reconsiderations and reformulations of cognitive development beyond Piaget's original model.

Neo-Piagian Theories of Case and Fischer

Numerous neo-Piagetian theorists could be selected to represent this spectrum of theories. For several reasons, two of the best choices are Robbie Case (1944–2000) of the Ontario Institute for Studies in Education, and Kurt Fischer of Harvard Graduate School of Education. They have both produced a large volume of work on the subject, their beingthey beingthey are both recognized as major contributors by other neo-Piagetian theorists, and they are the most contemporary representatives of this perspective.

Case's Theory of Cognitive Development

Robbie Case's theory is presented primarily in his two main works: *The Mind's Staircase* (1992) and *Intellectual Development: Birth to Adulthood* (1985). Case's central assumption is that children are thinkers and problem-solvers. He endeavors to explain how children become even better problem solvers through the development of higher levels of thought (Case, 1996a, 1996b, 1996c). This explanation is based on two ideas – that cognitive development occurs when (1) there is an increase in functional working memory, and (2) complex concepts depend on *central conceptual structures*, certain patterns of quantitative organization, narrative structure, and trans-domain development (Case, 1992a, 1992b, 1992c, 1992d). These central control structures for cognitive development consist of three components: (1) a problem situation, (2) an objective, i.e. solution to the problem, and (3) the ablility to create a sequence of operations to move from the problem to the solution.

The development of these control structures are represented in four major stages of cognitive development: Orienting, Sensorimotor, Interrelational, and Dimensional; as well as sub-stages of development represented as a staircase of development (Case, 1978; Case and Khanna, 1981; Case, 1992d), illustrated in Figure 3.

Figure 3

Case's "Staircase" of Development (adapted from Case, 1992d, p. 346)

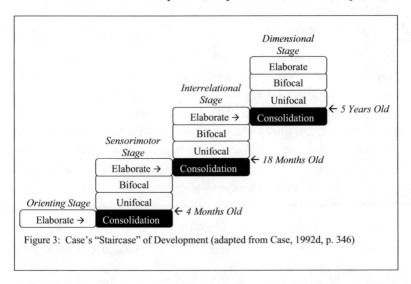

Figure 3: Case's "Staircase" of Development (adapted from Case, 1992d, p. 346)

Unlike Piaget's theory, Case's theory proposes transitional steps on the staircase; landings so to speak, wherein the completion of one step of development now provides the basis for the next, wherein the cognitive skills developed are *consolidated*, become routine and fixed mental capabilities. The steps in the staircase, stages of development, are composed and driven by the increase of relationship shared by the components in the control structures, until one is capable of dimensional or abstract thought; from unifocal to bifocal to elaborate coordination, i.e. the individual's ability to reason in an ever-increasing complexity of thought. The sub-stages are cyclical, reoccurring, and are the process whereby a child cognitively develops into an adolescent and eventually into an adult (Case, 1985; 1992a, 1992b, 1992c, 1992d). Hence, Case's book entitled *Mind's Staircase* is based on this fundamental depiction of cognitive development (Case, 1992d, p. 346). Case's last published work (2007) was completed posthumously and appeared in a book edited by Kurt Fischer.

Fischer's Theory of Cognitive Development

While Kurt Fischer's (1943–) publications list is quite voluminous, his two main works on the subject of cognitive development are *The Educated Brain: Essays on Neuro-education* (2008), written with

Arlyne Lazerson, and a previous work *Human Development from Conception through Adolescence* (1984). Fisher is a leading figure in *neuroeducation*, which gleans insights from and contributes toward the advancement of neo-Piagetian theories of cognitive development (Fischer and Dawson, 2002). His developmental theory is actually based on brain research, particularly the electrical impulses within the cortex. Unlike Piaget, who based his theory on observation of children, Fischer had the technological advantage of actually mapping and tracking neurological functions within the brain itself, using an electroencephalogram (EEG); upon which he could develop his theory. He noted that the amount of electrical activity in the cortex, which strengthens connections between parts and increases with cognition, shows periodic spurts, paralleling those times that new skills emerge, e.g. musical performance or spatial reasoning (Fischer, 2008).

Fischer proposed cognitive development as a constructive dynamic web so as to illustrate its dynamic and nonlinear nature. His basic assertion is that an individual dynamically, not statically, constructs skills in different given contexts, typically during social circumstances that require constant adaptation and reorganization of ideas (Geert and Fischer, 2009, p. 330). Fischer maintains that humans go through a series of three tiers, each with four stages, *but* with two being shared as transitional stages, totaling ten stages. Within each of these stages the same mental functioning occurs at a higher level, similar to that of Case's cycles, since a child develops the same skills over the course of a lifetime (Morra *et. al.*, 2008, pp. 158–59), as illustrated below in Figure 4.

Figure 4

Ficscher's Stages of Development

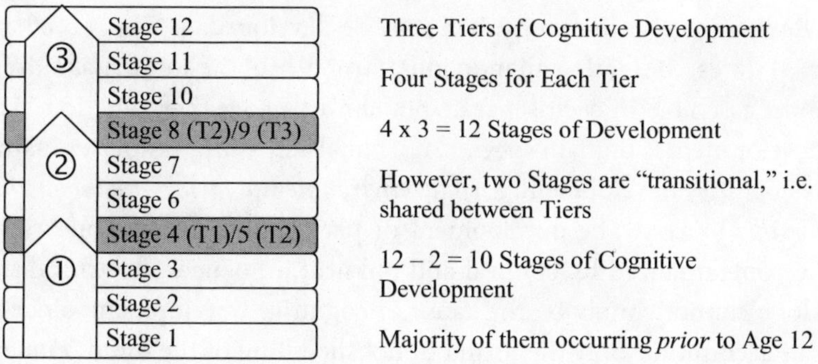

		Three Tiers of Cognitive Development
	Stage 12	
③	Stage 11	Four Stages for Each Tier
	Stage 10	
	Stage 8 (T2)/9 (T3)	4 x 3 = 12 Stages of Development
②	Stage 7	However, two Stages are "transitional," i.e.
	Stage 6	shared between Tiers
	Stage 4 (T1)/5 (T2)	
①	Stage 3	12 – 2 = 10 Stages of Cognitive Development
	Stage 2	
	Stage 1	Majority of them occurring *prior* to Age 12

However, cognition is more than stage related. Fischer distinguishes between *functional* and *optimal* levels of cognition, which are situational (Fischer and Pipp, 1984). Similar to Vygotsky's (1978; 1986) lower-spontaneous and higher-scientific ideas, *functional* is the normal level of cognition, but optimal cognitive thought requires the individual to actively engage in thinking beyond the normal functional level. For this reason optimal cognitive requires support for the circumstances, a situation that requires one to think, and hence aids in the connecting of various lines of development (cf. Morra *et. al.* 2008, pp. 154–57). For example, people usually do not normally think about statistics until they have to, their functional mind is not running statistical calculations in their normal activities of the day; but their mind could do it if so called upon in a given circumstance, such as a math class or conversing with an investment guide. So, whereas the functional level of cognition occurs routinely and has low support for any increase or alteration, i.e. normal level of cognition at any given period of time, the optimal level occurs in the context of high support for advancement and moves through stages of single abstraction, abstract mapping, abstract systems, and ultimately forms principles (Fischer and Rose, 1998, pp. 56–60; also Harvard Graduate School of Education, n.d.).

On what do Neo-Piagetian Theories Agree?

In the previous section the theories of Case and Fischer were summarized, but they represent only two voices among the full spectrum of neo-Piagetian theorists. In general, neo-Piagetians agree on at least three core essentials to their theories (cf. Case, 1987, pp. 784–87). *First, the cognitive development in humans is the result of independently assembled structures.* This means that cognitive structures are *not* wholly innate to humanity, but must be developed, as Case (1987, p. 784) states, "but rather an individual structure of the sort that children must assemble in each separate domain in which they function," i.e. development is domain specific, not equal across the various domains of cognitive development. *Second, environmental factors are important for this process.* The development of particular domains appears to be contextualized by cultural and physical influences. Structuralism alone cannot simply be the cause of cognitive development, since it can account for only the form but not the filling of the mind. *Finally, working memory is a common constraint in human cognitive development.* Memory capacity and functionality changes slowly with age, but is most available and functional during childhood. Like the hardware of a computer, we have to keep upgrading to grow.

The Value of Neo-Piagetian Theories for Childhood Spiritual Formation

The value of neo-Piagetian theories for the Christian educator are perhaps best found in their distinction from Piaget, the *neo* aspect of neo-Piagetian thought. Just as neo-Piagetian ideas reorient Piaget's theory, some of their ideas may reorient some of our developmentally-driven assumptions of spiritual formation in childhood. As was cautioned at the opening of this chapter, we cannot simply substitute spiritual formation with any given theory of development, but rather use developmental theories to shed light on the development of spiritual formation's cognitive dimension. It may simply cause us to question assumptions, or at least re-orient some of our thinking.

In so far as spiritual formation in childhood is connected to cognitive development, what is the value of neo-Piagetian theories to childhood spirituality? Several immediate implications are evident. *First, neo-Piagetian theories reaffirm the child as an individual, unique and distinctive.* There are two points to be made in this instance: (1) It calls the Christian educator to have a heighted concern for the individual as a whole person, not just his or her cognitive development or whether or not he or she is on an equivalent level of cognitive development with others in the class (Shulman, 1985, pp. xx–xi); and (2) these theories do not presume stage development simply based on the age of the student, but place an emphasis on the environmental factors that influence the life of the child, i.e. spiritual formation or potential is not purely a matter of chronological age, but is impacted by the life experiences of the child.

Second, these theories reconcile the implications for childhood spirituality made by the "two Piagets." The first is the *logical* Piaget with a view of cognitive development that was sequential stages, and the second is the *dialectical* Piaget that was more concerned with developmental processes; i.e. the structure and the process (Morra *et. al.*, 2008, p. 6). Those educators who have felt loyalty to the long established and embraced Piagetian tradition, but challenged by the insights and benefits of the theories of Lev Vygotsky (Estep, 2003), need not feel the extremes of tension often produced between them, and find a theoretical "home" in neo-Piagetianism. In short, neo-Piagetian perspective negotiates between the two points for the Christian educator, providing a more unified approach to development and education.

Third, neo-Piagetian theories affirm the value of environment and culture in development, which impacts our understanding of childhood spirituality through nurture. Spirituality and spiritual formation has often been tangentially linked to an individual's context, both in terms of adult believers and children. Neo-Piagetian theory is particularly valuable in terms of the two most immediate relational contexts of the child: (1) the child's immediate social context, begin considering an ecological view of spiritual formation more carefully, e.g. explaining the importance and impact of familial relationships, peer group, and the Church context in facilitating spiritual formation; and (2) the macro-context of the Child-in-Culture, e.g. the cultural context into which the child is born, which includes language, metaphors, symbols. For example, what symbols represent Christianity in your congregation? Crosses, Ichthus, ChiRo, dove . . . children would have to learn the meaning and significance of these from the church, it does not come naturally. A cross is a plus-sign, Ichthus is a fish, Chi Rho is an XP, and a dove is just a bird without the faith community's interpretation of them given to the child.

Fourth, neo-Piagetian developmental theories can not only be stage related, but likewise can affirm the value of the childhood experience of transformation. Neo-Piagetian ideas perhaps more readily move us toward James Loder's (1989) understanding of faith as the "transforming moment." The Christian educator can begin to glean insights into childhood spiritual formation through the implications of structuralism, but from attending to environmental factors and the child's personal experience.

Fifth, spiritual formation in children would be understood as a more dynamic process than typical developmental theories would suggest. With the advent of stage-based theories of human development, it has been commonplace to also explain spiritual formation as a stage-based process. However, without wholly abandoning these insights, the work of neo-Piagetian theorists provide insight beyond mere stages. For example, the idea of cognitive spurts in childhood development may explain the apparent spurts of faith expressions in children. A previous work of my own on childhood transformation, advocating a combination of nature and nurture approaches to the issue, would receive some developmental support from Fischer's idea of spurts in cognitive ability (Estep, 2002). [Anecdotally, we've probably all seen a child's suddenly catch on to an idea, or be able to reason more clearly on a spiritual matter; possibly due to a spurt in cognitive development.]

Finally, neo-Piagetian theories would require the Christian educator to develop multiple, individual-sensitive measurements for faith maturity. How do, or can, children express their faith in Christ? Christian educators have long affirmed that spiritual formation was more than cognition, and that there is more to cognition than any one set of measures can identify. Neo-Piagetian theorists would agree. We need to look for spiritual formation and growth with more than just one litmus test; we cannot assume that age alone is an indicator of spiritual maturity, nor that there is any one indicator of spiritual growth or maturity.

Practical Agenda for Childhood Education in the Church

Given the possible implications for spiritual formation provided by the insights of neo-Piagetian theories, particularly those of Case and Fischer, several practical implications are evident for the ministry to children for spiritual formation. *First, we must place an emphasis on the role of the teacher in childhood spiritual formation.* As a general approach to human development, structuralism somewhat gave the notion that children develop on their own, with no external stimuli necessary. However, neo-Piagetian theories suggest otherwise. "In other words: don't count on your cortex to do the work for you. Sustaining the highest level of performance supported by brain development takes practice and help from others" (Harvard Graduate School of Education, n.d.). Teachers aid in the advancement of the child by giving "support" to "optimal" functioning, which would be the case in religious instruction and faith nurture.

Second, we must place an emphasis on the setting and experiential activities of ministry in childhood spiritual formation. Neo-Piagetian theories suggests that even the context of a child's experience aids or detracts from their cognitive development, and this too could be an insight for the spiritual formation of a child, wherein the experiential context is part of our ministry. It is even more critical in terms of cross-cultural or multi-cultural ministry settings, wherein the significance or meaning of an experiential activity within a culture different from that of the instructor's or our own, and hence would have to be explored and its influence on spiritual formation assessed, rather than assuming that an change in setting has no effect on spiritual formation. Liturgy, symbol, rite, and ritual are all important to the child, and they are capable of understanding it earlier than formerly realized; but children do not do this alone and never is their understanding neutral, but rather contextually defined. This process emphasizes the teacher-student relationship as a means of guiding a student into meaning making within the socio-cultural context.

Third, we must place an emphasis on individualized attention to the child. While we may all recognize this on a practical level, neo-Piagetian emphasize it on a theoretical, developmental level. Also, they emphasize it more so than traditional Piagetian models of pedagogy and curriculum. As educators and pastors, we must see the tree and not just the forest; they are all similar, they are all not uniform; and not dismiss the uniqueness of the tree while viewing the forest. We should prepare an individual assessment of the child's spirituality, not a spiritual assessment of children in general.

Fourth, curriculum should place an emphasis on problem solving in the context of faith. Childhood education must become more than religious indoctrination or the mere recitation of factual information. Engaging students in faith issues and problems early in their lives will promote not only cognitive development, but also learning beyond rote memorization, as well as aid in the spiritual formation of the child. The cognitive dimension of childhood spiritual formation should in fact call us to engage in problem-solving methodologies in childhood. According to neo-Piagetian theory, children are capable of understanding and application at an earlier age than previously thought. Teachers should help students problem-solve in a faithful context, helping them grow toward the optimal level for their age! Viewing life through the lens of Scripture and theology can begin even in childhood, and can promote the spiritual formation of the child. For example, asking children to identify with a character in the biblical narrative taught in a lesson, or perhaps helping a child through a difficult situation by asking, "Where is God in all this? What can we learn about Him?", encouraging and enabling them to form a basic theology.

Fifth, we need to re-emphasize memory work as a teaching method. One limiting factor to cognitive development is a person's available memory. While much of this is determined genetically, i.e. neurological development in the brain, it is also in part a learned behavior. Teachers should prepare lessons that challenge development and press memory limitations (Buzzelli 1992). Memorization does not equal indoctrination, but is valuable for recall, and also in the development of a consistent knowledge base.

Sixth, nursery-preschool church becomes an essential aspect of ministry with children. More so than just a service to parents during the worship, or even quality childcare for the youngest members of the church, children need to be participants in the church. Cognition does indeed occur more dynamically and aggressively in early childhood than previously considered by traditional Piagetian thought. The importance of early childhood education becomes critical for neo-Piagetians. Vague. Source for this? While practitioners have espoused the pragmatic value of such programs as baby-church, nursery ministry, and the equipping of parents to raise their children in the faith, neo-Piagetian theory provides a developmental rationale for their inclusion in the congregation's overall education ministry with children.

Conclusion

Neo-Piagetian theory has virtually replaced the genetic epistemology of Piaget in the academy. It does indeed preserve what is best in Piaget's thoughts, while improving and even correcting some early assumptions, based both on new research in learning and advancement in knowledge of the workings of the brain. Just as Piaget provided a lens to our understanding of spiritual formation in childhood, so the neo-Piagetians may now provide a more precise prescription through which to understand cognition on children, with insights for the Christian education professional to use in better understanding childhood spiritual formation, and ministering to the children placed under their care.

References

Bidell, T. and Fischer, K. (1992). Cognitive development in educational contexts: Implications of skill theory. In A. Demetriou, M. Shayer, and A. Efklides (Eds), *Neo-Piagetian theories of cognitive development: Implications and applications for education* (pp. 11–30). London: Routledge.

Bullock, D. (1983). Seeking relations between cognitive and social-interactive transitions. In K. Fischer (Ed.) *Levels and transitions in children's development: New directions for child development* (Vol. 21, pp. 97–108). San Francisco: Jossey-Bass.

Buzzelli, C. (1992). Characteristics of school-aged children. In D. Ratcliff (Ed.), *Handbook of children's religious education* (pp. 1–20). Birmingham, AL: Religious Education Press.

Case. R. (2007). Approaches to behavioral and neurological research on learning disabilities: In search of a deeper synthesis. In K. Fisher, J. Bernstein, and M. Immordino (Eds), *Mind, brain, and education in reading disorders* (pp. 80–100). New York: Cambridge University Press.

———. (1996). Introduction: Reconceptualizing the nature of children's conceptual structures and their development in middle childhood. In R. Case and Y. Okamoto (Eds), *The role of central conceptual structures in the development of children's thought* (pp. 1–26). Monographs of the Society for Research in Child Development (Serial 246, Volume 61, Nos. 1–2).

———. (1996). Summary and conclusion. In R. Case and Y. Okamoto (Eds), *The role of central conceptual structures in the development of children's thought* (pp. 189–215). Monographs of the Society for Research in Child Development (Serial 246, Volume 61, Nos. 1–2).

———. (1996). Modeling the process of conceptual change in a continuously evolving hierarchical system. In R. Case and Y. Okamoto (Eds), *The role of central conceptual structures in the development of children's thought* (pp. 266–97). Monographs of the Society for Research in Child Development (Serial 246, Volume 61, Nos. 1–2).

———. (1992a). General and specific views of the mind, its structure and its development. In R. Case (Ed.), *The mind's staircase: Exploring the conceptual underpinnings of children's thought and knowledge* (pp. 3–15). Hillsdale, NJ: Lawrence Erlbaum Associates.

———. (1992b). A neo-piagetian approach to the issue of cognitive generality and specificity. In R. Case (Ed.), *The mind's staircase: Exploring the conceptual underpinnings of children's thought and knowledge* (pp. 17–35). Hillsdale, NJ: Lawrence Erlbaum Associates.

———. (1992c). Advantages and limitations of the neo-piagetian position. In R. Case (Ed.), *The mind's staircase: Exploring the conceptual underpinnings of children's thought and knowledge* (pp. 37–51). Hillsdale, NJ: Lawrence Erlbaum Associates.

———. (1992d). The mind and its modules: Toward a multi-level view of the development of human intelligence. In R. Case (Ed.), *The mind's staircase: Exploring the conceptual underpinnings of children's thought and knowledge* (pp. 343–76). Hillsdale, NJ: Lawrence Erlbaum Associates.

———. (1987). Neo-piagetian theory: Retrospect and prospect. *International Journal of Psychology, 22*, 773–91.

————. (1985). *Intellectual development: Birth to adulthood.* Orlando, FL: Academic Press.

————. (1984). The process of stage transition: A neo-piagetian view. In. R. Sternberg (Ed.), *Mechanism of cognitive development* (pp. 19–41). New York: Freeman.

Case, R. and Khanna, F. (1981). The missing links: Stages in children's progression from sensorimotor to logical thought. In K. Fischer (Ed.), *Cognitive development in new directions for child development* (pp. 21–32). San Francisco: Jossey-Bass.

————. (1978). Intellectual development from birth to adulthood: A neo-piagetian interpretation. In R. Seigler (Ed.), *Children's thinking: What develops?* (pp. 37–71). Hillsdale, NJ: Wiley.

Cully, I. (1984). *Education for spiritual growth.* New York: Harper and Row.

Downs, P. (1994). *Teaching for spiritual growth.* Grand Rapids: Zondervan.

Elkind, D. (1979). *The child and society.* New York: Oxford University Press.

Estep, J. (2003, June). *The social dynamics of childhood spirituality: A Vygotskyan paradigm for childhood spiritual formation.* Paper presented at the meeting of the Children's Spirituality Conference: Christian Perspectives. River Forest, IL.

————. (2002) Childhood transformation: Toward an educational theology of childhood conversion and spiritual formation. *Stone-Campbell Journal,* 5(2), 183–206.

Estep, J. Jr. and . Kim, J. (2010). *Christian formation: Integrating theology and human development.* Nashville: Broadman and Holman.

Finney, J. and Malony, H., Jr. (1985). Empirical studies of Christian prayer: A review of the literature. *Journal of Psychology and Theology,* 13(2), 104–15.

Fischer, K. (2008). Dynamics cycles of cognitive and brain development: Measuring growth in mind, brain, and education. In A. Battro, K. Fischer, and P. Léna (Eds), *The educated brain: Essays in neuroeducation* (pp. 127–50). New York: Cambridge University Press.

————. (1983). Developmental levels as periods of discontinuity: Levels and transitions in children's development. In K. Fischer (Ed), *New directions for child development* (Vol. 21, pp. 5–19). San Francisco: Jossey-Bass.

Fischer, K. and Canfield, R. (1986). The ambiguity of stage and structure in behavior: Person and environment in the development of psychological structures. In I. Levin (Ed), *Stage and structure: Reopening the debate* (pp. 246–67). Norwood, NJ: Ablex.

Fischer, K. and Dawson, T. (2002). A new kind of developmental science: Using models to integrate theory and research. *Monographs of the Society for Research in Child Development,* 67, (in press).

Fischer, K. and Lazerson, A. (1984). *Human development from conception through adolescence.* New York: Freeman.

Fischer, K. and Pipp, S. (1984). Processes of cognitive development: Optimal level and skill acquisition. In R. Sternberg (Ed.), *Mechanism of cognitive development* (pp. 45–80). New York: Freeman.

Fischer, K. and Rose, S. (1998). Growth cycles of brain and mind, *Educational Leadership,* 56(3), 56–60.

Fischer, K. and Silvern, L. (1985). Stages and individual differences in cognitive development. *Annual Review of Psychology,* 36, 613–48.

Fortosis, S. and Garland, K. (1990). Adolescent cognitive development: Piaget's idea of disequilibriation, and the issue of Christian nurture. *Religious Education,* 85(4), 631–44.

Fowler, J. (1989). Strength for the journey: Early childhood development in selfhood and faith. In D. Blazer (Ed.), *Faith development in early childhood* (pp. 1–36). Kansas City, MO: Sheed and Ward.

Geert, P. and Fischer, K. (2009). Dynamic system and the quest for individual-based models of change and development. In J. Spencer, M. Thomas, and J. McClennand (Eds.), *Toward a unified theory of development: Connectionism and dynamic systems theory re-considered* (pp. 313–36). New York: Oxford University Press.

Goldman, R. (1965). *Religious thinking from childhood to adolescence.* New York: Seabury.

———. (1964). *Readiness for religion: A basis for developmental religious education.* London: Routledge.

Gottlieb, E. (2006). Development of religious thinking. *Religious Education, 101*(2), 242–60.

Halford, G. (1980). Toward a redefinition of cognitive developmental stages. In J. Kirby and J. Biggs (Eds.), *Cognition, development, and instruction* (pp. 39–64). New York: Academic Press.

Harvard Graduate School of Education (nd), What's the brain got to do with it? Retrieved from http://www.uknow.gse.harvard.edu/learning/learning002a. html.

Heywood, D. (1986). Piaget and faith development: A true marriage of minds? *British Journal of Religious Education, 8*(2), 72–78.

Kim, J. (2010). Intellectual development and Christian formation. In J. Estep Jr. and J. Kim (Eds.), *Christian formation: Integrating theology and human development* (pp. 63–98). Nashville: Broadman and Holman.

———. (2007). Cognition and faith formation: A reflection on the interrelationship of schema, thema, and faith. *Christian Education Journal, Series 3,* 308–21.

Lewis, M. (1994). Reconciling stage and specificity in neo-piagetian theory: Self-organizing conceptual structures. *Human Development,37,*143–69.

Lewis, M. and Ash, A. (1992). Evidence for a neo-piagetian stage transition in early cognitive development. *International Journal of Behavioral Development, 15*(3), 337–58.

Lin, X. and Lesniak, K. (2006). Progression in children's understanding of the matter concept from elementary to high school. *Journal of Research in Science Teaching, 43*(3), 320–47.

Loder, J. (1989). *The transforming moment.* Colorado Springs: Helmers and Howard.

Mascolo, M., Kanner, B. and Griffin, S. (1998). Neo-piagetian systems theory and the education of young children. *Early Child Development and Care, 140,* 31–52.

McKeough, A. M. (1987). *Horizontal structure: A neo-piagetian analysis of structural parallels across domains.* Paper presented at the Ninth Biennial Meeting of the Society for the Study of Behavioral Development, Tokyo, Japan. ERIC Document: 292085.

Moran, G. (1983). *Religious education development.* Minneapolis: Winston Press.

Morra, S., Gobbo, C., Marini, Z, and Sheese, R. (2008). *Cognitive development: Neo-piagetian perspectives.* New York, NY: Erlbaum.

Ng, D. (1978). What children bring to worship. *Austin Seminary Bulletin: Faculty Edition, 94,* 5–30.

Pascual-Leone, J. and Smith, J. (1969). The encoding and decoding of symbols by children: A new experimental paradigm and a neo-piagetian model. *Journal of Experimental Child Psychology, 8*(2), 328–55.

Popp, N. and Portnow, K. (2001, August). Our developmental perspective on adulthood. *NCSALL Reports, 19,* 47–69.

Radcliffe, R. (1980). The relationship of theories of intellectual development to Christian educators. *Journal of Christian Education, 1*(1), 69–73.

Seibert, J. M. (1980a). *The development of pre-linguistic communication skills: A neo-piagetian analysis based on levels of cognitive organization.* Paper presented at the Tenth Annual Interdisciplinary Conference on Piagetian Theory and the Helping Professions, Los Angeles, CA. ERIC Document 190262.

———. (1980b). *Developmental assessment based on a structural stage model of early communication development: Some theoretical, methodological and practical issues.* Paper presented at the Thirteenth Annual Gatlinburg Conference on Research in Mental Retardation and Developmental Disabilities, Gatlinburg, Tennessee. ERIC Document 190265.

Shulman, V. (1985). Introduction. In V. Shulman, L. Restaino-Baumann, and L. Butler (Eds.), *The future of piagetian theory: The neo-piagetians* (pp. xv–xxv). New York: Plenum.

Sparkman, G. (1986). Proposals on religious development: A brief review. *Review and Expositor, 83*(1), 93–109.

Stonehouse, C. (1998). *Joining children on the spiritual journey.* Grand Rapids: Baker.

Suizzo, M. (2000). The social-emotional and cultural context of cognitive development: Neo-piagetian perspectives. *Child Development, 71*(4), 846–49.

Vygotsky, L. (1986). *Thought and language.* Alex Kozulin ed. Cambridge: MIT Press.

———. (1978). *Mind in society: The development of human psychological processes.* Cambridge: Harvard University Press.

Wollman, W. (1977). Controlling variables: A neo-piagetian developmental sequence. *Science Education, 61*(3), 385–91.

Section 2

Contexts of Children's Spirituality
Family, Church, and Community

10

How Parents Nurture the Spiritual Development of their Children
Insights from Recent Qualitative Research

Holly Catterton Allen
with Christa Adams, Kara Jenkins, and Jill Williams Meek

Introduction

In a recent family ministry course at our university, students interviewed parents of preschoolers regarding the changes parenting had brought into their lives. This pair of thirty-something couples had previewed the questions they would be asked, which included "How has having children altered your relationship as a couple?" and "How has your career been affected by having children?" Near the end of class time, students began asking questions not on the prepared list. One student asked: "What are you doing to nurture your children spiritually?" These very articulate, well-educated, strongly committed Christian parents seemed intimidated by this question. Sounding unsure, they scrambled for answers, eventually stating that they pray with their children before bed and read the Bible with them; but even as they answered, they seemed hesitant in their responses. Since that day, both couples have asked themselves what else they could do to nurture their children's spiritual growth and development. Their question is the one that this chapter addresses.

Most parents believe they have the primary responsibility for the moral and spiritual development of their children (Maccoby, 2000). Scripture indicates that parents are key agents as spiritual leaders for their children, and theologians throughout the ages have tended to agree. Martin Luther said, "Most certainly father and mother are apostles, bishops, and priests to their children, for it is they who make them acquainted with the gospel" (Holmen, 2005, p. 44). However, it is clear that complex forces are at work in children and adolescents as they develop spiritually. A child's personality and life experiences, the ethos of the child's community of faith, differences among particular Christian denominations and affiliations, and doctrinal variables all play roles in that child's religious and spiritual growth and development. While acknowledging that these and many other influences are at work, most parenting experts recognize that parents are certainly a crucial influence (see e.g., Boyatzis, Dollahite, & Marks, 2006; Maccoby, 2000). Therefore, the critical question that must be addressed is the question the two couples considered, "What can parents do to cultivate their children's spiritual growth and development?"

As this conference book illustrates, and as the literature indicates, the term "children's spirituality" can have a plethora of definitions. For the purposes of this chapter, two working definitions of children's spirituality from a Christian perspective have been constructed. These are amalgamations of keys elements found in (1) definitions of Christian spirituality[1] and (2) Rebecca Nye's description of children's spirituality which she calls "relational consciousness" (i.e., an awareness of relationship with self, others, world, and God, [Hay & Nye, 2006]). These key elements—awareness of relationship with the self, others, the world, and the Triune God, and participation in a believing community—form the basis for the two working definitions below:

> Children's spirituality is the ability of children to sense and explore a relationship with God in Christ through the Holy Spirit and to connect with self, others, and the world as nurtured by a sense of wonder and by identity with a believing community.[2]

1. Two excellent definitions of Christian spirituality are:
"the substantial gift of the Holy Spirit establishing a life-giving relationship with God in Christ within the believing community" (Schneiders, 1986, p. 266).
"a conscious relationship with God, in Jesus Christ, through the indwelling of the Spirit and in the context of community of believers" (Sheldrake, 2000, p. 40).

2. Jill Williams Meek, JBU graduate, Child and Family Studies degree; currently

> Children's spirituality is how children become aware of and
> develop a relationship with God in Christ through the power
> of the Holy Spirit. Children's spirituality also encompasses the
> development of children's understanding of themselves, their
> relationship with other people, their connections with a faith
> community, and their interactions with the world. [3]

This chapter will first explore several recurring themes in the literature for parents to consider as they cultivate spiritual growth and development in their children. The chapter will then present findings from recent field research with children, then conclude with implications from that research. Ultimately, central concepts and findings will be reframed into a more cohesive, holistic response—one that offers a fresh perspective as it addresses the question "What can parents do?"

Key Themes in the Literature

The recommendations repeated most frequently in the literature by children's spirituality and parenting researchers will not be surprising to most parents. Four ways commonly suggested to parents as they seek to nurture their children's religious and spiritual development are 1) to participate with children in religious activities and rituals as a family (e.g., prayer and Scripture reading), 2) to foster mutual conversation and discussion, 3) to model a congruent spiritual life before their children, and 4) to parent lovingly yet firmly. One other concept appearing more frequently in recent literature is the important role of active whole-family involvement in an intergenerational Christian community.

Intra-Familial Religious Activities or Rituals

A poignant chapter in Marjorie Thompson's *Family: The Forming Center* (1996, Upper Room Books) describes several rituals that families use to celebrate the presence of God in their lives. Some families light a candle when Scripture is read, make special foods for certain religious celebrations, say morning and evening prayers, decorate their homes for Christmas or Easter, or read a psalm before the evening

Director of Children's Ministries, National Presbyterian Church, Washington, DC.

3. Sarah Davis, JBU graduate, Children and Family Ministries degree; currently an Assistant Teacher with Little Light House, Tulsa, Oklahoma and a graduate student at Oklahoma State University.

meal. "Rituals are embodied ways of celebrating God's presence in the midst of ordinary life. They take the common stuff of life and reveal its sacramental capacity" (p. 88), Thompson says.

Well-known children's spirituality specialists such as Catherine Stonehouse (1998), Karen Marie Yust (2004a), and Don and Brenda Ratcliff (2010) strongly advocate such practices, offering a variety of family activities and rituals that nurture children spiritually. John Westerhoff (1980) recommends that families "tell and retell the biblical story . . . together"; celebrate faith and life as a family; pray together; "listen and talk to each other"; and be engaged in "faithful acts of service and witness" as a family (p. 37).

Beyond strong support from these spirituality experts and clear support from Scripture (e.g., instructions for Passover and other regular intergenerational feasts and celebrations), recent empirical research lends credence to the idea that basic family rituals do foster spiritual development in children. Retrospective reports from religiously committed adults indicate that regular rituals deeply influenced these adults in their childhood (McQuitty, 2008; Wuthnow, 1999). One of the interviews recorded by McQuitty (2008) tells of a boy who said that "whenever he left his house each morning, his mother would encourage him to remember 'whose you are and who you represent'" (p. 264).

Dollahite and Marks (2005, 2009), drawing on their interviews with 74 highly religious families, identify ten central processes these families employ to foster religious and spiritual development among family members. Their second process includes creating sacred times, places, and meanings at home "so that religion is not confined to a place of worship or a day of the week" (2005, p. 534). Dollahite and Marks give examples that include prayer, Scripture reading, and singing grace at dinner.

One last vital family practice recommended by experts (Beckwith, 2004; Ratcliff & Ratcliff, 2010; Stonehouse, 1998; Westerhoff, 2000), reported in retrospective studies (McQuitty, 2008; Wuthnow, 1999), named by "highly religious" parents (Marks, 2004), and noted by the currently faithful teens and emerging adults in Smith's studies (2005, 2009) is the importance of regularly attending worship services as a family—that is, going to church. As ordinary and mundane as it seems, going to church as a family is mentioned repeatedly by teens and adults who have maintained their Christian faith, as a family ritual that critically informed and shaped their spiritual journeys.

Everyday Conversation and Discussion

Though people tend to associate spirituality with a sense of other-worldliness—and indeed transcendent experiences certainly can contribute to faith and foster a relationship with God—commonplace, prosaic experiences also play a critical role in molding spirituality. Doing errands, driving to the next activity, completing chores and household projects together, and eating meals as a family provide opportunities for ordinary discussion and insight.

Chris Boyatzis (2004) asserts that parent-child conversations that occur within regular family interactions can be rich contexts for religious development. Reflection and questions are important parts of conversations that parents can use to engage children. Boyatzis shares the delightful story of his three-year-old at bath time talking about "bath-tizing" the soap; in the context of his daughter bath-tizing and re-bath-tizing the soap, Boyatzis shared with her the events surrounding her baptism when she was an infant, and that initial discussion led to subsequent conversations over the years regarding her baptism.

Brad Wigger (2003) encourages parents to reflect on daily situations and theological questions alike with their children. These reflections enable spiritual development for both parents and children, as children often have insight that is helpful and challenging for adults. Children are very inquisitive; they *want* to know more about God. They want to know what their parents think and believe; they *listen*. Certainly, Scripture offers clear understanding that ordinary but frequent parent-child conversation is a key means of fostering children's spiritual growth and development:

> Hear, O Israel: The LORD our God, the LORD is one. Love the LORD your God with all your heart and with all your soul and with all your strength. These commandments that I give you today are to be upon your hearts. Impress them on your children. *Talk about them when you sit at home and when you walk along the road, when you lie down and when you get up.* Tie them as symbols on your hands and bind them on your foreheads. Write them on the doorframes of your houses and on your gates. (Deut 6:4–9, emphasis mine)

Modeling

Thompson (1996) says that children need to see their parents setting time aside for prayer, worship, reflection, and open discussion about issues of faith. Ivy Beckwith (2004) states:

> If the child's parents and caregivers show that listening to and following God's story is a priority for them, then the child will model those attitudes. If the important adults in the child's life practice the spiritual disciplines, worship God, and make time to care for their own souls, then the child will find ways to mirror these behaviors in her own life. (p. 53)

Other children's spirituality experts such as Stonehouse (1998) and Yust (2004b) make the same point in their writings.

Albert Bandura's continuing work (1986, 1999, 2001) in social learning theory has emphasized the strong role of observation and modeling in the acquisition of basic mores and norms of a culture as well as the acquisition of personal lifestyles and values. In his recent work, Bandura (2003) extends his social learning theory into the spiritual realm, centering on the "the influential role of modeling in transmitting values, spiritual belief systems, and spiritual lifestyle practices" (p. 171). Oman and Thoresen (2003) make similar connections as they describe spiritual modeling as a neglected but important component of religious and spiritual traditions, citing specifically the powerful role of the family in modeling.

Marks (2004) reported the results of his first study exploring sacred practices of highly religious families in terms of three central themes. He described his first theme as "Practicing [and parenting] what you preach" (p. 222). One of the participants in the study, an African American Christian father of three said:

> It's not what you do in the [church] building; it's what you do outside the building. When everyday life struggles challenge you, are you able to overcome adversity, are you able to withstand the things that are being thrown at you. . . . Are you living the . . . walk of faith . . . or are you living like the world's living? . . . *Are you practicing what you preach?* (p. 222)

Other parents in the study repeatedly described the importance of living before their children the key tenets of their religion.

Ultimately, Marks, in further studies of highly religious families (Dollahite & Marks, 2009, 2005), identified other processes that reflect the importance of parents modeling a congruent spirituality before their children. These processes include "living religion at home," "loving and serving others in the family," and "abstaining from proscribed activities and substances" (2005, pp. 534–36).

Responsive Yet Firm Parenting

One widely used typology of parenting styles was developed by Diana Baumrind (1966, 1978, 1991, 1996). In 1966, Baumrind outlined three parenting styles which she called authoritarian, authoritative, and permissive, and later added a fourth, the neglecting-rejecting style. Baumrind (1991) describes these parenting styles along two dimensions—responsiveness and directiveness (or control). The first dimension, responsiveness, entails the degree to which parents respond to their children and provide affection. In the diagram below, this dimension forms the horizontal axis—responsiveness/affection. The second dimension, the vertical axis, involves the degree of control parents employ with children. The diagram below reveals Baumrind's four parenting styles that result from these two interfacing dimensions: authoritarian, authoritative, permissive, and neglectful.

Table 1

Responsive/Supportive

Directive/ Demanding	High	Low
High	AUTHORITATIVE *Responsive, supportive* *Directive, demanding*	AUTHORITARIAN *Unsupportive* *Demanding, controlling*
Low	PERMISSIVE/INDULGENT *Responsive, supportive* *Indulgent, non-demanding*	INDIFFERENT/NEGLECTFUL *Disengaged* *Little discipline*

Extremely *authoritarian* parents tend to be excessively controlling and almost indifferent to their children's need for support and affection; one real concern in this style is the tendency toward physical punishment without appropriate and balancing support and affection. Particularly *permissive* parents would exhibit opposite tendencies— little control and *over*-responsiveness—allowing the wants and needs of the child to dictate homelife. Very *neglectful* parents offer little direction to their children nor do they offer much support or affection. In Baumrind's work, *authoritative* parents offer the best blend of control and responsiveness (Baumrind, 1991).

Dozens of studies have been conducted over the past four decades correlating these parenting styles with various social, behavioral, academic, and spiritual outcomes in children and adolescents (Baumrind, 1996, overviews many of these studies). Sungwon Kim (2008) recently conducted a meta-analysis of the research over the last several decades regarding parenting styles and outcomes in children, focusing especially on religious and spiritual outcomes. In her summary of parenting styles literature, Kim states that "God's unconditional love and grace, including disciplinary action for his children, is the model for parenting that God provides" (p. 245). Ultimately, Kim (2008) concludes her meta-analysis by saying that the authoritative parenting style, one that combines a supportive, responsive approach with a directive, even demanding approach, is associated more frequently with healthy spiritual development than are other parenting styles. This style exhibits both loving support and strong boundaries and discipline for children.

Intergenerational Experiences

For decades well-known Christian education leaders and spiritual formation experts have been expounding the importance of intergenerational Christian experiences for spiritual growth and formation (Moran, 1978, 1981; Nelson, 1967, 1989; Fowler, 1991; Westerhoff, 2000). However, only in the last decade has strong empirical research been conducted that supports this notion. For the purposes of this chapter, intergenerational Christian experiences will be defined as including two or more different generations relating together in mutually influential activities with several from each of the generations present (Allen, 2002; White, 1988).

In the 2000s, Christian Smith (2005, 2009) conducted extensive sociological research with the National Study of Youth and Religion (NSYR) interviewing hundreds and surveying thousands of teenagers ages thirteen to seventeen, then interviewing and surveying many of these same participants again when they were EIGHTEEN TO twenty-three years old. From these interviews and surveys, Smith (2005) categorizes the participants in his study into four groups: the Devoted

(8 percent of the participants, whom Smith also refers to as "highly religious"), the Regulars (27 percent), the Sporadic (17 percent), and the Disengaged (12 percent). As Smith and his fellow researchers analyzed both the quantitative and the qualitative data, they found that, compared with less religious teenagers, the "highly religious" teens in the study exhibited significant (positive) differences in important life outcomes regarding relationships with parents and siblings, giving and volunteering, participation in organized activities, substance abuse, risky behaviors, mental and emotional well-being, life purpose, feeling gratitude, and educational achievement.

A basic finding in Smith's first study (2005) was that parents are the primary influence on teens' religious and spiritual lives. However, another key influence on teens ultimately emerged in Smith's study. After discussing the impressive findings of his study, Smith asks a critical question: "*What is it about religion that might produce positive outcomes in the lives of teenagers?*" (p. 240). In his detailed response to this question, Smith describes nine factors, two of which are intimately, integrally related to *intergenerationality.* The highly religious teens in the study frequently described the influence of older teens, young adults, middle adults, and older adults who had played important roles in their lives, who had provided accountability, or who had taught them explicitly or by example about Christian spiritual formation.

Furthermore Smith's (2009) study with eighteen to twenty-three-year-old emerging adults affirms this same basic premise—that it matters whether or not these emerging adults had nonparental adults in their congregation to whom they could turn for help and support: "Adult engagement with, role modeling for, and formation of youth simply matters a great deal for how they turn out after they leave the teenage years" (p. 285).

Other recent research also indicates the importance of inter-generational experiences for children and youth's spiritual development (see e.g., Allen, 2004; Fraze, 2009; Powell, 2009; Roberto, 2009). Extrapolating from these findings, a key strategy for parents as they seek important practices that foster spiritual formation in their children is to embed their family in an intentionally intergenerational Christian community.

Other Themes

Several other significant and worthy themes appear frequently in the literature, such as the importance of parents' participating with children in service projects and mission trips (Carr, 2008; Wigger, 2003; Yust, 2004b), explicitly teaching children (Caldwell, 2006; Dollahite & Marks, 2009; Ratcliff, 1995), and creating opportunities for wonder and silence (Berryman, 1991; Cain, 2002; Stonehouse, 1998). However, due to space limitations, these important themes will not be explored in this chapter.

Insights from Recent Qualitative Research

The research cited in this section is taken from the field data (Allen, 2001) that I collected for my doctoral thesis (Allen, 2002) on children's spirituality. Altogether, 40 nine-, ten-, and eleven-year-old children were interviewed from six churches in Tennessee and California in 2001–2002. All of the children attended church regularly with their parents. The children represented a cross-section of evangelical churches—two Vineyard churches (one large, one small), a Baptist church, a Bible church, a renewal Presbyterian church, and a progressive Church of Christ. In three churches, the children worshiped with the whole congregation, attended Sunday school, and participated in an intergenerational small group. In the other three churches, the children attended Sunday school and participated in children's church on Sundays while their parents and other adults worshiped. The purpose of the dissertation was to explore the connection between intergenerational Christian experiences and spiritual development in children. However, the children's responses to the interview questions offered insight into the question this chapter is addressing, that is, how parents nurture their children spiritually. Christa Adams, Kara Blood Jenkins, and Jill Williams Meek analyzed and coded the 250 pages of raw data collected in 2001, focusing particularly on what children said about their parents.

The entire interview protocol for the field research consisted of around twenty questions (see Appendix A). Among the first questions asked was, "Of all the people you know, who do you think knows God the best?" This question was followed by, "What is it about that person makes you think they know God?" The children had opportunity to name three or four different people whom they thought

knew God well. Altogether the children named 135 people. Of the
40 children, 25 named their mothers and 29 mentioned their fathers
or stepfathers. Twelve of the children named both their mother and
their father. Altogether 34 of the 40 participants in the study named
one or both parents among the people they think know God best. The
children responded with insights about their parents to various other
interview questions such as "Has your family ever needed special help
and you think God helped? "What is the difference between someone
who knows about God and someone who knows God?" and "Can you
tell me about a time when you were surprised or amazed by God?"

Interestingly, the children's comments and insights regarding
their parents reflect the themes that emerged in the literature.

Intra-familial Religious Rituals

To many children in the research, Bible reading, prayer, worship, and
church attendance are connected with knowing and experiencing
God. In the interviews, 13 of the 40 children mentioned praying with
their parents. Many of these instances involve ordinary events, such as
praying before dinner or praying before bedtime. Sara, 11, described
how her parents "always come in to pray with me at night before I go
to bed. . . . my dad normally comes in first. They keep telling me and
my sisters how much they love us" (Allen, 2001). Julia, 10, said, "I pray
every night with my mom before I go to bed" (Allen, 2001). Nathaniel,
10, shared that every night he prayed with his parents for several mis-
sionaries. Seth, 10, said "when I was little my parents taught me to
pray" (Allen, 2001). Priscilla, 11, said, "Each night my mom comes
into each of our rooms and prays about things with us and she prays
about that a lot of times when we are having trouble" (Allen, 2001).
[The children in the study chose biblical names as their pseudonyms
for purposes of anonymity in the research.]

Barnabas, 11, when asked if there was a specific time that his family needed special help from God described events around his dad's
death when he was seven years old. Barnabas said that God "helped us
get over it and get through the death. Mom prayed and I did" (Allen,
2001). Barnabas indicated in this reference—and others—that his
mom regularly sought God in prayer for help and guidance in her life,
and that consequently he did also.

Cornelius reported: "Every chance [my dad] gets . . . he wants to read the Bible with us" (Allen, 2001). Sara, 11, when describing why she thinks her dad knows God says, "He is a good example to us. He always reads the Bible; he reads it everywhere" (Allen, 2001). Scripture reading was a regular practice, even ritual, in these children's families.

The children also mentioned in a variety of ways the regular and important practice of attending church with their families. All 40 children mentioned attending church at least once during their interview, as a way that indicates one knows God, as a way to get to know God, or as a time when they felt close to God.

Mutual Conversation and Discussion (everyday experiences)

Children were quick to offer examples of regular conversational engagement with their parents about everyday events and spiritual matters. For example, Dorcas said, "I was being really stubborn because I wanted to have plans that day—I wanted to go with my friends and do something, and my dad said, 'But first you have to do these [chores]'" (Allen, 2001). When Boaz became interested in reading the Harry Potter books, he discussed the idea with his dad. Boaz noted, "My dad is reading the first Harry Potter book to see if it's okay" (Allen, 2001). Cornelius, 10, mentioned in his interview that he also discussed the Harry Potter books with his mom, and that they made a decision regarding the books after they had both prayed about the matter (Allen, 2001). These parents took the time to discuss everyday decisions with their children, and it clearly had a profound impact on their children's values.

When Joanna, 11, was asked what she would do if she wanted to get to know God, she said, "I would probably ask my parents [about] things I don't know about Him and I would tell them the things I do know about Him and they could tell me" (Allen, 2001). Lydia, 11, in response to the question, "Of all the people you know, who do you think knows God the best?" replied, "Mom, because of the way that she tells me about God . . . the way she talks about God, how she respects him" (Allen. 2001). Both Joanna's and Lydia's comments indicate that frequent easy conversations about God characterize their homes.

Modeling

The children offered a plethora of qualities that people who know God display. They said that people who know God are kind (or nice), calm, generous, patient, faithful, committed, disciplined, and loving. They do what is right, help people, and obey God. Several children offered a global description of character in general by saying that people who know God simply "act like it."

Among those who responded that their mother was one of the adults in their lives who knew God well, 12 children mentioned some aspect of their mother's character, and 13 mentioned their father's character, as evidence that they knew God. Noah commented about his dad, "Well, he's always kind of calm when there's strife going through the house" (Allen, 2001). Nathaniel added, "He (Dad) is very faithful to do what he says . . . he almost always tries . . . of course he has made mistakes. He has made mistakes like he has . . . forgotten his promise and not done it . . . but that happens sometimes. He always tries" (Allen, 2001).

The children interviewed were acutely aware of their parents' spiritual practices. Ten children responded that their mothers knew God because of her spiritual disciplines, while twelve children thought their father knew God because of his spiritual practices. Children expressed that they believed their parents knew God because of the amount of time they spent with God and the joy the parents demonstrated in worship. Sara recounted: "[My mom] spends a lot of time with [God]. She just had the last month off and she went to Sacramento. She spent the night there. She brought her notes, and her journal, and her music. She just will sit in her room sometimes and worship and write" (Allen, 2001). Tabitha said, "When I see her [my mom] worshiping she is not worried about everybody else around her. She really connects with God and she closes her eyes and really does not have a lot of social interactions with everyone else while we are supposed to be worshiping and I look to that as an example" (Allen, 2001). Another child, Hannah, said she thinks her dad knows God because "he likes to worship Him with his dance, and he reads the Bible a lot." (I interviewed Hannah at her father's dance studio where Hannah said he sometimes just turns on some music and dances "before the Lord.")

Children also mentioned parents bringing friends to church, praying and reading Scripture with other people, and reflecting their faith through their general actions toward other people. These obser-vations made the children think that their parents knew God well, and this has clearly had a significant impact in the children's lives. For example, Priscilla said, "all of [my mom's] friends, when they come over, she talks a lot with them and I think a lot of them know God because of her so a lot of them know God very well" (Allen, 2001). Martha recalled of her father, "He helped this guy become a Christian; when we were fishing and he started talking to him and he became a Christian and he gave him a Bible" (Allen, 2001).

Pricilla, 11, noted that her mom shares opinions about the ser-mon with a friend and says her mom "picks her up and brings her to church" (Allen, 2001). Tabitha, 10, writes about her dad and says, "I see him praying a lot actually and having quiet times with God" (Allen, 2001). All of these quotes illustrate how parents' examples im-pacted their children.

Altogether, 10 out of the 34 children who mentioned parents said that their parents knew God best because they went to church every Sunday; 15 out of the 34 children believed that their parents knew God because they read the Bible everyday; 10 connected their parents' prayer life with knowing God; 13 connected their parents' involvement in ministry or Bible studies to their knowledge of God; 14 mentioned a characteristic or personality trait of their parents that signified knowing God to them. The children were very aware of their parents' character and their spiritual lives.

Parenting Styles

Though children have a reputation for complaining or whining when being disciplined, the children in this study made surprising comments about discipline. For these children, being disciplined actually made them feel loved, and it communicated a knowledge of God to the child. Levi says he thinks his father knows God "because he disciplines us . . . because he knows that it's right" (Allen, 2001). Phillip acknowledged his mother wanted the best for him when he said, "She . . . wants me to do the right thing. She doesn't like me watching PG-13 movies . . . She's protective of me" (Allen, 2001). Caleb stated about his parents, "They're nice to other kids but they're tough and good when we do things that aren't right. When we do something bad, they come and tell us how we could do better, what we could do better" (Allen, 2001).

These children recognized that their parents discipline out of love and a desire for them to understand and become better people. The children in the study observed and appreciated their parents' tenderness, forgiveness, instruction, and even correction and connected these qualities to their parents' Christian beliefs.

Intergenerationality

Perhaps more than any other set of comments on a particular practice or subject, the children's comments concerning prayer shed light on the depth and quality of their spiritual lives. Also, this area yielded the largest differences between the two groups of children in the original research (i.e., between those who regularly participated in intergenerational settings and those who did not). The following samples are the "prayer files" of two of the participants. A "prayer file" consists of every comment the participant made concerning prayer, either in response to a question about their prayer life, or an "unprompted" remark made in response to some of the other questions. The following is the prayer file of Boaz, age eleven:

> Can you describe a time when you felt really happy about God? "Well, I've been praying for my great grandmother and she's been staying alive and that's pretty cool."
>
> Can you describe a time when you felt sad about God? "Well, sometimes I have prayed for somebody to get well and they don't."
>
> Can you describe a time when you felt angry at God? "Yes. Well, sometimes when I'm done praying for something and I don't get it, like something that I really wanted to happen."
>
> Can you describe a time when you felt an overwhelming love for God? "Well, a few nights ago I was just laying in my bed and I was just like, 'God you are so awesome.'"
>
> What does it mean to know God? "Like my friend Brandon, I can tell he knows God because I've been to church with him before and he just gets really into it." Gets into what? "The worship and prayer."
>
> How do you think someone gets to know God? "Praying, reading the Bible, listening to Him."

What are some things that you do that help you know that you know God? "Well, I just pretty much every night I just talk to him a lot. If there's anything I want to say to him I just say it."

What sort of things do you talk to God about? "I talk to him about Harry Potter and stuff like that, if he thinks I should stop reading it. So far I think he hasn't really told me anything about it, just kind of drawn me away from it just a little bit. . . . There's still only four but I have only read three of them. My dad's reading the first one to see if it's okay." What else do you pray about? "Well, if I like this girl or something I will pray that I don't go into anything bad or anything like that." What else do you talk to God about? "I pretty much pray about my family, if anybody is sick that they will get better." What else? "Sometimes I pray that I will get to know him better."

Were you ever afraid or alone, and you think God helped you? Would you tell me about that? "Yes. At night when I was going to bed when I was younger I would see the tree shadow and I would be scared. I would like see shadows on the wall and like be really afraid and ask him to protect me. There was one time where I think a month ago when it was really good weather and the lights went out and I was really scared and I asked him for protection."

Has your family ever needed special help and you think God helped? Would you tell me about that? "Well my other grandmother, my mom's mom had cancer and we prayed for her and she got better and now she's having cancer again but we don't think she's going to get better this time." How will you deal with it this time if she doesn't get better? "Well, I'll just ask God to comfort us. I think she's 74."

Boaz' prayer file is one of the longest and most eloquent. Boaz meets regularly in an intergenerational small group and worships on Sunday mornings with his family at the church he attends.

Below is the entire prayer file of Martha, 11:

Do you think you know God? "Yes." (strong answer) Tell me about that. "I know that I know God because my family grew up in a Christian home. Go to church. I asked him into my life. When I feel bad or something I sit in my room and talk to him."

What sort of things do you talk to God about? "When my grandpa died—about that. When my grandma died; when my friend had a problem. They had to move out of their house, their apartment, they didn't have anywhere to go. They lived with some people awhile, but they didn't know where to go. But now she's with her aunt." How did you know her? "She used to come here." What else do you pray about? "About the homeless; help me be safe; help when I'm sick."

Martha's prayer file is rather short, and her comments seem perfunctory. Martha has not had the opportunity to participate in intergenerational activities in the church she attends.

Some of the children from the non-intergenerational churches had fairly extensive prayer files; some did not. Though that was also true of the children in intergenerational settings, the intergenerational children referred to prayer more often and exhibited relationality in more of their discussions of prayer than did the children from non-intergenerational settings. (See Appendix B for further detail.) Analyses of the responses in other areas yielded differences also. For example, when asked what it means to know God, a larger number of intergenerational children gave relational descriptions of the concept of knowing God than did non-intergenerational children.

Though both groups of children gave profound and eloquent testimony to their relationships with God, the intergenerational children in this study generally were more aware of their relationship with God, that is, a larger number of them spoke more frequently and more reciprocally of that relationship (Allen, 2002).

Other Themes

Much of what the children said regarding their parents has been shared in the general themes above. Other categories developed by Adams, Jenkins, and Meek as well as other students who analyzed the raw data in light of children's comments regarding their parents include parents as teachers, parents as evangelists, and parents offering guidance.

Discussion

In considering the research, both from the literature and what has been gleaned from the interviews with the children, several clear recommendations seem to emerge. Those two young families asked what they can do to foster spiritual growth and health in their children; in response we will offer five specific recommendations; the first two are well known and should be continued; the third and fourth need to be reiterated; the fifth may be new to some, but it is crucial. We will spend more time describing and promoting this last recommendation.

Intra-Familial Rituals

Parents should pray with their children, read Scripture, tuck them in bed at night with a prayer and Bible story, and attend worship services as a family. The literature says that these are important family rituals that support a life of faith, and the children in the research confirmed that these repetitive outward religious activities conveyed to them that those who know God do these things.

I regularly teach a university course entitled Nurturing Spiritual Development in Children; an early assignment requires students to write a five-page reflection paper describing significant childhood spiritual influences. Typically about half of the students describe in loving detail the nightly routines of Bible story reading and prayer their mothers and/or fathers led them in. Though these bedtime routines seem mundane (and sometimes interminable) to the parents, the reflections of these students testify to the profound and abiding impact such ordinary rituals can have.

The Value of Ordinary Conversation and Activities

Parents need not manufacture spiritual experiences with their children; parental love and nurturing *is* positively affecting children's spirituality. Parents often think they aren't doing enough by spending time with their children, holding them, and showing them unconditional love. The literature shows otherwise: relationality, time, reciprocal conversation, and love make a lasting difference in the spiritual lives of their children; and the children in the research frequently described ordinary conversations as well as the loving things their families did for them and with them.

Modeling

Bandura's ongoing research regarding the importance of modeling plays out in the spiritual realm; parents need to model what they want their children to do and be. The children in the study were keenly aware of their parents' character and spiritual practices. Smith's studies (2009, 2005), as well as the Dollahite and Marks studies (2009,

2005), indicate the importance children place on the congruency of their parents' spiritual and religious lives.

A Healthy Parenting Style

Kim (2008) suggests that the authoritative parenting style nurtures children spiritually better than the other parenting styles. The warmth, love, responsiveness, and support, along with appropriate boundary setting, directive engagement with children, and appropriate discipline of this parenting style offer a balanced approach to parenting that is correlated with healthy social, achievement, and behavioral outcomes as well as spiritual outcomes. Amazingly, many children in the study indicated that they thought their parents knew God because of the way they disciplined, taught, and guided their children. The authoritative style of parenting balances truth and love as well as justice and mercy. The children in this study interpreted the disciplinary practices in their homes as parental demonstrations of love and faith.

The Role of Intergenerational Christian Communities

Though this chapter is focused on parents' roles in nurturing their children, the importance of the full body of Christ must not be ignored. Rather than abdicating their faith-nurturing role to the church as some parents do (see Barna, 2007; Beckwith, 2004), some parents may take total responsibility on themselves. This approach is also problematic. The church provides a complex, rich, diverse community for children as they learn about and experience their faith. Christ laid down his life for the church—not for the nuclear family. Parents cannot do it alone, nor were they meant to. Perhaps some parents, in their quest to take full responsibility for the spiritual growth of their children, have inadvertently diminished the role that the whole body of Christ should play in spiritual formation.

May, Posterski, Stonehouse, and Cannell (2005) believe that "children are nurtured most effectively in communities where they feel a sense of belonging, where they are able to participate in its life and ministry and where adult members model a vital faith" (p. 139). They found that relationships with parents and *other significant adults* provide the most formative influences for children. We know what Scripture says about parents' responsibility, but we cannot leave out what Jesus says about the new family and the communal aspect of the church. Intergenerational ministry embraces a holistic view of family and places all ages in the body of Christ as a family.

Intergenerational ministry places children in an atmosphere where they observe, interact, and participate in cross-generational worship, prayer, teaching, and learning. Children not only worship, pray, and learn alongside their parents, they observe and interact with other adults, teens, and children. Relationships across generational lines are established and fostered. Children discover what it means to be a part of the community of faith through *being* the body of Christ; they are not merely taught what the body of Christ is, they experience it fully.

A last recommendation, arising from the literature and the research, is that families need to actively participate in *intentional intergenerational faith communities*. In some ways this one umbrella recommendation can integrate key concepts and themes that have been developed thus far.

Conversation. In intergenerational settings, children will participate in ordinary conversation with other adults who believe as their parents do and see those adults relating in these ways with *their* children. The faith their parents are striving to teach them is reinforced through other significant adults in their church community.

Worship. Children who never worship with their parents and other adults have a limited understanding of the whole body of Christ. Worshiping together in close and intimate intergenerational settings reveal the inner spiritual lives of children, parents, and others to each other. Intergenerational worship experiences also give children a safe place to ask questions about what they are doing and seeing (e.g., What is that pretty silver cup [communion cup] on the table up there?) and a chance to lead as well as participate.

Prayer. As mentioned previously, the most significant differences between the two groups of children in the research was in the area of prayer. The children who met regularly in intergenerational small groups referred to prayer significantly more often than did the children from non-intergenerational settings. So if we believe that prayer nurtures spiritual growth and development, we want our children to be in settings where prayer is pervasive, where they hear other

Christians pray in intimate settings, and they begin to see that this is the first place to go when facing any challenge in life.

Definition of children's spirituality. A key aspect of most definitions of children's spirituality is *relationality*; our working definitions for this chapter include the child's relationship with self, others, and God. The *others* aspect of children's spirituality is nurtured through parents of course, but more fully in intergenerational faith community settings. Children are saturated there with the *others* component of spirituality.

In my dissertation research (Allen, 2002), when the children were asked, "Who do you know who knows God?" the children did respond often with a parent, but the children also mentioned dozens of *others*. One intriguing finding was that *eight* of the children mentioned that someone they knew who knew God was the *dad of their friend*. The interesting part is that often it is difficult for children to know anything about the spiritual aspects of their friends' *fathers*. So how would these children have known? All eight of the children who mentioned this were children who met in small intergenerational groups on a regular basis (Allen, 2002). For instance, Stephen, 11, describing one of these dads says, "Every [time] he will come up and greet [me] as if we were just equal people and I've seen him praying before. He's a very deep and wonderful Christian actually. He's a great example for everybody" (Allen, 2001).

Children see God in others' lives, they experience others' spirituality, and they come to know God better through these interactions. How children see their parents, other adults in their lives, teens, and other children influences their perception of God. Children see God in relation to the others in their Christian community, and they begin to pursue Him and experience Him personally in light of what they observe and experience not only in their homes, but among the whole community of believers.

Conclusion

Hundreds of participants in Smith's (2005, 2009) research repeatedly and unequivocally indicated that their parents have been the deepest and most profound influence on their spiritual lives. And indeed the literature and the children in the current study support the idea that parents powerfully impact their children through engaging them in regular spiritual rituals, recognizing the importance of frequent ordinary conversations and activities, modeling a congruent life—spiritually and religiously—and by parenting firmly yet lovingly. However, parents need not carry the entire weight of spiritually nurturing their children alone. Embedding their families in intentionally intergenerational believing communities will provide multiple opportunities for their children to become familiar with a broad age range of committed people who also know God; and in so doing, both their children and these parents will be blessed.

References

Allen, H. C. (2001). [Children's interviews.] Unpublished raw data.

———. (2002). *A qualitative study exploring the similarities and differences of the spirituality of children in intergenerational and non-intergenerational Christian contexts.* (Doctoral dissertation, Talbot School of Theology, Biola University, La Mirada, CA).

———. (Winter, 2004). Nurturing children's spirituality in intergenerational settings. *Lutheran Educational Journal, 139*(2), 111–24.

Bandura, A. (1986). *Social foundations of thought and action: A social cognitive theory.* Englewood Cliffs, NJ: Prentice Hall.

———. (1999). A social cognitive theory of personality. In L. A. Pervin & O. P. John (Eds.), *Handbook of personality: Theory and research* (2nd ed., pp. 154–96). New York: Guilford.

———. (2001). Social cognitive theory: An agentic perspective. *Annual Review of Psychology* (Vol. 52, pp. 1–26). Palo Alto, CA: Annual Reviews, Inc. Retrieved from http://search.ebscohost.com.ezproxy.jbu.edu/login.aspx?direct=true&db=afh&AN=4445594&site=ehost-live

———. (2003). On the psychosocial impact and mechanisms of spiritual modeling. *International Journal for the Psychology of Religion, 13*(3), 167–73. Retrieved from http://search.ebscohost.com.ezproxy.jbu.edu/login.aspx?direct=true&db=afh&AN=10797204&site=ehost-live

Baumrind, D. (1966). Effects of authoritative parental control on child behavior. *Child Development, 37*, 887–907.

———. (1978). Parental disciplinary patterns and social competence in children. *Youth and Society, 9*, 239–76.

———. (1991). The influence of parenting style on adolescent competence and substance use. *Journal of Early Adolescence, 11*, 56–95.

———. (1996). The discipline controversy revisited. *Family Relations, 45*, 405–14. Retrieved from http://www.jstor.org/stable/585170

Beckwith, I. (2004). *Postmodern children's ministry: Ministry to children in the 21st century.* Grand Rapids: Zondervan.

Berryman, J. (1991). *Godly play: A way of religious education.* San FranciscoL: Harper & Row.

Boyatzis, C. J. (2004). The co-construction of spiritual meaning in parent-child communication. In D. Ratcliff (Ed.), *Children's spirituality: Christian perspectives, research, and applications* (pp. 182–200). Eugene, OR: Cascade.

Boyatzis, C. J., Dollahite, D. C., & & Marks, L. D. (2006). The family as context for religious and spiritual development. In E. C. Roehlkepartain, P. E. King, L. Wagner, & P. L. Benson (Eds.), *The handbook of spiritual development in childhood and adolescence* (pp. 297–309). Thousand Oaks, CA: Sage.

Cain, J. D. (2002, March). Soul child: Seven ways to increase your child's spiritual awareness. *Essence*, 150–66.

Caldwell, E. F. (2006). At home with faith and family: A Protestant Christian perspective. In K. M. Yust, A. N. Johnson, S. E. Sasso, & E. C. Roehlkepartain (Eds.), *Nurturing child and adolescent spirituality: Perspectives from the world's religious traditions* (pp. 325–37). Lanham, MD: Rowman & Littlefield.

Carr, J. (2008). Equipping children for ministry. In H. C. Allen (Ed.), *Nurturing children's spirituality: Christian perspectives and best practices* (pp. 198–213). Eugene, OR: Cascade.

Dollahite, D. C., & Marks, L. D. (2005). How highly religious families strive to fulfill sacred purposes. In V. L. Bengston, D. Klein, A. Acock, K. Allen, & P. Dilworth-Anderson (Eds.), *Sourcebook of family theory and research* (pp. 533–37). Thousand Oaks, CA: Sage.

———. (2009). A conceptual model of family and religious processes in highly religious families. *Review of Religious Research, 50*(4), 373–91.

Fowler, J. W. (1991). *Weaving the new creation: Stages of faith and the public church.* New York: HarperCollins.

Fraze, D. (2009). Something is not right. http://fulleryouthinstitute.org/2009/01/something-is-not-right

Hay, D., with Nye, R. (2006). *The spirit of the child* (Rev. ed.). Philadelphia: Kingsley.

Holmen, M. (2005). *Faith begins at home: The family makeover with Christ at the center.* Ventura, CA: Regal.

Kim, S. (2008). Parenting styles and children's spiritual development. In H. C. Allen (Ed.), *Nurturing children's spirituality: Christian perspectives and best practices* (pp. 233–51). Eugene, OR: Cascade.

Maccoby, E. E. (2000). Parenting and its effects on children: On reading and misreading behavior genetics. *Annual Review of Psychology, 51*(1), 1.

Mahoney, A. (2010). Religion in families, 1999–2009: A relational spirituality framework, *Journal of Marriage and Family 72*, 805–27. doi: 10.1111/j.1741-3737.2010.00732.x

Marks, L. D. (2004). Sacred practices in highly religious families: Christian, Jewish, Mormon, and Muslim perspectives. *Family Processes, 43*, 217-231. Retrieved from http:// search.ebscohost.com/login.aspx?direct=true&db=afh&AN=1436 0297&site=ehost-live

May, S., Posterski, B., Stonehouse, C., & Cannell, L. (2005). *Children matter: Celebrating their place in the church, family and community.* Grand Rapids: Eerdmans.

McQuitty, M. (2008). A qualitative understanding of Deuteronomy 6. In H. C. Allen (Ed.), *Nurturing children's spirituality: Christian perspectives and best practices* (pp. 252–66). Eugene, OR: Cascade.

Moran, G. (1978). Where now, what next. In P. O'Hare (Ed.), *Foundations of Religious Education* (pp. 93–110). New York: Paulist.

————. *Interplay: A theory of religion and education.* Winona, MN: Saint Mary's College Press.

Nelson, C. E. (1967). *Where faith begins.* Atlanta: John Knox.

————. (1989). *How faith matures.* Louisville: Westminster/John Knox.

Oman, D., & Thoresen, C. E. (2003). Spiritual modeling: A key to spiritual and religious growth? *International Journal for the Psychology of Religion, 135*(3), 149–65.

Powell, K. (2009, Summer). Is the era of age segregation over? An interview with Kara Powell. *Leadership, 30*(3), 43–48.

Ratcliff, D. (1995). Parenting and religious education. In B. J. Neff & D. Ratcliff (Eds.), *Handbook of family religious education* (pp. 61–86). Birmingham, AL: Religious Education Press.

Ratcliff, D., & Ratcliff, B. (2010). *ChildFaith: Experiencing God and spiritual growth with your children.* Eugene, OR: Cascade.

Roberto, J. (2009). Faith formation 2010. *Lifelong Faith: The theory and Practice of Lifelong Faith Formation, 3*(2), 1–60.

Schneiders, S. (1986). Theology and spirituality: Strangers, rivals, and partners. *Horizon, 13*, 253–74.

Sheldrake, P. (2000). What is spirituality? In K. J. Collins (Ed.), *Exploring Christian Spirituality* (pp. 21–42). Grand Rapids: Baker.

Smith, C., with Denton, M. L. (2005). *Soul searching: The religious and spiritual lives of American teenagers.* Oxford: Oxford University Press.

Smith, C., with Snell, P. (2009). *Souls in transition: The religious and spiritual lives of emerging adults.* Oxford: Oxford University Press.

Stonehouse, C. (1998). *Joining children on the spiritual journey: Nurturing a life of faith.* Grand Rapids: Baker Academic.

Thompson, M. J. (1996). *Family: The forming center.* Nashville: Upper Room Books.

Westerhoff, J. L. (1980). *Bringing up children in the Christian faith.* San Francisco: Harper and Row.

————. (2000). *Will our children have faith?* (Rev. ed.). New York: Seabury.

White, J. (1988). *Intergenerational religious education.* Birmingham, AL: Religious Education Press.

Wigger, J. B. (2003). *The power of God at home: Nurturing our children in love and grace.* San Francisco: Jossey-Bass.

Wuthnow, R. (1999). *Growing up religious: Christians and Jews and their religious journeys of faith.* Boston: Beacon

Yust, K. M. (2004a). Creating a spiritual world for children to inhibit. *Family Ministry, 18*(4), 24–39.

————. (2004b). *Real kids, real faith: Practices for nurturing children's spiritual lives.* San Francisco: Jossey-Bass.

Appendix A

Interview Protocol

People who know God:

Of all the people you know, who do you think knows God the best?

Why do you think that person knows God?

Are there other reasons why you think knows God?

Is there someone else you know who knows God really well? Why do you think so?

Do you have any questions you want to ask me?

Feelings about God:

When you think about God, how do you feel?

Can you tell me about a time when YOU felt surprised or amazed about God?

Sorry or guilty toward God? Can you tell me about that time?

Happy about God? Can you tell me about that time?

Sad about God? Can you tell me about that time?

Scared about God? Can you tell me about that time?

Angry at God? Can you tell me about that time?

Love for God? Any time in particular?

Knowing God:

What is the difference between someone who knows *about* God and someone who *knows* God?

How do you think someone gets to know God?

Do you think you know God?

What are some things that you do that help you know that you know God?

Prayer:

Do you talk to God (prayer)? In your mind, in your imagination, out loud?

What sort of things do you talk to God about?

In what ways does God talk to us?

Have you ever thought God talked to you?

Other possible questions:

Have you ever felt God close to you? Would you tell me about that?

Were you ever afraid or alone, and you think God helped you?

Has your family ever needed special help and you think God helped?

Have you ever been at the mountains, or in a park, or at the ocean, and thought God was nearby? Would you tell me about that? (Allen, 2002, pp. 371–73)

Appendix B

Prayer and Intergenerational Experiences

I tallied the number of times the children mentioned prayer (before the questions about prayer) and did a statistical comparison. The t-test was significant, $t(38)=2.37$, $p=.02$.

Children who participated regularly in intergenerational settings.		Children who did not participate intergenerational settings.	
Participant	# times prayer mentioned	**Participant**	# times prayer mentioned
Elijah	4	Barnabas	2
Esther	3	Bartholomew	5
Eve	5	Cornelius	4
Caleb	5	Dorcas	4
Joseph	2	Joanna	6
Leah	5	Junia	0
Levi	4	Mark	3
Nathaniel	3	Paul	3
Noah	1	Priscilla	5
Rebecca	6	James	3
Sara	6	Luke	1
Abigail	6	Lydia	3
Adam	2	Martha	1
Benjamin	6	Mary	1
Boaz	6	Philip	2
Hannah	7	Stephen	4
Micah	2	Tabitha	5
Miriam	3	Thomas	4
Seth	3	Julia	2
Zipporah	7	Phoebe	2

11

Being Faithful Together
Families and Congregations as Intergenerational
Christian Communities

Karen Marie Yust

There is a debate raging in my home congregation: should children's church school continue in age-graded classrooms despite the small numbers the church has in each grade, or should we develop a multi-age Christian education program? Advocates of separate classes argue that older children do not receive adequate instruction in faith when mixed with younger children. Proponents of a multi-age program point out that classes consisting of just two or three participants do not provide sufficient numbers for most curricular activities or sustained discussion. What everyone acknowledges is that the Lenten "one room schoolhouse" series the church did last year was incredible – children were excitedly engaged in drama, music, storytelling, art, cooking, service, and reflection; parents were eager to volunteer as teaching the church assistants; and the entire congregation learned from the testimonies of faith depicted in the children's murals, outreach projects, and videography. However, this series was taught by a Christian education "expert" and the lay volunteers who usually teach church school cannot imagine themselves in a multi-age teaching role. They hold this opinion despite the fact that most of them are parents of children of varying ages and therefore, as teachers of Christian faith at home, are already working in a multi-age environment. That they have not realized this fact says much about the problematic division between congregational children's ministries and household faith practices.

Since 1861, when Horace Bushnell argued in *Christian Nurture* that families should be the primary locus of children's faith formation, North American Christians have struggled to understand the relationship between formal Christian education programs in congregations and informal Christian nurture in family homes. What is the appropriate balance between family spirituality and church-based experiences? The professionalization of religious education in the early twentieth century tipped the scale toward congregational settings and expert instruction in age-specific groups. Yet contemporary program and attendance patterns suggest that the home must be a place of faith formation if children are to have sufficient time and space to know God. Just as children do not learn how to play an instrument or excel at a sport with just one sixty minute lesson a week, they do not become faithful disciples of Christ based on an hour of instruction each Sunday once per week. Children (and adults) need daily practice in living their faith if they are to learn how to love God with all their heart, mind, soul, and strength.

However, many parents, grandparents, aunts, and uncles are unsure how to foster Christian spirituality in the home. Some recall raising children in an era when a wider culture largely reinforced Christian beliefs and practices and, they do not know how to cultivate Christian identity without this reinforcing structure. Some have no experience with household religious practices because their families of origin were not Christian or functioned as culturally Christian without active engagement in faith. Some have robust memories of family spirituality but cannot reconcile the schedules and demands of contemporary culture with the practices they recall from their own childhood. Some do not share Bushnell's belief that faith formation is primarily the responsibility of parents and need to be convinced that families and congregations must partner in this nurturing task. All would benefit from careful attention to how faith is elicited and supported within intergenerational Christian communities, whether in family rooms or fellowship halls, around dinner or communion tables, with immediate family members or among the family of God that call themselves "church."

In her Christian parenting handbook, *Home Grown*, Karen DeBoer notes, "My kids learned to swim from a certified instructor. They take piano lessons from a professional musician and learn to play basketball from an outstanding coach. As a parent I take full advantage of outsourcing when it comes to teaching my kids" (DeBoer, 2010, p. 9). What DeBoer and others have found is that parents frequently adopt this outsourcing approach for faith formation as well, even though children and youth repeatedly identify their parents as a primary source of religious information and spiritual counsel. A 2008 Search Institute study found that, globally, 44 percent of teens identify parents as the individuals who most help them spiritually; religious organizations were listed fourth (14 percent) out of six options, with "no one" (18 percent) and "friends" (15 percent) in second and third place (Benson, Roehlkepartain, & Hong, 2008, p. 35). Sixty-five percent of young people in the study said that they had talked with their parents about spiritual beliefs at least a few times in the last year, although only 24 percent reported that such conversations occurred at least monthly. A similar percentage (65–70 percent) identified specific parental religious activities, such as prayer, meditation, or expressions of spiritual joy, that they had witnessed (Benson, et al., p. 37). In addition, Christian Smith's 2005 study of American adolescents found that less than one-fifth (19 percent) of teens in the United States identify a religious youth leader as someone with whom they discuss personal spiritual questions, whereas the converse (81 percent) say that they engage in spiritual conversations or activities with their families at least a few times a year (Smith & Lundquist Denton, 2005, pp. 55, 64).

Smith's follow-up study with these young people five years later concluded that four factors consistently predicted which American teenagers will remain religiously engaged into young adulthood. Two of these factors—"strong parental religion" and "high importance of religious faith in daily life"—reinforce the point that family spirituality matters (Smith & Snell, 2010, p. 15). Smith notes that statistically, four of the six most likely combinations of factors that result in high religious engagement in emerging adulthood begin with "high parental religious service attendance and importance of faith" (Smith & Snell, 2010, pp. 17–18). Implicit in this factor is the assumption that parental participation in worship means they also took their children, and an expectation that the daily importance of faith means attention to spiritual practices at home during the rest of the week. While Smith's research does not include an observational component to confirm these assumptions, the information emerging adults and parents report in their interviews suggests that an active family faith life and familial participation in a religious community are key components in cultivating a lasting faith.

Family faith practices and congregational participation complement one another. Families provide a personalized experience of spirituality, in which God dwells intimately with a household like Jesus spent time with siblings Mary, Martha, and Lazarus. Congregations provide a broader, more diverse network of relationships within which to encounter God. As I wrote in *Real Kids, Real Faith*,

> Parents are the principal guides in children's spiritual formation, yet children need a religious community within which to experience God as something other than their own friend or possession. They need the benefit of others' discoveries about divine love and others' testimonies to the challenges of faithful living. They need to rub up against different ideas about God and experience the affirmation of shared understanding. They need opportunities to be shaped by communal rituals and practices that extend beyond the narrow confines of their immediate family so that they realize their kinship with other spiritual people (Yust, 2004, p. 164).

Children need the comfort of a shared family spiritual journey and the challenge of walking with a diverse group of congregational pilgrims in a lifelong process of faith formation.

The interaction between home and congregation is most nurturing when parents and religious leaders communicate effectively with multiple ages and yet within children's varied developmental capabilities. Catholic educator Thomas Groome refers to this kind of intergenerational partnership as "total community catechesis," in which understandings and practices of faith formation move "beyond children to all people; beyond teachers and taught to communities sharing faith together" (Groome, 2008, pp. 32–33). However, Groome still imagines this process as largely segregated and sequential in nature. Learning occurs on parallel tracks among separate age cohorts, with opportunities for interaction growing out of the common foci of age-segregated study rather than intergenerational exploration. What is needed are genuinely intergenerational learning events and practices that build learning communities of mixed ages capable of studying, worshipping, and praying together as one. As John Roberto observes, "In a culture increasingly segregated by ages, stages, generations, or developmental tasks, congregational gatherings may be some of the few or only opportunities for the generations to be with and learn from one another" (Roberto, 2006, p. 54).

African-American educator Anne Streaty Wimberly observes that congregational worship is a prime location of communal faith-sharing, and it is here that religious leaders can best model effective intergenerational approaches to faith formation. Wimberly specifically cites "preaching, prayer, and music" as the central educational "pathways" of worship (Wimberly, 2008, p. 8). Each of these pathways become a potential means by which worship leaders can demonstrate how parents and other adults engage children of all ages alongside older learners. However, as Nathan Frambach notes, "thinking and acting in an intentionally intergenerational manner does not seem to come naturally for many congregations" (Frambach, 2001, p. 253), so creating worship that models intergenerational preaching, prayer, and music requires careful attention.

Intergenerational Preaching

Preaching, according to Wimberly, has a threefold function in worship. It is "prophetic" in the sense that it generates "a heightened awareness of the meaning of a lived faith in God through Jesus Christ and the Holy Spirit, and an existence that exemplifies it" (Wimberly, 2008, p. 9). It is "priestly," drawing worshippers' attention to "a vision of Christian vocation and specific life skills that are critical to life" when their identity is threatened or coping abilities tested (Wimberly, 2008, p. 9). It is also "apostolic," marked by "the pastor's authentic modeling of the faith and hope about which he or she preaches" (Wimberly, 2008, p. 9). Each of these functions requires transposition across the keys of different age groups if the same sermon is to form an intergenerational community in faith.

To explore this idea, consider how one might preach the Emmaus resurrection story (Luke 24:13–35) with Wimberly's categories and an intergenerational body of Christ in mind. From a prophetic standpoint, young children can relate to the concept of a "surprise," so a sermon could play up this element as a means of connecting with child listeners. Older children and youth have likely heard many relatives and family friends declare, "You've grown so much, I hardly recognized you!" and thus might be drawn into sermonic specula-tion about why the Emmaus-bound disciples did not recognize Jesus. Many adults have experienced times when they are so caught up in the chaos of a family or work crisis that they do not think clearly and have trouble tracking details or listening carefully to others, and so can be invited to identify with the confusion of the disciples. In these ways, the prophetic call to enter the story and experience God's presence in one's life can reach all ages through the elements of the story that the preacher highlights.

The priestly aspect of proclamation is particularly easy to trans-late across generations with this story. The interaction between Jesus and the disciples imitates much that occurs in human relationships from a young age. Parents of preschoolers ask, "What did you do today?" when picking up children from daycare or returning home from work, and children often pour out a chronology of activities or exciting discoveries into the parent's willing ear, just as Jesus asked the disciples what they were doing and they told him. School-age children ask why something is true or an event is conducted a certain way, and parents suggest looking it up just as Jesus responded to the disciples' concerns with a lesson from the scriptures. Family members of all ages sit down to eat together—or wish that they could—and enjoy having friends over to share a meal, just as the disciples wanted to have supper with Jesus. A good sermon can emphasize the connections between the activities on the road to Emmaus and the predictable interactions of family life as a way of underscoring how these activities can also have spiritual significance.

Addressing the apostolic function of proclamation through this story is also fairly simple. Jesus patiently and through diverse methods helps the Emmaus-bound disciples discover the truth of the resurrec-tion just as children experience parents as responsive to their needs and parents try a variety of ways to help their children succeed in life. A two-year-old's ears may prick up if the preacher says, "The disciples were asking, 'why, why, why?' and Jesus said, 'because the prophets say so." A teen may pay attention if a sermon illustration likens the breaking of bread moment to the recognition that occurs when one sees an application icon ("app") on one's cell phone and knows it stands for something specific. Parents may connect to the sensation of their "hearts burning within" (Luke 24:32, NIB) when their children do something amazing and they fall in love with them all over again. Each of these references invites family members to experience a moment of recognition, to know that the biblical story is also "*my* story about *me*, and it is *our* story about *us*" (Brueggemann, 1979, p. 31).

For preachers who do not find that the practice of intergenerational preaching comes easily, Carolyn Brown's book, *You Can Preach to the Kids, Too*, offers numerous practical tips for crafting sermons that communicate across age groups. She identifies three questions that should shape sermon preparation: "What words does a child need to know in order to understand this text or topic?" (Brown, 1997, p. 33), "Are there obsolete practices, beliefs, or cultural realities children need to explore before they can understand this topic/text?" and "What does this text or topic say to children?" (Brown, 1997, p. 35). All of her advice is based on the assumption that those who proclaim the gospel should make an effort to recognize and understand the developmental capabilities and social circumstances of all their listeners. A developmental chart—like those used in pediatricians' offices—and at least a passing acquaintance with popular children's shows broadcast on public television can teach pastors some basics of effective communication with young children. Reviewing the local school district's "Standards of Learning" (SOL) document—often publicly available on the district's website or through the central office —offers a developmental picture of how school age children and youth approach learning and suggests age-appropriate topics and foci that preachers might tie to the texts they are preaching. Reading popular parenting magazines can provide further insight, as long as pastors' temper their interpretations of these popular parenting "gospels" with an awareness of the roles consumerism and other secular values play in shaping articles.

When worship leaders accept that intergenerational preaching is possible and craft sermons that proclaim the gospel to all ages, they model a kind of intergenerational conversation about faith that is also important for family life. Parents, grandparents, and other adults hear children's experiences validated as faithful connections with the gospel and can imitate the language used from the pulpit in their conversations with young people. They also see ways in which their own experience of a biblical story or theme overlaps or complements a child's engagement with the same text, offering ideas for family discussion. When a father says to his child, "Sometimes daddy gets distracted by work and doesn't notice what's going on around him—I wonder if the disciples going to Emmaus were distracted like daddy," he creates a space for a seven year old to say, "Yeah, like when I hit a homerun at t-ball and you missed it while you were talking on your cell phone – did the disciples have cell phones?" A teen may comment, "Maybe they were just caught up in their own conversation, working out what they thought and not really looking at the new guy on the road." When a mother shares that the Emmaus story reminds her of how much she enjoys family dinners because she can catch up on what everyone has been doing, her four-year-old may responds, "Can we have bread that we break tonight, too?" Such conversational exchanges reinforce the ways in which biblical stories are about contemporary lives as much as they are tales of past events. Good intergenerational preaching makes it easier for families to begin and sustain such conversations.

Brown affirms that preachers can assist families with this transition by suggesting conversational topics for parent-child discussion in the conclusion of the sermon. She offers the example of an invitation to "talk about the work that each member of the household does and then pray together about each person's work" as part of a Labor Day sermon on work (Brown, 1997, p. 107). Children hear this invitation issued and thus feel included in the "homework" assigned. Parents have the ideas about work expressed in the sermon as a springboard for the family conversation and thus, says Brown, are "prepared to tell their children about their own work and to help the children identify and value the work they do in school and at home" (Brown, 1997, p. 107).

Intergenerational Praying

Communal prayer is another primary faith practice that can be modeled intergenerationally in congregational worship. Wimberly notes, "Through the language of prayer in worship, we learn and validate who God is and how God acts" (Wimberly, 2008, p. 9). Contrary to the stereotype of prayer as a passive response employed when human initiative is insufficient or fails, Wimberly asserts that prayer is active. She argues that praying together offers all ages "practice in the vocabulary of prayer" and experience with a "model of conversations with God" (Wimberly, 2008, p. 9). Congregational prayer, then, teaches both the nature and method of praying.

A typical service contains several opportunities to pray together: prayers of invocation, confession, and thanksgiving (after the offering); a prayer following the children's moment (of blessing or conveying a desire to know and understand); baptismal or Eucharistic prayers (when those sacraments are celebrated); the Lord's Prayer; prayers of the people or a pastoral prayer (following the acknowledgement of congregational joys and concerns); and a benediction. Some of these prayers are scripted and others may be extemporaneously led by a worship leader or offered (aloud and silently) by various members of the congregation. The vocabulary and sentence structure attached to these prayers affects how well they engage persons of all ages. Scripted prayers constructed of complex sentences and challenging vocabulary will sail over the heads of many young participants. Very short sentences and overly simple vocabulary will seem irrelevant and disrespectful to older congregants. What are needed are prayers that combine Craig Dykstra's four principles of good religious language: clarity, richness, concreteness, and critical awareness (Dykstra, 2005, p. 124–25).

> *Clarity* uses terminology and logical reasoning appropriate to the age and developmental stage of the hearers. Everything that a child hears need not be cognitively clear, but a child must have some points of cognitive connection for religious language to be intelligent.
>
> *Richness* incorporates metaphors and other symbolic language, variations in tone, and combinations of simple and complex grammatical structures . . .
>
> *Concreteness* evokes a sense of personal relevance through intentional reference to children's experiences, as well as to the experiences of others . . .
>
> *Critical Awareness* makes room for analysis and inquiry, while providing a framework within which to ask, "Why?" (Yust, 2004, p. 84).

Scripted prayer that are truly intergenerational use: 1) clarity to appeal to varied levels of cognitive ability, 2) rich images and sounds that work alongside cognition and also offer other ways of knowing, 3) concrete life experiences from diverse age groups, and 4) the naming of possibilities that permit critical exploration of who God is, how God acts, and what God calls persons to do and be.

Caroline Fairless offers a practical approach to the prayers of the people that involves scripting prayers communally through the use of "prayer cards" (Fairless, 2000, p. 63). She suggests using index cards upon which people of all ages write or draw their prayer concerns and then place them in a prayer basket for inclusion in the formal prayer time. While acknowledging that some of these cards may require "creative interpretation on the part of the prayer leader," she also notes that, "[a]s often as not, they will reflect the kind of day it's becoming; reflect what the children have heard in the Liturgy of the Word, perhaps the music. Reflect perhaps, what they've overheard in casual conversation as people enter the church" (Fairless, 2000, p. 64). Since persons of various ages contribute to the construction of the prayers, they provide clarity at several cognitive levels and the richness of different grammatical structures. Young children can dictate the words of their prayer concern to an adult if desired. The pictorial submissions encourage the use of symbolic language as well as provide concrete connections to children's lives. The multiplicity of prayer concerns also generates thoughtfulness, as children and adults wonder how God will respond to their petitions in light of what they know about God and what others are asking God to do.

Sometimes the inclusion of children in congregational worship can be accomplished through bodily actions that accompany spoken prayers. Fairless describes using "confession stones" (2000, p. 87) that all congregants take and hold through the prayers of confession and then pass to the aisle for transfer to a bowl on the altar during the assurance of pardon, where the worship leader pours water over them as a sign of God's washing away of sin. Even an infant can be offered a stone (sized to avoid a choke hazard) to touch before it is passed for collection, initiating bodily knowledge of the practice well before cognitive knowledge develops. The symbolic items and actions provide intergenerational richness and raise critical questions about why the faith community uses stones, collects them into a single bowl, and pours water as part of the absolution ritual. Congregations that rely on traditional language from a book of worship or set liturgy—and thus may not have much latitude regarding multi-age clarity in the words used—can still extend understanding of the ritual through visual and bodily-kinesthetic knowledge paths.

Both prayer cards and confession stones are ritual prayer practices that families can adopt. Along the lines of intercessory prayer cards, families can also invite every member of the household to provide one or more thanksgiving prayer cards for mealtime blessings, invocation prayer cards for times when the family wants to acknowledge or call upon God's presence, and "sending forth" prayer cards for moving from home to school, work, or daycare. The family then can rotate through the prayers at appropriate times or "draw" from the "deck" of cards associated with a particular prayer time, ensuring that, over time, the prayers will connect with all cognitive levels. Asking the family member who created the card to lead the prayer may elicit the richness and concreteness of the family's diverse faith understandings and spiritual experiences. Families could also gather their own basket of confession stones, gathering rocks from special places (Fairless, 2000, p. 87), vacation spots, or just the backyard. A preschooler's precious bit of broken concrete can co-exist with dad's rosette stone, an older sibling's piece of sea glass, and grandmother's agate—all equally symbolic of biblical rocks (such as at Meribah and piled up beside the Jordan) that showed the way to faithfulness in the scriptures (Fairless, 2000, p. 89).

David Jensen points to a way in which the practice of praying the Lord's Prayer, whether at home or in congregational worship, levels the distinction between adults and children. Referencing the Heidelberg Catechism's interpretation of the prayer Jesus taught, he says, "We are to pray 'Our Father,' so that 'at the beginning of our prayer [God] may awaken in us the childlike reverence and trust toward God which should be the motivation of our prayer,'" (Jensen, 2005, p. 116). Congregations and families, then, become part of the same generation in relation to God, and "prayers are not detached adult musings, but the earnest desires of a child" (Jensen, 2005, p. 116). When the parental nature of God and the childlike nature of God's people are emphasized, prayer relies on a concept familiar to all but the very youngest of children (and even infants have an embodied experience of parental care). Add to this conceptual reality the use of both complex traditional language and paraphrases that simplify the vocabulary, and the practice of praying the Lord's Prayer together bridges generational differences effectively.

Intergenerational Singing

Music, particularly singing ourthe faith, also lends itself to intergenerational modeling. Wimberly asserts that "songs tell our communities' stories of faith and hope in God, Jesus Christ, the Holy Spirit, the valued self, and the movement from sin to salvation" (Wimberly, 2008, p. 10). Like most church musicians, she views congregational singing as a school in Christian ethics and faithful living. She also emphasizes the significance of church music in teaching all generations about sacramental practices. Aware that musical style can be a controversial issue, she advises worship leaders to ask: "How may nurturing faith and hope through music be an inclusive experience?" rather than divisive (Wimberly, 2008, p. 10).

Hymns and songs operate on multiple intelligences: rhythm, melody, and pitch appeal to musical intelligence, words tap into linguistic intelligence, and swaying to catchy tunes can evoke bodily-kinesthetic intelligence. Persons of different ages and intellectual development connect to spiritual music through these different intelligences. Infants may not know or recognize words but will attend to familiar tunes or respond to the emotional cues of minor and major keys, just as musically-inclined adults will do. Young children join kinesthetic adults in "feeling" the music in their bodies. Words repeated in a hymn may begin to make sense to children and form a bridge between their linguistic knowledge and the more advanced understanding of the adults around them. Thus the generations can meet through hymn-singing.

Letting the music move one's body or emotions is one aspect of intergenerational singing, but it does not necessarily result in shared faith formation. Coming to understand and embrace the theological ideas conveyed by congregational hymns also matters. Worship planners increase the odds that children will begin to make theological connections when they select hymns that are child-friendly. This does not mean that congregations must sing only simple choruses or pieces designated as Sunday School songs. Hymns that involve repetition of significant theological terms or phrases, such as *Holy, Holy, Holy* (where the word "holy" occurs 19 times) and *Great Is They Faithfulness* (in which the title phrase is repeated 10 times) resonate with children because hearing the same words reinforces their importance. The repetition may also prompt children to ask about the words they are hearing sung and beginning to sing themselves.

Taizé songs are also good choices for intergenerational singing during worship. Biblically based and theologically rich in content, these short songs are meant to be sung over and over until they get inside one's head and move one's heart. Singing "bless the Lord, my soul" or "in the Lord I'll be ever thankful" several times over not only teaches children (and adults) the words but also encourages meditation on those words. Praise songs that reflect a tradition's theology can have a similar effect, as can the choruses from African-American spirituals. These three types of songs also translate well into home life because they are easy to remember and sing without accompaniment. Just humming the tune can bring the words to mind for many children and adults, and the meditative style of singing can function as a form of prayer connected to family activities.

Hymn singing at home may be more difficult for families if an older child, youth, or adult is not a singer. Shyness about singing a cappella can stymie intergenerational faith formation through traditional church music even if congregational leaders are modeling broadly appealing hymn selections. Families may want to download hymns from iTunes or other sources for family sing-alongs in the car or music to sing with while doing household chores. Congregations might consider recording congregational singing during worship services and making DVDs available to families for home use (taking care to observe copyright restrictions).

Shared and Authentic Work

Joyce Mercer acknowledges that many adults fear a loss of adult connection when the topic of intergenerational worship is raised.

> Adults in mainline congregations often express fears about "dumbing down" the content of sermons or taking away from the dignity of liturgy in efforts to make worship more "child friendly." . . . But it is not difficult to think about ways to invite the participation of children that are in keeping with the general style or ethos of congregational worship in a particular place while at the same time inviting the presence of children

> to impact the congregation's liturgical practices. Using the
> model of mutual engagement of different cultures as a strategy,
> it is also all right for some aspects of worship to be more fitting
> to one group than to another. (Mercer, 2005, p. 235)

In this chapter, I have tried to illustrate how intergenerational worship
can meet the faith formation needs of all ages without compromising
those aspects of worship that signify a faith community's identity and
nurture its relationship with God. Furthermore, I have suggested that
quality intergenerational experiences within the worshipping community model a kind of intergenerational spiritual engagement essential
to Christian families at home. Christy Olson observes, "The concept
of moment-by-moment, day-by-day spiritual practice is new to most
families and quite intimidating" (Olson, 2010, p. 38). Congregational
worship that is effective in bridging generational differences without
diminishing or devaluing the experience of any particular age group
teaches ways of loving and serving God consistent with the intergenerational make-up of many households. When families begin to see
their intergenerational reality reflected and celebrated in congregational worship, they need look no further for models of household
religious practice. No longer will they wonder if children can learn to
be God's people in multi-age Sunday School classes instead of segregated age-specific classrooms. They will know experientially that the
body of Christ is intergenerational at its core, both in its gathered state
during church services and its scattered versions in multiple homes
throughout the week.

References

Benson, P. L., Roehlkepartain, E. C., and Hong, K. L. (2008). *Spiritual development: New directions for youth development.* San Francisco: Jossey-Bass.

Brown, C. (1997). *You can preach to the kids, too! Designing sermons for adults and children.* Nashville: Abingdon.

Brueggemann, W. (1979). *Belonging and growing in the Christian community: The first years of parenting.* Louisville: General Assembly Mission Board, Presbyterian Church in the United States.

Bushnell, H. (1861). *Christian nurture.* New York: Scribner.

DeBoer, K. (2010). *Home grown handbook for Christian parenting.* Grand Rapids: Faith Alive Christian Resources.

Dykstra, C. (2005). *Growing in the life of faith: Education and Christian practices, 2nd ed.* Louisville: Westminster/John Knox.

Fairless, C. (2000). *Children at worship: Congregations in bloom.* New York: Church Publishing.

Frambach, N. (2004). The ministry of children in congregations. *The ministry of children's education: Foundations, contexts, and practice* . Minneapolis: Fortress, 243–64.

Groome, T. (2008). Total community catechesis for lifelong faith formation. *Lifelong Faith, 2*(1), 30–38.

Jensen, D. H. (2005). *Graced vulnerability: A theology of childhood*. Cleveland: Pilgrim.

Mercer, J. A. (2005). *Welcoming children: A practical theology of childhood*. Atlanta: Chalice.

Olson, C. (2010). Family daily living faith practices. *Lifelong Faith, 4*(3), 33–43.

Roberto, J. (2006). "Part Four: Descriptions of the thirteen trends and forces influencing the future of faith formation in a changing church and world. *Lifelong Faith, 3*(2), 35–61.

Smith, C., and Lundquist Denton, M. (2005). *Soul searching: The religious and spiritual lives of American teenagers*. New York: Oxford University Press.

Smith, C., and Snell, P. (2010). *Souls in transition: The religious and spiritual lives of emerging adults*. New York: Oxford University Press.

Wimberly, A. E. S. (2008). Worship as a model for faith formation. *Lifelong Faith, 2*(1), 3–13.

Yust, K. M. (2004). *Real kids, real faith: Practices for nurturing children's spiritual lives*. San Francisco: Jossey-Bass.

12

Children's Place in the New Forms of Church[1]
An Exploratory Survey of these Forms' Ministry with Children and Families

Scottie May, Katie Stemp, and Grant Burns

Introduction

For academics with a long-standing interest in the spiritual formation of Christian children, the changing landscape of the North American evangelical church evoked a question: What is happening with children and families in the "new forms" of church that have been appearing in the past twenty years? This question was the impetus for this exploratory survey conducted in 2008–09. We coined the term "new forms," an intentionally vague phrase, to describe the way these churches function and conduct the life of their faith communities.

New-form churches, often started by young adults twenty to thirty-five years of age, meet in warehouses, shopping malls, homes, old church buildings, business complexes, theaters, even bars and pubs—anywhere people can gather regularly. They also vary widely in worship style; the names for these gatherings rarely contain the word church or the name of a denomination. Having a keen interest

---

1. This essay was originally published in slightly different form in the *Christian Education Journal*, Series 3, Vol. 8, No. 2 (Fall 2011). The essay is republished here with permission of the *Christian Education Journal*.

in children and their spiritual health, we became curious about this ecclesial phenomenon. Our investigation provides a snapshot of the ministry with children and families in these developing and evolving contexts.

New-form churches are alternative forms of church that seem to be reacting against what the leaders perceive as inadequate traditional evangelical or mainstream ministries. These inadequacies may include ways of being "in community," ways of living out God's mission, or ways of accommodating the surrounding culture. It is as if it is in the "DNA" of these churches to *do* church differently.

Many of these new churches are intentional about filling perceived ministry gaps of more familiar church models. For example, some of them appreciate symbols and ancient liturgical forms of worship. One common thread among their leaders, however, is the view that they are ministering in a postmodern, post-Christian cultural context and therefore need to focus ministries on emerging adults— people roughly eighteen to thirty-five years old. These are the churches to which in this survey the term "new forms" refers.

Because about twenty years have passed since this phenomenon was started, primarily for young adult singles or couples without children, we wanted to see what their ministries looked like as many in this original target population have since married and begun families. We wanted to investigate how individual new-form churches seek to nurture children and families as their target population matures, and in particular to identify patterns, themes, and contrasts within the churches we visited.

A Bit of History on New Forms of Church

Since the church is a living organism, change in form is inevitable because the culture in which the church is located is ever changing, and always will be. The twentieth-century saw new forms of church arise, such as the Gospel Tabernacles that sprang up under theologically conservative leadership in cities large and small all over the United States. Influenced by nineteenth century revivalism, barn-like structures were built for evangelistically oriented ministries. Some of the tabernacles were meeting halls on summer campgrounds, but many others were constructed as churches. Reacting against "mainline liberalism," these structures, able to seat hundreds of people, were sturdy shells usually devoid of Christian symbols or other traditional trappings. Evangelistic rallies and Sunday evening services would attract large crowds. Though tabernacles can still be found in many places, their popularity began to wane in the 1950s and early '60s as the culture shifted, making the architecture and the name "tabernacle" seem out of date to a new generation of Christians.

Robert Webber (2002) describes three shifts within evangelicalism since 1950. The first phase, which began after World War II, he calls Traditional. It is marked by strong Sunday schools in neighborhood churches, with traditional worship through hymns and gospel songs and accompanied by an emphasis on mass evangelism.

Although not identified by Webber as a phase, during the late 60s a new church form arose called "body life." Beginning in California, this form emphasized personal stories during Sunday evening services and was accompanied by a resurgence of small group ministry, an approach established centuries earlier. This period, occurring post-Vatican II, included a surge of church renewal that swept not only evangelical churches, but even more strongly among liturgical and sacramental churches.

Next came the Pragmatic phase, beginning in the mid-1970s after the social revolutions of the 1960s, which provided another new form—the "Jesus' People" and "seeker" movements. Its approach was to create ministries that would be attractive to the non-churched and to those who had been "turned off" by established ministries and worship styles. This phase is marked by megachurches, contemporary music and worship style, and teaching ministries that target the needs of specific age groups. Seeker services that were culturally sensitive and "market-driven" began to replace mass evangelism.

The third phase, according to Webber, is led by "Younger Evangelicals," and its growth was catalyzed by September 11, 2001. He describes what this study calls a "new-form" movement as an urban, intercultural ministry occurring in small churches with mixed or converging forms of worship. Importance is placed on "intergenerational formation in communities" including the "priesthood of all believers," as well as "process evangelism." Characteristics of these new-form churches include intentionally identifying with Jesus, having an impact on the surrounding culture, and exemplifying aspects of communal life—concepts that are compatible with many churches beyond this movement but often manifest themselves uniquely in twenty-first-century forms. Their forms of worship may include centuries-old symbols and practices (not usually associated with evangelical, non-sacramental churches) such as Stations of the Cross, candles, stained glass windows, and religious art, including icons. Or, contrastingly, contemporary props such as worship backdrops of cyclone fence, metal staging, electronic instruments, and elaborate media may be used to create the setting for the worship service. These churches value hospitality, generosity, creativity, productivity, and spirituality (McKnight, 2007; Gibbs and Bolger, 2005).

As with all things new, the new forms of church are not without controversy. Some criticism seems valid; other critiques seem reactionary and based on personal taste. Webber's assessment of the theological commitment of each category addresses his perception of the distinctives of the three different phases: Traditionals see Christian theology as a rational worldview accompanied by a response of "keeping the rules"; Pragmatics tend to see theology as therapy and answers to personal needs leading to "prosperity and success"; and Younger Evangelicals see it as a community of faith that seeks "authentic embodiment" (Webber, 2002, p. 18).[2]

Jim Wilhoit, an educator and observer of the evangelical church in North America, is concerned about the "erosion of intentional practices of spiritual formation" (Wilhoit, 2008) that had been present in earlier generations. Recognizing that the forms of those earlier practices may be outdated at best, he questions what has replaced these forms such as corporate times of testimonies, prayer services, shared meals, instruction on global missions, summer camps and conferences—all of which had usually been intergenerational. At the outset of this study, given the trends noted by Webber, we wondered if we would find restoration of these practices in new-form churches, albeit adapted for twenty-first-century application.

In preparation for visiting new-form churches, we speculated how the characteristics of Webber's phases of evangelicalism would be manifested. Would there be congruity among these new forms, or

2. Note that the term "emerging church" is deliberately not used to describe any of these new-form churches due to lack of consensus or application by new-form leaders. Additionally, that phrase has been used in the literature to describe the church since the mid-1960s. It is a descriptor intended to reveal that the church has never been static but is changing in ways and rates depending on the historical context.

would there be evidence of earlier phases of church form and style? How would these churches view children? Would intergenerational experiences be seen as influences on children's spiritual formation? Would ministry leaders be mindful in the visions for their churches of the spiritual nature and development of children? These are some of the issues we sought to investigate through the lens of the faith communities of new-form churches.

Children and the Faith Community

Before delving into our findings, it is important to consider Scripture's view of children in relationship to adults of that time. But it is also necessary to get an overview of contemporary perspectives on children's spiritual formation.

A Glimpse of Children in the Biblical Story

The Book of Deuteronomy instructs the people of God that children are to be taught to love, obey, and fear the Lord God in the context of life, and are to assemble with adults to learn the things of God (Deut 6:1–3; 11:18–21; 31:12–13). Other passages describe how children were present with the whole faith community as they stood to hear from God, to weep before God, and to celebrate together (2 Chr 20:13; Ezra 10:1; Neh 12:43).

In the New Testament, Jesus' interactions with and his words about children are especially helpful. As recorded in Matthew 11:25–26, Jesus was praying, and he acknowledged that things are revealed to children which sometimes are hidden from those who are wise. Another time he used children as the model for entering the Kingdom of Heaven (Matt 18:2–3). After Jesus' triumphal entry into Jerusalem, he entered the temple, overthrew the tables of the moneychangers, and then healed those in need. The children acknowledged who Jesus was by shouting, "Hosanna to the Son of David," while the religious leaders and teachers simply became angry (Matt 21:12–16), An especially significant incident with children is recorded in the Gospel of Mark. People were bringing their children to Jesus, but the disciples tried to keep them from doing that. This made Jesus indignant. Jesus told the disciples to stop interfering and let the children come to him. In a public gesture that was atypical for a Jewish male of that day, Jesus took the children in his arms and blessed them (Mark 10:13–16).

From these few passages it is evident that children occupied an important place within the people of God. Being among God's people was significant for the spiritual formation and nurture of those children. Jesus himself viewed children highly by welcoming them and, significantly, by telling the adults to become like them for their own spiritual health. In a way it is as if the text is saying that it is not truly a faith *community* if the children are not present.

Contemporary Scholars' Perspectives on Children's Spiritual Formation

In the past twenty years considerable scholarly work has focused on the spiritual formation and spirituality of children. The following sources, among many others, are helpful in this regard: Karen Marie Yust's *Real Kids, Real Faith: Practices for Nurturing Children's Spiritual Lives* (2004); *Will Our Children Have Faith?* (2000) by John Westerhoff; Cathy Stonehouse's *Joining Children on the Spiritual Journey* (1998); *Godly Play: An Imaginative Approach to Religious Education* (1995) by Jerome Berryman; *The Religious Potential of the Child* (1992) by Sofia Cavalletti; and *The Spiritual Life of Children* (1990) by Robert Coles. Common themes in these works include the incredible capacity that children—even young children—have to experience and reflect on God. These scholars emphasize the formative value for adults and children alike to worship together and the significance for intergenerational participation in God's story while also hearing each other's stories. They also point out the importance of equipping parents for the powerful, unique role that they have in the spiritual formation of their children.

Journal articles provide additional relevant viewpoints. One, written from a Quaker perspective over forty years ago by sociologist Elise Boulding, recognizes the need children have for solitude. Boulding writes, "It is possible to drown children and adults in a constant flow of stimuli, forcing them to spend so much energy responding to the outside world that the inward life and the creative imagination which flows from it become stunted or atrophied" (Boulding, 1967, p. 8). She calls for enabling times of solitude, even shared solitude within the home, so children may have "a sense of who and what they are, whence they came, [and] their place in God's world" (1967, p. 37). Homes where "silence is lived" become inviting and restorative, allowing the "spirit-illumined intellect" to be developed and utilized creatively.

In addition to the need for solitude, psychologists Keltner and Haidt (2003) emphasize the value of *awe*, something that is also identified by Cavalletti, Berryman, and others. Though not written from a Christian perspective, the authors note that awe is "easily felt in nonsocial situations" (2003, p. 300), and is often accompanied by an autonomic nervous system reaction in the form of piloerection (goosebumps). These researchers state that the "potential power of awe . . . may bring pleasure to those who cultivate it in their lives," and "awe-inducing events may be one of the fastest and most powerful methods of personal change and growth" (2003, p. 312). If these findings regarding awe and solitude are valid for children, the implications for ministry and spiritual formation are profound.

Perspectives on Children from Leaders of the New Forms of Church

Ivy Beckwith, an experienced pastor of children, in the introduction to her book *Postmodern Children's Ministry: Ministry to Children in the 21st Century* (2004, p. 13ff), vividly describes her perspective on the current state of children's ministry as broken. She views it as broken when church leaders and senior pastors see children's ministry primarily as a marketing tool; when the most outwardly attractive program is assumed to be the most effective; when God is trivialized; when children are excluded from worship with adults; when programs and curriculum are used to introduce children to God; when churches create expensive "playlands and entice children to God through food fights and baptisms in the back of fire trucks. And perhaps most importantly, it's broken when the church tells parents that its programs can spiritually nurture their children better than they can. . . . A church program can't spiritually form a child, but a family living in an intergenerational community of faith can" (2004, p. 14).

Supportive of Beckwith's position, Carla Barnhill, an author and overseer of children's ministry in a new-form church, writes, "Rather than seeing children as somehow unfinished and unable to participate in the life of the church until they have learned something, we can encourage children to contribute to the community" (Barnhill,

2007, p. 56). Many churches view children as inherently *capable* in age appropriate ways of loving the Lord Jesus and *wanting* to be obedient to his teachings out of their love for him. Therefore, they see their ministries as an open system of nurture in which the children have dozens of "relatives"—surrogate parents, grandparents, aunts, uncles, and cousins—who get to know, love, and "co-parent" them. Barnhill feels multigenerational ministry is foundational in a child's spiritual formation.

This philosophy is evident in a website from a new-form church that states: "We seek to make special effort to allow opportunities for the full involvement of children in our spiritual formation. Children are not seen as simply empty vessels that we pour information into, but full participants in life with God." Later it explains, "You are welcome to use the baby room, but we find that crying babies remind us that it is good to take time to listen to one another cry—even during the 'important' times of life." Stating further, "God is already working in [children's] lives. As adults, our role is to guide them to an understanding of what that work is about." This view of children is compatible with the consensus of the contemporary scholars cited earlier.

Michelle Anthony is another current voice speaking to these issues. As pastor to families and children in a large new-form church, she addresses the crucial link between home and church. She testifies to a significant shift in her approach to ministry with children from one that engaged children in fun learning activities, which she acknowledges have a place, to one in which the primary goal is to grow spiritually healthy families in order to foster a new generation of kids and parents who are in active relationship to God (Anthony, 2008).

One might assume that there would be consensus on the view of children among leaders of these new forms of churches, but that is not the case. Some leading thinkers of this movement—Dan Kimball, Eddie Gibbs, Tony Jones, Doug Pagitt, Ryan Bolger, to name a few—write books that mention the role of children, albeit with less emphasis than in Beckwith's and Barnhill's works. Yet, scores of other writings on the new forms of church—including books and blogs—make little or no mention of children. Ministry with families, if present, often merely includes parenting classes. And some of the largest churches within this new-forms movement have web sites that require following multiple links before finding any mention of children. Most striking were the number of websites that made no mention of children or families, stating that they target their ministry to emerging adults. The question must be raised about what these congregations will do in the next ten years as their members marry and have families.

Some of our visits revealed disheartening attitudes toward children. The following are three incidents experienced at similarly styled, new-form megachurches—each serving several thousand people. First, in a sermon anecdote, a pastor recounted a long plane trip he recently had taken on which there were restless children. He stated, to the laughter of the audience, that he wanted to scoop up those children and put them in the overhead luggage compartment. Another example occurred while we met with the staff of a church and asked when the whole faith community worshipped together. One of the pastors responded, "The only way we'd ever get our kids into worship would be to give them all Game Boys." When asked if there were opportunities for children to be with other generations of the congregation, the youth pastor excitedly told of his "intergenerational/family" small group in which several entire families meet together regularly. After enjoying dessert together, the children go upstairs to play as a college student supervises, while the adults study and pray. Only while eating dessert was this experience intergenerational. The third instance is from a church with a multi-staff children's ministry. Over a meal, the ministry team, whose members all have relevant advanced degrees, explained that they yearn to have children participate more actively and frequently with the whole faith community, but this is in opposition to the vision of the main teaching pastor. The staff stated that they have to content themselves with making experiences for the children as God-centered and formational as possible—in itself a good thing though falling short of their vision for children.

Since Scripture seems to take for granted the presence of children in the faith community, a view that has not been upheld in recent decades by many larger evangelical churches, we wondered what the practices would actually look like in the new forms of church.

Study Method

Beginning in April 2008, we conducted on-site visits (21) and phone interviews (4) to a range of these new forms of churches in order to observe ministry practices and to ascertain the philosophies behind their ministry with children and families. Prior to that, we explored websites of many new-form churches, gathering data regarding their theology and philosophy of ministry with children especially, but also for families. Whenever possible we visited churches that the team had read about or knew by reputation; in-depth phone conversations were conducted with recommended churches where travel was not possible. We sought to discern if the explicit intent of the church was being carried out in its view of and ministry with children. We intended this to be an exploratory, descriptive survey looking for patterns and contrasts in the ways these new forms of church minister with children. Because we would be considering a wide range of contexts, the following protocol guided our observations:

> Geographic location (state or province)
>
> Surrounding location or neighborhood (urban, residential, suburban, etc.)
>
> Building structure (traditional church, mall, warehouse, school, home)
>
> Media (extent of media usage in the church's ministries)
>
> Size (small=under 300; med=300–1000; large=1,000–3,000; mega=over 3,000)
>
> Mission statement of ministry with children
>
> Ministry to, for, or with children (relational, participative, passive, or observational)
>
> Intergenerational emphasis (present or not)
>
> Intentional, planned experiences for children (present or not)
>
> Intentional, planned nurture of parents (present or not)
>
> Curricular focus (cognitive, reflective, narrative, presentational, or a combination)

Most of the above items are self-explanatory, but one requires further clarification. Ministry "to, for, or with children" refers to John Westerhoff's (2000) designation of ways of working with children. Simply stated, ministry "to" children is similar to a transmissive, schooling model when adults do things such as using content focused workbooks, learning tasks, or rote recitation to teach children about Christianity. "For" ministry intends to teach children through engaging things to watch: adults provide skits, games, videos, or music *for* children. Both *to* and *for* ministries tend to employ passive and observational modes of learning, even if children are active doing motions to music, and so forth. By contrast, in "with" ministry, the adult and child are together exploring the biblical story, seeking to meet God within that story. The adult is more of a guide than a traditional teacher. The *with* approach is more relational and participative. Each of these approaches has a place, but *with* ministry seems to align with the values noted earlier of some of the new forms of church.[3]

What We Found

The majority of the twenty-one site visits took place in the western two-thirds of North America. Phone interviews occurred with an additional four churches that could not be visited. The churches[4] represented a wide range of Christian traditions, though almost half of the churches (twelve out of twenty-five) identified themselves as independent or nondenominational churches. Of those claiming roots in a specific faith tradition, five were Anglican, two each were Episcopal and Christian and Missionary Alliance, and one each was Covenant, Reformed, Methodist, and Presbyterian. The significance of the churches without denominational ties is that each congregation must establish its own set of practices or doctrines regarding children. Issues of concern for these more independent churches included the age at which a child can partake in Lord's Supper or Eucharist, the form of baptism, as well as the expected age or faith experience of the one being baptized. Ethnically, all churches but one (Church D) were primarily Caucasian both in leadership and attendees. Table 1 in the Appendix represents the overall findings.

For fear of being overly simplistic, a summary of our observations can be made thusly: two categories or varying distinctives were noted—churches tended to have "DNA" that was either developed from cultural qualities that the leaders perceived the attendees

---

3. We were not surprised, though disappointed, to find all three forms of children's ministry implemented during our visits to the new forms of church. Ideally, in a thoughtful children's ministry, all the forms would be present in a given church, but *with* ministry should be the dominant worship experience.

4. Note: Churches in this survey are identified by letters of the alphabet from A thru Y, ranking them by size, and the state or province in which each is located. For additional information about the churches, please contact the lead author: scottie.may@wheaton.edu.

expected and wanted, or the leaders developed their churches around what they perceived was important for spiritual growth even if it was counter cultural. That distinction did not follow tradition or denominational lines. For example, Churches G and T are part of the same denomination. While Church G follows trends of the culture; Church T seeks practices that follows more ancient traditions.

Significance of Size

The location of the churches—whether urban or suburban or according to type of structure the church used—did not correlate with any of our questions regarding ministry with children and families. Six patterns surfaced, however, based on size of the church.

a) Most large and mega-churches we visited did not promote intergenerational participation or encourage children to be part of the main worship service. Space in the service was reportedly needed for adults.

b) Although the majority of the churches planned experiences specifically for children, children's ministry was "intentionally relational" among small to medium sized churches; the form was "intentionally presentational" among larger churches.

c) Smaller churches were more intentional in nurturing parents beyond simply offering parenting classes.

d) The curricular focus was more Bible-fact based and physically active in the large churches; many of the smaller churches employed a reflective, responsive approach to the Bible story.

e) Even though the majority of churches used media in some way, the larger the church, the more media was a key part of the ministries with children.

f) Realizing that this survey was very limited, we found discrepancies in most megachurches between what they intend to do (or say they are doing) and what is actually happening.[5] This

5. One example is Church G that desires children to "encounter God" yet the environment is so loud and fast paced that discerning God's presence would be a challenge for anyone. Another is Church A whose pastor recently wrote a widely read book that describes the importance of slowness to be able to sense being in God's

was not the case in the smaller churches that we observed.

Significance of Founding Purpose

Seven of the twenty-five churches surveyed (Churches C, G, J, M, N, Q, and V) started out targeting emerging adults (twenty to thirty year olds), often near university campuses. As the attendees aged, married, and started families, their children became "attached" to the core program or vision of the church rather than woven intentionally into the original strategy. Consequently, their ministry with children often occurred in a "silo," separated from the adults. The style of these ministries were often high energy and activity laden in apparent conflict with the values upon which several of those churches were founded. The resulting practices for children in these churches varied considerably from the new-form churches described earlier that began with the intent of generational inclusivity.

Several churches began with a vision of intentionally integrating children and families into their core values. Churches M, O, T, and U are some of those. Church M, a non-denominational church, ministers to children in a separate space in a presentational style, yet includes the children around the table for the celebration of the Lord's Supper. When observing this weekly ritual, it was as if a very large family was being welcomed to the loving warmth of a kitchen table, the favorite gathering spot for many families. Children were embraced, encouraged to offer praise to God, and allowed to voice requests for prayer—even childlike requests. This ritual, practiced since the founding of the church, seemed sufficient to bring the generations together as they lingered around the table to converse long after the benediction had been pronounced. "Punk"-looking adolescents hanging around outside the worship space said that they love their church because they feel such a part of it.

Variance in Ministry Practices

There was a remarkably wide range of ministry practices among new-form churches. Some of them had intentional, consistent ways to nurture the spiritual formation of children; some also had the

---

presence. When asked how that works out in the life of the church, the response of the church staff was that they had not read the book nor ever thought about that.

same for parents. A few of the churches embraced full integration of the generations, while others kept the generations separated by age. As we visited these churches, we also found a wide range of set-ups for corporate worship. Some churches had chairs or pews arranged in rows facing a stage or platform; other churches were set up "in the round." Not surprisingly, for churches set up in rows, the entire service took place on the stage or platform. For the churches in the round, the focal point was either the table for the Lord's Supper or Eucharist, or it was the pastor in the center delivering the sermon. Interestingly, we noticed generational integration of the faith community if the focal point of worship was the Eucharist, the exception being Church M described earlier. Table 2 in the Appendix reflects these practices.

Churches with intergenerational nurture of children

Church O is a small church, intentionally established to bring together all generations of the faith community. Their weekly Sunday afternoon corporate gathering begins with a time of greeting, welcoming and blessings; then a shared meal, followed by sharing of evidence of God's work during the past week. During the time of sharing, when young children got restless, an adult took the toddlers to a corner of the large room to engage in quiet play; another adult took the preschoolers to a table to make a craft. Then came time for the worship service. The space for worship was set up in the round with an altar that also served as the table for the Lord's Supper in the center. As the adults listened to their sermon, the children (elementary and pre-school) went to their own prepared space for an age-appropriate homily that was participative and reflective, employing symbols to aid reflection. Afterwards, the children were welcomed back to the main worship service in time for the Eucharist and celebration. The congregants served each other the elements of the sacred meal. Then the people gathered in triads to pray for each other. Each group welcomed a child into their midst to pray with them.[6] Then, prior to a benediction of blessing, the service concluded with a circle dance around the altar in the ancient Jewish folk tradition. Because this church values complete integration of

6. When I (Scottie) visited this church, a 10-year-old girl invited herself to pray with me and another woman. I was a visitor and stranger; this child prayed first, a memorable prayer for me that focused with praise on God's work in my own life.

children, every work team that does tasks for the church and community includes a child as part of the team.

Church U has a similar view of the church and welcomes children to be present at every church event, including classes and committee meetings. During the worship service, families are especially encouraged to worship together, although children may go to a specially prepared space during the message. This worship space, in a traditional-looking old church, was filled with couches in the round, rather than pews or chairs, giving it the feel of a very large living room. Child-protective gated areas in the corners of the sanctuary had couches and quiet toys, so that families with very young children could stay together during worship as their little ones safely crawled or toddled around. If a baby fusses or cries, the congregation knows to use that noise as a signal to pray for those in our world who are in need or cannot care for themselves. The leaders of this church seek to impart "language acquisition" of the Christian life for faith formation, a reason why they desire children to be present during the service. The church is full of the congregants' art: the work of adults was displayed in the worship space, while children's work filled the hallways. Family retreats happen often because they believe that more often "formation happens in context without content"—where children see adults live and interact with them without explicit biblical teaching, like co-parenting in faith.

Church T, intentionally multi-generational and inclusive, has a worship space in the round with the altar and table in the center. Following a time of robust worship music, these children leave during the message for their own time of reflection and response to a biblical story that relates to the theme of the main worship service. With their own liturgy modeled after the main liturgy (including a child-sized altar), the children's worship time draws attention to the presence of the Spirit of God. This time for the children includes a blessing and a benediction before parents pick them up to be part of the corporate Eucharistic celebration. For both children and adults, the focal point of the worship in their separate areas is the altar. Children are so valued here that in order "to be part of the church, adults 'must' be involved in ministry with children."[7] Additionally, congregants meet weekly in house groups established by geographic proximity, several

7. Personal interview with the children's ministry leader, October 6, 2009.

of which are family groups with all ages present for the whole time. In warm weather, picnics and barbeques are held for the entire faith family on the church's extensive property.

Although children in Church I stay with the whole congregation only through the worship music, ministry leaders carefully attend to the children's spiritual formation. Using the rotation model, the children engage in the same story for several weeks, each week involving a different learning modality such as art, drama, or directly on the biblical text. One of the weeks is always spent in a large room that they call "Sacred Space." This special area is a beautiful dark wood paneled room with large pillows in deep, rich colors, a fireplace, a kneeling bench for prayer, candles, and classic religious art on the walls. The pillows form a circle around a low table with candles that serves as an altar. Here a child may request special prayer or to be anointed with oil. The leaders state that the children love this space. Adults have mid-week opportunities to attend an "Institute" that equips them to be disciples of Jesus. During this time, the children study and also practice spiritual disciplines. Parents can enroll in a course called "Playing in God's Story," the aim of which is to help parents engage the whole family in the biblical story. Intergenerational interaction occurs as the entire faith family worships together at least sixteen times every year in order to hear each other's faith stories. Children are always present for the Lord's Supper, and, during Lent, the children are provided the opportunity to serve the elements to the whole congregation.

Church P chooses to be small and to stay small. This church seeks to live out the role of the faith community differently than most North American churches: They intend to practice community living and a rule of life. When interviewed, the pastor stated that discipleship happens in "dinner circles" that include the deliberate discipling of children in that setting. When establishing this church, the leaders asked themselves, "How do we give children an experience that engages them in intentional community?" Pictures of kids are everywhere because "we value keeping our children with us." Also, during worship, the church asks adults to "lay down their rights" for the sake of the children, and for the adults to embrace the opportunity to strengthen their own ability to focus on God amidst the sounds of the youngsters. The same is asked of the children, meaning that sometimes they need to be quiet for the sake of the adults. To ensure that single parents get a respite, the church asks other adults to "adopt" the single parents' children during the worship time. The pastor said, "We value the experience of keeping our children among us during worship, considering the Lord's reminder that they hold for us something of the Kingdom."

Churches H, I, O, T, and Y have taken forms of liturgy established by the early church and modified them so that today's children can experience and understand them. This is in keeping with values held by many leaders in the movement toward new forms of church, and also supports observations made by Webber (2002, p. 18).

Churches without intergenerational nurture of children

The worship services of the mega new-form churches in this survey were presentational, and the worship spaces were virtually free of Christian symbols, although one prominently displayed a rustic cross. During the corporate worship time, the space was dark with spotlights on the speaker or musicians. Children were not part of these experiences. Each had a concert-like feel. Attendees stayed at their seats and watched except when then stood to sing. Participation by singing was expected, but not necessary because the volume of the instruments often drowned out the voices of the worshipers. These churches seemed remarkably like the description Webber gives of the pragmatic church that was characteristic of the evangelical period of the late twentieth century, even though the churches in this survey identified themselves as new and innovative. Since these churches had experienced significant attendance growth, perhaps that made it difficult to retain their original ecclesiological values.

No new-form large or megachurch in our survey exhibited generational integration in that there were no times when the generations of the faith community were together. In an interview with the founding pastor of Church N,[8] he stated that the church began with children present during the worship service, but parents did not like that, so the church now has a separate experience for the children. Yet, a couple of the large churches had begun to shift their view of their responsibility to the children of their congregations.

Church E, a well-known megachurch similar to Church C, is one of them. In recent years, since its founding in 1997, it has

---

8. Conducted January 19, 2010.

undergone a significant paradigm shift in its ministry with children and families. Even though children's ministry is still separate, the leaders have gone from a *to* ministry to one that is *for* and *with*. They dispensed with the children's store where kids could "buy" candy and other items with points they had earned for attendance, memorizing Bible verses, and other activities. In the space where the store used to be, the children's leaders have placed a large cross where children can kneel to pray, have created an area for "stones of remembrances" celebrating God's action in their lives, and have erected a prayer wall where requests and praises are displayed. According to the ministry staff, the children do not appear to miss the store—they do not ask about the store or the rewards they used to buy with their points. During the children's large group gathering, about ten minutes is provided for silence and reflection. Even though the generations are rarely together except for baptisms, the leadership is committed to equipping parents to be comfortable and skilled in the spiritual nurture of their children.

Church G provides a striking contrast to Church E. Established in 1999, Church G now has about 3,000 attendees, including 600 children each weekend.[9] The church desires that the children perceive this to be "the best hour of their week," so they provide a climbing wall and large inflatables for bouncing in order to offer "play with a purpose." On the Sunday morning of our observation, the lesson for the day was about Abraham. Children (ages 4–12) chose an activity such as Wii, crafts, puzzles, or Nintendo for the first 20–30 minutes. Then came "Spin and Shout," when adults in ridiculous clothes clown around and everyone does silly dances to music unrelated to God or worship. Next followed the "yucky Olympics" where Vaseline was spread on faces to see if marshmallows when tossed would stick so leaders could have beards like Abraham. The leader then asked a few Bible related questions of the whole group but answered them himself in short order. Small group time, called "Connect," came next and lasted about five minutes. After that, kids came back to large group for a game show, followed by a comedic skit about Abraham and Sarah. (The kids were "warmed up" for this part by the question: "If you could give your boogers a flavor, what would it be and why?") The skit was followed by

9. Note: This church has a Wednesday evening service when elementary-age children are present with their parents through the music portion of the service.

ten more minutes in small groups to discuss the story, and the rest of the nearly two hours was spent in activity zones until the main service was over. A six-year-old reported, "This church is fun, and the best part of being there is playing." Church G uses a curriculum that bills itself as "high energy children's ministry." It delivers on that claim. It is clearly evident that intentional practices with children among new-form churches vary greatly.

Observed Patterns; Ensuing Questions

Here are several patterns noted during the exploration of new-form churches followed by questions relating to each pattern:

- The size of a church correlated inversely with the level of children's involvement with the whole faith community—the larger the church, the more removed children were into their own separate spaces. *Since the North American culture tends to equate size with success and effectiveness, what might this mean for the children who are part of those huge churches now? Will they feel part of the faith community, or will they need to be re-evangelized as adults?*

- Churches established at the outset with children and families as part of their purpose were more successful in maintaining that involvement than churches that attempted to shift in this direction later. *If some churches are content to be intentionally small because they feel that a communal approach is a better way to nurture a child's faith, should large churches adapt their ministry approaches with children? If so, how?*

- The amount of media used in the worship service paralleled the amount of media used in children's ministry. Several churches employed "media-driven" presentations; others, primarily smaller churches, did not use media at all. *Does it matter if worship experiences are media-driven, media-enhanced, or without media? How might the impact of media usage in ministry on the church's children be assessed? Is engagement or attention effective evaluative criteria?*

- Churches that valued interaction between generations viewed children as full participants in the faith community. *What are possible explicit and implicit implications for children if they are not full participants?*

- Generational barriers seemed nonexistent if the focal point of worship was the communion table, whether or not the church was from a sacramental tradition (e.g., Church H and X were; Churches O and T were not). *In what ways might churches that place more emphasis on Bible teaching than on the sacraments achieve generational harmony?*

- New-form megachurches made quality use of media, sound, and staging but lacked visual symbols or banners that were explicitly Christian. *Given the belief among some traditions that those visual symbols are helpful, what difference does it make, if any, in a child's formation if Christian symbols are absent?*

Questions for Future Study

Since this was intended to be an exploratory survey, no attempt has been to draw definitive conclusions about new-form churches' ministry with children. Consequently, there are unanswered questions including the following that call for focused research:

- Is the place of children within the faith community as evidenced in both testaments applicable today? If so, in what form? If not, why not?

- What relevance does Jesus' view of children have for today's new-form churches and, for that matter, more traditional churches?

- If some churches are content to be intentionally small because they feel that is a better form of Christian community, why are other churches who also state they value community so focused on attracting large numbers of people that they end up ministering in generational and affinity silos?

- Does the size of a church in and of itself make a difference? Is size a factor that influences a person's choice of church?

- If "this church meets my needs" is a view characteristic of North America's consumer culture that influences the decision of many adults, what impact does that have on their children?

- What kinds of intentional, habitual practices in the life of the church enhance the formation of all the people of God toward conformity to the character of Christ?

- What long-term effects, if any, might church practices have on children?

- If there is validity in the writing of Boulding (1967, p. 8) that children can "drown" in a "constant flow of stimulation," and, if Keltner and Haidt (2003, p. 312) are correct that solitude and a sense of "awe" are powerful for personal change and growth, how are these concepts best communicated to parents and children's ministry leaders?

These questions are significant for any church to ask, but this is especially true for churches that seek to forge a new or renewed perspective of what it means to be the church in the twenty-first century. We challenge new-form churches, especially the large and megachurches because of our findings, to be sure that their *ministry practices* are actually fulfilling their *ministry purposes*.

Personal Reflection

For the past twenty years, I (Scottie) have taken delight in researching and writing about ways children are able to enter into sacred space and encounter the living God through the Holy Spirit in all kinds of contexts.[10] This survey of new-form churches has contributed significantly to my realization of the breadth of ways the church ministers with children. It has been especially encouraging to see many of the young new-form congregations with a "DNA" that seeks to bring the whole faith community, including children, into the presence of God during times of corporate worship, shared meals, and community service. I am very hopeful that these mainly small and mid-size churches can become voices that lead others to join them, as they seem to actively resist the influence of popular culture as much as possible as they seek to guide the people of God to be faithful and obedient followers of Jesus Christ.

---

10. I have written about this work in *Perspectives on Children's Spirituality: Four Views* (Michael Anthony, ed., Nashville: Broadman Holman, 2006), and coauthored with Cathy Stonehouse, *Listening to Children on Their Spiritual Journey* (Grand Rapids: Baker, 2010).

Table 1

Summary of the Data from the Survey of the New Forms of Church

Geog. Locat	Size	Mission Statement	Inter-gen. Emph	Ministry TO, FOR, WITH	Intentional Experiences for Children	Intentional Nurture for Parents	Curricular Focus
ChrchA -CA	Mega	Teach kids the Gospel for Gospel living. Conform to overarching biblical principles.	No	To	Yes, separate	Happens in their own Bible 'college'	Cognitive and presentational
ChrchB -WA	Mega	Know culture, love people, see lives transformed to live for Jesus. Nothing specifically relating to children or families.	No	To/For	Yes, separate	Parenting class	Cognitive and presentational
ChrchC -MI	Mega	We want kids to know God, and as part of our community, develop compassion and justice to serve.	No	To/With	Yes, separate	Parenting class	Biblical narrative w/ presentation
ChrchD -CA	Mega	To have a fun, safe place for kids to learn about Christ and Christ-like character.	No	To/With	Yes, separate	None	Cognitive, hands-on
ChrchE -CA	Mega	A community where kids can hear God's truth, experience His love, grace, and respond to Him with freedom; soul formation.	Yes	For/With	Yes, separate	Emphasizes equipping families	Story plus contemplation & response
Chrch F -GA	Mega	Strives to be biblical w/ relevant teaching, heart-felt worship, teaching kids to love God's word.	No	For	Yes, separate	Yes, 5x per year	Cognitive
Chrch G -KY	Mega	Spaces designed with kids in mind so that they'll have a chance to encounter a God who loves them in a way they understand.	On occasion	For	Yes, but mainly separate	None	High energy activities w/ presentation

Geog. Locat	Size	Mission Statement	Inter-gen. Emph	Ministry TO, FOR, WITH	Intentional Exper-iences for Children	Intentional Nurture for Parents	Curricular Focus
ChrchH -IL	Lrge	Sanctuary of Transformation: a safe place where people can meet God and be transformed into strong, confident, active servants of Jesus Christ. No statement for children.	No	With (but 'to' temporarily)	Yes Integrated &separate	Not much	Giving children an identity as beloved
ChrchI -MO	Lrge	Doesn't *have* a mission, *is* one. You can belong before believing. Sees children as part of community; wants them to enter into The Story.	Yes	With	Yes integrated &separate	"Institute" to help parents learn nurture	Rotation model plus reflection
ChrchJ -IL	Med	Passion for Jesus; transforming lives; globally reproducing churches. None specific for children.	Yes	To	Yes, Integrated &separate	Hopeful. Resource for family devos.	Cognitive (Hoping it's relational too.)
ChrchK -NE	Med	Gospel content, cause, and community. No for statement for children.	No	To	Yes, separate	Not evident	Cognitive
ChrchL -PA	Med	Loving community for children & families. Lead & equip parents. Goal: freedom and grace in Christ.	Yes	For	Yes, separate	Strong emphasis	Hands-on & presentational
ChrchM -IL	Med	Teach children Christian principles and the love of Jesus thru various modalities through drama, song, video, and games.	No	To/For	Yes integrated &separate	None	Cognitive, presentational
ChrchN -CA	Med	To care, shepherd, and be on the mission on which Jesus sent His disciples.	No	To/For	Yes	Being developed	Hands-on

Geog. Locat	Size	Mission Statement	Inter-gen. Emph	Ministry TO, FOR, WITH	Intentional Exper-iences for Children	Intentional Nurture for Parents	Curricular Focus
Chrch O -MN	Sm	Ancient way of Gospel living w/ all generations to discover what following Jesus faithfully as God's people looks like today.	Yes	With	Yes, integrated &separate	Holistic in context	Catechesis of the Good Shepherd
ChrchP -PA	Sm	Grace acknowledged in worship, shared in community; extended in service. None specific for children.	Yes	With	Yes, integrated	Holistic	Godly Play monthly for all ages
ChrchQ -WA	Sm	Focuses on young adults, calling them to friendship with God in Christ Jesus. Nothing for children.	No	None	No	None	N/A
ChrchR -WA	Sm	Called them to community to dream, play, relate in God's Kingdom, engaging w/ the Trinity to heal the world.	Yes	With	Yes, Integrated	Hopeful-target group: new parents	Non-programs w/ kindermusik & Godly Play
ChrchS -AB	Sm	A place to belong and to become closer to God, closer to each other and closer to the world in age appropriate ways.	Yes	For/With	Yes, separate	Family small groups	Hands-on & presentational
ChrchT -IL	Sm	No matter what age, we gather to learn about God and feed on his Word and nurture each other in the ways of Christ.	Yes	For/With	Yes integrated &separate	Holistic	Rotation w/ Reflection
ChrchU -MN	Sm	Has *dreams*; no mission statement. All ages are full participants.	Yes	For/With	Yes, integrated	Holistic	Rotation w/ Reflection
ChrchV -GA	Sm	A church for "people with worts." None for children.	No	N/A	No	None	N/A

Geog. Locat	Size	Mission Statement	Inter-gen. Emph	Ministry TO, FOR, WITH	Intentional Exper-iences for Children	Intentional Nurture for Parents	Curricular Focus
Chrch W -AB	Sm	Unclear Nothing specific regarding children	No	N/A	No	No	N/A
ChrchX -IL	Sm	To be a church that lives life together —all generations.	Yes	With	Yes, integrated &separate	Holistic	Cognitive
ChrchY -IL	Sm	To introduce non-churched children to the love of Jesus.	Yes	With	Church established *for* children	Holistic	Story, contemplation, liturgy

Grid Categories & Explanations:

The assigned letters are sequenced by church size: from largest to smallest.

Geographic Location (meaning state or province)

Physical Location (urban, residential, suburban, etc.)

Type of Structure (traditional church, mall, warehouse, etc.)

Size (sm=<300; med=300-1000; large = 1,000-3,000; mega=>3000)

Mission Statement

Intergenerational Emphasis

Ministry to, for, or with children (See John Westerhoff's *Will Our Children Have Faith?*)

Intentional Experiences for Children

Intentional Nurturing of Parents

Curricular Focus (if available—cognitive, reflective, narrative, etc.)

Contact made (V=Visit, T=Telephone interview)

References

Anthony, M. (2008, October). *New paradigms for ministry.* Presented at the Conference of the National Association of Professors of Christian Education, Atlanta, GA.

Barnhill, C. (2007). The postmodern parent: Shifting paradigms for the ultimate act of re-creation. In D. Pagitt and T. Jones (Eds.), *An emergent manifesto of hope* (pp. 51–58). Grand Rapids: Baker.

Beckwith, I. (2004). *Postmodern children's ministry: Ministry to children in the 21st century.* Grand Rapids: Zondervan.

Berryman, J. (1995). *Godly play: An imaginative approach to religious education.* Minneapolis: Augsburg.

Boulding, E. (1967). Children and solitude. *International Journal of Religious Education, 43* (1), 7–9 and 36–67.

Cavalletti, S. (1992). *The religious potential of the child.* Oak Park, IL: Catechesis of the Good Shepherd.

Coles, R. (1990). *The spiritual life of children.* Boston: Houghton Mifflin.

Gibbs, E., & Bolger, R. (2005). *Emerging churches: Creating Christian community in postmodern cultures.* Grand Rapids: Baker.

Hirsch, A. (2007. July 11). A working definition of missional church [Blog]. Retrieved from www.theforgottenways.org/blog/2007/07/11/a-working-definition-of-missional-church/.

Keltner, D., & Haidt, J. (2003). Approaching awe, a moral, spiritual, and aesthetic emotion. *Cognition and Emotion, 17* (2), 297–314.

McKnight, S. (2007, January 19). Five streams of the emerging church: Key elements of the most controversial and misunderstood movement in the church today. *Christianity Today, 51*(2). Retrieved from www.christianitytoday.com/ct/2007/february/11.35.html

Stonehouse, C. (1998). *Joining children on the spiritual journey.* Grand Rapids: Baker.

Sweet, L. (Ed.). (2003). *The church in emerging culture.* Grand Rapids: Zondervan.

Webber, R. (2002). *Younger evangelicals: Facing the challenges of the new world.* Grand Rapids: Baker.

Westerhoff, J. (2000). *Will our children have faith?* Revised edition, Harrisburg, PA: Morehouse.

Wilhoit, J. (2008). *Spiritual formation as if the church mattered: Growing in Christ through community.* Grand Rapids: Baker.

Yust, K. M. (2004). *Real kids, real faith: Practices for nurturing children's spiritual lives.* San Francisco: Jossey-Bass.

13

What's in a Name?
Forming the Identity of Children through Christian Naming Ceremonies

David M. Csinos

In 1959, the United Nations passed the declaration on the universal rights of the child, laying out what it believes to be central characteristics of childhood in need of protection. Item three reads: "The child shall be entitled from his [*sic*] birth to a name and a nationality." Evidently, the UN believes that one's name is an essential aspect of one's identity and well-being—it is a verbal and written symbol that speaks of one's self, and can provide much meaning into who a person is and from where a person has come.

Some Christian traditions recognize the importance of names by including a public declaration of a child's name at baptism.[1] Such declarations can have a strong sense of identity formation for

---

1. For example, the *Rites of the Catholic Church* instructs the celebrant of a child's baptism to begin with the following question: "What name do you give your child (or: have you given?)" (Bishop's Committee on Liturgy 1983, 214). The parents then announce the name they have chosen for the child that is about to be baptized. The *Book of Common Worship* for the Presbyterian Church (U.S.A.) includes a formal introduction of the child by the officiant after the opening scripture reading: "On behalf of the session, I present N., (son, daughter) of N., and N., to receive the sacrament of Baptism" (1993, 405). This formal introduction explicitly connects the child's identity—which is tied to one's name—to that of their family. While the liturgies for baptism in both of these traditions include a formal announcement of the child's name, a time for explaining the meaning behind the name of the child and the reason that this name was chosen is omitted.

children as they grow and learn about their name, and about the community in which it was formally bestowed on them. However, groups that practice believer's baptism—like Anabaptists and many evangelical denominations—do not always include an intentional and formal naming component in their infant and child dedication services. In fact, the meaning behind these dedications may be ambiguous, and can lack a sense of identity-formation for the child, parents, and community.

Research into children and the world's religious traditions demonstrates one way this problem may be remedied is by refashioning in appropriate contemporary forms, practices of Christian naming ceremonies that can provide children with a strong sense of identity. I have researched several religious traditions (Christianity, Judaism, Hinduism, and African religions, for example), Anabaptist theology, and the work of social scientists, and although this forms a relatively diverse base to draw information from, it cannot be denied that my thoughts in this chapter remain subject to my western cultural assumptions and Anabaptist religious biases. Nevertheless, this chapter is neither so narrow nor so exclusive as to be unfit for a wider audience. By stating clearly my biases and assumptions, I hope to engage a wide variety of individuals in meaningful conversation about how Christian traditions and groups can use naming ceremonies as a way of intentionally forming the identity of the children in their midst, specifically, an assigned collective identity that is appropriate for Anabaptists in the twenty-first century (Templeton and Eccles 2006).

To do this, it is important to begin with a brief overview of some distinctives of Anabaptist theology, followed by some recent social science research on identity and acculturation. These two sections will form the foundation for my discussion of naming ceremonies. The third section of this chapter focuses on naming ceremonies and includes some general ideas about how Christian naming ceremonies can be an appropriate way of providing children with an assigned collective identity as a member of an Anabaptist community and the wider Anabaptist tradition; an identity through which they can grow, develop, and explore the world around them.

For years, people have been saying that it takes a village to raise a child, but in contexts experiencing secularization, postmodernism, and a growing plurality of cultures, churches can no longer assume that the wider village or context will aid the church in fostering a Christian identity in children. Pretending this to be otherwise would be what Thomas Groome (2009) refers to as "naïve socialization" (86). Referring to his once-Catholic boyhood home in Ireland, Groome writes, "faith communities must be all the more intentional to social-ize/enculturate people into religious identity; what my old Irish village once did by osmosis now requires deliberate crafting and planning" (2009, 86).

By infusing child dedication services with intentional means of socializing children into a family, community, and identity, nam-ing ceremonies can play a key role in this "deliberate crafting and planning" for enculturating children into a Christian way of life. It transforms the "naïve socialization" of child dedication services— which may have been appropriate when Christianity was a dominant, widely-held aspect of Western societies—into practices that bestow on children not only a name, but the embryonic elements of an identity, all wrapped within a family, faith community, and religious tradition.

Naming ceremonies, as a way of intentionally and formally be-stowing names on children, can be a powerful means of forming chil-dren's identities very early in life. When paired with more typical child dedication services, they infuse these moments with meaning that can remain absent without a more formal naming ceremony. By bestow-ing names on a child in front of a community, parents claim for the child the family tradition into which he or she is born, the religious tradition in which he or she will be raised, and hopes and dreams for who the child is and who he or she is to become.

Anabaptist Theology and Community

The primary lens through which I will discuss Christian naming cer-emonies is the Anabaptist tradition. In addition to offering a theo-logical framework for understanding communities and the formation of religious identity, Anabaptist theology provides a foundation that can support Christian naming practices. As a theological tradition focused on the community of faith, Anabaptism offers much insight into socialization and the nature of the faith community into which children and other members are to be socialized. Furthermore, since this tradition seeks to foster a particular, often counter-cultural way of life, Anabaptists have given much thought to the issue of identity formation and the social dynamics of a community.

Anabaptism first arose in response to the Protestant Reformation of the sixteenth century. Early Anabaptists were initially followers of leaders of the Reformation, but they believed that the reformers compromised their agenda by setting up state churches and failing to address the issue of church discipline. They departed ways with these reformers and continued what the Reformation started by radically separating themselves from the state—thus, their movement became known as the Radical Reformation. These radical reformers saw themselves as part of the true, invisible church that is faithful to Christ through obedience and discipline, a view that has its roots in Augustine (Yoder, 251–52).

Since their opponents referred to them as ana-baptists—that is, those who are baptized again—many people believe that the main issue on the early Anabaptist agenda was believer's baptism, which Anabaptists saw as an act of obedience following conversion. Yet baptism was not the main focus of early Anabaptist leaders; it was simply an outward sign of a greater issue—church discipline. In this tradition, baptism indicates that a person commits oneself to a community in which that person lives a life of discipleship and to which that person is subject to discipline. Yoder (2004) noted that Anabaptists practiced believer's baptism based on personal testimony before the community, not because infants and young children could not understand anything about the faith, but because they could not be subjected to the community's discipline through confession as a member of the true, invisible church (274).

Discipline was important to the life of the Anabaptist community because they believed that what is most vital to the Christian life is not baptism, but obedience to God and the teachings of Jesus (Simons 1984b, 410–11). Radical reformers believed that the established churches had drifted from the initial vision of Jesus and early Anabaptists sought to reestablish the vision of the early Church. Thus, they fostered a strong sense of community, for their community was seen as the holy remnant that remained faithful to God. Discipline was an essential means for maintaining the community's integrity as this remnant. John Howard Yoder (2004) has noted that "when the Anabaptists were asked for the reasons for their 'separation' from the state church, their answer was not 'because you do not have the proper baptism,' but rather, 'because you have no discipline'" (228).

Menno Simons, one of the key leaders of the Anabaptist movement, used a number of metaphors to describe the importance and purpose of discipline within a community. He likened a church without discipline to a city without gates—anyone could enter and leave as they pleased (Simons 1984d, 724). He also stated that a little leaven leavens the whole lump and one bad sheep spoils the whole flock (Simons 1984a, 471), indicating that he believed in the power of socialization. That is why excommunication of the apostate was necessary and why he encouraged parents to keep their children from "good-for-nothing children" and other negative influences (Simons 1984c, 951). The leaders of the movement, including Simons, held that "parents and the Christian community together are responsible for nurturing children toward voluntary commitments of faith and discipleship" (Miller 2001, 195). Thus, Simons believed that it was vital for the entire faith community to protect children from harmful influences. Discipline and excommunication helped to ensure that those inside the community remained part of the pure and faithful remnant and that apostate members would not negatively affect the lives of group members and the integrity of the community.

Contemporary Anabaptists continue to foster a strong sense of community and at least some degree of separation (or distinction) from the world. Sara Wenger Shenk, an Anabaptist educator, notes that the main purpose of the church school—and the ministry of the church in general—is to nurture the loyalty of people to this alternative community of faith rather than loyalty to a particular nation or cultural ethos. She writes, "the church, if it is to be a nonconformed community, must socialize its young into its ethic and ethos" (Shenk 2003, 71), that is, the church is to be a formative place in which members are enculturated and socialized into a particular way of life, or *habitus*, that is modeled on the teachings and life of Jesus (Shenk 2003, 72, 77).

All people are formed by the cultures in which they engage, so it is important to foster a way of life that has a hand in forming people who identify themselves as members of this community known as the church. Yet within most contemporary Anabaptist traditions, it is expected that community members will regularly interact with the world, for Anabaptism stresses that the church should work for justice and peace in the world. What is more, Hauerwas (2001) is correct in stating that "Christians are never just members of the church but must rightly live in the world. As long as people have to make a living, there is no way to withdraw" (94).

Therefore, in order to nurture an identity as a member of a set-apart community that engages and constructively participates in the world, Anabaptists do well to foster a strong sense of community and in-group solidarity while also encouraging people to develop bicultural identities as members of the church who interact with the world. This is done, as Shenk has noted, by seeing Anabaptist practices and stories as centrally formative to the life of the faith community (2003, 18); that is, by "remembering who you are" and fostering identity as a member of the Anabaptist community (Shenk 1995).

One way to nurture such an identity early in one's life is through Christian naming ceremonies that help children to remember who they are—members of particular families, faith communities, and faith traditions. Names are loaded with meaning about the family, ethnicity, religion, and community to which children belong and, as they grow older and reflect on their names, children can recall that they are not random human beings—they are people who are members of communities and families. Such reflection can powerfully help children and adolescents to form their own identities. To explain this assertion further, it is helpful to draw from social science research into identity theory and acculturation in order to further strengthen the foundation generated by Anabaptist theology.

Insights from the Social Sciences

The past few decades have yielded a wealth of information about human identity that is useful for examining how Christian naming ceremonies can foster identity formation in young people. This information furthers our discussion of identity by adding a new voice to the conversation, one grounded on research into the area of identity formation and contexts that aid in forming appropriate identities. Even though much of this research is based on western views and assumptions, it remains useful providing that one acknowledges these biases.

One recent work that is helpful in understanding religious identity is Templeton and Eccles' essay on spiritual development and identity processes. These scholars identify key variables that affect identity as it relates to spiritual development. First, identity can be personal and identity can be collective (Templeton and Eccles 2006, 252)—and both are crucial aspects of an individual's identity (Phinney 2000, 28). The authors speak of personal identity as spiritual and they assert that, since all children have an inherent connection with the transcendent—what Hay and Nye (2006) refer to as relational consciousness—all people begin life with a personal identity (Templeton and Eccles 2006, 258).

Collective identity, on the other hand, deals with religious communities and traditions, and this aspect of identity can be assigned or chosen (Templeton and Eccles 2006, 253). When it is assigned, as is the case with infants and younger children, Templeton and Eccles argue that the child makes no choice about whether or not to be a member of a religious tradition or community. As the child grows, however, he or she can begin to make decisions about whether or not to attend religious services and be a member of a community and, thus, a child's assigned collective identity can gradually become a chosen collective identity—a religious self-identification through which one's spiritual life is interpreted, practiced, and nurtured (Templeton and Eccles 2006, 253–54).

Jean Phinney notes a similar trend in her research into ethnic identity. She identified three stages of ethnic identity: unexamined (which she connects with children), exploring (which she sees as most salient during adolescence),[2] and achieved ethnic identity (2003, 74). Phinney also holds that infants and young children are, for the most part, assigned their identity and largely begin to explore what it means to be a member of an ethnicity (or religion) as they reach adolescence (2003, 73). In all these stages, however, one's community plays an important role in identity formation. In Phinney's words (2003), "The community and larger setting in which ethnic group members live and work have an important impact on ethnic identity. . . . The vitality

2. Jeffrey Jensen Arnett's research into emerging adulthood has led him to speculate that many young people in today's industrialized nations engage in identity exploration not only during adolescence, but also during what he has called *emerging adulthood*, a new developmental phase beginning around the age of eighteen and lasting often until the mid- to late-twenties (Arnett 2004, 8-10).

of the ethnic community is clearly central to ethnic identity" (76). The same is true for religious identity—it is more likely to become chosen if it is fostered within a positive and supportive community. A child that is raised in a warm and encouraging community has a greater chance of moving from only having an assigned collective identity to also possessing a chosen collective identity, for example, as a person born into a faith community in the Mennonite tradition. As we will see, Christian naming ceremonies can be a powerful means of kick-starting the development of achieved and chosen collective identities.

The work of Templeton, Eccles, and Phinney clearly hold to some western assumptions, like a tendency to regard young children as passive and lacking in personal agency. Nevertheless, their work is helpful in recognizing that children exist and are shaped by cultures and communities of which they do not completely choose to be a part. All of this speaks of the important roles and responsibilities of parents and faith communities and it echoes Simons' advice to protect children from negative influences.

Since the concern in this chapter is naming ceremonies, the focus is on infants whose collective religious identity is assigned and unexamined. Yet the hope of most parents is that as the child grows and begins to explore identities, he or she will choose to stay within the religious tradition into which the child was born and will develop an achieved and chosen collective identity as a member of this community and tradition. My assertion is that naming ceremonies can help foster this progression from an assigned collective identity to one that is also chosen and achieved. The term *collective identity* must not lead one to think that one's religious identity is only played out in a religious community. As mentioned, an Anabaptist identity requires that people are able to maintain this identity while engaging and participating in one's surrounding context.

This brings us to the realm of acculturation, which refers to the process and the cultural changes that result from two cultures interacting with one another (Castro 2003, 9); when a minority culture comes into contact with a dominant culture, both cultures often experience changes (Castro 2003, 10). As a minority culture within the dominant landscape of North America or another host culture, Anabaptist communities (as well as many other religious traditions) can be examined through the lens of acculturation.

John Berry proposed four acculturation strategies that have been helpful in studying how people engage in multiple cultures, particularly from a Western standpoint. It is important to remember that his framework—like all good theories— is a tool for understanding human behavior; yet it is culturally-constructed and does not adequately address or describe human experience in all contexts. Nevertheless, with an awareness of its limitations, Berry's framework of acculturation strategies remains quite helpful in understanding different ways in which children form identities as members of a community or culture that exists within a wider context.

In his framework, he asserts that there are two key issues of acculturation of an individual or a group: a preference for preserving and maintaining one's culture and a preference for participating and having contact with the host culture, that is, the wider society as well as other minority cultures (Berry 2003, 22). As outlined in Table 1, the ways in which minority persons or groups deal with these two issues determines what Berry refers to as their acculturation strategy. Those who wish to have high levels of engagement and participation in the host culture and do not seek to uphold their minority cultural identity make use of the *assimilation* strategy. The *marginalization* strategy is used by those who do not wish to maintain their minority culture and are not interested in being involved or having relationships with the dominant culture. People or groups who highly value the maintenance of their heritage or culture and do not wish to participate in or associate with the wider society use the *separation* strategy. Finally, those who wish to maintain their heritage or culture as they engage with and participate in the wider society make use of the *integration* strategy (Berry 2003, 24).

Table 1
Acculturation Strategies of Minority Groups and Individuals
Adapted from Berry (2003, 23).

Preference to have relationships with other groups	Preference to maintain minority culture and identity	
	High	Low
High	Integration	Assimilation
Low	Separation	Marginalization

Multiple empirical studies demonstrate that integration (which can also be referred to as biculturalism) is the most preferred and adaptive of the acculturation strategies (Castro 2003, 20; Phinney et al. 2001, 502). This may not be surprising, for, as Vanessa Castro (2003) notes, "social groups provide individuals with a framework of reference for orientation in the social world and self-definition" (39). People who use the acculturation strategy of integration maintain a strong relationship with their original culture as they actively engage with the host or dominant culture. This provides a person with an identity that includes a solid sense of self-in-community, yet remains flexible and open enough to actively engage with other contexts and cultures.

Focusing our attention on children, Berry's framework highlights how a community's strategy for addressing difference (integration, assimilation, separation, or marginalization) can socialize children into developing a similar strategy in their personal encounters with difference. Thus, faith communities do well to help children develop identities that involve integration—that is, identities involving membership in a minority culture (like an Anabaptist community or tradition) that are strong enough to avoid assimilation and marginalization yet open enough to avoid separation. Without an integrated identity, a child whose religious identity differs from that of the wider context (for example, an Anabaptist in a an elementary school where many peers and teachers are not religious) may deal with this difference by shedding one's Anabaptist identity in order to assimilate into the wider nonreligious context or by holding tightly (too tightly) to one's identity as a member of an Anabaptist community and withdrawing from the wider society.

Likewise, the faith community or tradition into which a child is born can make use of these acculturation strategies in their encounters with wider society. For example, a community that utilizes the separation strategy can isolate itself with the hope of maintaining its purity amidst a world seen as secular and sinful. This can lead to the ghettoization of the community as members attempt to form their own worlds within the enclaves of society in which they can interact with other members of the community. As children engage in their communities, they pick up on cues offered by their communities about preferred acculturation strategies.

The issue of acculturation becomes more complex when one understands that not only do minority persons and groups use acculturation strategies, but the dominant or host culture also has expectations about acculturation (see Table 2). While integration is the preferred acculturation strategy for minorities, it is most successful when the dominant society accepts cultural diversity through the multicultural (or intercultural) strategy. In Berry's words (2003), "a mutual accommodation is required for integration to be attained" (24).

Table 2

Acculturation Expectations of the Dominant Society
Adapted from Berry (2003, 23).

Preference to have relationships with other groups	Preference to maintain minority culture and identity	
	High	Low
High	Multiculturalism	Melting Pot
Low	Segregation	Exclusion

Furthermore, integration is a collective strategy and, thus, it is most likely to occur when other individuals in one's minority group also seek to maintain their cultural heritage while participating in the wider society (Berry 2003, 25). Should they wish to abandon it through assimilation or marginalization, a person seeking to be integrative would find themselves struggling to maintain their culture when there is, at least in one's immediate circles, no minority culture left to maintain. When a person or culture uses an acculturation strategy that is not accepted or welcomed in the wider culture, they may experience acculturation stress (Berry 2003, 26).

All of this shows acculturation is not a purely individualistic phenomenon. Although individual persons may choose whether or not to engage the wider culture and maintain their minority culture, one's preference is influenced by one's network of relationships with those in the cultural group and the dominant society (Berry 2003, 30). That is, acculturation strategies are an outcome of both personal, psychological factors and interpersonal, sociocultural factors (Berry 2003, 5).

This is why acculturation strategies are helpful in understating the identity formation of children. Christian traditions and faith communities influence whether or not members participate in the wider society and whether or not they seek to maintain their identity as Christians. A faith community and religious tradition can encourage children to make use of particular acculturation strategies. Through Christian naming ceremonies, communities can offer a child a connection to his or her family, congregation, and religious tradition that can ground them as they interact with and become integrated into the wider society.

Over the years, a number of Anabaptists traditions and groups have been separatists. They have sought to maintain their Anabaptist identity and culture while remaining distant from and avoiding participation from the wider society. One need only think of the Amish in Pennsylvania or the Old Order Mennonites in southwestern Ontario to see the separatist strategy in action in particular Anabaptist communities.

However, in the contemporary world, where identity must be managed (Côté and Levine 2004, 126), a strategy of separation may be less effective than it has been in the past. Through globalization and technological advances, human beings now hold multiple identities and come into daily contact with countless other identities. Therefore, separation from the world is much more difficult to maintain, and does not prepare people for contact with difference that will surely occur in today's globalized world. Additionally, the Anabaptist commitment to furthering God's reign on earth through peacemaking and justice-seeking demands some degree of interaction with the world. Thus, Anabaptists do well to use the integration strategy as way of maintaining obedience to Christ within a Christian community as primary to one's identity, yet offering freedom to constructively and confidently engage in and explore the wider society. As I will show, naming ceremonies can help to foster such an identity—one that is chosen, achieved, and integrated.

Christian Naming Ceremonies

Having built a foundation using Anabaptist theology and theories from the social sciences, the focus of this chapter shifts once again to naming ceremonies. This section utilizes this theological and social scientific foundation to answer the following questions: How do naming ceremonies help to form children within an Anabaptist community into people who are part of a minority culture yet are also integrated into the world at large as they continually manage their identities as committed disciples of Christ? How can Christian naming ceremonies help children as they move from unexamined and assigned collective identities, through periods of identity exploration, towards achieved and chosen collective identities that can sustain and ground them as they engage in the world around them?

Since each tradition and faith community is unique and ought to form its own particular naming ceremonies, a detailed liturgy or order of service for Christian naming ceremonies is not offered here. However, what is offered are three central ways that naming ceremonies can help to form a child's assigned collective identity. These ideas can be used to form Christian naming ceremonies or simply add a naming component to existing child dedication ceremonies. In either case, a formal bestowing of a name on a child provides an early means for nurturing identity formation in the lives of young people.

The Meaning of Names

The meaning behind one's name can be a significant and formative influence on one's identity. In the Christian scriptures, one can read accounts of people whose names are given and changed in order to reflect who the person is and who the person will become. Throughout the contemporary world, many cultures still give names that have significant meaning to them. In India, for example, names are seen as loaded with power, so the meaning behind the names of a child has a hand in shaping who the child is to become (Gonda 1970, 5). Many Hindus give names to children to signify and form the character of the child (Pandey 1969, 78). Within the Jewish religion, it is held that "a person reflects the qualities and attributes of the name given to him or her. Names are suggestive of one's essence" (Goodman 2006, 145). This tradition stems from the Hebrew Bible. For example, the name Jacob, which means usurper, signified that the bearer of that name would seize his brother's rights (Gen. 25:26). In the book of Genesis, God changes Abram's name to Abraham (meaning "father of many") to reflect the future that God has planned for him (Gen. 17:5). A name and the blessing that comes with it provide a framework for one's life.

Thus, at an individual level, names and naming ceremonies speak of the character or qualities of the child's personal identity. In a sense, names can act as role models, giving children messages about character traits and ways of living with which children can identity. Such identifications can form the foundation of a child's identity as they grow and engage in identity formation (Phinney 2000, 28). Although they may not always live out or live into the meaning of their names, children can reflect on their names as they grow and remember that they have been called by a special name and have a special purpose and place in the family, community, and tradition that formally bestowed the name and blessings onto the child. This has certainly been the case in my life, for I was taught as a child that my first name speaks of the fact I am "beloved" by God and my family; furthermore, it may be more than coincidence that my vocation is in the field of theology and my middle name, Michael, rhetorically asks "who is like God?"

The Family Connection

A person's surname, or family name, is an important aspect of a one's identity. It speaks of the person's family, where the person has come from, the tribe, clan, or lineage to which a person belongs. From my birth, I have been a member of the Csinos family, who immigrated to Canada from Hungary in the early 1900s. There are not too many of us around, but as a Csinos, I share a connection with people in Canada, the United States, Romania, and Hungary who also carry this name. My surname provides me with a sense of belonging and commitment to my family that is an essential component of ethnic identity (Phinney et al. 2001, 496).

As an aspect of one's ethnic identity, the faith or religious tradition of a family can be passed on and formed through names that connect people to their family. This practice is common in Judaism, a tradition in which names connect people to their family's past and offer them a sense of identity as members of a family with a distinct history (Novak 1993, 22). Many Jewish children are given Hebrew names—like Rebecca, Israel, or Jacob—as a way of connecting them to their Jewish ancestry and strengthening familial ties. In Africa, where children have been given western names, many Christians are recognizing the importance of bestowing African names on their children in order to connect them to their roots. Taiye Aluko (1993) notes, "authentic African names must now reappear from beneath that cultural imperialism of the West with which Christians have undoubtedly been most closely linked" (26). By bestowing African names on their children, parents encourage them to connect with their ethnic and familial heritage and remember that they belong to and have a place within a particular family.

Phinney (2001) notes that the ethnic identity of children is significantly influenced by the messages that they receive from their family (501). Names, as important messages given to children by their parents, serve as constant reminders of one's roots and they can shape the identity of the child as a member of a particular family and heritage that may share a specific religious tradition. Names have the power to connect children to families that can guide them through childhood and adolescence, and can provide them with powerful ways of remembering who they are and from where they have come. As children grow older, they can reflect on their names and the ceremonies at which they were formally given these names in order to remind them of the family into which they have been born or adopted; names can connect children to a lineage and family that can sustain and ground them as they engage in identity exploration.

A Place within a Community

One of the most important aspects of a naming ceremony, especially in the context of the Anabaptist theology and social science research already discussed, is the fact that, within many religious traditions, naming ceremonies are a way of welcoming children into a faith community and tradition and providing newborns with an assigned collective identity as a member of a religious community. As Shenk (2003) has noted, fostering a way of life as a community member and nurturing loyalty to this alternative community of faith help to ensure that children, and all people, form identities as members of the community.

Many religions make use of naming ceremonies as a way of socializing children into their communities, lifestyles, and traditions. In Hinduism, for example, the samskaras—or life-cycle rituals—act as a means of gradually socializing a person into the Hindu way of life (Chaubay 1979, 49). The namakarana—or naming ceremony—is the fifth samskara (of the sixteen that are generally agreed upon), and one of its key sociological functions is to instill in the child a sense of belonging and identity within the community (Chaubay 1979, 47). Such a sense of belonging is an important factor in whether or not a child will form an identity as a member of a community.

Although identities are formed in many different ways and are based on a person's own idiosyncrasies and personality, "the typical developmental progression and the individual's choices are both shaped by events and opportunities afforded by the context" (Phinney 2000, 30). Furthermore, since acculturation strategies are influenced by one's community and integration is inherently a collectivist strategy, being a part of a community that is a positive influence on one's identity is important. By being named within a faith community that is a powerful influence of socialization into its particular way of life, children may come to form their primary identity as a member of this faith community. This is vital to people who have identities that are achieved and integrated, that is, individuals whose identities are strong enough to manage the challenges of interacting with other cultures and identities in the world.

Christian naming ceremonies can also allow the community to rally around a family and a particular child and commit themselves to being a part of an ecology that fosters the identity of the child as a member of the community and the wider faith tradition. This is a crucial aspect of naming ceremonies for, according to Simons, parents and the entire community are responsible for the spiritual nurture of children. Yet in the contemporary West, it can be challenging to be a counter-cultural Anabaptist. A community that supports children as they grow and explore their identities can help them to remember who they are as they wonder who they will become; it can foster integration and resolution and can encourage them to form identities as Anabaptists. Furthermore, since people who use a strategy of integration typically maintain strong connections with their childhood communities, helping young children—even infants—to belong to communities is vital. Naming ceremonies can help to nurture connections to a community and context that aid children in forming identities as community members who actively and constructively participate in the society around them.

One's name is vital to one's identity as an individual, a member of a family, and a part of a faith community and tradition. Speaking about African spirituality, Anthony Ephirim-Donker (1997) notes that "the name is the final seal of a complete person, without which the individual cannot exist" (63). Anabaptist families and communities (as well as those of other Christian traditions) can utilize Christian naming ceremonies as a way of providing a child with an assigned collective identity that begins at the earliest moments of life. They can serve as a continual reminder of who one is and from where one has come. Castro (2003) has found that high previous in-group involvement determines increased identification with a group in face of plurality and intergroup relations (47). Additionally, the research of Phinney and her colleagues has led them to conclude that the most positive outcomes of identity formation and exploration occur when individuals are members of a strong and supportive community (2001, 494).

Naming ceremonies, then, can not only be a means of socializing children and involving them in a particular faith community and tradition for their earliest days of life; they can also be a way for the community to gather around a child and a family and remind them that they are not alone, but belong to a wider community that offers support to them. As children grow, interact with the world, and form achieved and chosen collective identities, they can look back on their names and find their identities as members of a community and tradition that formally celebrated the giving of this name. As Sara Shenk (2003) has made clear, to have an identity is to remember who you are (13–14). As young people engage in a world that is becoming increasingly globalized, pluralistic, and heterogeneous, naming ceremonies help them to manage their identities by allowing them to remember their roots as valued members of a family, a faith community, and a religious tradition.

Conclusion

Phinney (2000) once wrote that "Among the various methods that can be used to study the complex interactions among these factors, personal narratives can provide a valuable perspective" (30). Through the connections to one's name, one's family, and one's faith community that are given and emphasized at Christian naming ceremonies, children receive these personal narratives as members of communities and families that have names that are all their own. In this way, Anabaptist, and many other Christian communities, can bestow on children an assigned collective identity, an identity that can provide a basis for the valuing of communal and cultural connections needed for identity achievement, management, and integration and it can support individuals in the midst of identity crises. Through Christian naming ceremonies, children can be formally bestowed with the embryonic potency of an identity that is strong and flexible enough to be maintained as they grow, engage with other people, explore different identities and cultures, and seek to be obedient to God and God's reign in the world.

References

Aluko, Taiye. (1993). Naming ceremony in African independent churches—A cultural revolution. *Indian Journal of Theology, 35*(2), 20–32.

Arnett, Jeffrey Jensen. (2004). *Emerging adulthood: The winding road from the late teens through the twenties.* Oxford: Oxford University Press.

Berry, John W. (2003). Conceptual approaches to acculturation. In K. M. Chun, P. B. Organista, and G. Marin (Eds.), *Acculturation: Advances in theory, measurement, and applied research* (pp. 17–37). Washington, D.C.: American Psychological Association.

Bishop's Committee on the Liturgy. (1983). *The rites of the Catholic Church as revised by the Second Vatican Ecumenical Council.* New York: Pueblo.

Castro, Vanessa Smith. (2003). *Acculturation and psychological adaptation.* Westport, CT: Greenwood.

Chaubay, B. B. (1979). Rituals and sacraments in Hinduism: A sociological perspective." In C. O. McMullen (Ed.), *Rituals and sacraments in Indian religions* (pp. 39–52). Delhi, India: I.S.P.C.K.

Côté, James F. and Charles G. Levine. (2004). *Identity formation, agency, and culture: A social psychological synthesis.* Mahwah, NJ: Lawrence Erlbaum Associates.

Ephirim-Donker, Anthony. (1997). My father and I are one. In A. Ephrim-Donker (Ed.), *African spirituality: On becoming ancestors* (pp. 49–68). Trenton, NJ: African World Press.

Gonda, J. (1970). *Notes on names and the name of God in ancient India.* Amsterdam: North-Holland.

Goodman, Roberta Louis. (2006). Entering the world, entering Torah: Moving from the natural to the sacred in the Jewish life cycle. In K. M. Yust (Ed.), *Nurturing child and adolescent spirituality: Perspectives from the world's religious traditions* (pp. 143–56). Lanham, MD: Rowman and Littlefield.

Groome, Thomas. (2009). Educating for religious identity in secularizing worlds. In W. Gräb and L. Charbonnier (Eds.), *Secularization theories, religious identity, and practical theology: Developing international practical theology for the 21st century* (pp. 85–91). Zürich/Berlin: Lit Verlag.

Hauerwas, Stanley. (2001). Why the 'sectarian tempation' is a misrepresentation: A response to James Gustafson. In J. Berkman and M. Cartwright (Eds.), *The Hauerwas reader* (pp. 90–110). Durham, NC: Duke University Press.

Hay, David and Rebecca Nye. (2006). *The spirit of the child*, revised ed. London: Jessica Kingsley.

Novak, David. (1993). 'Be fruitful and multiply': Issues relating to birth in Judaism. In R. M. Geffen (Ed.), *Celebration and renewal: Rites of passage in Judaism* (pp. 12–31). Philadelphia: Jewish Publication Society.

Miller, Keith Graber. (2001). Complex innocence, obligatory nurturance, and parental vigilance: 'The child' in the work of Menno Simons. In M. J. Bunge (Ed.), *The child in Christian thought* (pp. 194–226). Grand Rapids: Eerdmans.

Pandey, Rajbali. (1969). *Hindu Saṁskāras: Socio-religious study of the Hindu sacraments*. Delhi, India: Motilal Banarsidass.

Phinney, Jean S. (2003). Ethnic identity and acculturation. In K. M. Chun, P. B. Organista, and G. Marin (Eds.), *Acculturation: Advances in theory, measurement, and applied research* (pp. 63–81). Washington, D.C.: American Psychological Association.

————. (2000). Identity formation across cultures: The interaction of personal, societal, and historical change. *Human Development, 43*, 27–31.

Phinney, Jean S. et al. (2001). Ethnic identity, immigration, and well-being: An interactional perspective. *Journal of Social Issues, 57*(3), 493–510.

Presbyterian Church (U.S.A.). (1993). *Book of common worship*. Louisville: Westminster/John Knox.

Simons, Menno. (1984a). A clear account of excommunication. In J. C. Wenger (Ed.), *The complete writings of Menno Simons, c. 1496-1561* (Translated by Leonard Verdun, pp. 456–85). Scottdale, PA: Herald.

————. (1984b). A kind admonition on church discipline. In J. C. Wenger (Ed.), *The complete writings of Menno Simons, c. 1496-1561* (Translated by Leonard Verdun, pp. 408–418). Scottdale, PA: Herald.

————. (1984c). The nurture of children. In J. C. Wenger (Ed.), *The complete writings of Menno Simons, c. 1496-1561* (Translated by Leonard Verdun, pp. 945–52). Scottdale, PA: Herald.

————. (1984d). Reply to Gellius Faber. In J. C. Wenger (Ed.), *The complete writings of Menno Simons, c. 1496-1561* (Translated by Leonard Verdun, pp. 623–781). Scottdale, PA: Herald.

Shenk, Sara Wenger. (2003). *Anabaptist ways of knowing: A conversation about tradition-based critical education*. Telford, PA: Cascadia.

————. (1995). Remember who you are. *Mennonite Quarterly Review, 69*(3), 337–53.

Templeton, Janice L. and Jacquelynne S. Eccles. (2006). The relation between spiritual development and identity processes. In E. C. Roehlkepartain (Ed.), *The handbook of spiritual development in childhood and adolescence* (pp. 252–65). Thousand Oaks, CA: Sage.

Yoder, John Howard. (2004). *Anabaptism and reformation in Switzerland: An historical and theological analysis of the dialogues between Anabaptists and Reformers*. Kitchener, ON: Pandora.

14

Second Graders' Spirituality in the Context of the Sacrament of Reconciliation

Jennifer Beste

In the last five to ten years, religious scholars have begun to acknowledge their failure to attend seriously to children as a legitimate subject of academic inquiry (Bunge 2001; Haight 2002; Bales 2005; Orsi 2005). Influenced by the disciplines of psychology and sociology, many religious scholars are now recognizing that children are not passive recipients of a religious tradition, but complex social actors who creatively construct meaning and have religious perspectives and experiences distinct from adults (Hardman 1999; Bunge 2001; Miller-McLemore 2003; Bales 2005; Mercer 2005; Ridgely 2006; Browning and Miller-McLemore 2009).

Joining a growing number of religious scholars who stress the need to learn about children's religious and spiritual experiences from children themselves, I conducted a qualitative research study that explores how Catholic second graders interpret their first experiences of a particular religious ritual—the Sacrament of Reconciliation.[1] During

---

1. Sacraments are considered sacred rites in the Catholic Church in which God's love and grace is mediated in a special way to a Catholic believer; Baptism, Eucharist, Confirmation, and Penance (the Sacrament of Reconciliation) are significant rites of passage in Catholic children's and adolescent's socialization. I use the term, Sacrament of Reconciliation rather than Penance because it is used most regularly in religious education and pastoral practice to signify that the emphasis today is placed on one's reconciliation with God.

this sacrament, children confess their sins to a priest, express contrition, receive absolution, and perform a penance as reparation for wrongdoing. My interest in this research was sparked after I finished a separate research project analyzing the Catholic Church's historical and present perceptions of children's religious and moral nature.

From the thirteenth to the twentieth century there emerged two conflicting positions about when children attain sufficient reason to sin and need this sacrament: one group of theologians argued that children around seven attain sufficient reason to commit mortal sin, and therefore need the sacrament, while a second group argued that children are incapable of serious sin before puberty (Buckley 2000, 42). In his 1910 decree Quam Singulari, Pius X stated that children attain the age of reason around seven, can identify right from wrong, and have the right to receive the sacrament at this time (Pius X 1954, 245–50).[2] As a result of his decree, receiving Reconciliation in second grade became the traditional practice.

Later in the twentieth century, however, disagreement resurfaced among Catholic clergy, educators and theologians' about children's moral capacities and whether receiving the Sacrament in second grade effectively teaches children about sin and enhances their moral agency. The debate became most vocal after Vatican II's call for liturgical and sacramental renewal (O'Neill and Donovan 1966, 1–9; O'Neill & Donovan 1968; "Davenport" 1973, 159; "Baltimore" 1973, 157; "Introducing Children" 1974, 490–94; Mette 1987; Buckley 2000; Martos 2001, 318–19). Many U.S. and Western European religious educators warned of negative psychological effects of premature initiation into the sacrament. Without a consensus, more than half of U.S. parishes postponed the Sacrament of Reconciliation for several years, and the majority of religious educators and parents reported positive results (Martos 2001, 318–19; Mette 1987, 66). By 1973, the Vatican put an end to such experiments and stated that all churches should return to the practice of having second graders receive the Sacrament of Reconciliation prior to First Communion (Sacred Congregation for the Discipline of the Sacraments 1973, 4000). This declaration from Rome caused heated debate among clergy and educators throughout the 1970s, with some

2. Satisfying the precept means that one is obligated to receive the sacrament annually if one has committed a mortal sin.

bishops publishing statements that dissented from Rome's order ("Introducing Children" 1975, 490–95; "Authentic Theology" 1975, 567–68; "First Penance" 1977, 445–46). In my view, what is most noteworthy about this historical debate is the complete absence of children's own voices and perspectives about their experiences of this sacrament. Not a single research study during this time was conducted to determine the effects of this sacrament on second graders' relationship with God and their spiritual and moral development.

What light can children themselves shed on this debate about whether the Sacrament of Reconciliation in second grade fosters or actually hinders children's relationship with God and their moral and spiritual development? I decided to explore this question by visiting five second grade classrooms to observe and interview children about how they learn about sin and the Sacrament of Reconciliation. I was interested in several key questions. First, I wished to explore children's accounts of their overall experience and what meanings this sacrament has for them. Second, I wanted to examine whether this sacrament alters children's sense of self, their moral agency, and their relationship with God and others. Third, I wanted to explore whether children view reception of Reconciliation as an act they choose and desire and/or an act that conforms to the expectations of their Church, parents, teachers, and peers. It was my hope that asking these questions in a semi-structured interview format would offer second graders rich opportunities to express their spiritual and religious needs, their view of God and relationship with God, and their sense of themselves as moral agents.

The purpose of this chapter is, first, to share my research findings about Catholic children's diverse experiences and interpretations of this sacrament. Then, using emerging data from my interviews with children, I will analyze which factors foster or actually undermine children's spiritual growth as a result of this sacramental experience.

Methods

During the 2006–2007 academic year, I received approval from three Catholic schools to observe five second grade religion classes as students prepared to receive the Sacrament of Reconciliation. I then attended the Reconciliation services where the second graders received the sacrament for the first time. During the service, children, their families, and parish members sang songs, listened to a homily by a priest, recited prayers, and then received the sacrament individually. During the week following the Reconciliation service, I individually interviewed those children who returned their parental consent forms and assented to being interviewed.

Before beginning each interview, I emphasized to the second graders that there were no right or wrong answers to my questions, and that I was simply interested to learn what they thought and felt about their experiences of the sacrament. I was also careful during interviews to keep my responses and facial expressions neutral so that second graders would not be tempted to give what they perceived was the right answer. I also mentioned that no one would know what they said during the interview. I explained I would use a pseudonym for them if I included any of their comments in publications. Most second graders had drawn a picture trying to capture their experiences, and they began the interview by explaining their drawings (Beste 2010). I then asked follow-up questions about how the sacrament affected them and why they decided to receive the sacrament. After transcribing the 75 interviews, I realized two interviews were missing data on one question, so I analyzed the remaining 73 transcripts using Auerbach and Silverstein's method of qualitative analysis (Auerbach and Silverstein 2003).[3]

An obvious shortcoming of this study is its homogenous student sample: all but one of the second graders were Caucasian and were from families that could afford private school tuition. As a result, this study cannot analyze whether race and/or class significantly affects second graders' interpretations of this sacrament. During this past academic year, I observed an additional five religion classes at five parishes that had a more racially diverse group of children, but I have not yet analyzed those interviews.

---

3. Their method consists of five steps when interpreting transcribed interviews: 1) highlight the relevant text from the transcribed interviews; 2) identify repeating ideas in the relevant text; 3) organize repeating ideas into themes; 4) organize the themes into more abstract ideas called theoretical constructs; and 5) organize the theoretical constructs into a theoretical narrative that summarizes what one has learned about my initial research concerns.

Children's Experiences of the Sacrament of Reconciliation

When asked what the Sacrament of Reconciliation was like overall, the majority of second graders[4] first focused on their excitement, nervousness, or fear as they anticipated the sacrament. When asked why they felt nervous and scared, students offered the following reasons: they were nervous about sitting next to the priest and talking to him; it was their first time receiving the sacrament and they did not know how they would feel or what to expect; they were not sure what to say; and they were worried they would forget one or many of the components of this sacrament and were concerned that others in the parish would notice. Some students also felt uncomfortable about the process of revealing their sins to the priest, or were worried that the priest would get "mad" after hearing what they did wrong. Claire, for instance, stated: "You didn't really want to confess all your sins or anything because everybody's done something wrong and you feel bad about it. You feel like you want to keep it secret and no one should know about it." Trevor was concerned about the priest's reaction: "I thought if I said something that the priest was going to be mean. Like he would say 'Why'd you do that?!'"

Although the vast majority of second graders expressed feelings of nervousness and anxiety prior to the sacrament, their experiences during and afterwards became more diverse. Three overall responses emerged that I categorized as "lukewarm to negative," "positive," and "very positive." While the majority of second graders (80 percent) expressed either" positive" or "very positive" emotions and attitudes after they received the sacrament, a minority of second graders (20 percent) were mostly indifferent or focused on negative aspects of their experience. This minority emphasized feeling nervous or scared prior to the sacrament and did not volunteer how they felt during the sacrament.[5] Taking into consideration nonverbal cues such as facial expressions and gestures as well as their verbal responses to

4. 62 out of 75 second graders specifically reported feeling nervous or scared; the other 12 second graders described themselves as "not very nervous," "good," "happy," "fine," or not feeling anything.

5. 15 second graders expressed a lukewarm to negative response to the sacrament, 42 expressed positive views of the sacrament, and 16 expressed very positive views of the sacrament.

subsequent questions, I categorized these second graders' experiences as "lukewarm to negative." Jack, for instance, said he didn't remember feeling anything during the sacrament or remember much at all except the party afterwards. He thought kids should be older because "they have a bit more courage and understand it a bit more." Amy stated: "I felt glad to have it over. . . . I didn't need to worry about it anymore." Tim volunteered that he did not know if he wanted to receive the sacrament again. When asked how they would explain this sacrament to their peers, some of these students said they would tell second graders to "just do it and get it over with" or that they just have to "do this" if they wanted First Communion. "Lukewarm to negative" second graders also differed from their peers about the sacrament's impact on their relationship with God; 94 percent reported no change in their relationship with God.

In contrast, 58 percent of second graders reported a positive experience and 22 percent reported a very positive experience of the sacrament. I found it important to differentiate between the "positive" and "very positive" children's responses because the "very positive" students' enthusiasm and depth in their responses were qualitatively different. During the interviews, I was often caught off guard by the degree of joy and enthusiasm these second graders expressed when reflecting on what it was like to receive the sacrament. Brian, for instance, captured his rich emotions during the sacrament in the following way: "I felt like 'Hey, I've been forgiven. I'll go give my penance and then don't do the sins ever again.' My stomach was jumping up and down at the beginning and end. Because it was nervous then happy." All of Brian's responses were so enthusiastic that I found myself asking him a question I had not planned: "What was your least favorite part of your experience of the sacrament?" Brian paused, looked directly into my eyes, and said, "Leaving the Sacrament." These "very positive" student comments echo Emile Durkheim's descriptions of the "collective effervescence" and "extraordinary height of exaltation" felt by religious believers when they participate in religious rituals (Durkheim 1995, 216–18).

When asked whether receiving this sacrament affected their relationship with God, 67 percent of "positive" second graders reported a positive impact, with 20 (48 percent) explicitly mentioning that they were closer to God. By contrast, 94 percent of the "very positive" children expressed a positive impact, with 81 percent reporting that they were closer to God. The "very positive" children offered the most detail about how the sacrament affected their relationship with God. Emily, for instance, stated, "It brings you closer to God. You think it and feel it. I felt it in the sacrament, after, and when I got home." Catherine explained, "I want to make my relationship with God better than it is now. I think and feel it in my heart. I felt that way after the Sacrament. I felt happy and joyful and knew I was filled with God's grace because I was forgiven." Brian captured this same spirit when he said, "[The sacrament has affected] the way I believe in Him. Normally I would just read a book in Church but now I don't want to . . . I feel a lot closer. I can understand what the Gospel reading is and how He did the miracles." While the second graders' affective responses constitute an important variable for understanding their overall experience, this data is insufficient since it is unclear whether the children's affective responses were mostly connected to their particular experience of the sacrament and its impact, their personalities, family influences, or even relief that the sacrament was over and went well.

I decided it was essential to go deeper and assess how many children actually found the sacrament personally meaningful and relevant to their lives; since the concept of meaningfulness is so subjective, I defined a meaningful experience as having an effect on one's sense of self, on one's relationship with God or others, and/or an impact on one's moral behavior. If the children reported no impact in these three areas, their experience was coded as unmeaningful. If students reported one example of how the sacrament affected them in regard to one of these criteria, I coded their interview as meaningful. If students mentioned multiple ways they were affected, I coded their interview as very meaningful. Analyzing the interview transcripts with these criteria in mind, I noted that 67 percent of second graders affirmed that the sacrament either changed their sense of self, their relationship with God or others, or altered their moral behavior in other ways. Comparing the lukewarm, "positive," and "very positive" groups, I discovered striking differences among the groups: 94 percent of the "very positive" students had meaningful experiences, with 81 percent of these students reporting very meaningful experiences. 76 percent of" positive" second graders had meaningful experiences, with 16 percent percent reporting very meaningful experiences. 13 percent of the lukewarm children reported a meaningful experience, with none reporting a very meaningful experience.

When analyzing whether gender differences existed in regard to affective responses and meaningfulness, I noted that girls were more likely to experience a "positive" or "very positive" experience than boys. 80 percent of the lukewarm group were male and 69 percent of the "very positive" children were female." Positive" second graders were evenly split, with 22 boys and 20 girls. I did not notice very significant gender differences in regard to meaningfulness among the "positive" and "very positive" groups. In regard to the lukewarm group, however, all 12 boys lacked a meaningful experience while two out of the three girls had a meaningful experience.[6]

The Meaning and Significance of Reconciliation for Second Graders

As for the meaning of the sacrament, four salient points emerged: 1) The Sacrament is about confessing your sins to the priest; 2) the priest won't tell anyone your sins; 3) the priest (or God) forgives *all* of your sins completely, even the ones you forget to mention; and 4) being forgiven for your sins enables you to "start over" and brings you closer to God.

Out of all of the concepts involved in this sacrament, what struck many second graders and captured their imaginations most vividly was the power of the priest to forgive *all* of their sins *completely*. This theme frequently arose when second graders were asked whether they would agree or disagree with a friend who decided not to receive the sacrament because he chose instead to pray to God directly and say sorry for his sins. While several second graders thought this was fine, the vast majority disagreed with their hypothetical friend. Although some second graders could not explain why they disagreed, those who offered a reason typically responded in the following three ways.

The first and most common response was that, although God would forgive every sin confessed during prayer, it is simply impossible to remember to apologize for every sin committed: receiving the Sacrament was the only way to have *all* of one's sins forgiven. Second

6. For more detailed analysis of these research findings, see Jennifer Beste, "Children Speak: Catholic Second Graders' Agency and Experiences in the Sacrament of Reconciliation," *Sociology of Religion, forthcoming.*

graders believed that all of their sins committed thus far during their lives would be completely erased during the sacrament. A second group of students were not sure that God would forgive sins completely during individualized prayer and believed that confessing sins to a priest was essential for complete forgiveness of sins. For a third group of students, forgiveness was not the salient issue. These second graders believed that God forgave their sins if they asked God directly, but they still thought it was important to receive the sacrament because it assured them that they were forgiven and brought them closer to God.

The next common, salient feature of second graders' experience was the belief that being forgiven frees them from past sins, and enables them to "start over." Many children spoke about the moment in which the priest placed his hands on the children's shoulders as he absolved them of their sins and drew pictures about this particular moment; the laying on of hands was a powerful symbol of absolution for many of the children. In my interviews, I was struck by how many children seemed to experience being cleansed in a very visceral, physical sense. Cody for instance, stated: "[I felt] very happy and joyful because my body was rid of all my sins." When asked about the meaning of the sacrament, Jessica responded: "I'd say the Sacrament of Reconciliation is when you become clean. You'll be as pure as you can. Right now you might feel a little grey but you're going to be white and pure. You'll be washed inside and out." Catherine confided: "I can start clean again and I'm happy God's going to give me a second chance. I knew that if I was free from my sins I could start over again and be a better person." Such experiences of having one's sins dramatically wiped away and "starting over" was exhilarating and joyful.

Lastly, as noted above, a significant percentage of second graders stressed that feeling "sinless" and "starting over" brought them closer to God. For them, this represented the sacrament's greatest value. For example, Emily reflected, "It brings you closer to God. You think it and feel it. I felt it in the sacrament, after, and when I got home." When asked if the sacrament altered her relationship with God, Ellen stated, "I feel closer to God. When we apologize to Him, He accepts our apologies and He brings us closer to Him so He can hear us and we can hear Him." In fact, this theme of becoming closer to God surfaced in the second graders' responses to almost all of the interview questions. During the interviews, I became interested in whether this dominant

theme was primarily conceptual (arising from their teachers' instruction or highlighted in their textbooks) and/or primarily experiential.
To gain insight, I often asked the second graders whether they remember "thinking" that they were closer to God or whether they actually
"felt" closer. The majority responded that they felt (or both thought
and felt) closer to God. When rereading students' religion textbooks
and my field notes from class discussions, I found that the textbooks
and teachers never stated directly that this sacrament brings children
closer to God; the textbooks did, however, contain the parables of "the
prodigal son" and "the shepherd and the lost sheep." While this theme
of becoming closer to God is consistent with these parables, it was my
sense that this theme also arose from many children's personal experiences of feeling closer to God during or after the sacrament.

Why Did Second Graders Receive the Sacrament of Reconciliation?

When asked why they chose to receive this sacrament, second graders
offered a diversity of responses, with all mentioning at least one of the
following reasons: 1) They didn't know why they received the sacrament; 2) it was not their choice—it was their parents' decision; 3) they
had to receive the sacrament to avoid Hell or because they had done
"bad stuff;" 4) receiving the sacrament is part of being Catholic or they
just wanted to get the sacrament "done" or "over with;" 5) they needed
to receive this sacrament so they could receive First Communion; 6)
receiving the sacrament was the "right" thing to do; 7) their class was
receiving the sacrament together, and they wanted to be part of their
class and attend the party afterwards; 8) they desired God's forgiveness and wanted to start over; 9) they wanted to become closer to God;
and 10) they thought the sacrament would help them become better
persons and have a "new better life."

Different responses emerged when I compared the responses of
the attitudinal groups. None of the lukewarm second graders offered a
positive reason (reasons 8–10 above) expressing a desire for the sacrament. Forty percent offered a negative reason or one that viewed the
sacrament as obligatory or as a means to a different end (reasons 3–6).
Sixty percent did not view themselves as choosing the sacrament at
all; their parents decided or they did not know why they received the
sacrament.

In contrast, 62 percent of "positive" children chose a positive reason that indicated a desire for the sacrament itself, 10 percent offered reasons 3–6, and 29 percent did not perceive themselves as choosing the sacrament (reasons 1–2). Interestingly, all of the "very positive" group perceived themselves as choosing the sacrament; 69 percent reported a positive reason that indicated a desire for the sacrament (8–10), and 31 percent offered reasons 3–6. Such data reflect a strong association between one's reason for receiving the sacrament and one's affective and attitudinal response, and the sacrament's impact on one's relationship with God and others.

Furthermore, there was also a strong association among children between the degree of perceived agency (perceived oneself as desiring and choosing the sacrament) and the sacrament's impact on their relationship with God. Out of 37 children who reported a positive reason for the sacrament (reasons 7–9), 60 percent shared that they felt closer to God after the sacrament, and 17 percent reported a positive impact on their relationship with God (like believing in God more, feeling better about God, etc.). Regarding the children who reported reasons 3–6, 25 percent reported being closer to God, and 17 percent mentioned some positive impact on their relationship with God. In regard to the 21 second graders whose answers indicated no agency, only 18 percent reported being closer to God and 5 percent mentioned some positive impact. Such data demonstrate that the higher degree of agency, the greater the likelihood that children will experience a positive impact on their relationship with God.

Does the Sacrament of Reconciliation Foster Moral Development?

During my interviews at the first school with two classes, I did not ask students whether the sacrament impacted their moral behavior because I was initially interested in their overall experiences of the sacrament, its meanings, and its impact on their relationship with God. Since some second graders at the first school volunteered how the sacrament affects them morally and helps them be better people (motivating them to commit fewer sins and/or treat others better), I decided to ask the remaining students at the second and third schools whether receiving the sacrament helps them be a "better" person. I deliberately chose this vague question because I was interested in what "being a better person" means to second graders. When responding affirmatively to this question, second graders gave two primary reasons for believing they were better persons: they were treating others better and/or they reported committing fewer sins and doing "the good." Brian, who was at the first school and not asked this question, volunteered: "I feel like I should help other people the way I wanted to be treated. I want to start joining in things, and I gave up things for Lent." Hunter announced: "Now you're sinless. Now you'll try to not do as many sins as you did before." Kelly stated: "Sometimes I used to upset people, but it was hard for me to say sorry, but now I will say sorry. It has made me less stubborn." Catherine reflected: "I've been acting a lot better. I've been kind and obedient. It shows me what I'm doing wrong to make me do better. It makes me think about what I've been doing wrong and how I can do it better." Michael, along with other peers, made an interesting connection between being happier and committing fewer sins: "[The sacrament] makes me more happy and makes me not do sins again so I'm closer and closer to God. You're talking to the priest and telling him your sins and after that you try not to do the same sins again."

I found these responses fascinating because I never heard the second grade teachers suggest that the sacrament would help their students treat others better or avoid sin; the teachers seemed focused on preparing the children for the Reconciliation service, and did not focus on any effects of the sacrament after the service. Their textbooks also did not address the issue of experiencing moral effects from the sacrament. In regard to my analysis, if second graders offered an example of one of these reasons of treating others better or committing fewer sins, I coded their response as a "detectable" moral impact. If they offered more than one example, I coded their response as "very detectable" moral impact. If they answered negatively, their response was coded as "no moral impact." Of the 15 "very positive" children asked this question, 87 percent responded affirmatively, with 40 percent reporting "very detectable" moral impact. Out of the 36 "positive" students who responded to this question, 58 percent responded affirmatively and 17 percent reported a "very detectable" moral impact. Out of the 7 lukewarm children, 29 percent responded affirmatively and reported committing fewer sins. Some second graders also reported that it felt easier to do good and avoid sin since receiving the sacrament.[7]

Overall, a key theme that emerges from my data analysis is that children's sense of agency (whether they perceive themselves desiring and choosing the sacrament for a reason related to the sacrament itself) turns out to be a significant variable affecting their attitude, the sacrament's meaningfulness, and Reconciliation's impact on their relationship with God and others.

Children's Experiences of Spirituality within the Context of Reconciliation

What do children reveal about their experiences of spirituality throughout their reflections of the Sacrament of Reconciliation? As I sat listening to and conversing with these second graders throughout my interviewing weeks, I often had a sense that I was being transported into human reality "before the Fall." By this statement, I mean to convey that I was taken aback by second graders' deep degree of openness and receptivity to God, which enabled them to encounter and feel God's presence during this sacrament. For instance, when I asked Rachel how she felt during the Sacrament of Reconciliation, her eyes lit up and she enthusiastically responded: "Really happy because the Holy Spirit is inside me. I could feel it." When asked how she felt after receiving the sacrament, Rachel considered this question for a moment, and then replied: "I felt a lot holier. I felt I was more in God's family. I felt it after and when he put his hands on my head. I did my penance and I kneeled and started praying and thanking God for my life."

Another aspect of most children's spiritual experience was the deep way in which they trusted in God's love and forgiveness and the joy they felt when palpably experiencing being freed from their sins. Many children spoke about the moment in which the priest placed his hands on their shoulders as he absolved them of their sins, and they later drew pictures about this particular moment (Beste 2010). In my

7. When asked this question about whether Reconciliation helps them be better people, 75 percent of "very positive" second graders and 81 percent of positive second graders responded affirmatively. 2 out the 7 (25 percent) lukewarm children that were asked this question reported committing less sins since the sacrament but did not offer examples of treating others better.

interviews, I was struck by how many children seemed to experience being cleansed in a very visceral, physical sense. Jessica stated: "I'd say the sacrament of Reconciliation is when you become clean. You'll be as pure as you can. Right now you might feel a little grey but you're going to be white and pure. You'll be washed inside and out." Cody reflected: [I felt] very happy and joyful because my body was rid of all my sins. Similarly, Hunter echoed: [After receiving the sacrament] I asked my mom if I could do it again . . . I felt happy. I was so sinless, I just felt happy."

Such joy about being forgiven by God and freed from sin in turn brought about another aspect of children's spirituality: their openness to being altered by God's presence and their response of love for God and others. As noted above in regard to moral effects of the sacrament, many second graders shared that feeling freed from sin enables them to start over in their relationship with God and be better people. Claire, for instance, informed me: "It feels like I get to start over and try to be closer to God and it doesn't feel like you've done anything wrong and like you've just been born. Like you're a baby." Catherine stated: "I can start clean again and I'm happy God's going to give me a second chance. I knew that if I was free from my sins I could start over again and be a better person." When asked if the sacrament altered her relationship with God, Ellen stated, "I feel closer to Him. When we apologize to Him, he accepts our apologies and He brought us closer to Him so He could hear us and we could hear Him." Tara reflected on how her relationship to God changed: "I feel like I've come deeper into Him and more close to Him. I know what he wants of me. He wants me to believe in Him and go straight and do what he wants me to do." Tara's description of coming "deeper into Him and more close to him" evokes mystical language, challenging the adequacy of many adult perceptions of children's spirituality that minimize or trivialize children's ability to form a relationship with God.

Overall, my interviews with the "positive" and "very positive" children revealed that dominant aspects of children's spirituality are their deep desire to be closer to God, and their appreciation for religious experiences that foster their concrete experience of being with God. The depth of their desire to be with God and seek out religious experiences that bring them closer to God became most obvious when I attempted to separate students' concerns about conforming to parental or peer expectations from their desire to receive the sacrament. I asked them to imagine that their parents offered them the choice either to attend the Reconciliation Service or stay home and watch TV: the choice was up to them. I added that they found out that half of their friends were going to the Reconciliation service and half were staying home. Interestingly, the vast majority said they would go to Church and receive the sacrament.[8] I often acted surprised or skeptical by their answer, pressing them as to why they'd choose an activity that might make feel initially nervous when they could just choose a fun activity. The reasons they gave for choosing the sacrament rather than watching TV were similar to the reasons listed above about why they received the sacrament. Most focused on the value of the sacrament rather than social factors when explaining why they would choose the sacrament instead of staying home. Marissa decided: "I'd do the sacrament because it's much holier and just sitting around watching TV isn't really helping anything." Ryan said: "Go because when I get reconciliation, I feel really clean and I feel good. I don't want to have a sinful heart, so I would do the reconciliation." Marcus got to the heart of the matter: "Going home and playing isn't as much fun as receiving and talking to God." For Aubrey, the choice was simple: "I think that having Jesus near me and close to him is better than anything." Some students perceived the sacrament as a rare opportunity. Becca stated: "I'd go have it. Because you can always get to watch TV but you don't usually get to get your sins forgiven." Likewise, Nathan said: "I would go because watching TV is just boring. You don't get this sacrament a lot of times either. It's pretty hard to get." My surprise at the children's preferences made me aware that I had presumed children in general would prefer a "fun" (frivolous) activity rather than a religious experience—a presumption that caught me off guard since it undoubtedly trivializes children and what really matters to them.

After completing these interviews, I had the overriding impression that these second graders took themselves, sin, and their relationship with God seriously. It was not as though they glibly revealed their sins to a priest as if this act was "no big deal;" a significant number

---

8. Only one second grader reported that, if he were in the first grade, he would probably stay home and play with friends. He did not say what he would decide to do in second grade.

of children emphasized that the confidentiality of the priest greatly mattered to them. Once they were assured that the priest was under a strict oath never to tell an individual's sins to anyone, many second graders felt more comfortable at the prospect of confessing their sins. The high value they placed on confidentiality was also evident in *all* of the second graders' choices not to reveal to me which sins they had confessed to the priest. Interestingly, even though students knew that I would keep their comments confidential (similar to the priest), no one elected to share which sins they had committed or which penance the priest had given. Several students' eyes widened when I asked them what it was like to receive the sacrament, and their first response was essentially, "Well, I'm *not* going to tell you which sins I confessed." Such reserve about revealing their sins suggests that many second graders view their sins as a private matter and take themselves and their sins seriously. Their willingness to confide in a priest also reveals a great trust in priests' word to keep their sins confidential.

I had not anticipated how much second graders would appreciate the priest paying attention to them individually and taking them seriously. When asked what they liked most about the sacrament, many second graders spoke enthusiastically about being able to talk to the priest and how they liked confessing their sins; some enthusiastically described this process as "being important" to them and "fun." They described how exciting it was to talk to a priest and how they "never got to sit so close to the priest before." In 2010, after her first Reconciliation, my own daughter Anna echoed many of the children I interviewed. I watched her as she received the Sacrament of Reconciliation and noticed that she took quite a bit of time conversing with the priest. After he absolved her, she walked back to her pew and was absolutely beaming. When I asked her how everything went, Anna, who has never been much of a talker, said: "Mom, I'm so glad I had the priest who was a stranger. He spent so much time talking to me! Did you notice how the school priest absolved all of his kids so fast and got done so quickly? It was like he was just trying to get it over with. I'm so happy I had the stranger priest!"

Moreover, second graders' reflections on their spiritual experiences indicate that a great disparity exists between children's actual spiritual experiences and capacities and many Catholic adult perceptions of children. The perception I had formed from reading catechists' textbook guides, religious education articles, and interviewing priests and educators was that second graders are quite limited in what they can understand and experience when receiving the Sacrament of Reconciliation. Influenced by Piaget, some clergy, theologians and religious educators have argued that second graders are not developmentally ready to receive the Sacrament of Reconciliation; they have trouble understanding the basic concept of sin because many children only develop the capacity for critical value judgments at the age of nine to ten. Only at this time are children developmentally ready to express sorrow, seek forgiveness, and truly experience the fullness of the sacrament (Buckley, 2000; Martos, 2001, 318–19; Mette, 1987; O'Neil and Donovan, 1968; Betz, 1968; Corrigan, 1969; "In Context: First Confession 1. Why Worcester Delays It," 1971). It is also a common assumption in religious education literature, and in my conversations with priests and educators, that children even have trouble distinguishing between a mistake and intentional wrongdoing; thus, they cannot even grasp the basic concept of sin. In 2004, I emailed a questionnaire to DREs (Directors of Religious Education) and priests about their perceptions of second graders' experiences of Reconciliation. The 43 respondents were deeply divided about whether children ought to receive the sacrament in second grade: 20 approved of second graders receiving the Sacrament, 19 disapproved because they did not think the children understood the sacrament or did not think they were developmentally ready, and 3 did not express an opinion. When I spoke to ten priests who regularly administer this sacrament to second graders during First Reconciliation services, their conversations with me caused me to question whether I should even commit my research time to this project; all of them told me that second graders could not understand sin and forgiveness adequately and that they were too young to benefit from this sacrament. I found myself wondering whether I should abandon the research project because such conversations led me to doubt whether second graders would have anything to say during interviews beyond a few basic ideas they learned in class.

When reading the religions textbooks that were used in four of the five second grade classes after I conducted the interviews, I was struck by how basic and simple the explanations and class activities were in regard to sin, God's forgiveness and love, and the Sacrament of Reconciliation.[9] For instance, one recommended class activity is to choose one child to be a shepherd and send him or her out of the room. Another child hides a toy symbolizing a sheep. When the shepherd enters the room and looks for the sheep, the other children are to say "baa" if the shepherd is getting closer and should say "moo" when the shepherd gets farther away. When the shepherd finds the toy, children are supposed to cheer. This activity is designed to help the children understand that Jesus as the Shepherd will always look for them if they are lost (Dooley and McDade 2006, 16; Fragomeni and Hiesberger 2000; Jambor 2003).

I contacted several publishers of contemporary religion textbooks and asked them what philosophical view of the child underlies their Catholic religious textbook. Some mentioned that their view is informed by Piaget and other developmental psychologists, while others mentioned that a common assumption underlying Catholic education is that children are blank slates. According to these publishers, many Catholics assume it is the responsibility of the Catholic Church and religious educators to fill children with knowledge about Catholic teachings and form them in their faith by participating in the Church's liturgical and sacramental life.[10] Viewing children as blank slates, of course, constructs views of educators as actively instilling information and children as passive, "little sponges" who absorb the material (Bales 2005, 77).[11]

It is no wonder that I experienced such surprise during my interviews with second graders; it became clear to me when analyzing the transcripts and religious education literature that many Catholic adults currently underestimate children's intellectual, moral, and spiritual capacities. As noted above, many children experienced great joy when encountering God's presence during the sacrament, and they were more than capable of wrestling with challenging questions

9. For more in depth analysis of my ethnographic observations of religion classes and the content of textbooks, see Jennifer Beste, "Catholic Children's Encounter with the Bible through Catechesis of the Good Shepherd," *Children in Religion: A Methods Handbook*, Susan Ridgely Bales, ed. (New York: NYU Press, forthcoming).

10. Interviews with catechetical directors (March–April 2010).

11. In her ethnographic work with Catholic second graders preparing for First Communion, Susan Ridgely Bales also observed that Catholic adults viewed children as passive learners who could not fully understand what they were being taught and unable to reflect deeply on their faith.

and reflecting on whether and how this sacrament affected them. Of the religious education materials I read preparing clergy and religious educators for the possibility that children might experience profound spiritual experiences that would deeply affect their relationship with God and others.

While acknowledging second graders' spiritual capacities, I do not wish to perpetuate a romanticized image of these children as essentially "pure" or innocent.[12] While surprised by their depth of spirituality, I was simultaneously struck by how morally complicated second graders (like adults) truly were; my conversations with them and observations of them in classes and on playgrounds revealed their subtle and not-so-subtle capacities both to be kind and enjoy one another, and deceive, hurt, and exclude one another. For instance, during one particular day of interviews, I heard from many second graders in one classroom about how Becca had put a note in Audrey's desk that stated: "You are boring, and I don't ever want to play with you again. You are no longer my friend." Instead of signing her name, she signed the note: "From Connor." Becca knew this would cause significant distress and a rift between Audrey and Connor, and many second graders complained to me about how much she enjoyed the tears and drama that ensued. As noted above in my interviews, second graders know when they have deliberately done something wrong and how to act kinder if they so choose. It is my contention that Catholic educators and churches underestimate children's moral capacities to harm as well as to mediate Christ's love, and miss rich opportunities to challenge young Catholics to integrate children's religious faith and values into their everyday interactions with their family members and peers.

Implications of This Research Study: How Can We Foster Children's Spiritual Development?

My ethnographic observations and interviews with second graders prompt me to ask broader questions about how to foster children's spirituality and religious faith more generally. Let us return full circle

12. In regard to the dangers of depicting (and celebrating) children as innocent, see Robert Orsi, *Between Heaven and Earth* (Princeton: Princeton University Press, 2005).

to the question that prompted my research project: "What insights do we gain from second graders themselves about whether this sacrament in second grade fosters or harms their relationship with God and their moral and spiritual development?" In this study, second graders' diverse experiences suggest that the most important variable may well be each child's readiness, desire for the sacrament, and sense of agency about choosing this sacramental experience.[13]

While more research is needed to determine fully the reasons why a child has a lukewarm to negative, positive, or very positive response to this sacrament, a key theme in my data analysis is that children's sense of agency (whether they perceive themselves desiring and choosing the sacrament) turns out to be a significant variable that affects their overall experience of the sacrament, their attitude, and the sacrament's impact on their relationship with God and others (Beste, forthcoming). Comments made by the lukewarm to negative group suggest that a sense of coercion (a sense that one *must* receive the sacrament prior to First Communion) or lack of a desire for the sacrament correlates with a lukewarm to negative experience. While none of these second graders reported blatant harm or a negative impact on their relationship with God, it is possible that their anxiety about receiving the sacrament and lack of positive affect during and after the sacrament may negatively affect their faith and relationship with God in subtle ways.

If this qualitative analysis is representative of many second graders' experiences, and a correlation exists between desiring and choosing the sacrament and having a positive experience of the sacrament, my research data analysis casts doubt on the wisdom of the Catholic Church's current policy, which prioritizes conformity and unity (the normative expectation that all second graders receive Reconciliation prior to First Eucharist) over attention to the individual readiness and desire of each child for the sacrament when discerning the appropriate timing. In my field observations of second graders preparing for Reconciliation, as well as my research about how children are viewed and treated in American Catholicism, I sense a tension in the Catholic Church between the obligation to transmit religious beliefs and values

---

13. For more detailed analysis of the significance of second graders' sense of agency, see Jennifer Beste, "Children Speak: Catholic Second Graders' Agency and Experiences in the Sacrament of Reconciliation," *Sociology of Religion, forthcoming.*

and the obligation to foster children's moral agency and ability to make their own religious decisions. If the purpose of this sacrament is to experience a grace-filled encounter with a forgiving God, Church policy should focus more attention on the latter obligation of empowering children's agency: second graders should be invited to receive this sacrament, but there should be a space for the child to decide to choose the sacrament, a space to own this important religious decision.

These research findings have broad implications for fostering children's spirituality and religious faith throughout their childhood and adolescence. The very idea that children's own sense of agency greatly affects their religious experiences and faith formation should lead Christian denominations and other religious communities to reexamine our view of the child that undergirds our methods of religious education and religious practices involving children. Do we perceive children largely as passive vessels who absorb educational content imparted by adults, or do we perceive children as active learners who synthesize their communities' vision, beliefs, and values in ways that are distinct from adult perspectives? Next, with unbridled creativity, we need to brainstorm ways to foster an intentional space in which we as adults balance the tasks of sharing with children with the stories, values, and commitments of our religious traditions and offer children the space and time to experience the divine on their own terms. To meet children where they really are in their religious and spiritual capacities and offer them opportunities to respond to God entails listening to them and learning from them. It also requires consulting children in religion class and during Church activities about their ideas concerning worship, humanity's relationship with the divine, and Church outreach and activities. For instance, which service and social justice projects would be chosen by a religious community if children were presented with a range of options and ideas and offered their input? I suspect that more children and their families would participate in such communal projects if children and parents were part of the decision-making process, which would further strengthen social ties among generations within the religious community? New questions and possibilities are endless when religious believers begin examining their religious communities from a child-centered perspective.

Of course, I do not believe, based on my ethnographic observations and interview analysis that "the solution" is to simply advance a liberal agenda that promotes absolutizing children's own choices about their religious participation. We owe children far more than simply letting them dictate whatever they want. Instead, my proposal is to provide children with an inspiring, challenging religious education and religious communal life, listen seriously to their voices and perspectives, and create a space where children "own" their religious choices and experiences. For instance, within the Catholic context, let us imagine that James, a second grader, has prepared for the Sacrament of Reconciliation, but expresses anxiety about Reconciliation service and shows no desire to receive this sacrament. How should his parents, religious educators, and clergy respond? A pastoral response that honors James's own subjectivity and agency would be to engage in compassionate conversation, emphasize how the purpose of this sacrament is to experience God's love in a special way, listen to James's fears or apprehensions, and address the source of his fears. If James still seems anxious and shows no positive desire for the sacrament, his parents could ask James whether he would like to wait and receive Reconciliation at a later date. Perhaps it would help him to talk to his friends about their First Reconciliation. Simply offering James this option may lessen any pressure he could be feeling and sharing positive experiences of receiving this sacrament could keep him interested in moving forward when he feels ready. As my research findings indicate, James will be far more likely to experience God's grace if he waits until he is ready to choose the sacrament. It also seems far more likely that James's own sense of choosing the sacrament will more effectively inspire him to remain a faithful and active Catholic young adult than if he were to feel coerced to participate in religious activities until he was a young adult.

In summary, we need to stop underestimating children's spiritual, religious, and moral capacities, offer enriching religious education that promotes children's own creative input into their learning and worship, and honor and foster their agency to "own" their religious faith and choices. Relating to children with respect, honoring their dignity, and encouraging them to be authentic members of the Body of Christ who challenge and inspire their communities will advance our calling as as Christians to mediate Christ's grace and further actualize the Kingdom of God.

References

An inadequate response. (1973, August 2). *Origins*, 3(8), 120.

Auerbach, C., & Silverstein, L. (2003). *Qualitative data: An introduction to coding and analysis.* New York, NY: New York University Press.

Authentic theology and sound methodology. (1975, February 28). *Origins*, 3(36), 567–68.

Bales, S. R. (2005). *When I was a child: Children's interpretations of First Communion.* Chapel Hill, NC: University of North Carolina Press.

Baltimore-Washington/Regional guidelines. (1973, August 30). *Origins*, 3(10), 157.

Beste, J. (Forthcoming). Catholic children's encounter with the Bible through Catechesis of the Good Shepherd. In Bales, S. R. (Ed.), *Children in Religion: A Methods Handbook* (pages unknown). New York: New York University Press.

———.(2010, Spring). Catholic second graders' artistic expression of sin and forgiveness in the Sacrament of Reconciliation. *Practical Matters: Ethnography and Theology*, 3. Retrieved from http://practicalmattersjournal.org/issue/3/analyzing-matters/second-grade-children-speak

———.(Forthcoming). Children speak: Catholic second graders' agency and experiences in the Sacrament of Reconciliation. *Sociology of Religion.*

Betz, O. (1968). Penance and the child. In Betz, O. (Ed.), *Making sense of confession: A new approach for parents, teachers, and clergy* (pp. 13–26, Graef, H. Trans.): Franciscan Herald Press.

Browning, D., & Miller-McLemore, B. (Eds.). (2009). *Children and childhood in American religions.* Rutgers, NJ: Rutgers University Press.

Buckley, F. J. (2000). *Growing in the church.* Lanham, MD: University of America Press.

Bunge, M. (Ed.). (2001). *The child in Christian thought.* Grand Rapids: Eerdmans.

Corrigan, J. (1969). *Growing up Christian: Penance and moral development of children.* Dayton, OH: Pflaum.

Davenport/Ministry to Children. (1973, August 30). *Origins*, 3(10), 159.

Dooley, Sr. C., O.P., & McDade, T. (Eds.). (2006). *Reconciliation: Pardon and peace. Catechist edition.* Allen, TX: RCL Benziger.

Durkheim, E. (1912). (1995). *The elementary forms of religious life.* New York: Free Press.

First penance, First communion: Brooklyn. (1977, December 29). *Origins*, 7(28), 445–46.

Fragomeni, R., & Hiesberger, J. (2000). *The gift of reconciliation.* Chicago: Silver Burdett Ginn.

Haight, W. (2002). *African American children at church.* New York: Cambridge University Press.

Hardman, C. E., & Palmer, S.J. (Eds.). (1999). *Children in new religions.* Rutgers, NJ: Rutgers University Press.

In Context: First Confession 1. Why Worcester Delays It. (1971, December 33). *Origins*, 1(27), 456–57.

Introducing children to penance. (1974, January 31). *Origins*, 3(32), 490–95.

Jambor, M. (2003). *Reconciliation.* Allen, TX: Resources for Christian Living.

Martos, J. (2001). *Doors to the sacred: A historical introduction to sacraments in the Catholic Church.* Chicago: Triumph.

Mercer, J. (2005). *Welcoming children.* St. Louis: Chalice.

Mette, N. (1987). Children's confession: A plea for a child-centered practice of penance and reconciliation. In Collines, M. & Power, D. (Eds.), *The fate of confession* (pp. 64–73). Edinburgh: T & T Clark.

Miller-McLemore, B. J. (2003). *Let the children come.* San Francisco: Jossey-Bass.

———.(Forthcoming). Religious rites of passage. In Shweder, R. (Ed.), *The Chicago companion to the child* (pages unknown). Chicago: University of Chicago Press.

O'Neil, R., & Donovan, M. (1969). *Children and sin.* Washington, DC: Corpus.

Orsi, R. (2005). *Between heaven and earth.* Princeton: Princeton University Press.

Pius X. (1954). Quam Singulari. In Yzermans, V. A. (Ed.), *All things in Christ: Encyclicals and selected documents of Saint Pius X* (pp. 245–50). Westminster, MD: Newman.

Ridgely, S. (2006). Decentering sin: First reconciliation and the nurturing of post-Vatican II Catholics. *Journal of Religion, 86*(4), 606–34.

Sacred Congregation for the Discipline of the Sacraments. (1973). *Sanctus Pontifex. Declaration on children's confession prior to their First Communion,* 410.

15

Rebuilding the Walls of Protection
A Church's Response to the Spiritual Impact of Child Abuse

Melodie Bissell

Introduction

Over the past decade religious institutions have been questioned as to their efforts to protect the vulnerable in their midst. Newspapers are filled with stories of payouts in the billions of dollars compensating victims who have been exploited by clergy. The issue of abuse is not a new one and has rapidly become a leading area of concern for organizations responsible for the care and safely of children. "In the past 15 years, the issue of abuse has surfaced and is now the single most important issue facing insurance companies" (Hall, 2005, p. 1). However, to call for abuse prevention seemingly distracts from the mission of the church. But does it really?

Over the last twenty years, considerable research has been documented on the impact on psychological functioning. These studies demonstrate the negative effects of abuse on the survivor's psychological well-being, sexual identity, ability to handle stress, their ability to achieve life goals, and general life satisfaction. However, little published research has been done on the spiritual impact of abuse and their spiritual functioning. (Braver, 1992).

In this chapter, the spiritual impact of abuse will be identified, and a model will be introduced wherein the church can nurture spiritual healing and wholeness among a child's community. Two case studies will also be introduced to assist the reader in applying the model to real life incidences.

Spirituality Defined

According to Marilyn A. Ganje-Fling and Patricia McCarthy, in a 1996 journal article *"Impact of Childhood Sexual Abuse on Client Spiritual Development: Counselling Implications,"* the following definition of spirituality is offered: "Spirituality is a complex, multifaceted construct that involves ultimate and personal truths that individuals hold as inviolable in their lives. This definition of spirituality is broad enough to incorporate religious, existential, and unstructured orientation" (Ganje-Fling and McCarthy, 1996, p. 253).

Recognizing that this is a broad definition of spirituality, and that spirituality is often based upon one's worldview, including their cultural and sociological up-bringing, we will focus more specifically on how abuse impacts:

1. a child's belief in a higher being, a God who is holy, sovereign and loving;

2. a child's response to identifying with a community of believers; and

3. a child's spiritual formation as it relates to their purpose for living and hope for the future.

Please note that the author has a Christian worldview, therefore spirituality for this study will be narrowed to spirituality that has a Christian focus, where the Bible is the plumb line for establishing one's perspective of life, philosophy, and harmony of beliefs.

Child Abuse Defined

The following definition of child abuse, as adopted by the Children's Aid Society of London and Middlesex (Canada), will be used: "Child abuse refers to an act committed by a parent, caregiver or person in a position of trust which is not accidental and which harms or threatens to harm a child's physical or mental health or a child's welfare" (The Children's Aid Society of London and Middlesex, 2006, ¶4).

According to the same source, abuse is primarily categorized as "physical, sexual, emotional, or involving neglect" (The Children's Aid Society of London and Middlesex, 2006, ¶3).

The Spiritual Impact of Childhood Abuse

Child abuse is a sad phenomenon that impacts millions of children. Considerable attention has been paid to the immediate and long-term effects of abuse notably in relation to the impact on psycho-social functioning. Few studies, however, have focused on what may be called the spiritual impact of childhood abuse, despite the devastating consequences abuse has to the child's perception of and relationship with God.

According to Marilyn Ganje-Fling and Patricia McCarthy, many traumatized clients of sexual abuse that they have dealt with have experienced questions and conflicts regarding their spirituality. The impact to spiritual formation that they note includes striving to relate to a powerful, higher being. They also struggle with a sense of hope-lessness, lacking a sense of purpose, and are often ambivalent to connecting with a community (Ganje-Fling and McCarthy, 1996, p. 254).

Thomas and Susan Turrell's paper, *Where was God?*, supports that most psychological practice ignores the spiritual concerns of Christian victims and how these concerns influence psychological aspects of one's life. The study found that 60 percent of victims report an increased need for spirituality following the abuse, indicating that religion and spirituality can greatly impact victim recovery (Turrell, 2001, p. 133).

Though few studies have been done to determine the spiritual impact of child abuse (physical/sexual/emotion), virtually all of the studies that have been done show a negative effect spiritually. Most of the studies have been done among women (not children) survivors of sexual abuse. A significant impact noted is a sense of spiritual alienation.

David Pelzer in his first book "*A Child Called It*" speaks of his perception of God. A horrific first person account of one of the most severe child abuse cases in North America. Dave Pelzer was brutally beaten and starved by his own mother. In the chapter "The Lord's Prayer" Dave writes: "About a month before I entered the fifth grade, I came to believe that for me, there was no God. . . . No just God would leave me like this. I believed that I was alone in my own struggle and my battle was one of survival" (Pelzer, 1996, p. 131).

In the Amy Berg's 2006 film, "*Deliver Us From Evil*," a documentary of recent abuse within the Roman Catholic Church, you hear testimony after testimony of victims who have been abused at the hands of a Priest. They indicate they will never re-enter a church because in their eyes this was God abusing them.

A news report in the St. Louis Examiner addressed a report of a letter that surfaced indicating a cover up by the Catholic Church has raised the issue again of clergy related child sexual abuse; and the ramifications of how that affects someone's spirituality. SNAP's executive director, David Clohessy of St. Louis said, "Almost every victim of clergy sexual abuse—whether as a child or as an adult— struggles with spirituality at some point. A minority of them eventually find or restore some sort of faith life, but usually only after years of grappling and searching and working hard to recovery from the betrayal in and out of therapy. . . . But for the overwhelming majority of those assaulted by clergy, authentic spirituality is either impossible or possible only after long periods of inner doubt and conflict" (Weiman, 2011, ¶5).

Rossetti, in the journal article *The Impact of Child Sexual Abuse on Attitudes Toward God and the Catholic Church,* reports the outcome of a study he performed that focused on the abuse done by priests in Catholic churches and how that correlated to the victims views on commitment to Church leadership. It also deals with an assessment of the Church's response to Child Sexual Abuse, evaluation of the Church, trust in the priests, and relationship to God. He found that victims reported significantly less trust in the Church and the Catholic priests, and they lost faith in God after sexual abuse (Rossetti, 1995, p. 1469–81).

In the 2007 journal *Scientific Study of Religion*, Gall, Basque, Damasceno-Scott., and Vardy, specifically focused on both the effect abuse has on spirituality and the effect spirituality has on coping with abuse. Their findings demonstrate that spiritual beliefs can be a positive force of treatment. This study mentioned many positives of spirituality, such as protection against depression and shame, support, aid in understanding, inner strength, self-acceptance, belonging and attachment. This study also found that victims of child sexual abuse "reported having a negative image of God as being cruel, uncaring, and punishing" and "reported lower levels of spiritual well-being" (Gall, Basque, Damasceno-Scott and Vardy, 2007, p. 102).

Diane Langberg, in her article *The Spiritual Impact of Child Abuse,* identifies why these spiritual blocks and/or obstacles occur. The first block seems to be that a survivor's thinking often appears to be "frozen" in time. A woman who was chronically abused by her father for fifteen years thinks about herself, her life and her relationships through the grid of abuse. Trauma stops growth because it shuts everything down. The input of other experiences often does not alter the thinking that originated within the context of the abuse. So a woman may have encountered many trustworthy people since her childhood abuse, but she still does not trust. She may have heard thousands of words about how God loves her, but she believes she is trash and somehow an exception to that truth, (Langberg, p. 2,).

The second block according to Langberg is that the abuse was processed by a child's mind and children think concretely, not abstractly. Children learn about abstract concepts like trust, truth, and love, from the concrete experiences they have with significant others in their lives.

Third, children (like adults) learn about the unseen, or the spiritual, by way of the seen. God often teaches us eternal truths through the natural world. We grasp a bit of eternity through looking at the same. We learn about the shortness of life by the quick disappearance of a vapour. Jesus taught this way as well. He said He was bread, light, water, and a vine. Jesus, in His very essence, is an example of this. He is God in the flesh. God continually brings eternal truths to us in ways we can understand (Langberg, p. 2nd,).

Though the negative impact of abuse has been noted on spirituality, studies and testimonials likewise recognize the influence spirituality has on their healing.

Billye Graham Bowman shares with readers her own story of abuse, and the years she lived in darkness while suppressing her memories, without the knowledge of God's unconditional love. Once found, this love transformed her life. One of the keys identified in the book to finding healing is reading Scripture (Bowman, 2006, p. 97).

Galea, in *The Impact of Child Abuse on the Psycho-Spiritual and Religious Status of Maltese College Students,* notes both the negative effects of abuse as well as the reasoning behind why spirituality plays an important role in the treatment of child abuse. The reasoning identified is: "suffering stimulates the need for meaning because people analyse and question their suffering far more than their joys while beliefs counter hopelessness, such as religious beliefs, forming an important part in the treatment process" (Galea, 2008, p. 150).

It comes as no surprise to know there are long-term consequences to child abuse. We may no longer be surprised that children don't easily bounce back from abuse; they are not as resilient as we once believed. Learning that victims struggle spiritually after abuse left me to initially wonder what role, if any, the church could have in minimizing the impact. The following case studies demonstrate the influence spirituality has in the disclosure stage and the healing stages of recovery from abuse.

Case Study #1

Note: The Elliotts (including David) have chosen to use their real names both in this article and in their series of books as they desire to help other families that have been confronted with abuse and they firmly believe they have nothing to hide and are not responsible for the abuse that occurred. David wants his story to help other kids.

David Elliott was just shy of his nineteenth birthday when he was abused by a teenage friend of the family. The Elliotts are a strong godly Christian family that faced a Goliath that had every intent to destroy David. In the first of four books written by the Elliotts, *David's Sword*, and through phone interviews with David's parents, we will hear David's role in telling his story, the soldiers that have come around David and his family and the role of the therapist in nurturing and restoring David's faith, relationship with God, and his spiritual healing.

The Elliott's define themselves as evangelical Christians. Family makeup is Mom (Marybeth), Dad (Lee), and three sons of which David is the youngest. At the time of writing this article the boys are twenty, fourteen and eleven. The abuse occurred three years ago.

In the words of Marybeth Elliott: "David came to our bedroom at 11:00 p.m. at night. We were asleep and he knocked on our door and told us he had something urgent to tell us. David had been trying to read his children's devotional Bible with a desire to reach out to God. He knew he was in a dark place but he was having trouble being able to read it. The Holy Spirit was leading him. He came to tell us as he needed our help."

"When he told us, his words just spilled out very quickly and graphically, but we were able to listen and stay calm. We had learned this from caring for Mark, David's oldest brother who is now twenty and has autism. In our experience, it is best to remain calm and listen. We didn't want to react from concern that David would stop talking if he was afraid his words were hurting us."

"David gave his heart to the Lord when he was four years of age. He had attended church, Sunday School, and Bible clubs. The abuse plunged David into a dark time. David slept on the floor near our bed. As the story came out, more and more details were told. David would experience stomach aches, inability to focus in class, fear of being alone in a room, fear of outside, and many more things as well."

(M. Elliott, personal communication, May 2009)

Case Study #2

Note: the story of Jewel, Martin and Bella Sung is also a true story that the author of this paper encountered in the process of researching and writing this article. The names have been changed to protect the identity of the family and child.

Jewel is an eleven year old who was recently suspended from her school for stealing a piece of clothing. The piece of clothing was found in Jewel's position by school administration. The school called mom to report the theft and to inform mom that Jewel was suspended for two days. Jewel was also required to write a five-hundred word essay on stealing and lying. At home mom challenged Jewel on her behaviour. The child continued to lie and try to manipulate the events that led up to the theft. Mom called the Children's Pastor for help. She wanted someone to intervene in her daughter's life and do whatever was necessary to challenge Jewel. Dad was on an overseas business trip and had left mom home with three young children of which Jewel is the oldest. The family are of Asian descent.

In the course of meeting with Jewel the Children's Pastor addressed the concern about lying and stealing. Coming to the close of their time together they spoke about forgiveness and consequences to sin. The consequences to this behaviour were a two-day suspension, writing an essay, and the loss of allowance. The latter to Jewel was pretty difficult to swallow but she understood why. Jewel then disclosed further consequences: "this was not my only punishment." The following allegation and conversation took place:

J: "I had to sleep in the garage for two days and didn't get dinner."

J: "Mommy also beat me."

CP: "Do you mean mommy spanked you?"

J: "No, mommy beat me. She first started hitting me with a wooden spoon, then with a cane. Then she was punching and kicking me and pushing me against the wall. It lasted a really long time. It lasted over an hour."

As required by law, Children's Welfare was called and the abuse was reported. Over the course of the next 8 hours all parties were interviewed and questioned. Jewel was taken to the police station and she was interviewed and videotaped by a detective for 2.5 hours. That evening Jewel was placed into foster care and the detectives discussed the pending arrest of mom, possibly dad, and the apprehension of the siblings. Over the course of the next 12 weeks, Jewel was transferred into four different foster care homes. The Sungs lived with the fear that criminal charges would be laid for a few weeks, however the police officers decided not to lay charges after seeing Bella's remorse and the bruises had faded at the point of allegation and discovery.

Therapy

As abuse has long-term impact on a child—it is critical that parents and churches know that long term counselling needs to be provided. Short term pastoral care or counselling is often not enough to deal with the scars that a child will develop that are much more than skin deep. If abuse occurs outside of the family, the family may seek out a competent counsellor. They may contact the church for referrals.

Competent Christian counselling by a trained therapist/psychologist or psychiatrist can begin to help a child heal spiritually in light of the abuse.

As was the case with David Elliott, the parents immediately sought the assistance and counsel of the Church in dealing with the crisis. The morning after David disclosed his abuse, the parents shared it with the Pastor. They were then referred to a Christian therapist who began counselling sessions with David. The counselling continued for 20 months, after which time the therapist discontinued the therapy but with the commitment of being available whenever David felt he wanted follow-up sessions.

If a child is taken into foster care one of the first things that will occur is the child will be assigned a therapist. In most cases the therapist may be a non-Christian. The church can come alongside the family and child to provide pastoral care while the child is in therapy. This becomes a concrete example to the child that God is not silent. This is what occurred in the case study of the Sung family.

Cheryl Ettinger is the founder and President of House of Hope in Burlington, Canada. Cheryl herself served as a Children's Pastor for many years prior to completing her Masters of Christian Counselling. Today she is a psycho-therapist along with the group support she does at House of Hope. In an interview I asked Cheryl about the trauma children encounter. Cheryl spoke about their resiliency, "Many adults believe that because children are resilient, they don't need as much support. Adults hope the children will forget it. They don't forget! They stay there and then years later they will pick it up again and only then will you see how angry they are at God. They may look like they are doing fine, so the decision is made not to send the child to a professional counsellor. We do not count the spiritual cost of the crisis. It is true, children often bounce back, but years later the pain from their past re-surfaces if it has not been properly addressed. Even with counselling, children when they are adults will raise the question 'Why did God allow this to happen to me?'" (Ettinger, 2009). Cheryl stresses the importance of securing a counsellor for the child as soon after the trauma as possible.

Along with Marybeth Elliott in *David's Sword*, Cheryl encourages the children to be the teacher. The child can teach the adults how to interpret the abuse that happened. As a therapist, Cheryl wants to learn from the incident what happened. When we allow the child to be the teacher we can learn how to be a better parent, teacher, counsellor, or pastor. Children are comfortable with being in the teacher role. When questioning the child, ask the question, "what is it like to be you?" Cheryl also agrees with Marybeth that words are important. Healing begins to happen when you tell your story. Encourage the child to tell their story.

One area of concern that surfaced in my research and interviews was a form of therapy called theophostic counselling. The word "theophostic" comes from two Greek words: "Theos" (God) and "Phos" (light). Its originator, Ed smith, writes: "These two terms describe God bringing forth illumination into a previously darkened area of one's mind. Theophostic counselling offers a new and revolutionary means of accomplishing what traditional approaches to therapy" (Robinson, 2003, ¶1).

Theophostic therapists believe that Jesus was there with the child during the abuse, as a participant, and that children should rewrite their story at the point of abuse. If this model is used it should only be used by a trained counsellor. Research identifies that negative impact could occur when this model of counselling takes place (Robinson, 2003, ¶7). If you tell children that Jesus was right next to them when the abuse happened, they will ask, "was he watching me the whole time?" Theophostic therapists try to help the child see that Jesus is present within the counselling and is leading the way for truth to replace the darkness (Robinson, 2003, ¶3).

Memories of traumatic events, particularly those of childhood sexual abuse, are often repressed at the time of the incident. These memories are accurately stored in a part of the brain that is not readily accessible by the adult's conscious brain. Repressed memories of childhood abuse cause emotional problems in adults. Repressed memories can be accurately recovered via therapy or counselling.

Note: An effective means of counselling that can be done and is recommended by both professional counsellors and within a setting of pastoral counselling is narrative therapy. This model enables the child to rewrite their story from the point of counselling (see www.dulwich-centre.com). One specific method of narrative therapy which is done with children is The Tree of Life, developed in partnership by Ncazelo Ncube (REPSSI) and David Denborough (Dulwich Centre Foundation) has been used successfully among vulnerable children internationally. "The Tree of Life enables children to speak about their lives in ways that are not retraumatising, but instead strengthens their relationships with their own history, their culture, and significant people in their lives." (The

Dulwich Centre: Tree of Life, retrieved May 21, 2011, http://www.dul-wichcentre.com.au/tree-of-life.html)

Healing in Tandem with a Therapist

It has been said "It takes a village to raise a child." My position, which is reflected in my forth-coming model, is that it takes a circle of many to nurture the healing of an abused child.

In our case study of David Elliott, the parents shared with friends and family, seeking support and guidance. They also shared with the parents of David's friends believing strongly that if they continued to entrust David to them to play at their homes, then they could also trust them with this. If they trust David's physical care to them, they should also have no concern about trusting his emotional care.

The family also wanted to avoid secrecy about this. Sexual abuse, as we have all sadly discovered, is prevalent in society. David was very clear that this would be used to help other children, so no other kids would be hurt. He is a survivor of many crimes perpetrated against him, and he did nothing wrong. He received great encouragement from his parents, and they passed the litmus test with flying colors. Instead, he has been affirmed, and at Marybeth and Lee's request, they (parent's of David's friends) have held him to the same standard of manners and good behavior they hold their own children to. Essentially, this care of David and treating him normally, when he knows that they know the story, has been very edifying and strengthening for him. Along with the therapist, the supportive circle for the Elliott family has been the pastor, choir members, parents of David's friends, close friends, and family.

Whenever you invite people to share in your burden, you expose yourself to conflicting advice. We can learn a valuable lesson though from the Book of Job as we see his friends come around him and attempt to provide counselling. This raises the issue of having many voices speak into a family's life, all giving different counsel. Some of this counsel may be in the form of telling the parents the child is resilient and need not attend counselling, hoping the child will forget the trauma that has occurred.

With the Sung family, too many of the family friends wanted only to blame Jewel for her malicious and rebellious behaviour believing that she brought the abuse on herself. In an Asian setting many members of the community would want to help the mother not lose face but to support the family in causing the child to face shame. Rather than seeking counselling for healing of the abuse, the family chose to go to a therapist that focused on dealing with difficult adolescents, and how to respond appropriately. The community (friends, family, and school) quickly labelled the child and has supported an atmosphere of child maltreatment and emotional abuse, again making way for the church to either place blame in the wrong place or sweep the abuse under the carpet, hoping that the child will forget the painful memories.

The Response of the Church

An appropriate starting-point for a discussion of the relationship between childhood abuse and the church is the central role attributed to the child in Christian thought. Jesus' love for children is clearly expressed in the New Testament. One of the only two times reported in Scripture of Jesus showing anger is in his response to the disciples attempting to keep the children from him. Jesus said "let the children come" (Matt 19:14; Mark 10:14, Luke 18:6). In Matthew 18:5–6 we read a stern warning: "And whoever welcomes a little child like this in my name welcomes me. But if anyone causes one of these little ones who believe in me to sin, it would be better for him to have a large millstone hung around his neck and to be drowned in the depths of the sea."

God is not silent when it comes to abuse and neither should the church be. Diane Langberg states, "I believe members of the Body of Christ who have been called to walk with survivors become the representative of God to them. The reputation of God is at stake in our lives. We are called to live out in the seen, in flesh and blood what is true about who God is" (Langberg, 2009, p. 3).

The child needs to see and understand unconditional agape love. In other words, we are to demonstrate in the flesh the character of God over time so that who we are reveals the truth about God to the survivor. As we provide pastoral care to the survivor within community we are able to help the survivor or victim put down deep roots in the story of the crucifixion. The child will begin to identify with the suffering servant, "He was despised and rejected by mankind, a man of suffering, and familiar with pain," (Isa 53:3a, NIV, 2011). This will be a beginning to understand God's entrance into their suffering. This will require us in our teaching to linger on the story of the crucifixion for a time, not to be too anxious to move on to the story of the resurrection, allowing the child that is or has been suffering to consider and to identify with the suffering of Jesus.

As the church provides a safe place and a voice for the child they can "grasp God as their refuge. Out of their experience in the seen world they can better comprehend what is true in the unseen" (Langberg, 2009, p. 4).

Francis T. Murphy, Presiding Justice (Retired) of the New York Appellate Division states, "Children have neither power nor property. Voices other than their own must speak for them. If those voices are silent, then children who are victims of abuse may lean their heads against window panes and taste the bitter emptiness of violated childhoods" (F. T. Murphy, personal communication, September, 2007).

Unfortunately these voices too often speak in silos and work in isolation of each other. The model of The Healing Circle provides an impetus to bring these voices together.

A Model for the Church: The Healing Circle

In both of the case studies we have considered, the circle of care included family, friends, social services, guidance counsellors, educators, therapists, lawyers, medical doctors, and the church. Recognizing that the church has an unprecedented opportunity to be an instrument to nurture healing, hope and reconciliation, the remaining segment of this chapter will present a model which can be adopted for this purpose. We will end the chapter with the impact this had on our two case studies.

Prior to addressing the opportunity that the church has to be instrumental in nurturing a healing environment for the victim and their family, I would like to speak to the issue of the church both modelling and raising the bar on protection to vulnerable people. Faith organizations have been shamefully slow at implementing protective environments. Most of the efforts we have made would not have been made if it were not for the insurance companies having demanded it. Churches and faith organizations are now being held to the same standard of care in a court of law as any other organization. The church as a whole must also admit that we have been slow to respond to the issue of abuse within our walls and within many of our homes. We must take the same approach that the Lord Jesus did in Mark 10:13 and 14 and remove any barriers that would hinder a child coming to Jesus:

> "People were bringing little children to Jesus for him to place his hands on them, but the disciples rebuked them. When Jesus saw this, he was indignant. He said to them, 'Let the little children come to me, and do not hinder them, for the kingdom of God belongs to such as these'" (NIV, 2011).

There is no excuse for the church not to raise the bar on protection and demonstrate by example that protection is of utmost importance. The authors of *Plan to Protect® a Protection Manual for Children and Youth, a Protection Manual for churches*, state "the guidelines in this manual are written to help churches as they work toward fulfilling their responsibilities to provide a safe and nurturing environment for children and youth. . . . the manual is designed to assist church leaders in their recruitment of ministry personnel and, to the greatest extent possible, provide the safety of those served as well as those who serve" (Wiebe, Bissell & Cates, 2007, p. 22). With credibility, the church can then begin to reach out beyond the walls of the church and minister to the hurting.

The model of nurturing spiritual healing and wholeness in the life of an abused child is one where the church will engage a child's community for the purpose of rebuilding walls of protection. The church will be both incarnational and intentional in drawing together a child's community. The wise minister invites (seven pillars, Prov 9:1) family, teachers, therapist, church, friends, social, and legal systems to join a caring community around the victim in a safe neutral environment to do life together as a support to the child, family, and therapist/counsellor. An invitation is extended to the trained qualified Professional Counsellor/Therapist to participate in events and occasional meetings, to guide the community in supporting the healing process while still maintaining confidentiality. The Healing Circle is committed to supporting the Counsellor in his or her work with the child. Together, the Healing Circle will demonstrate grace and understanding. Grieving will be a natural part of the healing process. The child witnesses the strengthening and rebuilding of walls of protection.

Child abuse whether physical, emotion, sexual, or neglect can be devastating to a child. Once the abuse has been reported the governmental systems of the community and society kick in, family and friends can quickly feel out of control. The church has a tremendous opportunity to come alongside the victim, family, and community.

The role of the church in the Healing Circle will be to:

1. Help navigate through these troubled waters

2. Live incarnationally as they minister to a child and family during this turbulence.

3. Redeem the situation so that the child knows that God is not silent or distant but that God is taking the lead to rebuild walls of protection.

The Healing Circle is not another program of the church, rather an opportunity to draw together the family, friends and community of a child that has been abused with a desire to journey together to the place of healing and hope. The Healing Circle includes members who are trained and equipped to provide support to children who have been abused.

At the point that church is notified or becomes aware of the abuse, the church through its mandate begins to provide pastoral care. A recommended process includes:

1. Church being informed of the abuse and an opportunity arises to provide pastoral care

2. Church recommend a Healing Circle model

3. Pastoral and/or lay ministers begin slowly to build relationships with each group; ensuring confidentiality boundaries

4. Through pastoral care help the child see how all these "pillars" are rebuilding walls of protection

5. Initiate opportunity to bring the helping parties together for coaching by the Therapist

6. "Do life together" with the child helping to provide some normalcy to the child's life, i.e. providing transportation to counselling appointments, from the foster home to school, and legal appointments

7. With care help the child recognize and affirm commitment

to rebuild walls of protection

The Healing Circle is committed to:

- Engaging a child's community to model protection, support, and care during the weeks, months, and years after abuse has been revealed
- Bathing the ministry in prayer
- Maintaining confidentiality forever
- Initiating supportive networks for both the child and family
- Building strong partnerships with professionals and caregivers

The make-up of a Healing Circle could consist of: (see Illustration Appendix 1) Church community (Minister / pastoral staff, Sunday School teachers, and club leaders), Family (parents, siblings, and extended family), Educators (administration, guidance counsellors, and teachers), Social Services (protection workers), Legal (lawyers), Medical (doctors and therapist), and Friends (parents of friends, classmates, and neighbours).

The criteria for participation in the Healing Circle:

- A child that has been abused is either currently under professional care or with parents and caregivers desiring to build a support system.
- A group of 2 or more individuals (family, friends, or community members) who are willing to stand alongside of one needing protection. Early in the support network a primary contact and secondary contact for the Support Network will be identified.
- Commitment to assist in the development of desired goals and outcomes of the support network
- A commitment on behalf of the church to ministry beyond the walls of the church, encouraging and the silos of services offered to the family and child are broken down and build strong lines of communication to do life together moving in the same direction

A (lay) minister from the church may initially ask for the opportunity to meet with the social worker, teacher, parents making themselves available to walk alongside the child as the (lay) minister /

chaplain. Often great freedom is given to the (lay) minister / chaplain to sit with the child, participate in supervised visits, court appointments, etc.

Once strong relationships are formed, the (lay) minister could initiate an opportunity for all the parties to come together to hear from the therapist on how best to nurture the child through the stages of healing. This is when the Healing Circle begins to work together to rebuild the walls of healing.

Tips to a successful Healing Circle:

- Include the child in the Healing Circle.

- Seek permission to share their story. Ask the child what you can share and what you can't share.

- By including the child in the Healing Circle the therapist can offer to tell the story but if they make mistakes in the story the child can correct them.

- When ministering to the child predetermine a cue – to give you a sign to stop or I want to talk to you privately or that you are afraid. This gives comfort to the child that there is a way out.

Conclusion

In conclusion, the model of The Healing Circle provides the impetus to nurture healing of abuse, and cohesiveness within the community that is actively involved in the life of a victim. As we rebuild the walls of protection together we are also raising our voices on behalf of all children and youth, speaking against abuse and child maltreatment, striving to end child abuse. Victor Vieth states, "I believe we can end child abuse in the United States within three generations. If we start the clock ticking from this moment, this gives us 120 years to get the job done" (Vieth, 2006, p.6). Oh how I long to see the church leading the charge in the eradication of child abuse and nurturing the healing of abuse victims.

Jewel Sung was placed in foster care but Children's Aid Society permitted the Children's Minister to be her "life line" calling on her to assist the foster parents, and granting Jewel permission to call and visit her at any time, day or night, whenever she was needed.

Slowly additional people are being gathered into the circle including family friends, Child Welfare workers, the pastor, and principal.

Not everyone within the Healing Circle are Christians: the lawyer, therapist, kinship server, are not Christians. However, repentance, forgiveness, and reconciliation soon become evident to all.

The mother's initial response was bitterness, anger, and feelings of betrayal, while the father desired to help his family through the crisis and learn the lessons that God had for them through the journey. Within time reconciliation has taken place and friendships have been rebuilt, though there are still times when tension is felt within the relationship between the Children's Minister and the parents. The outcome is itself a testimony to God's intervention and healing for after ten weeks living within protective care, Jewel has returned home to her parents. The family has completed family counselling, and have become more transparent to the challenges they face in raising teens, and responding to family conflict. The parents vacillate between embarrassment and vulnerability, but today they are willing to call out for help and ask for prayer support.

As mentioned earlier, David Elliott was in counselling for 20 months. He still has some off-days. He struggles with some terms and phrases that pull back memories from the past. But he also now will say "this may be a remnant." He is learning the skills to recognize and implement the strategies he has been taught, to deal with these feelings and issues as they arise. He continues to talk as the occasion arises, and found out from an email that he was instrumental in saving an eleven year old boy's life who had experienced similar abuse, and was contemplating suicide. Through David's book, *David's Sword*, he has garnered strength, along with talking and journaling which helps him to learn the skills to build the life he deserves. David said "Mom if this book helps only this boy, it was all worth it" (M. Elliott, personal communication, May 2009).

Recently his therapist told him "David, you are doing so well." David asked the question "Why am I doing so well?" She told David because of the strong foundation from which he came, that because he was healthy to begin with, sought help early, and went through the painful process of dealing with it, his outcome is much healthier and stronger. He understands her door is always open to him, and he may want to call upon her as he grows and hits various milestones. He will revisit this issue, but he is equipped to know what to do when this happens, as are we (M. Elliott, personal communication, May 2009).

Marybeth communicates what David would want every victim to know in *David's Sword:*

> "David wants you to know that your words are your sword. And the people who love you are the sheath where your sword comes to res after its mighty work has been accomplished. Trust them with your secret and share your Goliath with them. They will help you. Keep sharing until you know you are believed and safe. You do not have to share with your parents; you can tell any adult whom you trust. They will help you! They will believe you, and they will work hard to set you free. Their swords will be their words, and you will no longer have to fight alone. They will be your protectors and your strength, and you will be free. You have the heart of a king, and your Father in Heaven is so very proud of you. No matter what beautiful name God has given you, when your words are spoken, you will be another David and your God will smile and say 'well done'" (Elliott, 2008, p. 38).

God receives the glory for the healing that has happened in David's life. His parents were committed to finding healing for him. David's community has helped David find healing and wholeness and rebuild his walls of protection (M. Elliott, personal communication, May 2009).

In conclusion, Marybeth Elliott (2009) recently stated:

> "No topic whatsoever should be off-limits to churches and to helping their people heal. In an environment of secrecy and perceived or real shame, abuse will flourish. Churches should be leading the way on results-oriented programming, and moreover churches should have the strongest voices of all with zero tolerance on this matter. Not only is it illegal, it is crushing to the victims to carry this burden. If churches will not address this issue, then this issue will confront churches in a way that is reactive and horrendous. It is much more proactive and healthy for churches to speak of this issue, as they would any other, to provide training, support and education as well as spiritual guidance in a mature environment for survivors of sexual abuse. Churches are embedded in communities, and their members come from communities. They have not only an obligation but an outstanding opportunity to shed light and promote health and support within their communities, and come alongside to partner with various agencies and enti-

ties, to strengthen the entire community." (M. Elliott, personal communication, May 2009)

"They will live in safety, and no one will make them afraid."

Ezekiel 37:4

References

Bowman, B. (2006). *Abuse buster: The second step.* Mustang, OK: Tate.

Children's Aid Society of London and Middlesex. (2011). *What is child abuse?*: Retrieved From: http://www.caslondon.on.ca/helping-families/what-child-abuse.

Elliot, D., Elliot L. & Elliot M, (2008). *David's sword.* Mustang, OK: Tate. Galea, M. (2008). The impact of child abuse on the psycho-spiritual and religious status of Maltese college students. *Pastoral Psychology, 57*(3), 147–59.

Gall, T. L. (2006). Spirituality and coping with life stress among adult survivors of childhood sexual abuse. *Child Abuse & Neglect, 30*(7), 829–44.

Gall, T. L., Basque, V., Damasceno-Scott, M., & Vardy, G. (2007). Spirituality and the current adjustment of adult survivors of childhood sexual abuse. *Journal for the Scientific Study of Religion, 46*(1), 101–17.

Ganje-Fling, M., & McCarthy, P. (1996). Impact of childhood sexual abuse on client spiritual development: Counseling implications. *Journal of Counseling & Development, 74*(3), 253–58.

Hall, K. (2005). *Abuse Prevention Newsletter.* London, ON: Robertson Hall Insurance.

Langberg, D. (2009). *The spiritual impact of abuse,* retrieved June 5, 2009, http://www.netgrace.org/content/images/The%20Spiritual%20Impact%20of%20Abuse.pdf

Pelzer, D. (1995). *A child called "It": One child's courage to survive.* Deerfield Beach, FL: Heath Communications.

Robinson, B. A. (2009). Theophostic© Counseling (TPM), retrieved June 6, 2009, http://www.religioustolerance.org/theophostic1.htm

Rossetti, S.J. (1995). The impact of child sexual abuse on attitudes toward God and the Catholic Church. *Child Abuse and Neglect, 19*(12), 1469–81.

Turell, S. C., & Thomas, C. R. (2001). Where was God? Utilizing spirituality with Christian survivors of sexual abuse. *Women & Therapy, 24*(3), 133–47.

Weiman, M. (2011). Still spiritual after trauma, *St. Louis Explorer,* January 23, 2011, http://www.examiner.com/spiritual-living-in-st-louis/still-spiritual-after-trauma

Wiebe, C., Bissell, M.,, & Cates, J. (2009). *Plan to protect: A protection plan for children and youth. A protection plan for churches.* Winnipeg, Canada: Word Alive Publishing.

Vieth, V., Bottoms, B., & Perona, A. (2006). *Ending child abuse: New efforts in prevention, investigation, and training.* Binghamton, NY: The Haworth Maltreatment and Trauma Press.

16

Divine Dialogue
Children's Spirituality Expressed Through Online
Discussion of Fantasy Literature

Catherine Posey

Introduction

Many books I encountered as a young reader increased my wonder and awareness of a world, both literal and figurative, beyond
my own. For example, some novels, such as Lucy Maud Montgomery's
Anne of Green Gables (1908) showed me that I was not the only one
who connected with God through the beauty of the natural world.
Other stories like *The Hobbit* (1937) provided me with the opportunity to consider how my own life held significance and purpose.
In other words, my spirituality was affected by what I read. I wish I
had been given the opportunity to share my responses to literature as
they related to my spiritual life, including my relationship with God,
the natural world, and other people. The connection I experienced
between literature and my spirituality is one of many reasons why I
became interested in children's spiritual expressions and literature,
both inside the classroom and outside of it.

As a result, at the beginning of 2009, I developed a qualitative
study exploring ten and eleven year old children's responses to several
novels in a fantasy series, *The City of Ember* (2003) by Jeanne DuPrau

within an online discussion forum. Before this, however, I identified a research problem to which my study responds.

The Problem

Within the field of education, some argue that the spiritual dimension of the individual is significant, and this perspective has cultivated an interest in expressions of children's spirituality (Coles, 1990; Houskamp, Fisher & Stuber, 2004; Hay with Nye, 1998; Hyde, 2008). Investigation into the literature about children's spirituality reveals a gap in descriptions of children's spiritual discourse about their responses to literary texts. Though I discovered a large amount of work on the broader area of children's spirituality and education, studies on how expressions of children's spirituality are generated through their responses to literature are few.

Myers & Myers discuss their ideas about encouraging children's spirituality through literature in the early childhood classroom, but their work is limited to a small study within a kindergarten classroom (1999). Pike and Schoonmaker have also explored children's and adolescents' spirituality as expressed through their engagement with literature. Pike's study concerned young adults reading and responding to poetry, and Schoonmaker's research focused on children's responses to picture books (Pike, 2000; Schoonmaker, 2009). Pike's case study research included students between the ages of thirteen and sixteen and their written responses to poetry. His findings revealed that young adults were engaging with spiritual and moral themes as they wrote about the poems in their journals. Schoonmaker, with some of her doctoral students, conducted a phenomenology of children's spiritual readings of picture books. As the researchers spoke with the children about different books, their initial conclusions were that the children did not bring up the spiritual aspects of the texts. However, after going over the transcripts, they realized they had often failed to listen to the children, and by so doing, they had missed significant moments of spirituality (2009). Schoonmaker's findings point to the importance of recognizing adult assumptions about children's spirituality, and that researchers should be intentional about listening carefully to children's ideas of a story.

Trousdale has conducted qualitative studies and written theoretical work about the ways that narrative can cultivate spiritual growth of children, but her research has not focused on descriptions of children's spirituality within online book group discussions (Trousdale, 2004a, 2004b, 2005a, 2005b, 2005c, 2006, 2007). Her work includes important discussion about reader-response theory, and she proposes that readers can bring their own spiritual identities into the book and reader equation (2006). One study employing a multiple case study design, during which children read and responded to picture books, reflected that different children draw various meanings from a text, interpreting the story on both literal and symbolic levels (2005a). Like Schoonmaker, Trousdale concluded that adults should listen to children in order to find out what they think about spiritual matters. Adults should be wary of expecting children to understand the same spiritual meaning they draw from the text. She also discovered in her case study research of children of seven and eight years old "that their perceptions of God were expanded through reading the text" (2004a, p. 183).

Based on my survey of research into children's spirituality and education, a gap exists in understanding children's spiritual discourse that is nurtured through their discussion of literary texts within online discussion forums. As a result, I developed a descriptive small-sample multiple case study focusing on describing children's spirituality as manifested through their responses to several fantasy novels within an online discussion forum.

Defining Spirituality

Various conceptions of the "spiritual" exists, but it is necessary to provide a clear definition for the purposes of this study, which include identifying expressions of children's spirituality through their discourse about literature. Many, including Hay, Nye, Coles, and Hyde agree with the notion of "spirituality as [a] fundamental aspect of human nature" (Hay with Nye, 1998; Coles, 1990; Hyde, 2008; McCreery, 1994). Though spirituality is a "contested concept," Hyde suggests that, "As an ontological category, spirituality is a natural human predisposition" (2008, pp. 235–36). I understand spirituality as a heightened awareness and a reaching out beyond the self. Nye has termed "relational consciousness" as "that awareness of an holistic relationship with the rest of reality" (Nye, 2006, pp. 131–32). This holistic relationship can encompass unity with the self, people, the world, or a divine being, such as God.

McCreery states: "It appears that the spiritual is to do with that aspect of human nature which reaches beyond; beyond the known and the ordinary, beyond the explainable to the mysterious to find answers" (1994, p. 98). The concept of a general spirituality encompasses that universal tendency within people to reach out for intangible, deep connection with something greater than themselves. This connection might manifest through a richer awareness of self, or through relationship to other people, the natural world, or to a divine source, such as God.

However, Christian spirituality specifically extends this notion of a general spirituality to also include a focus on God as revealed by the Trinity of the Father, the Son, Jesus, and the Holy Spirit. Catherine Stonehouse presents one way of conceptualizing Christian spirituality:

> Christian spirituality focuses on a growing love relationship with God that flows into the love and service of others. The model for that life of love for God and others is Jesus Christ, and spiritual growth is often identified as becoming more Christlike. (2006, p. 98)

Expressions of Christian spirituality in children, then, might reflect awareness of the significance of the person of Jesus as necessary for connection to God. Their spiritual expressions might also feature characteristics of the life of Jesus, as communicated through Biblical story. Additionally, these expressions might engage dialogue about the Holy Spirit, and reflect awareness of those blockages to relationship with God: "Within the Christian faith community they also learn that sin breaks our relationship with God, but that through Jesus' death and resurrection God offers forgiveness of sings to all who come to Jesus" (Stonehouse, 2006, p. 101). Though this study was not solely concerned with expressions of Christian spirituality as generated by children's responses to literary texts, it is helpful to consider how one particular perspective can influence its spiritual expressions.

Methodology

This qualitative study responded to the research question: What is the nature of children's spiritual talk as generated through their responses to fantasy texts? My study aimed to describe expressions of children's spirituality that were produced through their discussion within an on-line forum about the first two novels in the fantasy series, *The City of Ember*, by Jeanne DuPrau (2003–2008). Situated within my own defi-nition, spirituality as expressed by the children's discussion included their "reaching out beyond the self" and also included allusion to the otherworldly, mystical, and supernatural dimensions of life. This kind of talk could also reference the children's connection to God or a Divine Power, their connection with other people, the natural world, or themselves.

In order to collect data from an online forum, I used the web site, PICCLE. PICCLE, Pedagogy for Intercultural Critical Literacy, provides online space for international discussions for children and young adults, usually through a class project or discussion group. Faculty in the College of Education at Pennsylvania State University received a grant from the U.S. Department of Education in order to develop this electronic course environment, and the space provides multiple types of forums. Some of the different "categories" include classroom, open discussion, and a forum for "interpreting texts from intercultural perspectives." Teachers are able to develop forums for their students, and allow other teachers to take part in dialogue. The goal of the PICCLE online environment is "to form global communi-ties through online communication, and help global citizens develop new ideas about themselves, others, and the world" ("Pedagogy for Intercultural Critical Literacy"). PICCLE thus represented an effective tool for creating a secure discussion space for the children to share their ideas about selected fantasy novels.

Online book clubs provide educators with a method for build-ing links between old and new literacy practices (Scharber, 2009). Scharber highlights the fact that new technology has influenced chil-dren's reading, but she suggests that, "online book clubs may offer a motivating and convenient environment to encourage voluntary book reading" (p. 433). When children read books for pleasure, they can socialize with other children of similar ages and share their opinions about the texts. Scharber provides instructions for creating an online space for a book club using the tool, Moodle (p. 434). Those who are interested in creating an online forum for young people to discuss literature can navigate to www.moodle.org and discover a secure and free online environment where book club facilitators can create and manage online forums. In addition to discussion forums, Moodle also provides the opportunity to conduct real-time chats with book club members and students can also create profiles. Scharber points out the flexibility and security of Moodle that makes it an ideal space on the web for the development of book clubs for young people (p. 435). If I had not gained access to PICCLE through Penn State, I would certainly have utilized Moodle to conduct my study; as a result, those interested in creating their own online book clubs are encouraged to explore the benefits of this resource.

I used a descriptive multiple case study design in order to answer my research question about children, children's literature, and spirituality. Case studies can provide an in-depth and rich description of a phenomenon, resulting in an increased understanding of a situation or process (Rossman & Rallis, 2003, p. 104). I recruited participants from classrooms and home school communities within the United States and England. My contacts included a fifth grade teacher at a Christian elementary school in Northern California, a children's librarian at a school in England, and a home school mother in Central Pennsylvania. The fifth grade teacher in Northern California was introduced to me by a family member, while the other two contacts were personal friends of mine. These gatekeepers assisted me by e-mailing flyers to parents about the book club, and also helped with distributing consent forms and other information about the study. The one participant from England that had originally expressed interest in the study never participated in any of the discussion forums once the study began, and so my participants were all living in America at the time of the study.

On PICCLE, I created three forums about each book with questions to which the children could respond. During the first month I labeled the first discussion forum, "Entering Ember," the second "Inside the City of Ember (1st half of the book)," and the third, "Inside the City of Ember (2nd half of the book)." The second month concerned the same types of forums for *The People of Sparks*. The first forum included questions concerning assumptions about the cover and speculations about the story's focus while the other two forums included open-ended questions about the content of the texts.

I chose to use open-ended questions for the book club because I was interested in whether children talk about spirituality in a text without explicit promptings from an adult. Furthermore, I found the spiritual aspects of DuPrau's novels implicit rather than explicit, though I do not think this makes the likelihood of children's spiritual talk about a story any less frequent. These questions followed the *Tell Me* framework, introduced by Aidan Chambers in his book on talking to children about literature, *Tell Me* (1996). I asked the children to share their likes, dislikes, patterns/connections they noticed in the story, and questions/puzzles they developed. Then, at the end of the month, I doubled the number of questions, repeating the ones from the first half, but adding prompts related to the conclusion of the story, significant ideas the children noticed, and whether or not the reader would recommend the text to someone else.

Method of Analysis

During the analysis phase, I used thematic analysis to explore the data. Braun and Clarke (2006) emphasize the theoretical flexibility of this approach: "thematic analysis provides a flexible and useful research tool, which can potentially provide a rich and detailed, yet complex account of data" (p. 78). Braun & Clarke state that a theme in the data is identified as something connected to the research question and reflects "some level of patterned response or meaning" (p. 82). I focused on the content of the children's responses in order to identify themes within the discussion, using my own understanding of how some spiritual themes in literature emerge.

Researcher Identity

This study is shaped by the researcher's background, worldview, gender, and social class. The researcher necessarily influences the research, and I am viewing the participants, the setting, and the data through my unique lens as an individual. Rather than hide that fact, as a researcher, I recognize how my own background is an integral part of my study. My education and experience influence my approach to children's books and might also influence my responses to the children's comments about those books. By making biases and assumptions explicit, researchers can strengthen their studies by considering how the researcher's identity affects the study.

Limitations of Study

This study does not aim to make generalizations about children's spirituality or to develop a theory about how children express their spirituality as they respond to literary texts. What it does intend to provide, however, is a description of the spiritual talk that is generated through a small group of children's responses to several fantasy novels in a series within an online book club. A similar study might concern a larger group of participants over a lengthier amount of time, but this descriptive case study sought to understand more deeply the kind of spiritual discussion that was produced as children shared their ideas about the first two novels in *The City of Ember* series. The texts are not explicitly religious, but like other fantasy novels, these stories engage with some spiritual themes and ideas. Before discussing the findings of my study, the reader may benefit from a brief summary of both novels.

Summaries of Novels

The City of Ember (2003) introduces readers to an underground city, rapidly losing its electric power. Two twelve year-old children, Lina and Doon, discover a secret message that may enable them to find a way out of Ember. Ember was originally created due to a catastrophic event above ground, but because those living underground have existed there for over 200 years, no one is aware of an outside world. The situation at the beginning of the novel is dire, with increasing black outs that are growing in length and frequency. The novel charts the journey of Lina and Doon as they piece together the meaning of the mysterious message and search for a way out of the city.

The People of Sparks (2004) concerns the life of those inhabitants of the city of Ember who made their way out of the underground city, thanks to discovery of Lina and Doon in the first novel. Bewildered and challenged by their new environment in the outdoors, the people eventually discover the city of Sparks, where they attempt to live and work within the community. However, conflicts and issues arise as two groups of people who don't understand each other are forced to coexist and share limited resources.

Results

In all, six children participated in the study, and of these six, five children attended a private school and one was homeschooled. Five of the children were in the fifth grade, around the ages of ten or eleven, and lived in northern California. One child was in the fourth grade, and lived in central Pennsylvania. I recruited both boys and girls, not to explore gender differences, but because I was interested in the perspectives of both genders. Four boys and two girls made up the online book club. One boy was homeschooled, in central Pennsylvania, while the other five children attended a private Christian school in northern California.

Not all of the children replied to questions on all of the forums in the book club. For example, only four participants posted on the forum concerned with the first half of the first novel, but a different group of four replied to the forum for the second half. However, some of the children did reply to all of the questions on each forum, and some posted replies to other participants' responses. Pseudonyms are used in order to protect the identities of the children in the study.

The children's comments illuminated several themes related to expressions of the children's spirituality. Their responses indicated at least an implicit awareness of some spiritual dimensions of the novels, and these included the significance of connection with others and the importance of hope/perseverance within difficult circumstances.

Connections with Others

Several of the participants discussed the significance of the characters' connections and relationships for the unfolding of the plot. The theme of working together, sometimes in sacrificial ways, runs throughout all of the *City of Ember* books, and DuPrau manages to illuminate this theme from the very beginning of the series.

Two participants commented on the two central characters in the story, and both focused specifically on an important and pivotal opening episode, "Assignment Day," where Lina and Doon discover what roles they will play in helping the city of Ember to run efficiently. "Philip" shared one of his "likes" of the first novel: "I like assignment day and remembering when they were young." "Colin," stated: "I liked how at the beginning, Lina and Doon picked the job that the other person wanted, and that they cooperated and traded." Duncan stated what he liked about the second half of the first book: "Lina and Doon discover more secrets about the city." Cassie echoed this idea in her forum post with "I liked the second half of the book because they started to discover more things!" "Josh" posed the question about the second part of *The City of Ember*, "Why is it so lonesome for them?" He included a sad faced emoticon at the end of his sentence, indicating the feelings associated with his question about Lina and Doon. Though Josh did not further elaborate on his question, his comment reflected an insightful perspective of the difficulties surrounding the two main characters in the story.

Some of the participants' comments also reflected the realization that the children's connectedness and commitment could accomplish significant victories. Duncan shared his idea about the second novel in the series: "Guessing from reading the back cover of the book, I think the two children will prevent a big war from happening." Cassie also posted a comment that pointed to her understanding of the power of the children as depicted in the story: "It is important to know that even kids can save a city." Cassie's statement linked to an idea that Duncan shared: "I think it is important to know that no matter your age, you can accomplish anything that isn't beyond human reach, if you have enough determination and will." Both the participants tapped into the idea that age does not have to be a barrier to bringing about significant change. In the case of the Ember series, two children working together helped bring about these changes. Duncan's comment crossed both spiritual themes by also illuminating the importance of perseverance.

To summarize, the children's comments from several of the forums indicated their awareness of the importance of relationships for the resolution of the central conflict in the novel. Many of the children's "likes" in the story concerned situations where both Lina and Doon were involved, and in some cases these "likes" were the only ones mentioned. The emoticon that Josh used at the end of his question about the loneliness surrounding the characters points to his awareness of the plight of the characters. Some of the children's comments also concerned the benefit of Lina and Doon's working together in order for both their desires to be fulfilled.

Perseverance/Hope

In the discussion of the second half of the novel, three of the four participants said that perseverance, determination, and never giving up all represented important aspects of the text. Jason identified "eagerness" as one of the main ideas of the story and articulated an important idea as "Never give up." In her post about the first novel Cassie said, "Some main ideas I noticed were that Lina was determined to save the city and whenever something failed she kept going. If she and Doon did not have that the city of Ember could have been forever in eternal blackness." In response to the question about the second novel, "Is there anything about this story that you think is important for people in our world?", Cassie said, "Yes, I think there is something important for people in our world, and it is to always have hope." Duncan depicted the cover of *The People of Sparks* as "A new life springing," a phrase that conjures hope and the possibility of something new. These comments reflected the understanding that hope and the will to go on were both necessary for the positive outcome in the plot, and as its significance in the story emerged, the children connected it to an overall idea that was important for readers.

To summarize this aspect of the children's discussion, the theme generated through their responses included the notion that inner strength, perseverance, and hope help individuals to achieve the impossible. As a spiritual trait, hope can play a vital role in the human experience. Though most of the children's responses concerned the content of the story, Duncan made a comment pointing to the story's effect on his own life: "I think others should read this book because it inspired me to do better things." This reflects Duncan's sociocultural literacy, that ability of readers to see the world from a different perspective based on their experience of the text (Mikkelson, 2005, p. 4). His statement illuminates the idea that the story allowed him to consider the notion that he might "do better things."

These books are clearly within the fantasy genre, but good fantasy, as Mikkelson points out, engages the reader's reality. "Reading fantasy is both a way to make meaning about life and literature and a way of altering the world, and children exposed to rich narrative coding in fantasy works internalize many new ways of seeing for stories of their own" (Mikkelson, 2005, p. 179). Fantasy texts for children offer rich opportunities for the exploration of children's spiritual expression through their discussion of those stories.

Difficulties with Data Collection

Unanticipated difficulties arose during this study, but helped to facilitate learning and further understanding of the issues and challenges related to collecting data through an online tool. Though there were nine children who provided consent forms, only six actually logged onto the forum and shared their ideas. Secondly, though the children were asked for several paragraphs of responses per forum, often participants would only write several sentences, and occasionally only one sentence. It was a struggle to elicit lengthier responses from the children, and even though I replied to members' posts in order to ask for further ideas about their initial posts, I very rarely received responses. I provided each participant and his/her parent with instructions for the study, and these instructions included a timeline for the discussions in the book club, but participants did not seem to follow the directions regarding frequency of logging onto the forum and when to contribute to discussion.

In light of these difficulties, it may be advantageous to have real contact with participants and their parents before the study begins in order to communicate expectations and to discover the extent to which the children can be involved. One of the disadvantages of online studies is that children may not always provide an immediate reply to a question on the discussion forum. Regardless, online forums do have their advantages in that participants can reflect on prompts before sharing their ideas, and this can result in detailed and thoughtful responses to questions.

Conclusion

Though the collecting of data through this online book club was difficult at times, the children's responses indicated their engagement with some spiritual themes, as elicited by their reading of two fantasy novels. Rather than ask the children specific questions about spiritual concepts identified in the text, using open-ended questions about a story can also encourage expressions of their spirituality. Children can tap into spiritual dimensions of texts of which the researcher may not even be aware, as I discovered within this study. Researchers working with children in book clubs should maintain flexibility and openness to the direction the discussions may take, but at the same time, be aware of opportunities to probe further about spiritual ideas children highlight. I anticipate developing a future study using online resources for exploring children's ideas about their literature, but this study would most likely include a larger number of participants and take place over a longer period of time.

Using online forums as space for literature discussion with young readers offers both advantages and disadvantages. Researchers choosing to use this tool may face challenges, but the discovery of unexpected kinds of spiritual discourse generated by children's discussion in response to any kind of "text" is rewarding and worthy of investigation. Other researchers might carefully consider strategies to help guide discussion on forums, but at the same time avoid pressuring participants to respond when they have nothing to post. Additionally, if some children are hesitant to share their thoughts with everyone in the book club, an option to email the researcher their ideas could be provided.

My experience conducting this qualitative study has led me to encourage other scholars of children's spirituality to take advantage of online resources for exploring children's and young people's spiritual expressions as revealed through their engagement with texts. Additionally, discussion forums developed on the web do not necessarily have to be about literary texts; they might concern artwork, music, or film. Though there are challenges and difficulties with studies conducted online, book clubs on the web can provide space for the expressions of children's spirituality that might not emerge through other means.

References

Chambers, A. (1996). *Tell me*. Portland, ME: Stenhouse.

Coles, R. (1990). *The spiritual life of children*. Boston: Houghton Mifflin.

DeVries, D. (2001). "Be converted and become as little children": Friedrich Schleiermacher on the religious significance of childhood. In M. J. Bunge (Ed.), *The child in Christian thought* (pp. 329–49). Grand Rapids: Eerdmans.

Groome, T. (1998). *Educating for life*. Allen, TX: Thomas Moore.

Hade, D. (2002). Living well in a time of terror and tests: A meditation on teaching and learning with literature. *The New Advocate, 15*(4), 292–303.

Hay, D., and Nye, R. (2006). *The spirit of the child*. London: Kingsley (Original work published 1998).

Houskamp, B. M. Fisher, L. & Stuber, M. (2004). Spirituality in children and adolescents: Research findings and implications for clinicians and researchers. *Child and Adolescent Psychiatric Clinics of North America*, 13(1), 221–30.

Hyde, B. (2008). *Children and spirituality*. London: Kingsley. McCreery, E. (1994). Towards an understanding of the notion of the spiritual in education. *Early Child Development and Care*, 100, 93–99.

Mikkelson, N. (2005). *Powerful magic*. New York,: Teacher's College Press.

Montgomery, L. M. (2004). *Anne of Green Gables*. Ontario, Canada: Broadview. (Original Work Published 1908.)

Myers, B.K. & Myers, M.E. (1999). Engaging children's spirit and spirituality through literature. *Childhood Education*, 76(1), 28–32.

Myers, B.K. (1997). *Young children and spirituality*. London: Routledge.

Nye, R. (2006). Listening to children talking. In D. Hay and R. Nye, *The spirit of the child* (pp. 92–107). London: Kingsley Publishers. (Original Work Published 1998.)

"Pedagogy for intercultural critical literacy." In PICCLE. Retrieved March 2009, from http://piccle.ed.psu.edu/.

Pike, M. A. (2000). Spirituality, morality and poetry. *International Journal of Children's Spirituality*, 5(2), 177–91.

Riessman, C. K. (2008). *Narrative methods for the human sciences*. Los Angeles,: Sage.

Schoonmaker, F. (2009). Only those who see take off their shoes: Seeing the classroom as a spiritual space. *Teacher's College Record*, 111(12), 2713–31.

Stonehouse, C. (2006). After a child's first dance with God: Accompanying children on a Protestant spiritual journey. In K. M. Yust, A. N. Johnson, S. E. Sasso, & E. C. Roehlkepartain (Eds.), *Nurturing child and adolescent spirituality* (pp. 95–107). New York: Rowman & Littlefield.

Trousdale, A. M. (2005a). And what do the children say? Children's responses to books about spiritual matters. In C. Ota & C. Erricker (Eds.), *Spiritual education: Literary, empirical, and pedagogical approaches* (pp. 23–29). Brighton, UK: Sussex Academic Press.

———. (2007). An endangered relationship. *Journal of Children's Literature*, 34(1), 37–44.

———. (2004a). Black and white fire: The interplay of stories, imagination and children's spirituality. *International Journal of Children's Spirituality*, 9(2), 177–88.

———. (2005b). Intersections of spirituality, religion and gender in children's literature. *International Journal of Children's Spirituality*, 10(1), 61–79.

Trousdale, A. M. & DeMoor, E. A. (2005c). Literature that helps children connect with the earth. *Encounter: Education for Meaning and Social Justice*, 18(3), 44–49.

———. (2006). The role of literature in children's spiritual development. In M. deSouza, G. Durka, K. Engebretson, R. Jackson, & A. McGrady (Eds.), *The international handbook on the religious, moral, and spiritual dimensions in education* (pp. 1225–35). New York: Springer.

———. (2004b). Using children's literature for spiritual development. In H. A. Alexander (Ed.), *Spirituality and ethics in education* (pp. 130–39). Brighton, UK: Sussex Academic Press.

Tolkien, J. R. R. (2001). *The Hobbit*. Boston: Houghton Mifflin. (Original Work Published, 1937.)

17

How Am I To Believe?
The Relation of Religion and Gender in Contemporary Children's Literature

Ann M. Trousdale

Perspectives on religion and on religiously sanctioned gender roles have undergone a dramatic shift in children's literature in recent years. These developments also reveal a shift in the role which children's literature plays in society as a whole. In this chapter I discuss contemporary works of children's literature that treat the relation of religion and gender, providing a historic background for the two issues: the role of religion in children's books and intersections between religion and gender.

Historical Background: Religion in Children's Books

"In Adam's fall / We sinned all." Thus did the alphabet, and early reading instruction, begin for children in the New England colonies. Once children had mastered the alphabet, the *New England Primer* took them on to more extended text, which included the Ten Commandments, stories of Christian martyrs, and a catechism. The catechism commonly used in the colonies, John Cotton's *Spiritual Milk for Boston Babes in Either England, Drawn from the Breasts of Both Testaments for Their Souls' Nourishment* (1646), included exchanges that followed a similar theological vein to the rhymed verse of the *Primer*: The catechist asks, "How did God make you?" The child learns to respond, "I was conceived in sin and born in iniquity."

Religious teaching continued to permeate reading matter published for children into the nineteenth and early twentieth-centuries. A typical 19th century passage, from the popular Elsie Dinsmore series, is this father's admonition to his daughter: "My child . . . my great desire for you is that . . . you may become meek and lowly in heart, patient and gentle like the Lord Jesus. . . . Do you never feel any desire to be like him?" (Finley, 1884, pp. 187–88). Even in less overtly didactic literature, young protagonists and their families, in the ordinary course of life, attended church, prayed before meals, read the Bible, and feared God.

In the 20th century, the world of children's literature in the United States became an increasingly secular world, reflecting a generally more secular society. At the same time, children's authors began writing about topics that had formerly been considered taboo in children's literature: divorce, drug and alcohol addiction, teenage pregnancy, death of a parent or friend, physical or mental disability. Religious belief was no longer assumed and didacticism of any sort went out of style. In fact, by mid-century, so nearly absent from children's books was any mention of religion that the prominent children's author Jane Yolen commented that religion had become "the last taboo" in children's literature (cited in Schmidt, 2000).

The last quarter of the twentieth century saw the beginning of a re-emergence of religion in books for children, but with a distinctive difference. When religion was mentioned, it was often in a critical vein. Religion was no longer presented as having definitive answers, nor were religious leaders necessarily held up for emulation or respect. Books from mainline publishing houses that mentioned religion tended to focus less on religious answers and more on young people's questions. These questions cover a wide range, including books in which religious leaders or institutions become stumbling blocks to the young protagonists' faith (M.E. Kerr's *Is That You, Miss Blue?*, 1975; Cynthia Rylant's *A Fine White Dust*, 1986; Jane Yolen and Bruce Coville's *Armageddon Summer*, 1998; Nikki Grimes' *Dark Sons*, 2005); books in which intellectual questions bring about a crisis of faith (Miriam Bat-Ami's *Dear Elijah*, 1995; Stephanie Tolan's *Ordinary Miracles*, 1999); books in which young people struggle to find a religious tradition with which they are comfortable (Rita

Williams-Garcia's *Like Sisters on the Homefront*, 1995; Sarah Darer Littman's *Confessions of a Closet Catholic*, 2005); and books in which young people contend with religiously sanctioned restrictive gender roles (Katherine Paterson's *Jacob Have I Loved*, 1980; Stephanie Tolan's *Save Halloween!*, 1993; Katherine Paterson's *Preacher's Boy*, 1999; and Trudy Kriser's *Uncommon Faith*, 2003). Many of these books reflect a theological shift as well, providing critiques of the kind of judgmental, punitive theology that framed *The New England Primer* and John Cotton's catechism.

Historical Background: Religion and Gender

Five New Testament passages lie at the center of controversy surrounding women's roles in the Church:

> ". . . [W]e went into the house of Philip the evangelist, one of the seven, and stayed with him. He had four unmarried daughters who had the gift of prophesy." (Acts 21:8b–9)

> "The gifts that he gave were that some would be apostles, some prophets, some evangelists, some pastors and teachers, to equip the saints for the work of ministry, for building up of the body of Christ, until all of us come to the unity of the faith and of the knowledge of the Son to God, to maturity, to the measure of the full stature of Christ." (Eph 4:11–13)

> ". . . [A]ny woman who prays or prophesies with her head unveiled disgraces her head." (1 Cor 11:5b)

> "There is no longer Jew or Greek, there is no longer slave or free, there is no longer male and female; for all of you are one in Christ Jesus." (Gal 3:28)

> "Let a woman learn in silence with full submission. I permit no woman to teach or to have authority over a man; she is to keep silent." (1 Tim 2:11–12)

The first four passages indicate that women enjoyed equal status with men in the early church, and did in fact speak with authority during public worship; the fourth has the effect of silencing women and relegating them to a role subservient to that of men. Contemporary religious traditions whose practices are shaped by the belief that women as well as men are called into leadership roles often cite the first four passages as providing scriptural evidence for the ordination of women; those denominations that deny women ordination or equal status with men tend to focus on the 1 Timothy passage.

A look at the history of the church reveals an ongoing struggle between culture and religion and the ways in which the church has accommodated itself to cultural norms, beginning in the fourth century when the Roman Emperor Constantine declared Christianity a legally-sanctioned religion. Before this sanction, Christians had suffered massive persecution in Rome. In resisting, the young church had struggled to maintain its identity in the face of "pagan" beliefs and values. One of the radical differences between the early church and the pervasive Roman culture was the equality practiced by women and men in church leadership. But once Christianity was sanctioned by Rome and Roman citizens began to adopt Christianity as their religion, the church began to assimilate Roman cultural mores, which included an assumption of a male hierarchical leadership and a concomitant subservient role for women. In the ensuing centuries the church persisted as a hierarchical structure with male leadership, silencing women in the public arena, and generally relegating women to secondary status in the home, in the church and in society as a whole (Reuther, 1983; Bristow, 1988; Torjesen, 1993; Fiorenza, 1998).

The letters of St. Paul have been widely used to support such views. Yet many contemporary scholars have pointed out discrepancies and contradictions in letters ascribed to Paul. In the above-cited 1 Corinthians, Ephesians and Galatians letters Paul writes openly of women leaders in the church and proclaims equality for women. Yet there is the contradictory 1 Timothy passage, also historically ascribed to Paul. Some biblical scholars consider 1 Timothy among the "disputed" letters of Paul, written by another later writer who borrowed Paul's authority to write "in his name," a not uncommon practice at the time. Nevertheless, regardless of its authorship, the 1 Timothy passage has been used in the church down through the ages to silence women's voices and to relegate women to subservient roles in the church.

Such issues have been the topic of a great deal of feminist theological scholarship and feminist secular scholarship, too lengthy to go into in this chapter, but some of which has been cited above. The effect of centuries of religiously-sanctioned views of women's roles as subservient in the home, in the church, and in society have been deep and far-reaching in Western society. In recent years, women have made significant progress in social, economic, political, and religious arenas, including the ordination of women in some, but not all, mainline denominations.

Children's literature has historically played a conservative role in society, and has not tended to challenge the social order. Even as a heavily didactic tone gave way to a desire to entertain children, polarized gender roles continued to be assumed and, implicitly, taught. John Newbery's *A Little Pretty Pocket-Book,* published in 1744, is commonly regarded as a landmark in this shift from didacticism to amusement. As the title page says, the book was intended "for the Instruction and Amusement of Little Master TOMMY and Pretty Miss POLLY. With Two Letters from JACK the Giant-Killer; AS ALSO A Ball and Pincushion; The Use of which will infallibly make *Tommy* a good Boy, and *Polly* a good Girl." Adding an intent to amuse to the intent to instruct was a revolutionary concept at the time. Seldom commented on is the difference in assumptions about "Tommy" and "Polly"; Tommy will be made a good boy by playful, active, outdoor activity, and Polly a good girl by useful, sedentary, domestic activity.

Such differences in expectations for the Tommys and Pollys of the world was not directly challenged in children's books in the United States until 1868, when Louisa May Alcott's *Little Women* was published. *Little Women* was a forward-looking book for its time both in the absence of overt didacticism and in Jo March's chafing under the restrictions placed upon females and longing for the freedom and wider sphere of activity available to males. Yet even Jo March was eventually tamed and transformed into a properly domesticated young wife.

With few exceptions, children's literature reflected and projected very different kinds of activities for boys and for girls well into the twentieth century, when, along with the secularization of children's literature and the removing of long-held taboos in books for children, spunky, independent, capable young female protagonists began to appear. As children's books providing critical perspectives on religion emerged, so did challenges to religiously sanctioned restrictive gender roles. I turn now to an examination of such literature.

Uncommon Faith

Uncommon Faith (2003) reflects community life in Millbrook, Massachusetts, in the years 1837–1838. The story is told from the alternating points of view of 10 townspeople; we come to know Faith Common, the protagonist, only through their perspectives. Like many children's books set in the early nineteenth century, *Uncommon Faith* reflects widespread religious belief among its characters. Faith's father is an itinerant Methodist bishop and her mother's father is a Calvinist minister. Traditional understandings about women's submissive role are accepted in the family as well as by the townspeople, with the exception of Faith herself and Amanda Putnam, an outspoken advocate of social justice and the wife of the newspaper owner.

Emma Common, Faith's mother, is a model of the exemplary wife described in the 31st chapter of Proverbs; her virtues are also reflected in the often quoted 1Timothy 2:11 passage. She is submissive, quiet, industrious, full of charity and good works. She is dismayed at Faith's challenges to such expectations for all women.

Neither Faith nor her younger brother John conforms to gendered expectations. Bishop Common is grooming John to follow in his footsteps and study for the ministry. But John has no taste or aptitude for public speaking or the study of Greek. It is Faith who has is a natural leader, who is comfortable speaking in public, and who has a passion for learning Greek, the better to translate the Christian Testament accurately. John suffers from embarrassment at his seeming failures–though he is a gifted musician–and Faith suffers because her father doesn't see her for who she is.

Bishop Cannon, a compelling preacher, has brought many to a confession of faith. His daughter, however, has made no declaration of faith herself. She is an outspoken, independent young woman, determined to live by her own lights, to seek knowledge, and to realize her gifts.

Faith is not allowed to go on from the local grammar school to the district school so that she might stay at home to help her mother with domestic chores. She is the oldest student in the local school. A new schoolmaster is hired, a cruel and lazy man, a hypocrite and a religious bigot, who determines that girls are not capable of the kind of abstract thinking required in the study of geometry. He sets the girls to sewing while he instructs the boys in mathematics. Faith leads the girls in designing a quilt based on patterns using geometric shapes—trapezoids, rectangles, squares, and equilateral triangles. The quilt squares are the girls' statement of intellectual equality.

A range of feminist issues come to the fore in the lives of the various characters in the book: the silencing of women in public arenas, spousal abuse, women's lack of legal rights and recourse, women's suffrage, equal economic and educational opportunity. Scripture, particularly the 1 Timothy passage, is used to justify this widespread oppression. Faith, who has begun to teach herself Greek, refutes such teaching by challenging the translation of the 1 Timothy passage, and quoting the Bible herself, using Galatians 3:28, which has been the bedrock of feminist theologians, "There is neither Jew nor Greek, there is neither slave nor free, there is neither male nor female. . . ."

The oppression of women is paralleled with slavery in the book. Jacob and Hetty White, a Quaker couple, are stationmasters in the Underground Railroad. Mentors to both Faith and John Common, they involve John is hiding and transporting runaway slaves. Rufus Thomas, a free man of color, has had his papers of manumission seized and is in danger of being sold into slavery by bounty hunters. The themes of slavery and the oppression of women are woven together at the end of the book when Faith and Celia Tanner, another local girl, leave town to enter Mount Holyoke Female Seminary on the same wagon in which Rufus and his family are taken to the next safe house; Faith gives the geometric-patterned quilt made by the girls to Rufus, thus symbolically uniting the two causes, and two victories.

Allusions to religion in this novel also present a tension between Faith's parents' gracious and merciful version of Methodism and Faith's grandfather's narrow, punitive version of Calvinism. The grandfather, Mrs. Common's father, is an embittered man, having been blinded in one eye in an accident and suffering the infirmities of old age. His version of evangelism is confronting people with their sinfulness. He assumes the worst in others' behavior and cites biblical passages that shame and demean them. His religious convictions are strongly misogynistic. As he tells one elderly woman, "she was just like Eve. Her disobedience caused all the world's trouble . . . all the sins of the world pointed straight back to that first female. . . ." (p. 11). Finally his daughter, the otherwise passive Mrs. Common, stands up to him. In a scene related by young John Cannon,

While my grandfather banged his cane, describing ours as the
very family cursed by Scripture, recommending the rod of
punishment for my sister, my mother stepped up to him.

"Scripture, Father," she declared, "says that ours is a God
ready to pardon, gracious and merciful" (p. 220).

Through many such dramatic scenes, *Uncommon Faith* presents tensions inherent in the struggle for female liberation in the church and
in society as well as tensions between a theology of judgment and
damnation and a theology of mercy and grace.

Save Halloween!

While women made many advances in the 150 years between the
setting of *Uncommon Faith* and Stephanie Tolan's *Save Halloween!*
(1993), the limitations placed on girls and women in many conservative Christian traditions had not—and have not—changed significantly. The female protagonists of both *Uncommon Faith* and *Save
Halloween!* are born into churches that do not permit women to
preach; despite these restrictions, both girls manifest the spiritual gifts
that are recognized as those equipping one to preach. And both girls
are caught between a fear-based fundamentalist theology and a more
tolerant and flexible view of God.

Rev. Filkins and his wife intended to raise a family of preachers. Their first three children—Matthew, Mark, and Luke—are being
groomed for the ministry. When the fourth child was born a girl,
they continued the tradition, naming her Johnna, but concluded that
she, being female, would not qualify for the ministry. Rev. Filkins'
refusal to allow women to speak in church is not addressed directly
in *Save Halloween!*, but it is made clear in the prequel, *Ordinary
Miracles* (1999).

There has been a belief in the Filkins family that one person in
every generation is bestowed with a special gift for preaching. It has
been assumed that Luke, the third son, is the gifted one in this generation, though Matthew and Mark also assist Rev. Filkins in leading
worship by reading the scriptures, an honor not accorded Johnna.

Johnna and her friend Brian have been chosen to write the
Halloween play at school, the performance of which is a sixth grade
rite of passage. Being chosen to write the play is a significant event
in Johnna's life; until now she has tended to fade into the social

background of her class. Johnna and Brian enthusiastically set to work researching the history of Halloween, but when Johnna's Uncle T.T., a well-known evangelist, comes for a visit, he holds a revival and stirs up a campaign to ban any Halloween activities in the town.

Johnna and Brian's play explores the pagan roots of Halloween and dramatizes the psychological reasons why the holiday is so popular. Johnna believes in the play, and her determination to see it produced brings her into conflict with her family's efforts on Uncle T.T.'s behalf. When pressures in town mount and it looks as if the play will indeed be banned, Johnna finds herself speaking powerfully for it, moving her audience to enthusiastic support. The next day she prays about the experience:

> *Preaching, Brian called it, and I guess it was, sort of. What was amazing was how it happened. Like a miracle. It felt as if I just opened my mouth, and the words came. I didn't even have time to think what to say. I know this is strange, because I was talking about the pageant, about Halloween, that Uncle T.T. says is so bad. But for some reason, it felt as if the words were coming from You. Was it You? It was, wasn't it? This is what they mean when they talk about the gift. I have it too!* (p. 138)

This newly realized gift manifests itself on another occasion when Johnna organizes a petition to reinstate the play. The ban is revoked and the play is successfully produced. Johnna's father recognizes that perhaps more than one member of the younger generation has the gift of preaching. He asks Johnna to read the scriptures in church the following Sunday.

Allowing a female to speak in church represents quite a breakthrough for Rev. Filkins. In the novel we see both Johnna and her father working through the complexities and ambiguities that are often involved in seeking spiritual understanding. Tolan avoids demonizing or oversimplifying Johnna's father's conservative religious beliefs and provides a satisfying ending to the Halloween crisis.

Uncle T.T.'s brand of religion comes under greater critique, in two points that are made concerning similarities and differences between Johnna's play and Uncle T.T.'s revival services. Johnna notes the special lighting, the carefully staged dramatic entrance, the effective use of voice, and other theatrical effects that Uncle T.T. uses in his revival services. She adapts these dramatic aids for her play, thus highlighting the staginess and affectation of Uncle T.T.'s preaching. More subtle is the contrast between the ways Uncle T.T.'s preaching and Johnna's play treat the subject of fear. Uncle T. T. explains to the Filkins children that his success is grounded in a message that capitalizes on people's fears, in this case fear of the Devil. He manipulates people into donating money to the church and starting the campaign against the observance of Halloween through playing on their fear. Johnna, on the other hand, realizes that one of the benefits of Halloween is that it allows people to make fun of their fear. "Kids—and maybe everybody else too—like to get scared of stuff they know isn't real, because it helps them not be scared of stuff that is" (p. 103). Uncle T.T. uses people's fear to control them; Johnna's approach is to bring fear into the open so that it loses its control over people.

Jacob Have I Loved

As Elizabeth Cady Stanton pointed out as far back as 1890, patriarchal and misogynistic interpretations of the Bible have been used to relegate women to secondary roles not only in the church but in Western society as a whole. In Katherine Paterson's *Jacob Have I Loved* (1980), Louise Bradshaw suffers from restricted gender roles and from punitive, narrow, and shaming uses of religion, but the connection between the two is not so overtly intertwined as they are in *Uncommon Grace* and *Save Halloween!* The gender restrictions that affect Louise Bradshaw's life permeate society.

   Jacob Have I Loved is set in the early twentieth century on an island in the Chesapeake Bay. Louise is the elder of twin girls. The younger twin, Caroline, almost died at birth and is pampered by her parents through her childhood and into adolescence. The family often tells the story of Caroline's birth, but when Louise asks about her own birth, no one seems to remember; she must have been put in a basket somewhere, they say. Caroline is also strikingly beautiful and musically gifted. Louise grows up in the shadow of all the attention shown to Caroline, increasingly resentful of the preference she sees always being shown to her twin. Their father is a fisherman whose family have lived on the island for generations; their mother is a refined, educated woman who had come to the island as a schoolteacher. The two had fallen in love and married, but Louise wonders how a woman like her mother can be happy in such a place.

The family attend the one church on the island, a Methodist church which presents a rigid, fear-based, judgmental version of the Gospel. The household is further subject to the grandmother's cruel and shaming use of the Bible. Paterson takes the title of the book from the story in Genesis of the twins Jacob and Esau, the younger of whom "rules over" the elder—a parallel which Louise recognizes in her own life. Her grandmother taunts her with the passage from Romans 9:13, "Jacob have I loved, but Esau have I hated." Louise tries to dismiss her grandmother's cruelty, but when she realizes that it is God who is quoted in the Bible as speaking these words, she interprets the passage to mean that God hates her as God hated Esau. She turns her back on God, on church, on religion.

Louise also suffers rejection because of her gender. She loves the water and would like to help her father on his fishing boat, but as a female, such "men's work" is not permitted to her. Instead her father teaches her how to pole a skiff and net crabs in the shallow waters near the island. She turns her income over to her parents to help with their meager livelihood, while a friend on the island donates the money needed to send Caroline to music school on the mainland.

Eventually Louise also leaves the island. Her dream is to be a doctor, but she is told that, as a female, she has no chance of being admitted to medical school. Instead she becomes a nurse-midwife and takes a job in a town in a remote Appalachian valley. There she meets Joseph, a widower with three children. Joseph wonders, in much the same way that Louise had wondered about her own mother, what had brought such a woman to such a remote place. He answers his own question: God had been preparing her all her life to come to that valley.

Louise and Joseph marry, and she finds deep satisfaction both in her work and in her role as wife and mother. Joseph is a Roman Catholic, but Louise does not attend church with him or attend the other, Protestant, church in the valley.

One evening Louise is summoned to attend a young woman who is giving birth to twins. The first is born strong and healthy, but the second has a difficult birth and almost dies. Louise wraps the infant in a blanket and places her on the warm open oven door, sitting by her and refusing to leave until she is sure the baby will survive. But she remembers the first twin and instructs the father to pick him up and hold him as well.

This experience of primary concern for a sickly twin seems to bring some healing to the issues which had made Louise's childhood and adolescence so painful. As she walks home under the stars, the melody of a song that Caroline had once sung as a solo in church comes to her: "*I wonder as I wander out under the sky . . .*" (p. 244). The novel ends with this line. The entire verse, as rendered earlier in the novel, is

> *I wonder as I wander out under the sky*
> *Why Jesus the Savior did come for to die*
> *For poor on'ry people like you and like I*
> *I wonder as I wander–out under the sky* (p. 35).

The novel presents a strong critique of a punitive, shaming use of religion. Despite the religious abuse she has suffered, however, there is a hint that Louise may find her way back to some degree of belief. Indeed, if one is to give credence to Joseph's insight about God's leading Louise to the valley, there is a suggestion that there has been a merciful and caring God watching over her all along. The book clearly portrays the strongly polarized roles for men and women in early and mid-twentieth-century America, but it also presents women as capable of making choices and finding meaning in their lives. Both Louise's father and her husband support her in that process.

Preacher's Boy

In Katherine Paterson's later novel, *Preacher's Boy* (1999), tensions between theologies of grace and of wrath are connected with tensions surrounding gender expectations, but here the family is not theologically conservative but liberal. In this book religion is not used to sanction socially accepted gender norms but to challenge them, and the gender norms in question are male norms.

Ten-year-old Robert Burns Hewitt is the son of a Congregationalist minister at the turn of the twentieth century. Robbie's older brother Elliot is mentally and physically handicapped. Robbie, a rough-and-tumble boy, has a hard time dealing with the townspeople's expectations of him as the "preacher's boy," but his central struggle has to do with his father's religious beliefs which derive from his strongly held convictions about God's universal mercy and grace.

Robbie loves and admires his father, but Rev. Hewitt fails to conform to Robbie's notions of manliness as well as the community's notions of a "successful" preacher: one that preaches "hellfire and brimstone." Rev. Hewitt is a pacifist. He humiliates Robbie by pulling him out of fights—even when he is fighting to defend Elliot from the taunts of other boys. He decries the United States' involvement in the Spanish-American War, and, to Robbie's horror, actually prays for his country's "enemies."

Moreover, Rev. Hewitt reads Darwin, which is a scandal among the townsfolk, who regard Darwin's work as coming from the Devil himself. But the final blow to Robbie's estimation of his father comes when he sees his father cry. Elliot has wandered away, and after a long search Rev. Hewitt finds him and brings him home. His relief is so great that he collapses, weeping, in his wife's arms. Robbie is appalled at his father's lack of manliness.

Rev. Hewitt, preaching a gospel of grace, has followed a 'hellfire and brimstone" preacher in the pulpit of the local church. The members of the congregation do not care for Rev. Hewitt's version of the Gospel and long for the fear-based, judgmental preaching of the former preacher, Rev. Pelham. They insist that he be invited to come back to town to preach a "Revival Sunday." As he listens to Rev. Pelham's condemnatory and judgmental sermon, Robbie realizes that if Heaven was going to be populated with people like Rev. Pelham, "who judge every word you say and think and condemn most of what you do" (p. 19), he wants no part of it. He decides to give up trying to be a Christian at all and becomes a self-proclaimed "apeist."

The arrival in town of a vagrant alcoholic and his spunky and resourceful daughter present Robbie with a moral crisis. He sets out to correct a potential miscarriage of justice, and, miraculously it seems to him, an automobile (rare in those days) appears to take him to his destination just in time. With this manifestation of divine aid, Robbie gives up being an "apeist" and decides to "sign on as a true believer for all eternity" (156). There is a sense, as the story concludes, that Robbie will continue to negotiate his way between socially and religiously sanctioned notions of manliness and the kind of integrity and compassion that mark his father's response to the Gospel.

Concluding Thoughts

The treatment of religion in these contemporary works of children's literature reveal a significant shift from perspectives on religion in books for children in the past. They do not assume—indeed they challenge—religious authority, while honoring young people's questions and struggles with faith. Rather than taking a conservative stance toward societal and religious mores, they offer a critique of oppressive practices, indeed taking an almost prophetic stance in their challenge to inequities, particularly oppressive gender constraints, and pointing to a time when such inequity will be dissolved.

These books present protagonists who struggle with the question "How am I to believe?" on two levels. First, polarized views of gender become stumbling blocks to belief. How is one to embrace a religious faith that is oppressive, limiting, rejecting? Second, the theological issues raised cause the protagonist to wonder, In what way am I to believe? What view of God can I accept? When there is a sense of God's mercy and compassion, a door to belief seems to open. The novels discussed here offer satisfying resolutions to the conflicts the young protagonists experience, and their questions are answered, at least tentatively. But these answers are discovered by the characters themselves rather than dictated by religious authority

The resolutions occur in varying ways. Grace Common and Johnna Filkins, the two female protagonists who struggle with gender-based restrictions in the church, do not find resolution by accommodating themselves to imposed limitations; both girls resolve their difficulties by standing up to adult authority figures and fighting for what they believe in. Louise Bradshaw finds fulfillment through work that is at least close to what her dream has been, and finds healing of her childhood pain through that work as well. In *Preacher's Boy*, a seemingly supernatural event allows Robbie Hewitt to "sign on as a true believer for all eternity."

In two of the novels–*Save Halloween!* and *Preacher's Boy*—the resolution includes the retaining or regaining of religious belief. This issue is less clear in *Uncommon Faith* and *Jacob Have I Loved*. At the end of *Uncommon Faith*, Faith Common has still not made a confession of faith; the resolution of her struggles is the opportunity to further her education. An informed contemporary reader would know that whatever her religious journey might entail in the future, it will not be as an ordained clergy person in her denomination; women would not be allowed to preach in the Methodist Church for another hundred years. Yet one senses that Faith will persist in seeking liberating rather than oppressive interpretations of the Bible and that her interest in the equality of women will be fostered and strengthened at Mount Holyoke. At the conclusion of *Jacob Have I Loved*, there is only a hint that Louise, who had rejected both religion and God, may find a way to some degree of rapprochement.

In all four books a punitive, judgmental view of God is critiqued, and the proponents of such a theology are depicted as otherwise unappealing characters. In *Save Halloween!* a fundamentalist approach is questioned, but one of its representatives, Johnna's father, is a compassionate and "teachable" man. It is Uncle T.T.'s manipulative, fear-based theology that Johnna must see through and challenge to find her own voice. In *Uncommon Grace* and *Preacher's Boy* the "hellfire and brimstone" theology is contrasted with a theology of grace. In *Jacob Have I Loved*, there is no ameliorative religious perspective offered to Louise in her time of spiritual crisis, and she falls away from belief.

The fact that all of the protagonists emerge from their crises as more mature individuals on a healthy path of life gives the reader the sense that questions and doubts about religion are not to be feared, but are to be embraced and worked through. Two of the four characters emerge with an ability to believe in God; and even in the two novels that do not end with a return to faith, there is a sense of hope at the end.

For young people who are experiencing such religious questions, finding sympathetic characters with whom to identify can provide a sense of companionship on their own journeys. Such books can offer young people encouragement to engage the issues rather than to repress or avoid them or to abandon religious faith altogether.

References

Children's Books

Alcott, Louisa May. (1868/1983). *Little women.* New York: Bantam.
Bat-Ami, Miriam. (1995). *Dear Elijah.* New York: Farrar Straus Giroux.
Grimes, Nikki. (2005). *Dark sons.* New York: Hyperion.
Kerr, M.E. (1975). *Is that you, Miss Blue?* New York: Harper & Row.
Krisher, Trudy. (2003). *Uncommon faith.* New York: Holiday House.
Littman, Sarah Darer. (2005). *Confessions of a closet Catholic.* New York: Scholastic.
Paterson, Katherine. (1980). *Jacob have I loved.* New York: HarperCollins.

————. (1999). *Preacher's boy*. New York: Clarion.

Rylant, Cynthia. (1986). *A fine white dust*. New York: Bradbury.

Tolan, Stephanie S. (1999). *Ordinary miracles*. New York: HarperCollins.

————. (1993). *Save Halloween!* New York: Morrow Junior Books.

Williams-Garcia, Rita. (1995). *Like sisters on the homefront*. New York: Puffin.

Yolen, Jane and Bruce Coville. (1998) *Armageddon summer*. San Diego: Harcourt Brace.

Professional Resources

Bristow, John Temple, (1988). *What Paul really said about Women: An Apostle's liberating views on equality, marriage, leadership, and love*. San Francisco: HarperSanFrancisco.

Crossan, John Dominic and Jonathan L. Reed. (2004). *In search of Paul: How Jesus' apostle opposed Rome's empire with God's Kingdom*. San Francisco: HarperSanFrancisco.

Fiorenza, Elisabeth Schussler. (1998). *In memory of her: A Christian theological reconstruction of Christian origins*, Tenth Anniversary Edition, New York: Crossroad.

The New Oxford annotated Bible, New Revised Standard version. (1999). Bruce M. Metzger and Roland E. Murphy, Eds. New York: Oxford University Press.

Reuther, Rosemary Radford. (1983). *Sexism and God talk: Toward a feminist theology*. Boston: Beacon Press.

Schmidt, Gary (2000). The last taboo: The spiritual life in children's literature, *The Five Owls*, *10*(2), 25–34.

Stanton, Elizabeth Cady Stanton and the Revising Committee (1898). *The woman's Bible*. New York: European Publishing.

Torjesen, Karen Jo. (1993). *When women were priests: Women's leadership in the early church & the scandal of their subordination in the rise of Christianity*. San Francisco: HarperSanFrancisco.

18

Orphans Among Us
Evaluating the Ministry Needs of African American Children in Foster Care

La Verne Tolbert

There is a crisis in America. According to the most current AFCARS (Adoption and Foster Care Analysis and Reporting System Report) Report, released in September 2010, there were approximately 423,773 children in the U. S. in foster care on September 30, 2009. The largest state in the nation, California, has the highest number of children in foster care— approximately 105,000. Although only twelve percent of the overall United States population is black, forty to fifty percent of all foster care children are African-American. These are the most difficult children to place in foster or adoptive homes. As a result, black children remain in the system longer (Hough, Landsverk, McCabe, Yeh, Ganger, & Reynolds, 2000), averaging ten years or more and represent the largest proportion of children in out-of-home care nationally (Smith and Devore, 2004). The result: too many African-American children grow up institutionalized (Singleton & Roseman, 2004).

Why are children in the system? The answer is threefold: abandonment, abuse, and neglect. Abandonment is desertion by a parent or primary caregiver who has neither made provisions for childcare nor has any apparent intention to return to take care of his or her child. Abuse and neglect encompass physical, sexual, or emotional maltreatment by a parent or caretaker who is responsible for the child's welfare—food, clothing, shelter (www.cakidsconnection.com).

Of the total number of children in the system, almost half are living with relatives in what's termed "kinship foster care." In this mutual arrangement, once the problem that caused the separation from the birth parents is resolved, children are returned to their birth family.

Unfortunately, many children do not enjoy kinship foster care and will never be reunited with their families. The result is that every day, 3,000 children need either permanent adoptive families, connections with adults that will last once they are emancipated from the system, or both.

How well is the Church participating in solving this crisis? What roles can volunteers in churches across America play to help the orphan? This study includes field interviews along with a case study to examine how the church can improve its response to children in foster care.

Why Care About Orphans?

Christians have a specific mandate from the Lord to care for the fatherless:

This is pure and undefiled religion in the sight of our God and Father, to visit orphans and widows in their distress, and to keep oneself unstained by the world. (Jas 1:27, NASB)

This passage, written by James the brother of Jesus, is considered to be among the first letters penned to the church at Jerusalem and is dated AD 46. In it, the author challenges believers about what they do with what they believe. Action is imperative because faith is not just a matter of orthodox belief. Faith is also evident in an orthodox lifestyle.

In other words, as faith produces *inner* transformation it is expressed in *outer* demonstration.

But someone may well say, "You have faith, and I have works; show me your faith without the works, and I will show you my faith by my works." (Jas 2:18, NASB)

Genuine faith cannot ignore the orphan. This faith will, as James admonishes, *visit* the orphan. Visit means to *help* (Vine, 1985, p. 662) because the orphan is in distress . . . suffering severe pressure of pain and sorrow and anguished with severe bodily or mental pain (Concise Oxford Dictionary, 1995, p. 301).

At the time of this letter, many Jewish believers had been disowned by their families and were ejected from their traditional Jewish communities. They had to rely upon their new church family for the basics—food, clothing, shelter. Widows and orphans were the most vulnerable and were especially dependent upon the generosity of the faithful.

Today, children remain the most vulnerable in our society. Who better to respond to their needs than those of us who have that faith of which James writes?

A History of Helping

Not surprisingly, the faith community has an extensive history of caring for those who have been orphaned. In antebellum America prior to the Industrial Revolution, most families lived in rural settings. If a problem surfaced within the household, both the immediate and extended families assumed responsibility for taking care of the children.

Churches stepped in to help when families experienced stress. They provided resources that included relocating orphans to larger homes that allowed them to continue living within rural communities.

With the influx of Western European immigrants into America cities grew and orphanages and "children's asylums" were birthed around the 1830s. There were seventy-one orphanages in the United States by 1851 with a large proportion located in New York. These were established by private, Protestant philanthropic associations to provide alternatives to public almshouses where children had been thrown together with adult paupers, the aged, the widowed, the mentally-retarded, and the unemployed.

Because of the racial disparity that existed during that time, "colored" orphans were not allowed to live in the same orphanages as white children. These orphans fared worse than others. But in 1836, the Colored Orphan Asylum was established by two white, Protestant activists in New York City. Soon, this racially-segregated model of orphan care spread to other urban centers.

From 1848 to 1860, there were ninety-three Jewish welfare societies to aid widows and orphans in the Jewish community, which comprised less than 5 percent of New York's population. The Hebrew Orphan Asylum was founded in 1863.

The Wrong Emphasis?

By the Civil War, orphanages and children's asylums sponsored by faith communities were generally regarded as failures because as custodial institutions they had the wrong emphasis. Strict discipline and staunch regimentation were the norm while these malnourished children lived in squalid, overcrowded dormitories with poor education.

In the late nineteenth century, alternative visions for child welfare began to emerge within the context of Christian Socialism and the American Social Gospel. Almost all modern professional services for children were conceived in the period between 1890 and World War I—a period marked by social criticism and faith-driven institutional innovation.

During this era, the Settlement House Movement that had begun in London expanded to the United States. Attached to churches and religious philanthropies, settlement houses provided residential living that included gymnasiums, pools, libraries, dispensaries, medical clinics, and soup kitchens. Here, the homeless or disadvantaged found help with employment services, educational programs, and financial aid provided by scholars who were driven by a social philosophy.

By the twentieth century, religiously affiliated orphanages and children's asylums were disappearing as networks of specialized institutions began to flourish. Their focus was to help children who were delinquents or who were developmentally disabled. These were precursors to what we know today as group homes or multi-service residential treatment centers.

Catholic and Jewish religious groups established alternatives to Protestant public schools by establishing supplementary school systems and creating networks of social welfare agencies. In addition to parochial schools, Catholics established centers for orphans in large urban areas and served children whose parents could not provide adequate care. These soon became specialized service centers designed to help pregnant teenagers, battered women and children, the homeless, and families abused by drug or alcohol addiction. Day care and adoption services were also available.

A New Deal

President Roosevelt's New Deal, fanned by the devastating conditions of the Depression, expanded the nation's publicly-funded social services safety net. The government realized that faith communities and private philanthropies were simply not equipped to handle the large number of distressed families.

As responsibility for child welfare services began to be seen as the responsibility of the state instead of faith-based agencies, Christians found new ways to help. They opened residential treatment centers for families and children with cottage-based dormitories for a homelike environment; recreational activities were also included.

During the 1960s, thanks to the Civil Rights and child advocacy movements, services increasingly focused on the child. Priorities shifted from institutionalizing orphans to preserving families in their own neighborhoods and keeping them within their own religious traditions.

By mid-1960s, President Johnson instituted a War on Poverty that designated funds for faith-based organizations and other community-based organizations that provided either services for children or built senior housing. Many inner-city African-American churches received these funds to help them with the unpaid work they were doing in their impoverished communities.

The family preservation and reunification movement was born in the mid-1970s in response to President Carter's mission to protect fragile families. Child welfare professionals had complained about chronic problems in the nation's foster care and adoption system prompting the Adoption Assistance and Child Welfare Act of 1980 as well as laws that were enacted in a number of states. A 1982 California law mandated treatment services for families to prevent removing children, whenever possible, from their homes and focused on reuniting foster children with their families as quickly as possible (Orr, Dryness, and Spoto, 2004).

With the church's role now limited, states experienced an increase in the number of children who were remaining in foster care far too long. In Los Angeles, for example, the Department of Children and Family Services (DCFS) realized that recruiting foster and adoptive parents was problematic without the direct help and encouragement of leaders in the faith community (Sari Grant, personal interview).

They shifted their focus to involving churches and ministries who are concerned about helping the orphan.

Unfortunately today, Christians face serious challenges despite their sincerest desires and heartfelt efforts to help youth who have been in the system for extended periods of time. Foster youth carry heavy emotional baggage. They've learned the self-protective mechanisms of social distance and detachment—the result of multiple placements during their childhood. With few adults in their lives permanently and even fewer meaningful ties to people who can help them navigate to adulthood, adolescents step out of foster care with a suitcase and some money in their pockets to stare into a vacant, hopeless future.

The Freedom of Emancipation

When children are raised in the system, they are "emancipated" or re-leased as adults at age eighteen. Some refuse to follow rules and feel they have matured/grown up at earlier ages. Thinking they are able to take care of themselves and having no idea of the difficulties that await them, they choose to run away with only the clothes on their backs. These foster youth are now considered emancipated, and even if they wanted to go back to the foster care system, they may not be allowed to return.

Even when they wait until the age of emancipation, youth may lack practical social skills like cooking, cleaning, balancing a checking account, doing laundry, or completing a job application. So along with their newfound freedom, many youth experience extreme emotional crises. To prepare them for the real world, foster/adoption agencies such as Olive Crest have a transitional housing placement program or THPP to prepare teens for emancipation. Youth live in supervised housing in an apartment. A director, who also has an apartment in that same complex, goes from apartment to apartment acting as a house parent teaching how to clean, how to shop for groceries, etc.

Even with this support, emancipation for some is still frustrating and frightening. One emancipated male could not get a job because he did not have any proof of identification such as a birth certificate (Dr. Phil Show, May 25, 2009). How could he find his mother to get this document? And who would help him? Another youth, upon learning that he was to be emancipated, became so distraught that he tried to commit suicide by standing in the middle of railroad tracks. He was rescued and immediately hospitalized (La Nelle Powlis, THPP caretaker, personal communication).

College tuition for all children in foster care is fully subsidized by the state, but since most have poor grades because they may have attended as many as fifteen different schools by the time they reach 7th grade, most drop out of high school. Only 3 percent of foster children complete college.

Foster care youth are at high risk of "rotten outcomes" because once emancipated, they end up homeless, unemployed, welfare dependent, with out-of-wedlock births, alcoholic, drug-addicted, or incarcerated (Inglehart & Becerra, 2002). The statistics are troublesome:

- 50 percent of youth become homeless within eighteen months of leaving the system;

- 70 percent of all prisoners were raised in the foster care system. (Dr. Phil Show, May 25, 2009)

Foster children need real help . . . they need to be adopted or at the least . . . they need lifelong mentors. But the hurdles of abandonment, multiple placements, poor grades, and even poorer attitudes demand more than what well-meaning short-term programs can provide as the following Case Study demonstrates.

"Let Me Tell You" Case Study

The "Let Me Tell You" Foster Theatre Project was a collaborative effort between the Los Angeles Department of Children and Family Services, the Jahi ANT Production Company, and a mega church—Crenshaw Christian Center (CCC) located in Inglewood. This pilot program had a multi-level purpose:

1. To develop an opportunity for 30 mentors to interact with 12 foster/adoptive children, ages twelve to fifteen by driving them to and from Saturday rehearsals at the church;

2. To enable foster care children to build their esteem through theatre—dance, singing, drama—by providing a forum for them to tell the stories of why they were in foster care;

3. To put faces and stories to the statistics by providing prospective adoptive parents the opportunity to meet real children who are immediately adoptable.

A program liaison recruited 30 CCC mentors who were finger-printed and received DCFS clearance. Specialized training instructed volunteers on the do's and don'ts, which included not giving money to the children, how to respond if a child runs away, how to listen and other important and essential information. On Saturday mornings working in teams, mentors had the responsibility to drive to foster homes to pick up children and bring them to and from the church for half-day rehearsals.

The program began with twleve teenagers, but only eight completed the project and performed their stories. Sharing was voluntary. Some children were too heart-broken to tell why they were in foster care. Others found the voice and the courage to share their experiences. The program liaison and mentors listened to stories that broke our hearts . . .

> "When I was 3 years old, my mother felt that she was too young to be a mother, so she put me in foster care . . . She was on drugs . . ."

> "I've been in foster care my whole life. My mother was abusive . . . Isn't there someone out there who wants a daughter?"

> "I was walking home from school . . . the social worker told me to get my clothes . . . my mom was in handcuffs, my dad across the street in a police car . . ."

> "My brother died right in front of me . . . He was 18; I was six . . . I didn't know what to do . . . he [was shot and] just died right in front of my face . . . my dad didn't care . . ."

> "My mother is doing her own thing. My father travels a lot for work, so he put me back into foster care . . ."

Mentors sought ways to build bridges with these children, to establish meaningful relationships that would last a lifetime. Preparing for the performance meant assuring the children that they sing, dance, or act, handling crying spells or emotional breakdowns, encouraging a child to rejoin the group if he or she decided to isolate, dealing with temper tantrums and outbursts of frustration, congratulating every small victory such a child remembering his or her lines, applauding the child who made even the slightest improvement, shopping for the perfect outfit, praying with and for children, and watching the transformation from the first to the final rehearsal.

Was the six-month project a success? Here are the responses of the mentors in the program.

***

This experience as a mentor has been a positive one for me and the youngster with whom I was paired. Our relationship has grown from the awkward first "road trip" from the foster home to a comfortable growing relationship of trust and sharing. I will continue to build on the relationship we have established. I am interested in other programs such as KidSave, the week-end care program that allows children to stay with adults who have clearance so that foster parents have a mini-break from their fostering responsibilities.

***

I was blessed with the opportunity to work with Barbara [not her real name]. During the twenty-minute drive to and from church, Barbara and I talked and she shared with me her hopes and dreams for her future. I quickly found that she was just like any other teen. She loved to listen to music. Her favorite artist was Beyoncé! I often allowed her to listen to songs as we drove to and from church. At times, we would discuss the music, and I cautioned her that while the beat was nice some of the lyrics were inappropriate.

Most of the time that we spent together I would allow her to talk. Sometimes it's just important to listen, which is what I did. There came a point in time when I asked Barbara if I might share about my faith with her. She gladly welcomed it.

As the program began to draw to an end, I saw Barbara differently. I wanted more than just a mentor/mentee relationship. I wanted to help make her dreams come true and for her to have a forever family of her own. I told Barbara that my husband and I wanted to get to know her better. Her question to me was, "Does this mean that you want to adopt me?" I told her that my heart was open to it. My husband and I had already begun the process for adoption . . .

***

Ariel [not her real name] was my mentee, and she told me that she was an atheist. The one thing that we had in common was music, so to introduce her to Gospel music or even just positive music to listen to, I first allowed her to listen to whatever she wanted to on the radio whenever she was in the car with me. She had her stations locked in and we would listen to music and sing together.

One Saturday when I had to pick her up I was on a fast. I listen only to Gospel when I'm fasting. She got into the car, and I told her about my fast. She asked what it meant and I explained that I wanted to be clear about a few things so I wanted to hear from God. I further explained that the fast was my way of getting out of the way so that Father would know I was sincere and really wanted to hear from Him. She listened to the music and enjoyed it. She was also a lot calmer that particular Saturday, too.

She enjoyed listening to Gospel music with me. I told her that "God is good, and He has good music, too!" That was a wonderful experience for me and for her.

***

Hearing what some of the youth had gone through in their young lives was heart-breaking at times, yet it inspired me to make whatever difference I can make in their lives. It stretched me and grew me on a couple of levels. First, I am remaining in contact with my mentee and will be present in his life as much or as little as he wants. I also told the other youth that they can call on me if necessary. Secondly, I enjoyed watching him and the others grow. What a difference from when they started the theatre program! Seeing them blossom in their own way was rewarding.

I think Donald [not his real name] learned and saw that others cared and were vested in him succeeding in life. With the consistent encouragement that he received from me and his other mentor, I believe he became more confident with his ability to achieve his goals and dreams.

***

Initially, my husband didn't want to attend the mentor meetings because in gatherings like this, he's usually the only male. In the end however, he thanked me because he found it very rewarding.

Andrea [not her real name] was the child that we drove to and from rehearsals. Even though the project ended a few weeks ago, we are still maintaining contact with her. This past weekend, with the social worker's approval, Andrea spent some time with us at our home. On Sunday, she came to church with us.

Besides that great news, we are currently going through the process to adopt Andrea. We're working with the social workers, but Andrea doesn't want to wait to live with us. She's fifteen and she wants a family now. So we are becoming her foster parents while we wait for the adoption process to finalize. The social worker says that Andrea is really resilient and very good in school.

Andrea has never had anyone sit down and talk with her. She feels that she is just moved from place to place. She needs someone to love her, care for her, and give her stability.

We've always been told that we would be the perfect parents. Now, we have an immediate opportunity, so we thought, why not contribute something to another child's life? This is right for us. She has a forever family now. We thank God for this opportunity to change a child's life.

***

Project Outcomes

Of the children who participated in this project, two females and one male were to be adopted by their respective mentor families. The male refused adoption immediately, even though he was legally "free." His dream was to be reunited with his birth mother, a reality that social workers said was highly unlikely.

Hope remained for the two females, but unfortunately, after expressing initial excitement and enthusiasm, both decided not to continue the adoption process for similar reasons. Each spent the weekend at her soon-to-be permanent family's home during the adoption process. One child shopped and completely decorated her room in a lavish home in an upscale neighborhood. But she decided she wanted to "bond" with her foster mother rather than be adopted by the married couple who were her mentors in the theatre project. Her goal was to emancipate . . . Counseling was offered but she rejected any intervention.

Similarly, the other female found it difficult to live within the structure of her prospective parents. She wanted their financial assistance but didn't want anyone telling her not to go to dances or parties, which she was permitted to do in the foster home. The mounting frustration strained communication. Both sets of mentors continue to be involved in the lives of these young girls, but they are disappointed and discouraged about the aborted adoption process.

These children have been in foster care so long that perhaps they are unable to cope with the prospect of a change as permanent as adoption. That not one child was adopted as a result of this intense six-month project was disheartening, but our expectations though well-intentioned, may have been unrealistic given the complex individual stories and circumstances of the youth.

Implications for Ministry

Mentoring children at younger ages and beginning the adoption process prior to teenage years may increase the potential for successful outcomes and bridge the gap between failure and a productive future. To be successful, churches might commit to being actively involved in the life of a foster child long-term by engaging these children in their youth programs, Children's Church or Sunday school.

In the African-American setting, Sunday school is a significant context for children's socialization (Haight, 2002). Not only does this introduce a child to Christian faith, but it also helps build relationships with peers and other caring adults. Perhaps then the prospect of change may seem less threatening. Most of all, exposure to a faith-filled environment provides the healing balm to mend fragmented minds and revive crushed spirits.

A pilot project—Covenants for Kids, "churches helping children in foster care"—is being launched by Teaching Like Jesus Ministries, Inc., a parachurch ministry. In Los Angeles County alone there are 11,000 children in the foster care system. Of these, 7,000 children are destined to grow up without ever being placed in a permanent home. Presently, 500 children are immediately adoptable and over 30 percent of these are African-American (Sari Grant, personal interview, April 25, 2011).

In partnership with the Department of Children and Family Services (DCFS), Covenants for Kids is an intentional effort to integrate youth into the congregational life of a local church close to where the foster youth resides. Similar to the theatre project, volunteers are recruited, DCFS cleared and trained to be mentors to foster youth ages nine to seventeen. They drive to the foster homes and bring youth to Sunday services, youth meetings, choir rehearsals, and special outings. Ultimately, the goal is that the child will be adopted by the mentor or by another family in the church. If adoption does not occur, youth will have developed meaningful life-long relationships that will hopefully endure after emancipation from the foster care system.

Nationally, models for similar efforts that are working within this community include the Institute for Black Parenting, which recruits and trains prospective parents, and One Church One Child (OCOC), which began in Chicago in 1979 by Father George Clements, an African-American Catholic priest. OCOC has expanded to over twenty-six states resulting in the adoption of hundreds of children (Belanger, Copeland, & Cheung, 2008).

Summary

Despite the challenges, churches and faith communities of all ethnicities must hear the cries and address the crisis of orphans. Actively and intentionally mobilizing churches to minister to the needs of children in foster care is as urgent today as it was during biblical times.

The good news is that faith increases the likelihood of successful placements. Religiosity is significantly related to the total number of foster/adopted children in the home including and especially African-American children (Belanger, Copeland, & Cheung, 2008).

One remarkable example is Bennett Chapel Missionary Baptist Church in Possum Trot, Texas. Since 1998, 70 African-American children have been adopted by church members when they learned of the need for adoptive families from their pastor, Bishop WC Martin and his wife, Donna. Once a week for twelve weeks the Martins drove 120 miles for classes. They adopted two children and then two more. Meanwhile, Bishop Martin preached and preached about the need for and value of adoption in obedience to scripture. A total of twenty-three families responded.

Bishop Martin arranged for classes to be taught locally to save parishioners the tedious drive. Twelve families completed the first set of classes, and then eleven completed a second set of classes. In the words of Donna Martin, the children are "here but not healed," (Belanger, Copeland, Cheung, 2008, p. 100). So this church community depends upon their faith, prayer and the word of God to encourage one another. The children are thriving.

Focus on the Family published the Bennett Chapel story (Martin, 2007), and they were featured on Oprah and CBS' 48 Hours. The television program, Renovate My Family, went to Texas and built a 10,000 square foot center that provides after-school tutoring, sports activities, summer camp, and a food bank program. (Possum Trot residents live below the poverty level. Each week, Bishop Martin drives sixty minutes to the food bank in Tyler, returning with a truckload of food to disburse to those in need including some of the adoptive families).

Now that the center is completed, the biggest challenge is keeping it opened and operating. Expenses for liability and car insurance, water, gas, and electricity, plus general upkeep have taken a financial toll on the church and on Bishop Martin personally. Every month he depends on a miracle while seeking donations and a permanent means of support for the center. (Bishop Martin, personal interview, April 25, 2011).

Bennett Chapel is an example of the potential within the Black church. Researchers estimate that 8.7 million adults attend predominantly Black churches. "The African American church has not fully recognized itself as a potential focus for the efforts in providing for Black children in need of formal adoptive families," (Singleton, & Roseman, 2004, p.84). An overwhelming majority—nearly 96 percent of respondents—reported that "the church mission statement did not include a focus on the adoption or foster care need for Black children. . . . 83 percent of the ministers reported that they did not address the need in their sermons," (Singleton & Roseman, 2004, p. 84). Imagine the impact of hundreds of churches like Bennett Chapel!

Together, people of faith must aggressively seek creative ways to rescue the orphan, especially older children who are least likely to be adopted or to be permanently placed.

"It's not a glamour story. It's ministry work. You're taking in children who have been molested . . . children who would eat like animals, down on the floor. You have to train them all over again as if they were one-year-olds. You've gotta be up at odd hours to attend to them when they're crying out in the night. And when you leave for the grocery store, you've gotta deal with their very real fear—a fear that you'll never come back, that you'll leave them all alone again" (Martin, 2007, p. 53–54).

The children do recover. They learn to trust. They learn not to be afraid.

They don't have to worry about having food on the table or clothes on their backs. Now they have a place to stay and food to eat. They have a family. . . . If a family is having trouble with a child and needs some help, they don't call Child Protective Services. They call on a neighbor or a nearby relative. Sometimes, that child may stay with someone else for a while till things get straightened out. It's how we relate as family. We're in this together. (Martin, 2007, p. 54)

Doesn't this sound like the heart of Christ? "Jesus took the children in his arms, put his hands on them, and blessed them. Are we ready now to do the same?" (Martin, 2007, p. 106).

References

Adoption and Foster Care Analysis and Reporting System Report. (2009, September 30). http://www.acf.hhs.gov/programs/cb/stats_research/afcars/tar/report17.htm

Belanger, K. Copeland, S. and Cheung, M. (2008). The role of faith in adoption: Achieving positive adoption outcomes for African American children. In Racial Disproportionality in Child Welfare: A Special Issue. *Child Welfare Journal of Policy, Practice, and Program, 87*(2), 99–123. *http://www.cwla.org/pubs/pubdetails.asp?pubid=J872*

Davis, L. P. (2009). Olive Crest Transitional Housing Placement Program. Personal communication.

Dr. Phil Show, May 25, 2009.

Grant, S. (June, 2009). Department of Children's and Family Services, Los Angeles, CA. Personal communication.

Haight, W. L. (2002). *African–American children at church: A sociocultural perspective.* New York: Cambridge University Press.

Hough, R. L., Landsverk, J.A., McCabe, K. M., Yeh, M., Ganger, W.C., & Reynolds, B. J. (2000). Racial and ethnic variations in mental health care utilization among children in foster care. *Children's Service: Social Policy, Research, & Practice. 3*(3), 133–46.

Iglehart, A. & Becerra, R. (2002). Hispanic and African American youth: Life after foster care emancipation. *Journal of Ethnic & Cultural Diversity in Social Work, 11*(1, 2), 79–107.

Martin, WC. (2007). *Small town big miracle.* Focus on the Family. Carol Stream, IL: Tyndale.

Orr, J., Dryness, G. R., & Spoto, P. W. (2004). Faith–based adoptive/foster services: Faith communities' role in child welfare. *Center for Religion and Civic Culture, University of Southern California*, 3–6. Retrieved from http://crcc.usc.edu/docs/childwelfare.pdf

Singleton, S. & Roseman, F. (2004). Minister's perceptions of foster care, adoptions, and the role of the black church. *Adoption Quarterly. 7*(3), 79–91.

Smith, C. J. & Devore, W. (2004). African American children in the child welfare and kinship system: From exclusion to over inclusion. *Children and Youth Services Review*. 26(5), 427–46.

Thompson, D. (Ed.). (1995). *The Concise Oxford Dictionary of Current English*, (9th edition). Oxford, UK: Oxford University Press.

Vine, W. E. (1985). *Vine's Expository Dictionary of New Testament Words*. Virginia: MacDonald & Co. www.cakidsconnection.com

19

Forgiveness, Peer Relations, and Children's Spirituality

Kelly S. Flanagan and Rebecca L. Loveall

Introduction

. . . forgiveness involves the lifelong process of learning a craft. There are no shortcuts; and those who genuinely seek to embody Christian forgiveness will find that it involves profoundly disorienting yet life-giving transformations of their life, their world, and their capacity for truthful communion.

(L Gregory Jones, 1995, p. xiii)

Having been created in God's image, we are called by God to live our relationships in a way that reflects the presence of his eternal love, which is intended for friends and enemies alike (Matt 5:44, 18:35). In our relationships God is revealed to us when we are loved by others, and the challenge of loving those around us sharpens and shapes us, developing virtuous traits for the treatment of others and the expression of God's love to them (1 John 4:7–12). Yet because of our sinful nature, even in the healthiest of intimate relationships (i.e., satisfied, stable marriages and supportive childhood friendships), conflict is present (Lundberg, 2002; Smedes, 1984). Although the natural human impulse is to escalate the conflict through such responses as retaliation, retribution, avoidance, or exclusion, one profound way to cope with such hurt is through forgiveness (Jones, 1995; Worthington, 2006). As Christians we are emphatically and undisputedly called to extend forgiveness to others as God has forgiven us. When engaged in faithfully, forgiveness is integral to the lifelong process of spirituality and is associated with psychological health.

Childhood, from the preschool years to adolescence, is a fertile ground for nurturing the spiritual craft of forgiveness. Children's peer relationships, in particular, are fraught with conflict that increases in frequency and intensity from the preschool years and throughout formal schooling (Denham, Wilson, Pickering, & Boyatzis, 2005; Parker, Rubin, Erath, Wojslawowicz, & Buskirk, 2006). Even in the early child years, conflicts over objects, moral issues and control are common. Conflict becomes more hostile and retaliatory, and attempts to harm others through relational means such as gossip and exclusion from groups becomes an increasingly normative experience of youth. Throughout childhood, friendships necessitate an appreciation and understanding of the need to coordinate different needs, thoughts, feelings, and behaviors in dyadic relationships. On a more commu-nal level, children have to navigate an increasingly more complex social world that involves negative group dynamics (e.g., exclusion, victimization, intergroup biases) which can cause anxiety, fears, and relational harm.

The complexity and conflict inherent in these peer experiences can have a multitude of negative effects upon a child's self-image and capacity to relate to others. Children must choose how to live in this world, and how to emotionally, behaviorally, and cognitively respond to these conflictual, interpersonal dynamics. Viewing this harm as a challenge and being motivated to actively deal with it through forgive-ness may allow a child a sense of efficacy in response to the offense, thereby reducing the negative impact of such wounds. Over time, the ability to forgive should positively impact the way in which a child generally responds to relational difficulties—a craft that will carry over into adulthood. Thus, engaging in forgiveness could both heal the wounds a child experiences and also contribute to their social competence and their spiritual calling to love others including those who hurt them (Matthew 22:39; Luke 6:27–36).

In this chapter, we explicate the theological and psychological un-derpinnings of forgiveness as a response to the interpersonal conflicts that children increasingly face throughout their development. The literature on children's spirituality and social development will advance the argument that we *must* attend to the facilitation of forgiveness among children. Finally, a research example will be presented that provides initial evidence for the proposed interconnections between children's forgiveness in peer relationships and their spirituality. We espouse a view of children as spiritual beings who are fully capable of understanding and engaging in forgiveness, to come *alongside* them in their spiritual growth as they work through conflict with peers, and to foster a community that facilitates forgiveness among children.

The Gift of Forgiveness

Forgiveness can be separated into two essential elements: 1) naming the offense and condemning it, and 2) not counting the offense against the offender but rather releasing any debt (Volf, 2005). Thus, by offering forgiveness one is practicing love in a radical form—disrupting a cycle of conflict and extending God's love to others. Divine forgiveness of our sins includes both elements through God's grace (Heb 7:27) and permits reconciliation with him. Forgiveness is a gift from God in response to original sin—not something we have earned but something He freely gives through his grace, mercy, and love. In turn, we are able to forgive our enemies through God's embrace of us on the cross and through the working of the Holy Spirit (Volf, 1996). Thus, forgiveness is also *being love* to others. In the same way that we have received this gift of healing and loving communion with God, we are called to be an agent of the same kind of healing and communion (Matt 6:12). Forgiveness of others can be both a healing response to relational conflict reflecting the abundance of grace that we have received, and an intentional and faithful response to God's spiritual command. If we are unable to engage in this process then the offense continues to burden both the offender and us, and prohibits us from living as God intended us to live—in communion with Him and with others as a part of Christ's communal body. In the giving and receiving of forgiveness, we can develop a more complete understanding of the depth of God's love for us, leading to spiritual growth.

Within psychological literature, definitions of forgiveness abound (see Worthington, 2006), although relative to faith traditions, the theoretical and empirical study of forgiveness in psychology is in its infancy (i.e., the past two decades). A commonly cited definition of forgiveness highlights the cognitive, behavioral, and emotional changes of the forgiver from negative to positive towards the person forgiven (Enright & Fitzgibbons, 2000). Worthington's stress-and-coping theory of forgiveness suggests that individuals must cope with interpersonal stressors (i.e., transgressions) and that forgiveness is one way in which to cope. Other responses include rumination or holding a grudge, revenge, and avoidance (Worthington, 2006). Worthington posits that these responses are developmentally solidified over time to impact individuals' personality characteristics and social relationships.

Forgiveness that is extended and received is mutually beneficial for all involved in a relational offense (i.e., offenders and offended; Rom 4:7; Ps 32:1; Isa 44:22; Isa 43:25). Indeed, we are called to forgiveness and unforgiveness has significant consequences (Matt 6:14; Mark 11:25). We are called to not take revenge ourselves but instead to overcome evil with good (Rom 12:19–21). Retributive justice alone, without forgiveness, can cause significant relational splits and problems in the community (e.g., Goins, 2008) and can cause those who avenge themselves to be overcome by evil. Justice without forgiveness cannot truly bring about a transformation of those involved or reconciliation between the parties. We may reflect God's just nature, but our motive for justice is often perverted (Worthington, 2006); therefore, we must be encouraged to unconditionally practice the spiritual craft of forgiveness.

Psychological research provides evidence of the benefits of forgiveness and potential maladjustment associated with unforgiveness. Forgiveness is related to indices of positive adjustment, such as reductions in stress, anger, depression and anxiety, and an increase in self-esteem (Al-Malbuk, Enright, & Cardis, 1995; Freedman & Enright, 1996; Seybold, Hill, Neuman, & Chi, 2001; Toussaint & Webb, 2005; Witviliet, 2001). Forgiveness is also associated with prosocial motivations, social competence, and restoration of interpersonal relationships (McCullough & Worthington, 1995; McCullough, Worthington, & Rachal, 1997; Zechmeister & Romero, 2002). In contrast, immediate negative emotions in response to an interpersonal offense may include anger, fear, hatred and/or shame. Experimental evidence suggests that these immediate negative emotions can develop into unforgiveness over time (Worthington, 2006). Unforgiveness is physically and mentally stressful and can harm relationships (e.g., Witvliet, Ludwig, & Vander Laan, 2001). The process an individual goes through in order to forgive may be a means of reducing the stress reaction and employing more adaptive ways to respond and cope with hurt.

It has been argued that forgiveness is the ultimate characteristic and necessary requirement of a Christian life (Jones, 1995; Volf, 1996). Volf (2005) suggests that the ability and willingness to forgive is a powerful indicator of our reception of God's forgiveness, thus highlighting the critical role of forgiveness in spirituality. Jesus called everyone (both powerful and powerless) to love and repentance (Matt 5:44; Luke 6:27, 29–31; Luke 13:3, 15:7, 17:3; Mark 6:12) through his offering of forgiveness. Jesus' example of forgiveness includes a tender, valuing of the others, creating safety to realize our need for repentance (Matt 9:2–7, 10–13; Luke 23:24; John 8:9–11). The question is whether we are able to offer that same mercy and kindness to our enemies, as "[h]is command to love our enemies shakes the foundations of social control" (Alter, 1997). Yet his example insists upon the universal need in our relationships for forgiveness, as it can restore communion between ourselves and others, our community and God (Alter, 1997; Lundberg, 2002). In sum, forgiveness is given to us through God's grace and love and we are to offer that forgiveness to others. As we engage in forgiveness, we mature spiritually, and as we mature spiritually, our capacity for forgiveness grows.

Spirituality

From a Christian perspective, the role of forgiveness in spiritual growth is crucial. Yet are children capable of this spiritual imperative, and should we call them to engage in forgiveness? How might it interact with their spirituality? Much ambiguity exists in defining the term spirituality, and spirituality and spiritual development have often been defined and used separately (Benson, Roehlkepartain, & Rude, 2003). However, we will use the term spirituality as it has been proposed by Yust and colleagues (2006) to highlight the inherent, universal aspect of spirituality that involves growth, maturation, and change that must be actively nurtured (i.e., the changes inherent in the process of spirituality are not an inevitable aspect of development). The term spirituality can be understood with the following definition:

Spirituality is the intrinsic human capacity for self-transcendence in which the individual participates in the sacred—something greater than the self. It propels the search for connectedness, meaning, purpose, and ethical responsibility. It is experienced, formed, shaped, and expressed through a wide range of religious narratives, beliefs, and practices, and is shaped by many influences in family, community, society, culture, and nature. (Yust, Johnson, Sasso, & Roehlkepartain, 2006; p. 8).

Implied in this definition is that spirituality is embedded in an individual's cultural and social contexts (Benson et al., 2003; Yust et al., 2006). Religion as one part of this context provides a coherent worldview, belief system, and behavioral norms that are embodied in the religious community's norms (Furrow, King, & White, 2004; King, 2003; Markstrom, 1999; Yust et al., 2006). Yet the contexts that impact how spirituality plays out are both within and outside of religious beliefs and practices. The social world (e.g., school, neighborhood, youth group, extracurricular activities) is another important context in which spirituality is embedded. The relational aspects of spirituality ultimately lead one to act in a certain way (lovingly) toward others beyond imposed or learned "rules" and thus affects the individual's relationships and the larger community (Yust et al.). Ratcliff and Nye (2006) suggest that spirituality is a holistic characteristic that is affected by and affects cognitive, physical and social development. Coles makes the point further that the moral life and spiritual life naturally overlap (Coles, 1990). The dynamic, intertwined nature of children's social, moral, and spiritual lives is notable.

Childhood Spirituality

As we consider the role of forgiveness in childhood and its interface with children's spiritual wholeness, it is important to recognize the inherently relational aspect of children's spirituality. It has been proposed that children's spirituality is embedded in how they perceive, understand and relate to things, self, others, and God (Hay & Nye, 1998). That is, children's other-oriented reflections promote self-understanding and connection with the transcendent, thus implicating social processes and influences in children's spirituality. Children's spirituality is based within relationships and thus there are transactional interconnections between how they handle difficulties in peer relationships and their spiritual growth (Hart, 2006; Lerner, 2002; Reimer & Furrow, 2001; Worthington, Sharp, Lerner, & Sharp, 2006). Children's spirituality is present in their encounters and connections with others, most often experienced as deep empathy and compassion for another (i.e., self-transcendence and connection with something greater) (Hart, 2006).

Theological views of children also suggest a rich and nuanced view of childhood and children's spiritual nature. Simplistic views of children as either entirely sinful or entirely innocent are not wholly accurate (Bunge, 2006; Miller-McLemore, 2003); children are not fully depraved or virtuous, not solely victims or villains, and they are not merely passive recipients of adults' spiritual teachings. Theologians across the ages have portrayed children as humble and vulnerable, but also corrupted by sin and needing guidance and intervention (e.g., Bunge, 2006; Gundry-Volf, 2001; Stortz, 2001; Pitkin, 2001). Feminist theologian Miller-McLemore (2003) further recognizes the agency of children as a source of spiritual insight, and identifies their innate ability to be in loving relationship with God, self and others. Children can have rich spiritual lives and they might even be less resistant to or have fewer obstacles to the movement of the Holy Spirit in their hearts than adults (Bunge, 2001).

Spirituality and Peer Relations

Though the reality and importance of children's spirituality is difficult to contest, much of the research does not consider the role of the social context in their spirituality (Benson et al. 2003; Regnerus, Smith, & Smith, 2004). However, the emerging field of child and adolescent spirituality is more often framed within a developmental systems theory with a focus on ecological forces that affect the developmental process (Benson, 2004). A small but growing body of research indicates interconnections between peer relations and various measures of spirituality (Erickson, 1992; Gunnoe & Moore, 2002; King, Furrow, & Roth, 2002; Martin, White, & Perlman, 2003; Ozorak, 1989; Regnerus et al., 2004; Schwartz, 2006). For example, Schwartz (2006) found that friends' modeling of faith and their faith dialogue (e.g., "My friends are consistent in how they live out their faith," "My friends encourage me to grow closer to God in my own way") significantly contributed to adolescents' religious faith above parents' faith support. In qualitative interviews, friends were more frequently identified as important to goals, moral values, and sense of identity among Christian youth than among non-Christian youth who more often mentioned the importance of teachers and family members (Good & Willoughby, 2007).[1]

Based on the extant literature, we can hypothesize how children's peer relations interact with their spirituality (Schwartz, Bukowski, & Aoki, 2006). Keep in mind the definition of spirituality being used, which involves the connectedness, meaning, purpose, and contribution that is embedded in relationships. Peer relations are characterized by more equal and mutual relationships than adult-child relationships which are more hierarchical in nature. Peer relationships help children learn how to think of others' feelings, to engage in perspective-taking, to be sensitive to others' needs, and to protect each other and help each other with emotional support (Parker et al., 2006). They learn to resolve conflicts and regulate emotions in order to preserve relationships. Thus, these relationships might contribute to the growth of children's sensitivity for and love of others, as well as their moral behavior that is a part of spirituality. Peer relationships provide children with the opportunity to develop a sense of how they fit and function within the social world, particularly as peer acceptance becomes more important. It has been hypothesized within the peer relations literature that the importance of peer acceptance reflects a human need for belonging (Baumeister & Leary, 1995), which is clearly linked to the sense of connectedness involved in spirituality (Schwartz et al., 2006). Given the hypothesized associations, empathy, perspective-taking, and meaning making, which are necessary in all relationships that include conflict and require forgiveness, are likely then to facilitate children's spiritual experience and growth. Likewise, aspects of spirituality (e.g., the valuing of others, connection with others, and God's calling for how to live in community, espoused moral behavior as part of a belief system) will positively impact children's peer relations and social competence. Indeed, research with adolescent populations shows a link between religiosity and peer relationships that is played out in shared activities, social interactions and trusting relationships

1. Many of these studies, though not all, assessed youth's religiosity versus their spirituality, though the two constructs are related and spirituality itself is associated with positive adjustment (Good & Willoughby, 2008; King & Boyatzis, 2004). Measures included items asking about church attendance, the importance of religion to the youth, and engagement in various activities including prayer.

(i.e., connection with God and others), shared worldview, beliefs and religious commitment (i.e., meaning and purpose), and the reinforcement of values and behaviors (i.e., contribution) (King, 2003).

Less explored in any literature are the potential negative connections between peer relations and children's spirituality. Any parent upon reflection can recognize the impact of children's peer interactions on their well-being when they come home from school upset that they were picked on, or that a friend ignored or was mean to them. Understanding these connections is complicated, given the multifaceted nature of children's social world. At the same time that prosocial behaviors and the ability to resolve conflicts increases, the frequency and intensity of conflict among friends also increases throughout childhood (Parker et al., 2006). Similarly, physical aggression declines as verbal and relational aggression increases (Bierman, 2004). Gossip, or comments about others when they are not present, also increases in frequency (Parker et al.). Unfortunately, even more substantial difficulties, including victimization and neglect by peers, and rejection by the larger peer group, are not uncommon experiences (Asher & Coie, 1990; Bierman; Juvonen & Graham, 2001; Nasel et al., 2001).

It has been suggested that being hurt by another can alter the offended party's worldview in the realization that the world is not wholly just and kind. This altered worldview can lead to confusion, sadness, and even anger and hatred (Enright, Santos, & Al-Mabuk, 1989). Further, children's view that they are created in God's image can be negatively impacted by others' treatment of them (Charry, 2006). Negative experiences with peers would likely impact their understanding of themselves, their sense of the world, and their feeling of connection with others, and lead to deeper spiritual questions and a feeling of disconnect with God and others. Likewise, an inability to make sense of peer difficulties, or to hold onto a larger meaning of the world and one's place in it, may lead to rumination on hurts, and rumination can in turn lead to anxiety and depression, and subsequent maladaptive coping responses and behavior (e.g., Burwell & Shirk, 2007; Muris, Roelofs, Meesters, & Boomsma, 2004; Skitch & Abela, 2008; Worthington, 2006). Psychological research indicates associations between negative peer experiences and maladjustment, including poor self-esteem, loneliness and depression, negative cognitions about their ability to handle the situation, and increases in rumination, and vengeful or aggressive behavior (e.g., Boivin & Hymel, 1997; Deater-Deckard, 2001; Hawker & Boulton, 2000; Juvonen & Graham, 2001; Kochenderfer & Ladd, 1996; Sandstrom & Coie, 1999). Not having roots in a set of values that upholds a respectful, accepting and loving approach to others, or viewing maladaptive coping such as revenge, avoidance, and aggression as positive coping responses could lead to further rejection or victimization by peers.

Forgiveness in Childhood

A Theological View

As spiritual beings created in God's image, children's spirituality is affected by all of their experiences and choices, including those within their social context (Stonehouse, 2006). For spiritual growth to occur children must develop a loving relationship with God that flows into love of others (Mark 12:30–31). Conflict with peers is one aspect of this fallen world that highlights for children that relationships are not perfectly safe, just, or caring. Children learn about the complications of life as well as the difficulty of forgiveness and recognize that they too need forgiveness. If children learn to focus on God and God's love of others then they will be able to grow in their moral capacities and spirituality. Spiritual growth is dependent on relationship with God that requires forgiveness extended from Him to us, and through us to others. Negative peer influences may lead to children's difficulty in engaging in the forgiveness process and thus impact their spiritual and psychological wholeness. If we view forgiveness as the essence of being a Christian and as a response that can alleviate psychological problems (Smedes, 1984), then it should be a crucial component in children's peer interactions. Their treatment of others and moving beyond their own needs in a purposeful way that is informed by their spirituality will help them to grow in their connection with others and God and in turn will nurture their spirituality.

A complex but affirming view of children's spirituality suggests that children are fully capable of forgiveness. Theologian Friedrich Schleiermacher viewed children as being flexible and forgiving (as cited in DeVries, 2001, p 341). As DeVries reviews, in his sermons regarding raising children and parenting he recognized children's dependency on others, which he believed helps them to live simply and in connection with others, offering others' blessings. He argued that children have a spiritual perspective (e.g., present-focused, trusting, accepting) necessary for Christian faith. Further, because children are less powerful in many relationships, they are in the constant functional position of having to forgive others. They are subject to orders, adult-imposed structure, and adult irritation and frustration. They are often overlooked, ignored, and their needs may not be taken into account. In addition, they can be chastised and even shamed for their lack of knowledge and understanding even if age-appropriate. It has been argued that this makes them naturally able to bless others because their resilient and flexible nature allows them to be loving and warm in spite of their position of dependence (Matthew 5–7; Berryman, 2004). The elder is blessed by the younger. This complex view suggests that children may actually be more capable of forgiveness than are adults, though they may not be able to articulate it as well. It has been argued that children are innately capable of sophisticated theological thinking and should be taught both scripture and its application to their lives (Coles, 1990; DeVries, 2001). However, they need to continue to develop and understand the forgiveness process and how it fits with their beliefs in order to continue growth in this spiritual craft.

A strong religious faith, which emphasizes forgiveness, might help a child to forgive and release negative emotions toward a peer offender. Additionally, being forgiven and accepting forgiveness (in the case of the offender) can set in motion a process of self-forgiving and other positive outcomes (e.g., overcoming feelings of self-hatred and shame) and help children to be other-directed in their perspective, emotions, and behaviors (North, 1998), communicating love and grace. Through attempts to understand others and choose cognitive, emotional and behavioral responses that promote reconciliation, children might feel more connected with their peers and God. The forgiveness process can be informed by and in turn reinforce the meaning of their faith and how it should be demonstrated in their love of others (e.g., because God forgave me, I will love my enemy). Their relationships with others will include a sense of contribution in acting for another's sake and promote self-transcendence. In summary, the process of forgiveness among children and their peers has the potential to contribute to their understanding making meaning of events in relationships, their purpose in relating to others in an empathic and loving manner, and their connection with others (i.e., spirituality).

A Psychological View

Developmental psychologist Robert Enright, with the Human Development Study Group (1991, 1994), conducted several studies to evaluate a cognitive developmental model of forgiveness. In response to hypothetical moral dilemmas, the reasoning of fourth grade children about forgiveness could most often be categorized in the proposed stage that requires restitution in order for forgiveness to occur (e.g., "I can forgive someone only if I can punish him/her to the extent that I have been hurt") whereas adolescents' reasoning most often fell into a stage reflecting the influence of others (e.g., "I can forgive someone when other people expect me to forgive") (Enright et al., 1989). Only adults endorsed the stage of reasoning about forgiveness that was more complex (e.g., to restore relational harmony, to truly love and care for another). Drawing from Piaget, Enright and colleagues (1994) suggest that children might have difficulty understanding forgiveness, as immature cognitive abilities would not allow children to move from the more concrete, inflexible view of justice to more abstract understandings of forgiveness. Interestingly, as Enright and colleagues point out, Piaget also identified other features that might impact children's ability to understand forgiveness, including practicing forgiveness and social input (e.g., religious beliefs, cultural supports), and suggested that forgiveness can be placed within a moral realm because it requires charity and love for others. These findings suggest that the community in which children are surrounded is important. They also suggest that youth rely on others to clarify the situation and/or encourage them to forgive.

Concerns have been raised about the cognitive-developmental perspective (Denham et al., 2005; Estep & Breckenridge, 2004; Worthington, 2006). The most significant concern is that asking children to reason about forgiveness requires logical, abstract thought and the verbal ability to express this thought, though forgiveness involves much more than reasoning skills. Further, the capacity to think about forgiveness might not translate into actual forgiveness (Worthington, 2006). An ecological view would emphasize systemic rather than stage-like changes of forgiveness development, as moving through various contexts and developmental periods requires adaptation to and incorporation of various influences over time (Estep & Breckenridge, 2004). It is crucial to understand the transactional relationships between children's social development, the forgiveness process, and their spiritual development. Children's engagement in the forgiveness process at times may be outside of their cognitive abilities but can still be an experiential and emotional process enabled by God and embodied by their moral communities.

Denham and colleagues (2005) have embarked on research that links forgiveness to social competence. They provide three reasons it is necessary for children to engage in forgiveness: 1) to maintain close relationships, 2) to decrease the use of violence, and 3) to promote well-being. They suggest that at school entry children may be less capable of understanding forgiveness; however, by middle childhood the nature of the peer context increases the potentiality of forgiveness while maturation in social and cognitive abilities and emotion regulation make it "easier" to engage in forgiveness. Indeed their preliminary research indicates that forgiveness is positively associated with social competence (e.g., status in the peer group, prosocial behavior, empathy) and negatively related to aggression (Denham et al.). Using hypothetical scenarios, these researchers found that children's motivation for or propensity to forgive did not vary by age; that is, age may be related to children's abstract reasoning about forgiveness but not their ability to engage in forgiveness.[2]

In a program of research at Wheaton College, forgiveness and spirituality have been explored within an early adolescent population from middle schools (public, rural and private, suburban). We used a modified version of the Enright Forgiveness Inventory for Children (EFI-C), which is based on the well-validated and widely used Enright Forgiveness Inventory (EFI) for adults (Subkoviak et al., 1995). Although there is no published data on its reliability and validity, in the current study this measure was found to have high internal consistency (α = .89 – .94 for the three subscales and Total score). It was also meaningfully related to other constructs (i.e., general coping strategies, empathy, self-esteem) that gave some evidence of its validity. This measure uses a definition of forgiveness that involves the

2. These researchers did find that children were more likely to endorse forgiveness in these hypothetical scenarios when it was an accidental offense or when the offender apologized or felt bad. North (1998) reasons that an apology places the offender and offended in a position of moral equality, which allows the injured person to esteem the offender as worthy of respect and consideration because of the offender's acknowledgment of the offense and intention to make amends and to change.

change of affect, cognition and behavior from positive to negative towards an offender. The modified measure asked about a specific time that a peer bullied or hurt the adolescent, with responses indicating strong disagreement to strong agreement on a five-point Likert scale to 30 items that comprised three subscales (Affect, Cognition, and Behavior) and a Total Forgiveness score. A subgroup of these adolescents who attended a private Christian school ($N = 136$ with an 88 percent participation rate) also completed a measurement of spirituality (the Multidimensional Measurement of Religiousness/Spirituality for Use in Health Research; Fetzer, 1999) that has been primarily used with adults, but has shown adequate reliability and validity in research with adolescents (Desrosiers & Miller, 2007; Harris et al., 2008; Pearce, Little, & Perez, 2003). This multidimensional measure provided assessment of adolescents' perception of and involvement with the transcendent (Daily Spiritual Experiences subscale; $\alpha = .86$), perceived forgiveness by God, and forgiveness of oneself and others (Spiritual Forgiveness Beliefs subscale; $\alpha = .72$), engagement in private spiritual practices (Spiritual Practices subscale; $\alpha = .57$), self-ranking of religiousness and organized religious attendance.

The larger sample of early adolescents from grades 6–8 ($N = 777$) were first asked to provide a definition of forgiveness. Findings validate previous literature with adolescents more frequently conceptualizing forgiveness as apology-facilitated and in less complex and more behavioral terms (e.g., "Forgiveness is when you move on and go on with life," "To be kind and act like they didn't do anything") than as changes in feelings and thoughts or perspective-taking (Reich, 2009; Reich, Flanagan, & Wright, 2009). Additionally, older adolescents (eighth-graders) tended to provide more complex definitions of forgiveness than did younger adolescents (sixth-graders), which suggests that developmental differences exist even among such a small age range. Although these findings support the cognitive-developmental framework (e.g., Park & Enright, 1997), it is important to note that a sizeable proportion of this sample provided definitions that were indeed more cognitively mature (Reich et al, 2009). That is, some early adolescents understand and are capable of describing forgiveness as involving changes in thoughts and feelings, perspective-taking, and reconciliation.

Although the majority of early adolescents did not provide complex definitions of forgiveness, the current results indicate that they may in fact be engaging in the forgiveness process in response to an actual, self-selected instance of a peer offense (Reich, 2009). They did not strongly endorse overt aggressive behavioral responses or negative thoughts and feelings that would be typified in revengeful forgiveness or rumination. Instead, the majority endorsed more neutral feelings, thoughts, and behaviors, and about one-fifth of the adolescents who indicated "Yes" to the question "Have you forgiven the kid who hurt you?" (79 percent of the sample) agreed or strongly agreed that they had *positive* feelings, thoughts, and behaviors toward the peer who hurt them (Reich, Wright, Flanagan, Carter, Post, & Andrews, 2007).

Overall, the comparison of these early adolescents' definitions of forgiveness and their endorsement of forgiveness-related thoughts, behaviors, and feelings, indicate that youth are able to engage in the forgiveness process more readily than researchers have previously concluded (Reich et al., 2009). A difference may exist between a youth's actual response and how he or she is linguistically able to define forgiveness. Because a stage theory of child development tends to rely heavily on cognitive abilities to articulate beliefs, evaluation of actual relational experiences may provide more insight into their abilities and experiences (Boyatzis, 2005).

In our sample of Christian middle school students, we examined associations between early adolescents' experience of forgiveness and their spirituality. Findings indicate that spirituality is significantly associated with forgiveness (Flanagan, 2009; Reich et al., 2007). Specifically, Daily Spiritual Beliefs (e.g., "I feel close to God," "I find strength and comfort in my religion") and Spiritual Forgiveness Beliefs (e.g., "I know God forgives me," "I believe that when people say they forgive me for something I did, they really mean it") were positively though modestly associated with adolescents' report of greater levels of forgiveness of a peer (range of $r = .20$ to $.31$; $p < .05$ or $.01$). Higher levels of self-ranking of religiousness ("I consider myself to be a spiritual or religious person") and private spiritual practices were also modestly associated with higher levels of forgiveness thoughts and behaviors (range of $r = .18$ to $.22$; $p < .05$ or $.01$).

Examination of the responses provided by the Christian sample to the statement, *Explain what forgiveness is*, shows the potential impact of spirituality on the ability to articulate forgiveness (Flanagan, 2009). Although many of the responses were pat or displayed a lack of understanding of the intricacies of the forgiveness process, we were impressed by some of the responses that showed a mature understanding of this abstract concept and an understanding that was clearly informed by their faith (e.g., "Forgiveness is what God wants us to do when someone hurts us. It's being kind and letting them know that you forgive them," "To show mercy or grace, giving them something they don't deserve," "When you move on and forget their wrongs, like what Jesus did for us.") These qualitative data suggest that there are interconnections between youth's spirituality and their understanding of the spiritual craft of forgiveness.

In summary, from both theological views as well as the limited psychological evidence, children are clearly capable of experiencing and thinking about the hurt and forgiveness required within interpersonal relationships. Forgiveness is not just merely possessing different thoughts or feelings about others or enacting positive behaviors toward those who have hurt us, but a way of being in a transformative relationship with God and with others (Jones, 1995). We can thus envisage the potential of forgiveness in children's peer relations. If giving and accepting the gift of forgiveness is crucial to spiritual growth then children's engagement in the forgiveness process with their peers will be intertwined with their spirituality.

Facilitation of Forgiveness

> ... the craft of forgiveness involves the ongoing and ever-deepening process of unlearning sin [of domination and diminution of others] through forgiveness and learning, through specific habits and practices, to live in communion—with the Triune God, with one another, and with the whole Creation. (Jones, 1995, p. xii)

Interpersonal relationships, whether they are between children, children and adults, or two adults require forgiveness. Learning how to forgive is God's gift for abundant living in this fallen world, and learning how to forgive well has direct implications for spiritual growth. Forgiveness has two components: 1) naming the offense and condemning it, and 2) choosing to release the other from the debt of the offense (Volf 1996). How can we facilitate the growth of this skill at home, in our churches and in our communities? Children "need to be taught what is right and just and to develop particular virtues and habits that enable them to behave properly, to develop friendships, and to contribute to the common good" (Bunge, 2004, p. 48). We offer three sets of suggestions and end with some ideas for adults to ponder. Recognizing that each child is unique, the suggestions given will need to be tailored to suit individual children. If a child's typical pattern of interpersonal behavior is one of acquiescence, then he/she may need to be encouraged to take ownership of difficult emotions. If a child seeks control of the situation then he/she may need to be more actively encouraged in perspective taking.

Cognitive: Teaching, Modeling, Labeling

Given children's rapid cognitive development over the course of childhood, several methods for facilitating their understanding and recognition of forgiveness are necessary. As with any other spiritual discipline, information regarding the importance of forgiveness from scripture, stories, videos and/or games need to be shared with children. Discussions regarding what forgiveness is and is not are imperative. Stories in particular are an extremely effective way for children to learn about the process of and need for forgiveness. Children respond to and are influenced by stories, which provide meaning and structure for interpreting life. In addition, adults cannot facilitate learning about forgiveness if they do not themselves find it important. Openness about situations that require forgiveness and the difficulty of going through the process of forgiveness will facilitate children's depth of understanding. It is important to understand that we cannot truly teach forgiveness unless we realize that we too need forgiveness, are forgiven, and need to forgive others. Malcolm & Ramsey (2006) discuss the painful awareness that we do not often live lives that embody forgiveness. The more we embrace this skill ourselves the more able we are to be transparent and authentic with children. Children must not only learn to look at others as needing their forgiveness; they need to recognize that they also enact hurts on others and that they are ultimately loved and forgiven of their offenses as well.

Yust (2006) encourages modeling when teaching children. The modeling of forgiveness occurs through our own loving and accepting relationships. It is important to remember that the skill of forgiveness is used daily, and not pulled out only for the most conflictual circumstances. Offenses exist on a continuum between accidental and intentional. "Honey, I forgot to stop and buy milk on my way home" becomes an opportunity to model forgiveness and label it as such. Modeling and then labeling forgiving behavior on a daily basis makes the idea of forgiveness real for children in their relationships. A child's revelation that "Sally was mad at me today but then we decided to play dolls" is in fact an opportunity to point out the underlying mechanism of forgiveness that allowed the two friends to continue to enact love with each other. Adult interactions model and label forgiveness, and our awareness of children's peer relationships allow us the opportunity to teach about forgiveness.

Over time children will be increasingly able to understand and recognize the need for forgiveness, and engage in the specific cognitive skill of perspective-taking. Perspective-taking is the cognitive ability to see and understand another person's point of view. The degree to which a child will be able to understand that his/her peer has a different point of view is contingent on his/her age. This ability is slowly acquired in childhood and must be used in conjunction with the emotional and behavioral aspects of forgiveness mentioned in this paper. Perspective-taking can increase empathy and thus the desire and ability to forgive.

Emotions: Affirmation, Validation, Permission

Often when I am trying to explain to my young son that he needs to forgive his friend, I focus almost entirely on his friend's point of view because I don't want him to be hurting. My son usually responds with "Mom, you're not listening to me!" What he is trying to say is "Mom, I am hurt, don't talk to me about Sam!" The cognitive skill of perspective-taking must be used in conjunction with affirming the hurt, validating the child's emotional response, and giving the child permission to sit with those emotions. Allowing the process of forgiveness to take time is crucial. Further, children need to identify their feelings of hurt, anger, guilt, and/or mourning and be assured that these feelings are valid (e.g., "I would be hurt too if my friend had not invited me to the party.") Be patient with the child's process and encourage patience. Resilience, our ability to bounce back from hard circumstances, is determined by how much support we receive from others. The degree of support and protection from others during and after conflict directly impacts children's long term ability to cope with stress (Boyden & Mann, 2005; Goins, 2008).

Worthington (2006) hypothesizes that negative emotions and positive emotions each have their own command center. Thus, focusing on controlling negative emotions like anger or vengefulness does not necessary correlate with an increase in positive emotions. In general increasing other-focused emotions like gratitude, humility, contrition, and altruism increase the child's ability to use all positive emotions, which in turn helps displace feelings of unforgiveness. If we want to increase children's ability to forgive we can also encourage them to be more grateful, to be realistic about their own abilities, and to accept and forgive themselves. Involvement in peer-oriented activities can increase children's sense of altruism because they are able to contribute to others' well-being within a context of equality. Over time as we encourage children's understanding of their own emotions, and the process through which emotions dissipate and change, they will grow in their ability to empathize and have compassion for others. As we affirm, validate and allow children to feel difficult emotions and encourage the growth of positive other-oriented emotions, forgiveness will come more easily.

Behaviors: Empowerment, Decision-making, Responsibility

Once we allow children to acknowledge and feel the negative emotions involved in being hurt or in hurting others, we need to focus on the action component of forgiveness. This is the hardest part of the forgiveness process to actually enact with children because it gives a certain measure of control to the child and also leaves them open to pain that we would prefer children not experience. First, we should recognize that regardless of the situation every child has a choice in how to respond. Second, we can engage children in brainstorming the range of choices available for possible response. Third, allow the child to choose the option that seems best to him/her and then follow up with the child to evaluate the outcome of this response with your discussion guided by an understanding of the spiritual craft of forgiveness. If we remember that forgiveness is not just for "big" problems but also for everyday occurrences, this three step process seems less intimidating. The more hurtful the offense the longer the forgiveness process may take. There are so many chances to slow down and help children think about what happened with friends that day. "Sam is mad at me and is ignoring me" becomes an opportunity to sit and brainstorm, "How do you think you can respond?" This trial and error behavioral posture allows children to develop their decision, making ability.

Unforgiveness can be manifested in such behaviors as retaliation, retribution, avoidance and exclusion. Although retaliation and retribution are generally not encouraged within the Christian context, often behaviors of avoidance and exclusion are (e.g., "If Sam is mad at you then just find another boy to play with at recess."). In fact, patterns of avoidance and exclusion can be seen in unforgiving people and do not serve to alleviate psychological distress. Encouraging personal responsibility and engaging others in proactive responses (e.g., conflict resolution) minimizes feelings of shame and the vilification of others. Encourage children to engage their peers whenever possible, and they will find it easier to do so in response to even significant hurts. Over time children will become more skilled and comfortable with approaching conflict, misunderstanding and painful situations with a sense of personal responsibility and self-efficacy.

Christian living can be reduced in principle to learning to love God and love our neighbor (Matthew 22:37–40). The practical application is visible in how we apply God's forgiveness to ourselves and increasingly love God as our gratitude for his active and persevering love grows. This same perseverance and action must be employed in our loving interactions with others; "If it is possible, as far as it depends on you, live at peace with everyone" (Rom 12:18). The peace called for in this chapter of Romans involves forgiving attitudes and actions such as offering yourself as a living sacrifice, resisting the patterns of this world, loving your enemy, blessing those who curse you and admonishment not to repay evil for evil. These are some of the principles that God lays out for establishing peace. God's peace is active and persevering. Living at peace with others is not only possible with an ample view of forgiveness, but it is necessary and powerful. Embodying forgiveness is a life-long endeavor which we are wise to employ early with our children. "Blessed are the peacemakers for they will be called children of God" (Matt 5:9).

References

Al-Mabuk, R. H., Enright, R. D., & Cardis, P. A. (1995). Forgiving education with parentally love-deprived late adolescents. *Journal of Moral Education, 24,* 427–44.

Alter, M. G. (1997). The unnatural act of forgiveness: Exploring Jesus' radical method of restoration. *Christianity Today, 41*(7), 28–30.

Asher, S. R., & Coie, J. D. (1990). *Peer rejection in childhood.* New York: Cambridge University Press.

Baumeister, R. F., & Leary, M. R. (1995). The need to belong: Desire for interpersonal attachments as a fundamental human motivation. *Psychological Bulletin, 117,* 497–529.

Benson, P. L. (2004). Commentary: Emerging themes in research on adolescent spiritual and religious development. *Applied Developmental Science, 8,* 47–50.

Benson, P. L., Roehlkepartain, E. C., & Rude, S. P. (2003). Spiritual development in childhood and adolescence: Toward a field of inquiry. *Applied Developmental Science, 7,* 205–13.

Berryman, J. (2004). Children and mature spirituality. In D. Ratcliff (Ed.), *Children's spirituality: Christian perspectives, research, and application* (pp. 22–41). Eugene, OR: Cascade.

Bierman, K. L. (2004).*Peer rejection: Developmental processes and intervention.* New York: Guilford.

Boivin, M., & Hymel, S. (1997). Peer experiences and social self-perceptions: A sequential model. *Developmental Psychology, 33,* 135–45.

Boyatzis, C. J. (2005). Religious and spiritual development in childhood. In R. F. Paloutzian & C. L. Park (Eds.), *Handbook of the psychology of religion and spirituality* (pp. 123–43). New York: Guilford.

Bunge, M. J. (2001). Education and the child in Eighteenth-century German Pietism: Perspectives from the work of A. H. Francke. In M. J. Bunge (Ed.), *The child in Christian thought* (pp. 247–78). Grand Rapids: Eerdmans.

———. (2006). The dignity and complexity of children: Constructing Christian theologies of childhood. In K. M. Yust, A. N. Johnson, S. E. Sasso, & E. C. Roehlkepartain (Eds.), *Nurturing child and adolescent spirituality: Perspectives from the world's religious traditions* (pp. 53–68). Lanham, MD: Rowman & Littlefield.

Burwell, R. A., & Shirk, S. R. (2007). Subtypes of rumination in adolescence: Associations between brooding, reflection, depressive symptoms, and coping. *Journal of Clinical Child and Adolescent Psychology, 36,* 56–65.

Charry, E. T. (2006). Countering a malforming culture: Christian theological formation of adolescents in North America. In K. M. Yust, A. N. Johnson, S. E. Sasso, & E. C. Roehlkepartain (Eds.), *Nurturing child and adolescent spirituality: Perspectives from the world's religious traditions* (pp. 437–48). Lanham, MD: Rowman & Littlefield.

Coles, R. (1990). *The spiritual life of children.* Boston: Houghton Mifflin.

Deater-Deckard, K. (2001). Annotation: Recent research examining the role of peer relations in the development of psychopathology. *Journal of Child Psychology and Psychiatry, 42,* 565–79.

Denham, S., Neal, K., Wilson, B. J., Pickering, S. R., & Boyatzis, C. (2005). Emotional development and forgiveness in children: Emerging evidence. In E. Worthington (Ed.) *Handbook of Forgiveness* (pp. 127–42). New York: Brunner Routledge.

Desrosiers, A. & Miller, L. (2007). Relational spirituality and depression in adolescent girls. *Journal of Clinical Psychology, 63*(10), 1021–37.

DeVries, D. (2001). "Be converted and become as little children": Friedrich Schleiermacher on the religious significance of childhood. In M. J. Bunge (Ed.), *The child in Christian thought* (pp. 247–99). Grand Rapids: Eerdmans.

Enright, R. D. & Fitzgibbons, R. P. (2000). *Helping clients forgive: An empirical guide for resolving anger and restoring hope.* Washington, DC: American Psychological Association.

Enright, R. D. and the Human Development Study Group. (1991). The moral development of forgiveness. In W. Kurtines & J. Gewirtz (Eds.), *Handbook of Moral Behavior and Development* (Vol. 1, pp. 123–52). Hillsdale, NJ: Erlbaum.

———. (1994). Piaget on the moral development of forgiveness: Identity or reciprocity? *Human Development, 37,* 63–80.

Enright, R. D., Santos, M. J. D., & Al-Mabuk, R. (1989). The adolescent as forgiver. *Journal of Adolescence, 12,* 95–110.

Erickson, J. A. (1992). Adolescent religious development and commitment: A structural equation model of the role of family, peer group, and educational influences. *Journal for the Scientific Study of Religion, 31,* 131–52.

Estep & Breckenridge (2004). The ecology and social dynamics of childhood spirituality. In D. Ratcliff (Ed.), *Children's spirituality: Christian perspectives, research, and application* (pp. 324–42). Eugene, OR: Cascade.

Fetzer Institute (1999). Multidimensional measurement of religiousness/spirituality for use in health research. Kalamazoo, MI: Author.

Flanagan, K. S. (2009, June). *Fighting the good fight: Children's spirituality manifested as forgiveness of their peers.* Invited presentation at the Children's Spirituality Conference: Christian Perspectives, Chicago, Illinois.

Freedman, S. R., & Enright, R. D. (1996). Forgiveness as an intervention goal with incest survivors. *Journal of Consulting and Clinical Psychology, 64,* 983–92.

Furrow, J. L., King, P. E., & White (2004). Religion and positive youth development: Identity, meaning, and prosocial concerns. *Applied Developmental Science, 8,* 17–26.

Goins, S. (2008). The Place of forgiveness in the reintegration of former child soldiers in Sierra Leone. In H. C. Allen (Ed.), *Nurturing children's spirituality: Christian perspectives and best practices.* Eugene, OR: Cascade.

Good, M., & Willoughby, T. (2007). The identity formation experiences of church-attending rural adolescents. *Journal of Adolescent Research, 22,* 387–412.

———. (2008). Adolescence as a sensitive period for spiritual development. *Child Development Perspectives, 2,* 32–37.

Gundry-Volf, J. M. (2001). The least and the greatest: Children in the New Testament. In M. J. Bunge (Ed.), *The child in Christian thought* (pp. 29–60). Grand Rapids: Eerdmans.

Gunnoe, M. L., & Moore, K. A. (2002). Predictors of religiosity among youth aged 17–22; A longitudinal study of the national survey of children. *Journal for the Scientific Study of Religion, 41,* 613–22.

Harris, S. K, Sherritt, L. R., Holder, D. W., Kulig, J., Shrier, L. A., & Knight, J. R. (2008). Reliability and validity of the Brief Multidimensional Measure of Religiousness/ Spirituality among adolescents. *Journal of Religion and Health, 47*(4), 438–57.

Hart, T. (2006). Spiritual experiences and capacities of children and youth. In E. C. Roehlkepartain, P. E. King, L. Wagener, & P. L. Benson (Eds.), *The handbook of spiritual development in childhood and adolescence* (pp. 163–77). Thousand Oaks, CA: Sage.

Hay, D., & Nye, R. (1998). *The spirit of the child.* London: Fount.

Hawker, D. S., & Boulton, M. J. (2000). Twenty years' research on peer victimization and psychosocial maladjustment: A meta-analytic review of cross-sectional studies. *Journal of Child Psychology and Psychiatry and Allied Disciplines, 41,* 441–55.

Jones, L. G. (1995). *Embodying forgiveness: A theological analysis.* Grand Rapids: Eerdmans.

Juvonen, J., & Graham, S. (2001). *Peer harassment in school: The plight of the vulnerable and victimized.* New York: Guilford.

King, P. E. (2003). Religion and identity: The role of ideological, social and spiritual contexts. *Applied Developmental Science, 7,* 197–204.

King, P. E., & Boyatzis, C. J. (2004). Exploring adolescent spiritual and religious development: Current and future theoretical and empirical perspectives. *Applied Developmental Science, 8,* 2–6.

King, P. E., Furrow, J. L., & Roth, N. (2002). The influence of families and peers on adolescent religiousness. *The Journal for Psychology and Christianity, 21,* 109–20.

Kochenderfer, B. J., & Ladd, G. W. (1996). Peer victimization: Cause or consequence of school maladjustment? *Child Development, 67,* 1305–17.

Kochenderfer-Ladd, B. J. (2004). Peer victimization: The role of emotions in adaptive and maladaptive coping. *Social Development, 13*(3), 329–49.

Lerner, R. M. (2002). *Concepts and theories of human development (3rd ed.).* Mahway, NJ: Erlbaum.

Lundberg, M. D. (2002). From conflict to communion: An examination of Christian forgiveness. *Word & World, 22 (3),* 295–303.

Malcolm, L., & Ramsey, J. (2006). Teaching and learning forgiveness: A multidimensional approach. *Teaching Theology and Religion, 9,* 175–85.

Markstrom, C. A. (1999). Religious involvement and adolescent psychosocial development. *Journal of Adolescence, 22,* 205–21.

Martin, T. F., White, J. M., & Perlman, D. (2003). Religious socialization: A test of the channeling hypothesis of parental influence on adolescent faith maturity. *Journal of Adolescent Research, 18,* 169–87.

McCullough, M. E., & Worthington, E. L., Jr. (1995). Promoting forgiveness: Psychoeducational group interventions with a wait-list control. *Counseling and Values, 4,* 55–68.

McCullough, M. E., Worthington, E. L., Jr., & Rachal, K. C. (1997). Interpersonal forgiving in close relationships. *Journal of Personality and Social Psychology, 73,* 3211–336.

Miller-McLemore, B. J. (2003). *Let the children come: Reimagining childhood from a Christian perspective.* San Francisco: Wiley.

Muris, P., Roelofs, J., Meesters, C., & Boomsma, P. (2004). Rumination and worry in nonclinical adolescents *Cognitive Therapy and Research, 28,* 539–54.

Nasel, T. R., Overpeck, M., Pilla, R. S., Ruan, W. J., Simons-Morton, B., Scheidt, P. (2001). Bullying behaviors among U.S. youth: Prevalence and association with psychosocial adjustment. *Journal of the American Medical Association, 285,* 2094–2100.

North, J. (1998). The "ideal" of forgiveness: A philosopher's exploration. In R. D. Enright & J. North (Eds.), *Exploring forgiveness* (pp. 15–34). Madison: University of Wisconsin Press.

Ozorak, E. W. (1989). Social and cognitive influences on the development of religious beliefs and commitment in adolescence. *Journal for the Scientific Study of Religion, 28,* 448–63.

Park, Y. O., & Enright, R. D. (1997). The development of forgiveness in the context of adolescent friendship conflict in Korea. *Journal of Adolescence, 20,* 393–402.

Parker, J. G., Rubin, K. H., Erath, S. A., Wojslawowicz, J. C., & Buskirk, A. A. (2006). Peer relationships, child development, and adjustment: A developmental psychopathology perspective. In D. Cicchetti & D.J. Cohen (Eds.), *Developmental psychopathology: Vol. 1: Theory and Methods, 2nd Edition* (pp. 96–161). New York: Wiley.

Pearce, M. J., Little, T. D., & Perez, J. E. (2003). Religiousness and depressive symptoms among adolescents. *Journal of Clinical Child and Adolescent Psychology, 32*(2), 267–76.

Pitkin, B. (2001). "'The heritage of the Lord": Children in the theology of John Calvin. In M. J. Bunge (Ed.), *The child in Christian thought* (pp. 160–93). Grand Rapids: Eerdmans.

Ratcliff, D., & Nye, R. (2006). Childhood spirituality: Strengthening the research foundation. In E. C. Roehlkepartain, P. E. King, L. Wagener, & P. L. Benson (Eds.), *The handbook of spiritual development in childhood and adolescence* (pp. 473–83). Thousand Oaks, CA: Sage.

Regnerus, M. D., Smith, C., & Smith, B. (2004). Social context in the development of adolescent religiosity. *Applied Developmental Science, 8,* 27–38.

Reich, H. (2009). *Forgiveness in early adolescence: Coping and conceptualization.* Unpublished doctoral dissertation. Wheaton, IL: Wheaton College.

Reich, H. A., Flanagan, K. S., & Wright, J. B. (2009). *Early adolescents' use and understanding of forgiveness in response to peer hurts.* Poster presented at the biennial meeting of the Society for Research in Child Development, Denver, CO.

Reich, H., Wright, J. B., Flanagan, K. S., Carter, C., Post, D., & Andrews, K. D. (2007). *Spirituality and forgiveness in relation to socioemotional adjustment among early adolescents: A developmentally informed perspective.* Paper presented at the annual meeting of the Christian Association for Psychological Studies, King of Prussia, PA.

Reimer, K. S., & Furrow, J. L. (2001). A qualitative exploration of relational consciousness in Christian children. *International Journal of Children's Spirituality, 6,* 7–23.

Sandstrom, M. J., & Colie, J. D. (1999). A developmental perspective on peer rejection: Mechanisms of stability and change. *Child Development, 70,* 955–66.

Schwartz, K. D. (2006). Transformations in parent and friend faith support predicting adolescents' religious faith. *The international journal for the psychology of religion, 16,* 311–26.

Schwartz, K. D., Bukowski, W. M., & Aoki, W. T. (2006). Mentors, friends and gurus: Peer and nonparent influences on spiritual development. In E. C. Roehlkepartain, P. E. King, L.M. Wagener, & P. L. Benson (Eds.), *The handbook of spiritual development in childhood and adolescence* (pp. 310–23). Thousand Oaks, CA: Sage Publications, Inc.

Seybold, K. S., Hill, P. C., Neumann, J. K., & Chi, D. S. (2001). Physiological and psychological correlates of forgiveness. *Journal of Psychology and Christianity, 20,* 250–59.

Skitch, S. A., & Abela, J. R. Z. (2008). Rumination in response to stress as a common vulnerability factor to depression and substance misuse in adolescence. *Journal of Abnormal Child Psychology, 36,* 1029–45.

Smedes, L. B. (1984). *Forgive and forget: Healing the hurts we don't deserve.* San Francisco: Harper & Row.

Stonehouse, C. (2006). After a child's first dance with God: Accompanying children on a Protestant spiritual journey. In K. M. Yust, A. N. Johnson, S. E. Sasso, & E. C. Roehlkepartain (Eds.), *Nurturing child and adolescent spirituality: Perspectives from the world's religious traditions* (pp. 95–107). Lanham, MD: Rowman & Littlefield.

Stortz, M. E. (2001). "Where or when was your servant innocent?": Augustine on childhood. In M. J. Bunge (Ed.), *The child in Christian thought* (pp. 78–102). Grand Rapids: Eerdmans.

Subkoviak, M. J., Enright, R. D., Wu, C.-R, Gassin, E. A., Freedman, S., Olson, L. M., & Sarinopoulos, I. (1995). Measuring interpersonal forgiveness in late adolescence and middle adulthood. *Journal of Adolescence, 18*(6), 641–55.

Toussaint, L., & Webb, J. R. (2005). Theoretical and empirical connections between forgiveness, mental health, and well-being In E. Worthington (Ed.) *Handbook of Forgiveness* (pp. 349–62). New York: Routledge.

Volf, M. (1996). *Exclusion and embrace: A theological exploration of identity, otherness, and reconciliation.* Nashville: Abingdon.

———. (2005). *Free of charge: Giving and forgiving in a culture stripped of grace.* Grand Rapids: Zondervan.

Witvliet, C. V. O. (2001). Forgiveness and health: review and reflections on a matter of faith, feelings, and physiology. *Journal of Psychology & Theology, 29*(3), 212–24.

Witvliet, C. V. O., Ludwig, T. E., & Vander Laan, K. L. (2001). Granting forgiveness or harboring grudges: Implications for emotion, physiology, and health. *Psychological Science, 121,* 117–23.

Worthington, E. L., Jr. (2006). *Forgiveness and reconciliation: Theory and application.* New York: Routledge.

Worthington, E. L., Jr., Sharp, C. B., Lerner, A. J., & Sharp, J. R. (2006). Interpersonal forgiveness as an example of loving one's enemies. *Journal of Psychology & Theology, 34*(1), 32–42.

Worthington, E. L., Jr. & Wade, N. G. (1999). The social psychology of unforgiveness and forgiveness and implications for clinical practice. *Journal of Social and Clinical Psychology, 18,* 385–418.

Yust, K. M., Johnson, A. N., Sasso, S. E., & Roehlkepartain, E. C. (2006). Traditional wisdom: Creating space for religious reflection on child and adolescent spirituality. In K. M. Yust, A. N. Johnson, S. E. Sasso, & E. C. Roehlkepartain (Eds.), *Nurturing child and adolescent spirituality: Perspectives from the world's religious traditions* (pp. 1–14). Lanham, MD: Rowman & Littlefield.

Zechmeister, J. S. & Romero, C. (2002). Victim and offender accounts of interpersonal conflict: Autobiographical narrative of forgiveness and unforgiveness. *Journal of Personality and Social Psychology, 82*(4), 675–86.

20

The Roles of Identity and Wisdom in a Spirituality of Hope Among Children with End-Stage Renal Disease[1]

Duane R. Bidwell and Donald L. Batisky

The Pauline literature of the New Testament presents hope as a constitutive element of abundant life (John 10:10), and recent theologies have emphasized the role of hope, especially in relation to the doctrine of eschatology.[2] These developments have been enriched by attention to faith practices that contribute to hopefulness in Christian contexts. As pastoral theologian Duane Bidwell (2010) notes, an interdisciplinary group of theologians—including Donald Capps (1995), Russell Herbert (2006), Flora A. Keshgegian (2006), Andrew D. Lester (1995), and Ellen Ott Marshall (2006)—has recently proposed theological and pastoral practices that can nurture hope as a spiritual resource.[3] This literature primarily addresses adult

1. This essay was originally published in slightly different form in the *Journal of Childhood and Religion*, Vol. 2 (2011) (www.childhoodandreligion.com). The essay is republished here with permission of the *Journal of Childhood and Religion*.

2. See, for example, 1 Cor. 13:13, Rom. 5:2 and 8:24, Heb. 10:23, Eph. 1:18 and 4:4, Col. 1:27, Titus 2:13, 1 Thess. 4:13, 1 John 3:2, 1 Pet. 1:3 and 3:15, and 1 Tim. 1:1.

3. Contemporary theological interest in "Christian hope," especially in pastoral theology, may be traced to Jürgen Moltmann's early work, *Theology of Hope*. Moltmann was influenced by the Marxist-Existentialist philosopher Ernst Bloch, who also informed Latin American liberation theologies. See *Jürgen Moltmann, Theology of Hope: On the Ground and the Implications of a Christian Eschatology*, Trans. James W. Leitch (New York: Harper and Row, 1967).

experience through a Christian existential lens; its emphasis on the future and its eschatological assumptions may prevent it from being useful for children (Bidwell & Batisky, 2009). Yet no theologians have engaged children's own accounts of hopefulness or explored the practices that children themselves say nourish hope.[4]

This chapter describes and reflects on a preliminary theological-spiritual understanding of hope that is grounded in, and accountable to, the experiences of particular children living with end-stage renal disease. Our understanding emerges from a grounded-theory study of hope among chronically ill children (see Bidwell & Batisky, 2009) and these findings should not be generalized beyond the particular healthcare setting where the research occurred.

Nonetheless, this model might have a pragmatic, heuristic value for conversations about hope as a spiritual resource among children (Bidwell & Batisky, 2009). For example, it resonates with a broader framework for understanding childhood and adolescent spirituality that has emerged from a large-scale empirical study of children across cultures and faith traditions (Roehlkepartain, et. al., 2008). Our model might also inform an emerging biomedical and psychosocial consensus that chronic, life-threatening illness is "fundamentally a spiritual crisis" (Doka, 2009, p. 163) that involves making meaning, finding hope, and facing death (Doka, 1993, pp. 160–161).

In this chapter, we use the terms "spiritual" and "spirituality" to refer to an embodied pattern of response to a dynamic, ultimate reality—a reality that may approach human beings from beyond a transcendent horizon and manifest through the mundane, material world. Human experiences of the ultimate—which for Christians is the liberating God revealed by Jesus—happen within social and cultural realities (see Hopkins, 2005). Our use of "spirituality" follows Joseph D. Driskill (2007), professor of spirituality at Pacific School of Religion, for whom spirituality is a lived experience of faith "concerned with the community that shapes and celebrates [it], the spiritual practices which sustain it, and the moral life which embodies it" (p. 74). Thus, spirituality refers to a socio-cultural/existential phenomenon and a

---

4. In general, psychologists, nurses and early-childhood specialists have done a better job than theologians of attending to children's experiences of hope, but they primarily—although not exclusively—propose non-contextual models of childhood hopefulness focused on cognition and emotion. These models have limited utility for contemporary theology.

dimension of experience recognized in many Eastern and Western cultures. We approach this phenomenon from a descriptive-critical rather than prescriptive-normative stance (Schneiders, 1989), which entails a critical appraisal of a person's accounts of spiritual experiences. The word "resource" denotes a wellspring or site of understanding, energy, and consolation that can enhance people's natural capacities (to endure suffering, for example) or provide the power and resources to accomplish what people could not achieve on their own.

Contextual Factors

The accounts of our research partners—seven girls and five boys ranging from nine to nineteen years—lead us to envision hope as a contextual spiritual resource that manifests through the interplay of social processes, an individual's internalized resources, and a transcendent presence. Like all children, our research partners live in a paradox of strengths and vulnerabilities (see Bunge, 2009), a childhood reality that theologian David Jensen (2005) calls "graced vulnerability." As we have written elsewhere (Bidwell and Batisky, 2009), three contextual factors shape the strengths and vulnerabilities of our research partners: end-stage renal disease itself, the interdisciplinary treatment team, and experiences of suffering. These contextual factors particularly shape the ways in which our research partners understand hope.

End-stage Renal Disease

End-stage renal disease is an incurable and potentially fatal chronic illness that requires medical intervention to replace some functions of the kidneys so that the body can be cleansed of excessive toxins. The best treatment is a kidney transplant, but a transplant is not a cure; on average, a transplanted kidney functions well for only fifteen years. The disease and its treatment can also create additional long-term health concerns, especially in the cardiovascular system (U.S. Renal Data System, 2008).

Interdisciplinary Team

An interdisciplinary treatment team serves as an ongoing web of supportive resources for children and parents. The team also constitutes a particular culture or community into which patients and families are welcomed. Through intentional and unintentional practices, team members create a community of hope and socialize patients and their families into that community. The team's expectation that patients of all ages can and will participate in managing the disease contributes to the hopefulness identified by our research partners.

Suffering

The most influential contextual factor for our research partners is suffering—physical, psychosocial, and intra-psychic. Psychosocial and intra-psychic sufferings were mentioned twice as often as physical suffering. While coping with chronic physical pain, our research partners also experience disrupted peer relationships, restriction of normal activities, awareness of being different from other children, and a sense of losing a part of themselves. Intra-psychic suffering manifests primarily as fear, loss, and worry.

The Multifaceted Nature of Hope

Shaped by these contextual factors, our research partners provided descriptions of hope that have a richness and depth missing from the primarily existential understandings of recent pastoral theologies, the cognitive model privileged by psychology, and the emotional understanding central to the literature of nursing (see Snyder, 1994; Snyder, 2005; Connelly, 2005; Farran, Herth & Popovich, 1995).

Hope does have existential, cognitive and emotional dimensions for these children. But they also experience it as participatory, relational, kinesthetic, perceptual, and—perhaps most significantly—conative. The will—that is, the ability to choose—has a prominent place in their accounts of hope; hope is not a passive experience for them but an active decision that often precedes or informs other dimensions of hope. This finding is consistent with research that suggests children perceive an element of choice in their spiritual development (Roehlkepartain, et. al., 2008). For example, Bradley, a fifteen-year-old dialysis patient, describes the relationship between end-stage renal disease and hope:

> It ain't a part of me; I'm a part of it. Well, it is a part of me, but it doesn't have control over me. I have control of it. . . . I don't let pain or my disease take control over me. I know there's something better; I know there's something else rather than just

letting it come over me. . . . I just live day by day, year by year.
I don't think about the now; I think about the future—how I
can do stuff . . . how I can give back. . . . I believe there is hope
(Bidwell & Batisky, 2009, p. 43).

Our research partners often describe an immediate manifestation of
hope—an awareness of the abundance that surrounds them day by
day—represented primarily by supportive family, friends, and members
of the interdisciplinary team. Eighteen-year-old Tom is a transplant
recipient:

Hope is keeping up, looking forward, being happy and joyful
while you still can. [It is] looking to the bright side of life and
enjoying life and your family—all the good things in life. . . .
Just hanging out with my friends and family and looking to
the bright side of life—all the good things in life (Bidwell &
Batisky, 2009, p. 44).

Stated in these terms, hope seems to become an aspect of noetic or sapiential eschatology (Bidwell, 2010), what pastoral theologian Peggy
Way (2005) calls the "ordinary grace" that places "ultimacy and im-
mediacy in the same sentence" (pp. 41–42).

For our research partners, hope often entails being aware, in the
moment, of the fullness of life, relationships, and caring community
amidst the finitude of disease. This understanding resonates with the
three elements of children's spirituality—awareness or awakening,
interconnecting and belonging, and living an integrated life—proposed by the Center for Spiritual Development in Childhood and
Adolescence, based on a world-wide empirical study (Roehlkepartain,
et. al., 2008, pp. 40–47).

Pathways to Hope

In the accounts of our research partners, we identified five pathways
to hope: maintaining identity, realizing connections, claiming power,
attending to God, and learning wisdom. (See Fig. 1) We believe that
he greater the overlap between pathways, the more likely hope is to
be present for a particular child. Interventions to nurture hope can
focus on (a) strengthening pathways already apparent in a child's life
and (b) activating pathways that seem weak or absent. We also suspect
that the more pathways "activated" for a particular child, the more

hope that child feels. Developing and testing these hypotheses will be a focus of future research.

Figure 1

Pathways to Hope: A Preliminary Theological Model

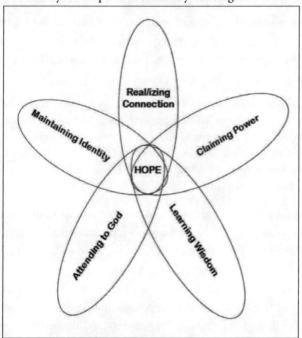

Theoretical descriptions of each pathway appear below, providing a broad overview of the tentative model. Each pathway can also be developed in greater detail, using the words of our research partners to illustrate particular concepts. We provide detailed descriptions of "real/izing connections" and "attending to God" elsewhere (Bidwell & Batisky, 2009). This chapter offers expanded descriptions of "maintaining identity" and "learning wisdom" and also identifies practices that can help nurture these two pathways among children with end-stage renal disease.

Maintaining identity reflects the desire and efforts of children with end-stage renal disease to continue to participate in the activities and relationships that shaped their sense of self prior to diagnosis and treatment. This facet of hopefulness is primarily performative and agential; it focuses on what a child can do despite limitations created by the disease and treatment. Children with the disease are keenly aware of being different from healthy peers; behaviors that maintain pre-disease identities allow them to remain "normal" (or to become "more normal," in the words of one research partner) despite the illness. Internalized norms about being a child (established through particular socio-cultural contexts) are a motivation to participate in treatment and can become a source of tension when the disease creates barriers to "being normal." Some children also discover new and positive facets of identity as they cope with the disease, seeking to integrate these new self understandings into their pre-disease identities. One way that children maintain identity in the midst of treatment is by externalizing end-stage renal disease, speaking of it as an entity and force separate from and alien to themselves.

Realizing connections weaves children who have end-stage renal disease into a community of mutuality and trust that assures them that they are not alone in living with the illness. This facet of hopefulness is primarily relational; by "making real" their connections to others, children participate in the creation of social capital that provides resources for coping with the psychosocial, spiritual, and intra-psychic aspects of the disease. While relationships with members of the interdisciplinary treatment team are primary in this process, the illness also leads many children to develop multifaceted connections to a broader community. These connections can be formal or informal. Children especially value connections to other children and adults living with kidney disease. Connections to others are made real through conversation, visitation, consultation, and participation in daily activities; in the process, children receive (and often give) guidance, empowerment, reassurance, and encouragement. Some relationships offer children a broader vision of future possibilities despite the ongoing effects of kidney disease. Social artifacts generated through these relationships can be internalized to increase agency and clarify identity in the midst of the disease; thus, relationality is constitutive element of claiming power and maintaining identity, two other pathways to hope.

Claiming power allows children with end-stage renal disease to take an active role in treatment by setting goals, advocating for themselves, and monitoring and maintaining their own health. This facet of hopefulness is primarily agential; it focuses on children's abilities to influence outcomes, access resources, and participate meaningfully as a member of the interdisciplinary team. Children claim power by refusing to be an object that passively experiences the disease and its treatment; instead, they assert themselves as subjects in relation to other members of the interdisciplinary team and in relation to the effects of the disease. For some children, claiming power includes identifying and enacting strategies to control anxiety as a means of resisting the intra-psychic suffering that can accompany the illness. By acting to claim power in relationship to the disease, children can influence health outcomes and thereby obtain more freedom from the limitations imposed by the disease and its treatment.

Attending to God provides spiritual consolation to children with end-stage renal disease by assuring them that God is present during their suffering and participates in the treatment process. This facet of hope is primarily relational and sapiential; it is activated through religious and spiritual practices such as prayer, worship, visitation, blessing, and the reading of scripture. Some children invoke a family wisdom figure, such as a grandparent, as a spiritual guide to help them attend to God. Children with end-stage renal disease tend toward an instrumental understanding of religious resources (using prayer, for example, to relieve anxiety during dialysis), but speak intimately and personally of God's availability and presence with them in the midst of illness. Prayer is the primary way that these children connect to God.

Learning wisdom allows children with end-stage renal disease to integrate technical information from the interdisciplinary team with a noetic assurance about their own well-being to relieve immediate intra-psychic and spiritual suffering, enhance agency, and generate possibilities for the future. This facet of hopefulness is agential, relational, and resource-oriented; it can also have a transpersonal dimension. Children seem unaware of pre-diagnosis resources and knowledge that help them cope with kidney disease; they perceive wisdom as evolving primarily from the team's expertise and secondarily from the child's own transpersonal awareness of a positive personal future. Among older children whose diagnosis occurred when they were young, this integrative awareness can create a vocational desire to use their experiential wisdom to benefit others. In this way, learning wisdom moves children beyond egoic concern for their own well-being to a generative focus on the well-being of other children living with chronic illness. Finding ways to "give back" what they have received and to activate a special, noetic connection with caregivers and other chronically ill patients are significant ways that these children make meaning of their illness.

Richer Descriptions of "Maintaining Identity" and "Learning Wisdom"

Maintaining Identity

Describing the Pathway. As a pathway toward hope, "maintaining identity" reflects children's desires and efforts to "be normal"—or, in the words of fourteen-year-old Sally, who lives with a transplanted kidney, to be "more normal." Most often, "being (more) normal" means to participate again or more frequently in the activities and relationships that shaped identity prior to diagnosis and treatment. Thirteen-year-old Gina, a transplant recipient, speaks of it this way:

> I thought with all this, you know, in about ten or twelve years, I would still have to be taking medication—extra medication or something—but instead they had to come out with dialysis; then I had to have a tube put in; so then I didn't have much hope. Then my parents were like, "Oh, no, you'll get better. You are going to be able to go out and play and hang out with friends. Don't just focus on that one little thing, getting through all this." Then I will be able to have most of my normal life . . . just to be able not to be getting hooked up [to dialysis] every night; then I could, like, stay over at a friend's house and stuff. Be a normal teenager.

Children with end-stage renal disease are keenly aware of being different from healthy peers. Their bodies and activities remind them daily of their differences, and any practice that encourages them to remember and rehearse who they are apart from the diagnosis seems to nurture this pathway to hope. This facet of hopefulness is primarily performative and agential; it focuses on what a child can *do* despite limitations created by the disease and its treatment. Yet it can also involve normalizing the ways the disease shapes a child's life. For example, our research partners delight in Kidney Kamp, an annual, week-long overnight camp organized by members of the interdisciplinary team. Camp, says fifteen-year-old William, provides an opportunity to be with peers:

> who had the same problem as you and don't make fun of each other about it. . . . They don't sit and stare at you and point and laugh and whisper to each other about you. They just ask you when you started dialysis, how long you had been on dialysis. Sometimes they show each other scars or [ask] about what point that they go through and how they got started on dialysis, when they got the transplant and how long they had it. . . . like it is normal for kids. . . . When I first started, [I] thought it only happened in grownups and older people—like I didn't think it happened to kids. . . . It is kind of a relief when you are around people . . . , [and] everybody has the same thing. It is not that they can't make fun of each other; it is just like they don't bother to make fun of each other because it is not funny. . . . They think I am the same, normal kid.

Some children, of course, discover positive, new facets of identity as they cope with the disease; the pathway of maintaining identity includes efforts to integrate these insights into their pre-disease identities. The practices of the interdisciplinary team help make this possible.

Practices that Maintain Identity. A primary practice that helps children maintain identity and integrate new insights in the midst of treatment is, in the language of narrative psychotherapy and pastoral counseling, the "externalization" of end-stage renal disease. Children speak of the disease as an entity and force separate from and somewhat alien to themselves, as something they have a relationship with rather than as something they "are." Bradley, a fifteen-year-old dialysis patient, says:

> It ain't a part of me. I'm a part of it. It is a part of me . . . but it doesn't have control over me. I have control of it . . . I don't let pain or my disease take control over me. I know there's something better. I know there's something else rather than just letting it come over me.

When thirteen-year-old Gina reflects on the relationship between hope and end-stage renal disease, she immediately externalizes the illness: "It's just pulling you back," she says. "You go forward."

Members of the interdisciplinary team can use externalizing language intentionally to help children maintain pre-diagnosis identities and strengthen a sense of agency is relation to the disease. But there is a simpler practice as well: becoming curious about, and helping "re-member," (see White, 2007) children's lives outside the dialysis unit and transplant clinic. Our research partners emphasized that their hope is nurtured most by the ways that nurses, doctors, and other members of the interdisciplinary team ask informally about friends, family, school, vacation, and weekend plans. Such conversations are not focused on gathering information for medical purposes, but on relationships and day-to-day living in the community of the dialysis unit and transplant clinic.

The concept of re-membering has a rich history in the Christian traditions of pastoral and spiritual care, but here we are using the term as employed in the traditions of narrative psychotherapy and pastoral counseling. For narrative practitioners, re-membering is short-hand for helping a person identify and enrich relationships with people they claim as personal "cheerleaders" and "consultants"—people who constitute a circle of influence and are supportive, wise and bring strength for positive change. Re-membering conversations contribute at least two strategies for our research partners. First, they distract children from the immediate medical context, re-focusing them on their identities and daily lives apart from end-stage renal disease. Second, they communicate the team's belief that a child has a present and future that include but are broader than the disease. Both effects, our research partners say, nurture hope by helping them maintain their pre-disease identities.

Learning Wisdom

Describing the Pathway. Even as they maintain pre-disease identities, our research partners encounter and integrate new types of knowledge that contribute to a hopeful stance by expanding and enriching their understandings of self and world. We call this knowledge-based pathway "learning wisdom." The process can move beyond cognitive and content-oriented knowing to encompass a greater awareness of non-empirical realities that shape a child's experience with the disease. When our research partners talk about this process, they describe two types of wisdom: First, a pragmatic, medical wisdom that develops as they integrate technical information from the interdisciplinary team with a noetic assurance of their own well-being. This type of wisdom seems to relieve immediate intra-psychic and spiritual suffering, enhance agency, and generate possibilities for the future. The second is an altruistic wisdom expressed as special knowledge or responsibility, including a sense of "connection" with other ill children; sometimes, this altruistic wisdom is expressed in transpersonal terms, and almost always in terms of career and vocation.

These two types of wisdom seem to be sequential. Our research partners first develop a pragmatic (or "practical") wisdom focused on health skills and medical information; some go on to develop an altruistic wisdom motivated by gratitude and focused on their sense of connection with other suffering people. Thus, learning wisdom as a pathway to hope is agential, relational, and resource-oriented; and for children who actively engage the pathway of "attending to God," it can also be transpersonal.

All children have, at the point of diagnosis, existing resources and knowledge that help them cope with kidney disease. But our research partners seem either unaware of or unimpressed by their prior resources. Instead, they perceive wisdom as evolving primarily from the expertise of the interdisciplinary treatment expertise and secondarily from a transpersonal awareness of a positive personal future. The team's contribution consists primarily of educating children so that they can understand their experiences and claim power in relation to the disease. For example, Suzy, an eighteen-year-old diagnosed at infancy, talk about her transition to dialysis as an adolescent:

> It was terrifying because I did not really know much about [dialysis] until they explained it to me. . . . They told me how it worked and what it can do for me and stuff like that . . . the parts of the machine, and what they do. . . . Then they showed me some doll that had the dialysis catheter in it. . . . When they explained it to me, it actually made me feel better. It did not seem as scary after they told me what they had to do and all that, to put the catheter in and stuff. . . . I guess it made me have more hope . . . .

In addition to teaching how dialysis can "take out the toxins and stuff" (as thirteen-year-old Gina describes it), the team also teaches necessary health-care skills. Fourteen-year-old Sally named this didactic function as the most important thing that a new team member could do to nurture hope:

> Give the patient all the information and all the guidance that
> they need for after the transplant and before the transplant.
> Just tell them what to expect and teach yourself what they
> should expect. . . . Just give them the skills to do it. Yeah, give
> them the skills.

This sort of education, she says, helps children have:

> more maturity and more confidence. The more maturity is
> because, like, you've been through, like, a lot, and you're more
> confident because you know, like, everything is going to be
> OK. . . . Like if the doctor tells you that you have to start doing
> something, or you, like, have to change medications or doses
> . . . it's like, OK, and then you have to like, mature and stand up
> and do it to make yourself better.

Some older children diagnosed at a young age also develop a type of
integrative wisdom that manifests as a desire to draw on their experiences to benefit others medically and psychosocially, which pastor
and death educator Kenneth J. Doka (2009) notes is a common phenomenon among patients with life-threatening illnesses. Many of our
research partners want to become pediatric doctors or nurses. It is
at this point that learning wisdom moves beyond egoic concern for
a child's own well-being to a generative, altruistic focus on the well-
being of other children living with chronic illness. Inspired by gratitude for what they have received from the team, our research partners
seek to "give back" to others. Bradley, the fifteen-year-old awaiting a
transplant, said, "In a way, it's kind of like karma; because the hospital's given to me, and I want to try to give back. . . . I know they've done
a lot for me—everybody here has—which I really appreciate."

Our research partners also talk about a special, noetic and
empathic connection with caregivers and other chronically ill patients—an altruistic wisdom that provides a significant way of making
meaning of illness. Fourteen-year-old Rob, who received a transplant
eighteen months before our conversation, put it this way:

> I felt like I needed to survive to help other people. . . . I know
> how they feel when they're sick and stuff. So that's the connec-
> tion between us and other people—of what pain is and stuff.
> So. That helps me a whole lot. . . . Some people don't under-
> stand, you know; you say it, but you might not really know,
> you know—so: When I say it, you know, I really mean it—so
> that might give that person a big, you know, joy. . . .

Likewise, 14-year-old Sally wants to become a nurse because the illness has given her a special empathy and gift for understanding human suffering:

> I just want to, like—if anybody has questions, then, yeah, I'll answer them, because I have been there. And, like, most of the nurses and doctors haven't been there, so . . . just saying, "I know it hurts" and being truthful about it. . . . Like, I could say I know what you're going through and like, mean it, instead of just those doctors saying, "I know it hurts" or whatever. I could say I know it hurts . . . I'd have a personal, like, I already went through it. . . . They know somebody there actually knows what they're going through, and they can have somebody to talk to . . . .

Some research partners do not simply imagine a future where they "give back," but already take an active role in mentoring newly diagnosed children. When fifteen-year-old William began dialysis, for example, he suffered acute anxiety that caused him to pull dialysis catheters from his arm in the midst of treatment; the interdisciplinary team taught him ways to self-regulate to manage anxiety. William now teaches those skills to other anxious patients:

> They had a new boy who came . . . he had the same problems I had, and I talked to him about how to overcome his panic attacks and stuff. . . . I asked his parents if it was OK to do with him, and they said yeah. So I did help him with that. That helped him out.

As a pathway to hope, learning wisdom is clearly related to the pathways of realizing connections, claiming power, and attending to God. All four can be nurtured by the team through a particular set of intentional practices.

Practices that Contribute to Learning Wisdom. Our research partners say the most important practices for learning wisdom are the honest sharing of medical information, the teaching of health-management skills, and medical actions consistent with the words of team members. Two additional practices seem to contribute to the growth of altruistic wisdom. The first is conversation with team members that helps children (a) name the gifts they have developed as a result of their relationship with end-stage renal disease and (b) discern how they want to respond. The second is the facilitation of mentoring relationships between children at different stages of the disease process. Both practices are primarily spontaneous and informal at the hospital where our research partners are treated; if team members become more intentional and formal about these practices, it could result in more robust hopefulness among children with end-stage renal disease.

Eschatology and Children's Accounts of Hope

Elsewhere, we propose the ancient Semitic tradition of the sojourner as a useful biblical and theological frame for understanding the experiences of children with end-stage renal disease (Bidwell & Batisky, 2009, pp. 49–51). Children with the disease enter a foreign territory as sojourners—strangers asking for protection and support from local patrons. They dwell in that territory for the rest of their lives, pitching their tents in the midst of a community that offers local wisdom without expecting the children to give up the identities, traditions or resources of their native places. Rather, those gifts and resources become woven into, and benefit, the life of that local community. Hope emerges when and where a child's gifts to the community overlap with and amplify the wisdom of the interdisciplinary team. These communities can become outposts or manifestations of eschatological abundance in the finitude of the present moment (see Brock and Parker, 2008), demonstrating the common wealth (Hopkins, 2005) or "kin-dom" of God.

Our research partners repeatedly locate hope in the present, experienced during ordinary moments in community, especially unstructured time enjoying family, friends, and team members—what eighteen-year-old Tom, a transplant recipient, calls "all the good things in life." In the midst of suffering, some research partners also experience God as a comforting, kinesthetic presence that reassures them about their ultimate well-being. The emphasis that chronically ill children place on the present when talking about hope contrasts significantly with recent theologies that emphasize the future and topocentric—that is, "heaven-centered"—dimensions of hopefulness (Bidwell, 2010). Certainly, the dominant North American culture is suffused with an apocalyptic, futurist, and topocentric eschatology.

Children's recognition of day-by-day abundance in the midst of the finitude of illness might reflect a lived experience of the "latitudinal eschatology"—local, particular, contextual, fleeting—of some Latin American liberation theologians (Westhelle, 2008; see also Bidwell, 2010). Children's accounts of hope might also resonate with sapiential or wisdom eschatologies evident in John Dominic Crossan (1994) and other contemporary wisdom theologians, in which the whole of creation is being transformed—through divine and human action—to manifest here-and-now, in the midst of brokenness, the wisdom, beauty and goodness of God (Crossan, 1994; see also Bidwell, 2010).

And it is God, not Jesus, on whom our research partners focus. Although the locus of hope in the Christian traditions is almost always found in the person and work of Jesus Christ, none of our research partners made explicitly Christological claims in relation to hope. For them, eschatology is neither an ultimate, apocalyptic event nor an ultimate, soteriological person or place; rather, it seems similar to, but not exactly like, Dodd's "kingdom version" of realized eschatology in which the common wealth of God is an ongoing, historical and contextual manifestation of God's promises made real through the actions of a called and gathered community (Dodd, 1969). The sojourner participates *now* in the realities of the future promise through a "bond of hospitality" with a community whose practices in a particular context reflect God's role as the special protector of the poor, weak, and disinherited (Knauth, 1962).

Conclusion

Hope manifests among some children with end-stage renal disease through the pathways of vision, voice, faith, community, and identity. It is received and perceived in the present moment through awareness of God's abundance in the midst of chronic illness. Additional research could assess how well theological, psychosocial, and medical literatures address the elements of hope identified by these particular children living with end-stage renal disease. Their accounts may require a re-interpretation of predominately Christological, future-oriented, and individualistic understandings of hope. Finally, these accounts suggest that hope-nurturing practices can be taught to, and intentionally employed by, members of the interdisciplinary team. When this occurs, the practices must remain relational, contextual, and mutual in order to preserve the character of the actions that children describe as helpful.

Implications for Pastoral, Clinical, and Community Practice

Previous research suggests that hopeful children—those who find meaning in their disease, feel empowered to manage their illness, successfully integrate chronicity into previous identities, develop a sense of altruism as a result of their illness, and anticipate future achievements—are more likely to take their medications; follow medical instructions to avoid rejecting a transplanted kidney; and manage their illness to maintain good kidney function, increase independence, avoid hospitalization, and qualify for less-demanding dialysis schedules (Maikranz, et. al., 2007). Without question, the health and economic benefits of nurturing hope among children with chronic illness deserve the attention of spiritual caregivers, religious leaders, and members of the interdisciplinary treatment team.

Beyond material benefit, however, there are also significant spiritual, existential, relational, and communal reasons to become more intentional about nurturing hope among chronically ill children and adults. Our research has at least three primary implications for this goal in relation to pastoral, clinical, and community practice.

First, our work makes clear that children with end-stage renal disease are aware of what's going on with their bodies, their psychosocial circumstances, and their medical care; they also reflect with insight on their experiences of illness. Chronically ill children make meaning of their suffering in creative and nuanced ways. Having clear, honest, and accurate information from members of the interdisciplinary team facilitates this process, and children with end-stage renal disease trust and value adults who know that children are, as pastoral theologian Bonnie Miller-McLemore (2003) argues, responsible, knowing agents who have ever-emerging and ever-maturing spiritual, moral, communal and health-related powers. Again and again, children demonstrate that they know more about their health and illness than team members tend to assume, and children say that accurate, honest medical information provides them with another, especially effective tool, for coping with their illness. This suggests that caregivers of all types should provide specific, detailed and developmentally appropriate information to children living with chronic illness, paying as much or more attention to their needs for information than they might with adults with the same disease.

Second, this research suggests that spiritual caregivers, medical team members, clinicians, and faith communities could do more to cultivate noetic awareness in children with chronic illness, opening them "to knowledge that comes . . . directly through . . . subjective experiences or inner authority" (Schlitz, et. al., 2007, p. 4) rather than through discursive thought. Such knowledge can be cultivated and accessed through intuition, imagination, creative processes, spiritual insights and practices, and other epistemological events. This type of direct and spiritual knowing contributes significantly to the pathway of "learning wisdom," as well as to other pathways in our preliminary model; it also seems operative in children's eschatological descriptions of moments when hope is most present (see Bidwell, 2010). Children who say the disease has clarified their vocation, bestowed special gifts or knowledge, and created altruistic motivation often attribute their insights to a noetic awareness that carries significant authority for them. Practices of curiosity, prayer, mindfulness, creativity, and introspection (in both the psychological and spiritual uses of the term), among others, can help cultivate noetic awareness (Schlitz, et. al., 2007, pp. 66–114).

Finally, our work clarifies that hope is nurtured in many, idiosyncratic ways; singular or mono-dimensional understandings of hopefulness cannot be effective for all people. Because no child or family hopes in the same manner, it is essential that pastoral, spiritual, clinical, and community caregivers identify the specific pathways to hope already present to each patient and family and intervene to access and strengthen those pathways in relation to the experience of chronic illness.

References

Bidwell, D. R. (2010). Eschatology and childhood hope: Reflections from work in progress. *The Journal of Pastoral Theology, 20*(2): in press.

Bidwell, D. R. & Batisky, D. L. (2009). Abundance in finitude: An exploratory study of children's accounts of hope in chronic illness. *The Journal of Pastoral Theology, 19*(1): 38–59.

Brock, R. N. & Parker, R. A. (2008). *Saving paradise: How Christianity traded love of this world for crucifixion and empire.* Boston: Beacon.

Bunge, M. J. (2009, June 14). Reexamining children's paradoxical strengths and vulnerabilities: Biblical and theological perspectives. Keynote address at the Third Triennial Children's Spirituality Conference, Concordia University, River Forest, IL, June 14–17, 2009.

Capps, D. (1995). *Agents of hope: A pastoral psychology*. Minneapolis: Fortress.

Connelly, T. W. (2005). Family functioning and hope in children with juvenile rheumatoid arthritis. *MCN: The American Journal of Maternal/Child Nursing, 30*, 245–50.

Crossan, J. D. (1994). *The essential Jesus: Original sayings and earliest images*. Edison, NJ: Castle Books.

Dodd, C. H. (1969). *The parables of the kingdom*. London: Collins.

Doka, K. J. (1993). *Living with life-threatening illness: A guide for patients, their families, and caregivers*. San Francisco: Jossey-Bass.

———. (2009). *Counseling individuals with life-threatening illness*. New York: Springer Publishing Co.Driskill, J. D. (2007). Spirituality and the formation of pastoral counselors. In D. R. Bidwell & J. L. Marshall (Eds.), *The formation of pastoral counselors: Challenges and opportunities* (pp. 69–86). New York: Routledge.

Farran, C. J., Herth, K. A., & Popovich, J. M. (1995). *Hope and hopelessness: Critical clinical constructs*. Thousand Oaks, CA: Sage.

Herbert, R. (2006). *Living hope: A practical theology of hope for the dying*. Peterborough, UK: Epworth.

Hopkins, D. N. (2005). *Being human: Race, culture, and religion*. Minneapolis: Fortress.

Jensen, D. H. (2005). *Graced vulnerability: A theology of childhood*. Cleveland: Pilgrim.

Keshgegian, F. A. (2006). *Time for hope: Practices for living in today's world*. New York: Continuum.

Knauth, R. J. D. (2003). Alien, foreign resident. In T. D. Alexander & D. W. Baker (Eds.), *Dictionary of the Old Testament: Pentateuch* (pp. 26–33). Downers Grove: InterVarsity.

Lake, V. E. (2003). Children's stories of hope: Moving toward an expanded understanding of the world children live in. *Early Child Development and Care, 173*(5), 509–18.

Lester, A. D. (1995). *Hope in pastoral care and counseling*. Louisville: Westminster John Knox.

Maikranz, J. M., Steele, R. G., Dreyer, M. L., Stratman, A. C., and Bovaird, J. A. (2007). The relationship of hope and illness-related uncertainty to emotional adjustment and adherence among pediatric renal and liver transplant recipients. *Journal of Pediatric Psychology, 32*(5), 571–81.

Marshall, E. O. (2006). *Though the fig tree does not blossom: Toward a responsible theology of Christian hope*. Nashville: Abingdon.

Mauch, T. M. (1962). Sojourner. In *The interpreter's dictionary of the Bible, Vol. 4* (p. 397–98). Nashville: Abingdon.

Miller-McLemore, B. J. (2003). *Let the children come: Reimagining childhood from a christian perspective*. San Francisco: Jossey-Bass, 2003.

Moltmann, J. (1967). *Theology of hope: On the ground and the implications of a Christian eschatology* (J.W. Leitch, Trans.). New York: Harper and Row.

Roehlkepartain, E.C., Benson, P. L., Scales, P. C., Kimball, L., & Ebstyne King, P. (2008). With their own voices: A global exploration of how today's young people experience and think about spiritual development. Minneapolis, MN: Search Institute Center for Spiritual Development in Childhood and Adolescence.

Schlitz, M. M., Vieten, C., and Amorok, T. (2007). *Living deeply: The art and science of transformation in everyday life*. Oakland, CA: Noetic Books and New Harbinger Publications, Inc.

Schneiders, S. M. (1989). Spirituality in the academy. *Theological Studies, 50*, 676–97.

418   Duane R. Bidwell and Donald L. Batisky

Snyder, C. R. (1994). *The psychology of hope: You can get there from here.* New York: Free Press.

———. (2005). Measuring hope in children. In K. A. Moore & L. Lippmann (Eds.), *What do children need to flourish: Conceptualizing and measuring indicators of positive development* (pp. 61–73). New York: Springer Science and Business Media.

U.S. Renal Data System. (2008). *USRDS 2008 Annual Data Report: Atlas of Chronic Kidney Disease and End-Stage Renal Disease in the United States.* Bethesda, MD: National Institutes of Health, National Institute of Diabetes and Digestive and Kidney Diseases.

Way, P. (2005). *Created by God: Pastoral care for all god's people.* St. Louis: Chalice.

Westhelle, V. (2008). Liberation theology: A latitudinal perspective. In J. L. Walls (Ed.), *The Oxford handbook of eschatology* (pp. 311–27). Oxford: Oxford University Press.

White, M. (2007). *Maps of narrative practice.* New York: Norton.

21

What Children and Adolescents Think about Theodicy and How the Book of Job Can Help
The Case for Using Job in Children's Bibles

Eva Jenny Korneck

Research Goal and Main Thesis

What ideas of "theodicy" do children and young people have? The question of how to justify God in the face of innocent suffering has long been the domain of philosophers and theologians. Is this topic even suitable for children and young people? Does it hold any interest for them? In the following, I aim to show what religious pedagogical research has to say on the issue. The various positions—each supported by their own empirical data—are ambivalent. This has consequences for Christian education, and impacts the kind of material parents and teachers may want to use, especially for the design of children's Bibles. I believe that including the book of Job in children's Bibles can provide an appropriate framework in which the perspectives and needs of children can be taken more seriously. The ultimate goal always constitutes assisting children and young people with their experiences of suffering.

For a better understanding of this article, it commences by describing the special situation of Christian educational possibilities in Germany, so that the reader may integrate the following consulted research studies, which were held in public schools in the subject of Religious Education, in a better way. By exploring the topic of sorrow out of the perspective of children and teenagers and concluding possible consequences for the creation of the medium children's Bible, the article accosts to a broad readership, beyond the borders of the German-speaking world.

Christian Education in German Schools

In contrast to countries such as France and the USA, in which the constitution stipulates a strict separation between church and state, the situation in Germany is different. According to the national law of the Federal Republic of Germany, religion is a regular subject in public schools (German Constitution, 2000/2001). The responsibility is taken by the state as well as the church and religion is taught at schools in accordance with the fundamentals of the Christian churches (Ministerium für Kultus, Jugend und Sport Baden-Württemberg, 2004, p. 23). Therefore Christian Education is the business of church *and* state.

It is essentially structured as follows: While the contents of the formal curriculum for the subjects evangelic and catholic Religion are formulated by the particular churches, state-approved colleges educate teachers on the subject of Religious Education. After their state exam they obtain a church teaching allowance (*Vocatio* or rather *Missio*) and teach the subject with two lessons weekly in regular state schools.

A Theology for and by Children

Within a German context, the topic of "Kindertheologie" (i.e. theology for and by children) has been the subject of much recent debate and academic interest. Prompted by "doing philosophy with children," primarily from within an English speaking context, institutions of post secondary education have started to ask what a "theology for children, by children and with children" could be. Basic existential and theological questions were placed in the centre of dialogue with children. Children are not exempt when it comes to fear, joy, disappointment and loving care. Because of these experiences, they—no different than adults—ask about the final meaning underlying everything. In their own way, they are even more radical than adults, as they cannot be impressed by complicated philosophical phrases.

Children are serious partners in theological dialogue. They are able and willing to be pushed into experimental, creative, original and individual systematic thought, thus becoming "potential" theologians (".. . experimentell-kreativ, eigenständig und individuell zu systematisch relevantem Denken herausfordern zu lassen und so selbst zu ‚potentiellen' Theologinnen und Theologen zu werden") (Büttner & Schreiner, 2008, p. 8). It would be a mistake to underestimate this ability. Their answers can often open new perspectives for their adult counterparts. Theology with children is a process of religious education where first and second naivité influence each other ("Kindertheologie . . . ist ein religiös bildender Prozess, indem sich erste und zweite Naivität wechselwirkend gegenseitig beeinflussen") (p. 8). The vast amount of literature that exists on this topic shows the intensity of research done in this area, especially with empirical surveys.

Most religious education leaders agree that asking questions is the most important methodological tool for this task. A true question defines itself by refusing to be silenced by an easy answer. On the contrary, a true question continues to stimulate reflection and produce many more questions in response and opposition. A quick and easy answer, on the other hand, only leads to stagnation of thought. We must work towards keeping children alert in their questioning, furthering the process of thinking and remaining partners in dialogue. Such partners cannot be afraid to continually re-examine their own set theories and critically reflect on long held positions and presuppositions.

The question of suffering is one of these "large questions." Why do individuals have to suffer without cause if a good and almighty God exists? How do children and young people approach this topic?

Theodicy

In 1710, G. W. Leibniz (1744) coined the term "theodicy" which originally referred to the justification of God in the face of a reality shaped by the experience of suffering without human cause. The problem of theodicy arises out of the logical conflict between two attributes of God: "his goodness" and "his omnipotence." This conflict was artfully expressed by the Greek poet Epikur (341–270 BC):

Either God wants to remove evil and cannot
or he can and does not want to
or he cannot and does not want to
or he can and wants to.
If he wants to and cannot, then he is weak—this is not God
If he can and does not want to, then he is begrudging—this
too is foreign to God.
If he does not want to and cannot, then he is weak and begrudging—and not God.
Yet if he can and wants to, and this alone is worthy of God,
where does evil come from and why does he not take it away?

The history of theology and philosophy has provided us with numer-ous answers to this question. Many of the answers tend to either limit God's omnipotence, his goodness, or the suffering experienced by humanity.

How do children and adolescents deal with this issue?

Children experience suffering

Children suffer the harshest consequences of military conflict and natural disaster. Even in peaceful countries of Western Europe, such the Federal Republic of Germany, there are many factors that lead to the suffering of children:

- an increasing number of children live in poverty

- children increasingly suffer illness, especially chronic illness

- children suffer from inadequate or absent relationships

- children live in an environment that fills them with fear

- children today live with the awareness that their future is being threatened (Oberthür, 2006, pp. 44–45).

In addition, the life of each child—as with adults—is never protected from unexpected and unavoidable blows of fate, such as sickness and death. Children are by no means more isolated than adults from the suffering that each life contains—but they are very often less protect-ed, because they do not yet have many strategies to absorb and react to suffering.

Children are faced with suffering. Individual experiences with suffering can thus be used as a starting point for reflection on theodicy.

The goal for religious education and theological reflection should be acquiring greater competence in dealing with suffering.

But how do children connect suffering with God? Do they believe that God is somehow responsible for what they have encountered or encounter? Do they expect God's help?

Two Different Approaches

A) Empirical Study A

In an extensive survey (Gerichhausen, 1993) of twelve rural and urban primary schools in north western Germany, children were asked "What I would ask God . . .," with no further thematic specification. The 2,634 questions collected were subsequently analysed and classified according to strict categories. The result of this survey showed that the deep need of children to ask theological questions increases during their primary education and moves more and more towards questions of suffering and theodicy. More than 56 percent of all questions concerned suffering. Almost half of all questions (46 percent) can be read as a reflection on theodicy. Questions about suffering within an immediate personal context are more frequent than reflections on indirect suffering (i.e. as communicated in the media) by a ratio of 67 to 33 percent Regarding the question posed above, we can refer to this study and give a clear answer: Yes, children connect experiences of suffering, especially those from their immediate context, with God within the parameters of theodicy. They ask about the "why" of suffering. This "why" is addressed to God. As the proponents of a theology with children suggest, children show great interest in the large questions of human existence, such as suffering, while searching for ultimate meaning. Religious education should consequently be interested in supporting these questions already at an early age and not wait until later stages of development, at which the young adult seems "mature enough," as is currently done in most German curricula. At this point, the disappointment over the absence of divine help may have already become a breaking point (Nipkow, 1988), leading to the loss of faith in God. Primary education in Germany has thus recently engaged the topic of theodicy with renewed interest.

B) Empirical Study B

A second recent study on the issue of children and suffering has proved an irritation to the above mentioned conclusions (Ritter, Hanisch, Nestler & Gramzow, 2006). A survey was taken in schools in Nuremberg and Leipzig that collected data from 392 children and young people aged 8 to 18. They were read a story in class dealing with a young boy suffering from cancer. In response they engaged in independent dialogue about the story, guided by several thematic questions.

Five basic tendencies regarding the question of theodicy became evident in these conversations:

The participants

- do not mention the issue (*the vast majority*)
- reflect on the issue in passing without mentioning grave problems
- resolve the issue by giving suffering some kind of meaning
- turn away from their faith (*happened on two occasions*)
- seem to find other issues more important

From the fact that the children and young people in this study seldom addressed the issue of theodicy, the authors of this study conclude that they do not connect God and suffering. This is a very different outcome than the consensus opinion and study A!

With their analysis, the authors believe that they are able to show that children and young people regardless of age, gender and place of residence no longer consider God to be almighty and merciful in the traditional sense. Instead, they refer back to American studies in religious sociology (Smith & Lundquist, 2005) and propose a kind of "mainstream religion" in Germany. This moral-therapeutic deism forgoes the omnipotence of God in favour of a "nice God."

The Necessity of the Omnipotence Idea to Handle Sorrow

Any successful interaction with theodicy that might increase competence in dealing with suffering must include the issue of omnipotence. Suffering in this world is limited in its temporal scope and its effectiveness by the power of God (Ritter, Hanisch, Nestler & Gramzow, 2006, pp.17–18).

The predication of omnipotence only occurs on the fringes of biblical tradition, yet it occurs primarily in situations of challenge and oppression by foreign powers; this oppression leads to an increased trust in God's capabilities. Stated forcefully: trust in God's rule intensifies in extreme situations; it then becomes a confession of God's omnipotence (Feldermeir, 1997, p. 37). God's power is mightier than the power of suffering.

Omnipotence is not a theoretical description of God's being, it is a veto against the apparent reality that suggests that not God, but rather suffering and death wield ultimate power in this world. Omnipotence in this context means: the powers of this world do not hold ultimate sway, but rather God who gives life to the dead and calls what does not exist into being (Rom 4, 17) (Schoberth, 1997, pp. 43–67). It would thus be a consequence for Christian education that God's omnipotence cannot be abandoned in favour of the kindness of God.

The Intervention of Omnipotence and Kindness in Children's Bibles

Do we have to blame religious instruction for creating and relaying this one-sided portrait of God? If we survey material for Christian education of children we notice that the topic of God and suffering or theodicy is absent for the most part.[1] This coincides with many children's Bibles published in the last few decades; they hardly contain any stories that have problems in conveying the image of a "nice" God. All throughout, the portrait of God is very homogeneous, if not to say one-sided. If challenging stories such as Cain and Able or the sacrifice of Isaac are included at all, they are "cleansed" from the outset and given an interpretation that does not provoke further thought in any way.

The Appearance of the Book of Job in Children's Bibles

Older Children's Bibles

In reviewing older editions of children's Bibles one finds the book of Job quite frequently. Up to the first decades of the twentieth century

---

1. Lesson plans for this subject exist—and there are exceptions—almost only for secondary education. Recently this seems to be changing.

it often existed in children's and school Bibles. In older editions of the Bible, Job stands for an example of abasing the self in suffering. As one example, the Kratzensteiner Bible of the year 1737 (see illustration below) is mentioned in this case, which clarifies this for such a long time indisputable interpretation of the book of Job, in the illustration signature „Hiobs stille seyn im Leiden / Kan uns zur Gedult bereiten" ("Job's silence in suffering / may prepare us to be patient").

In the text component on the opposite side it is assured by question and answer, that the reader gets to know Job exclusively as the silent sufferer, as the biblical text in chapter one introduces him. They are not introduced to the screaming, complaining revolution-izer of the remaining chapters 2–42. In consideration of the strong overbalance of these chapters, in which Job is not silent anymore, it is a displacement or rather falsification of the original, in favor of a repressive pedagogical quintessence, which educates children as well as adults to a so called "sacrificial lamb mentality." Exemplary for it is the verse of the chant, with which the disquisition of the book of Job finishes:

> Selig, ja selig, wer willig ertraget
> dieser Zeit Leiden, Verachtung und Streit,
> welches nach dieser Vergänglichkeit
> pfleget mit sich zu bringen die ewige Freud.
> Selig, wer hier was um Jesum erduldet,
> droben im Himmel wirds doppelt verschuldet.
> Blessedly, yes blessedly, who willingly bears
> This time's suffering, contumeliousness and conflict,
> Which after this caducity
> Administer to implicate the eternal delight
> Blessedly, who suffers here anything for Jesus
> Up in the sky it will be doubly compensated

Children and Picture Bible of Christoph Heinrich Kratzenstein
(Erfurt 1773)

Modern Children's Bibles

In children's Bibles of the last few decades, the book of Job appears rather seldom. A more detailed research is just being completed; still this article is going to share some preliminary results. An analysis of the extensive children's Bible collection "Regine Schindler" at the theological department of the University of Zurich in September 2009 resulted in the following picture: Only 15 out of 111 existing exemplars of German speaking overall views (NT and OT) or compendiums of Old Testament stories from the last 70 years contain descriptions of the book of Job. That makes a percentage of 6.9 percent. In summary, it can be said that, in the last decades, the book in general has been paid little attention in published children's Bibles.

This analysis is strictly quantitative. Yet, by inspecting individual Bibles, it became quite apparent that they contain very different interpretations of the subject of Job. Accordingly, some authors attempt to summarize the 42 chapters of the Book of Job shortly on a double page (Westhoff & Birkenstock, 2006, pp. 92–93), whereas others write comparatively long versions, which concede much more space to the book (Oberthür & Burrichter, 2004, pp. 129–40).

The distinct versions also differ in the varying choice of pictures, which are emphasizing and forming the interpretation. (Illustration of the suffering, submissive or accusing Job or rather of the recovered Job; Job and the friends, Job's wife, Job and God, and so on). Often, there is a selection of headings and sub-headings, which reveal how strongly the children Bibles differ in their chosen interpretation. Still, without penetrating too deeply into the text analysis, one can conclude that the title "Job-the indulgent" (Inkinow & Briswalter, 2008) conveys a different meaning than "Job in a struggle with God" (Merckel-Braun & Arndt, 2006)

In regard of the perspective of God's image there is a huge difference if and, if yes, how the prolog is affiliated[2]. But especially the interpretations of the speeches of God decide, in my opinion, strongly about what is understood and remembered by the reader. This requires a more extensive and precise analysis.

Reasons for the Gathering of Resistive Stories in Current Children's Bibles

But why should children be confronted with stories that transmit a rather uncomfortable image of God? Wouldn't talking about the almighty, destructive God scare them? They might be overburdened by the questions that these stories cause, even for adults; questions even grown-ups are unable to answer instantly. Isn't "The Dear Lord" the quintessence of our didactic approach to simplify God's complex scriptural image and, therefore, perfectly fine for our children?

When I was working at a publishing house of children's books, I received an e-mail from an angry mother, who had bought the publisher's children's Bible for her daughter. Ever since the girl found out about the story of Abraham being ordered, by God, to immolate his son, she was no longer able to sleep calmly. The mother wondered how someone could be as irresponsible as to include such a story in a children's Bible.

2. All the here listed children Bibles work with the prolog; only Westhof & Birkenstock (2006) constitute an exception.

Surely, that is a legitimate concern. Children are sensitive and in need of protection. Thus it is important to offer them a safe setting in which they can have their own experiences with the variety of the biblical texts. Together with parents and educators they can make a first acquaintance and express their questions in a confident atmosphere. In addition, there clearly is an interest of many children in just these "dark" stories.[3] Children find themselves and their life situations in these stories. They realize that these texts have something to do with their life (Weth, 2003, p. 155). Is it our right to simply defraud these stories? There are good reasons not to deprive children of these "dark stories" of the Bible. By considering and differentiating the stories precisely under exegetical principles, it becomes clear why (pp. 156).

Texts that cause fear. The description of a hopeless situation activates fear in the audience. Nevertheless, stories such as the immolation of Isaac, the flood and the exodus from Egypt end with the liberation from fear by God, because, fundamentally, they are supposed to be rescue stories. "According to this, the descriptions of horror belong directly to the aspiration story of the Old Testament (Weth, 2003, p. 157)," because where there is no misery, there is no need for rescue. We can assume that children's experiences with reality are already (or rather especially) containing sufficient contradictories and distressing moments to understand situations like that.

To talk about God as the one who is in control of hopeless situations and who is able to turn them around is an important task that we are not allowed to avoid by simply hiding the misery. Children will, and justifiably so—when they are becoming older at least—classify biblical stories as meaningless and "childish," if they are not able to describe their reality comprehensively or even just euphemistically. In the stories that cause fear, children take part in the whole range of human experience, which people in the Old Testament have made with God and which children already know, based on their everyday life.

Texts that contain violence. It cannot be denied that especially in the Old Testament a lot of stories contain violence. "In more than 6000 passages we read of destruction and extinction of entire peoples. In

---

3. After a girl was read Genesis 22, she said: "That is my favorite story! Because it has got such a good ending!" Here it is about an occurrence, which Irmgard Weth (1994, p. 28) experienced and described.

this book, nearly 1000 times God is introduced as the God of anger, of revenge and of the court (Weth, 2003, p. 158; Schwager, 1986, pp. 58, 65, 70)." The description of the conquest of Israel in the book of Josua is described bloodily. Nowadays, the necessity of the levy execution appears as unintelligible. Therefore the question is, shall one introduce an – similar to cinema films with corresponding contents—age limit for these biblical texts? In this connection, it is important that God is on the side of the weak, poor and oppressed ones in Israel. The stories are reflections of someone's own experience of helplessness and suffering. They tell, in denomination of the own disability, in a continued history of the suffering Israel, how God takes away the fear of dying. Without him, all would have been lost. Thereby the protagonists of the stories are described as victims as well as offenders, who cause their situation on their own; they have to be rescued of an as "told confession" (Weth, 2003, p. 160) so to speak.

A discussion with a first grade class in a primary school with incessant input by the pupils on the topic "always against the little" made obvious to me how especially the topic "violence towards weaker people" is relevant among children. Although children are the weaker ones in doing so, according to their definitions, they still have got a very clear understanding for the fact that violence can proceed from them, i.e., they can be victims as well as offenders. They, for instance, told about incidents, in which the first grade was maltreated by the fourth graders or about conflicts among siblings.

Would we fade out biblical texts that contain violence for children, we would once again take away possibilities of identification with situations in their life that we would not be able to prevent them from experiencing anyway. However, I think it is very helpful to link the "cinema visit" to parental guidance and to transfer that idea to the use of scriptural stories.

Reasons for Including the Story of Job in Children's Bibles

Texts that talk of the despair of God. Finally, texts in which the suffering proceeds from God, in which he appears as enemy and the sufferer must doubt about him, do not really seem to be suitable for children, do they? They do not only result in a logical-indissoluble, but rather in an emotional contradiction to the conventional image of God. The book of Job questions exactly this contradiction. The Bible chooses a form, which opens for children an entry to the theme: It tells a *story* here. And in this story, Job does something very simple: he addresses his complaint to God. He finds a way of expression and an attachment figure. Right here a way is proposed how children can handle sorrow and doubt as well. In the end, Job retains "in defiant confidence" "against God with God" until he changes the situation. That really is an imposition for our belief, which can and shall challenge us with regard to our own praxis. However, it surely is no danger we have to save our children from.

Conclusions

If we are interested in conveying Christian modes of interpreting suffering, we will not be able to avoid dealing with the "dark sides" of God. A renewed, intentional, and increased focus on challenging biblical stories would be congruous with the results of both studies, as different as their outcomes are! It would be congruous as well with the just shown exegetical results of resistive stories of the Old Testament, especially the book of Job.

Any successful interaction with the issue of theodicy, which might be used as the basis for further faith development in which the child will inevitably be confronted by suffering, can only occur if we do not avoid the topic (*as shown in study A*) and if we succeed in relating two aspects—kindness and omnipotence—in the context of theodicy (*as suggested by study B*).

The goal would be to avoid creating barriers for children with ready made answers and well intentioned interpretations. We cannot leave children alone when they search for answers in this area. Religious education can provide a protective framework, in which questions may be raised, questions that arise from the tension between God's goodness *and* his omnipotence. In honest dialogue, the educator should not put down any position, but motivate all participants to think further. Like Job, children are able to ask questions. The discursive character of the book invites its readers to enter into the process of "doing theology."

References

Ministerium für Kultus, Jugend und Sport Baden-Württemberg. (2004). Bildungsplan für die Grundschule (Formal curriculum for the primary school). *Kultus und*

Unterricht – Amtsblatt des Ministeriums für Kultus, Jugend und Sport Baden-Württemberg, Lehrplanheft 1/2004 (Cult and Class- Official Register of the Administration of Cult, Adolescence and Sports Baden-Württemberg, Curricular Booklet 1/2004).

Büttner, G., and Schreiner, M. (2008). Im spannungsfeld systematisch-theologischer wissenschaft und kindlicher intuition: Mit kindern grundaussagen des Christlichen glaubens deuten. einleitende überlegungen. (In the area of conflict of systematic-theological science and childish intuition: Interpret general statements of the Christian belief with children. Incipient thoughts). In G. Buttner and M. Schreiner (Eds.), *Jahrbuch für kindertheologie, sonderband, "Manche sachen glaube ich nicht." mit kindern das glaubensbekenntnis erschließen (Yearbook for children's theology, register book, "Some things I do not believe." To develop with children the Credo)* (pp. 7–14). Stuttgart: Calwer.

Deutschland Grundgesetz. (2001). Deutschland. Sonderausgabe, 36., neubearbeitete auflage, Stand: 15. Oktober 2000 (German constitution/ Germany. Special edition, 36, newly edited, updated: 15. October 2000). Munich.

Feldmeier, R. (1997). Nicht übermacht noch omnipotenz (Neither superiority nor omnipotence). In W. H. Ritter, R. Feldmeier, W. Schoberth and G. Altner, (Eds.), *Der Allmächtige (The Almighty One)* (2nd edition, pp. 13–42). Göttingen, Germany: Vandenhoeck&Ruprecht.

Gerichhausen, S. (1993). *Kinder fragen nach dem leid. theodizeeproblem im grundschulalter? (Children ask for the suffering. The problem of theodicy in the primary school age?).* Unpublished examination work, exhibited at the University of Cologne, Cologne, Germany.

Inkinow, D., and Briswalter, M. (2008). *Die Bibel für kinder (The Bible for children).* Munich, Germany: Deutscher Taschenbuch.

Kratzenstein, C. H. (1773). *Kinder- und Bilderbibel (Children's and picture Bible).* Erfurt, Germany: Sauerländer.

Leibniz, G. W. (1774). *Essais de théodicée – la liberté de l'homme et l'origine du mal.* Leipzig, Germany: Suhrkamp.

Merckel-Braun, M., and Arndt, J. (2006). *Elberfelder kinderbibel (Elberfelder children's Bible).* Wuppertal, Germany: Brockhaus.

Nipkow, K. E. (1988). *Erwachsenwerden ohne Gott. Gotteserfahrungen im lebenslauf (To grow up without God. Experiences with God in biography),* 2nd edition. Munich: Kaiser.

Oberthür, R., and Burrichter, R. (2004). *Die Bibel für kinder und alle im haus (The Bible for children and everyone at home).* Munich, Germany: Kösel-Verlag.

Oberthür, R. (2006). Kinder fragen nach leid und Gott: Lernen mit der Bibel im religionsunterricht (Children ask for suffering and God: Learning with the Bible in religious education), 5th edition. Munich: Kösel.

Ritter, W. H., Hanisch, H., Nestler, E., and Gramzow, C. (2006). Leid und Gott – aus der perspektive von kindern und jugendlichen (Suffering and God – out of the perspective of children and teenagers). Göttingen, Germany: Vandenhoeck & Ruprecht.

Schoberth, W. (1997). Gottes allmacht und das leiden (God's almightiness and suffering). In W. H. Ritter, R. Feldmeier, W. Schoberth, and G. Altner (Eds.), *Der Allmächtige (The Almighty One)* (2nd ed., pp. 43–67). Göttingen, Germany: Vandenhoeck & Ruprecht.

Schwager, R. (1986). Brauchen wir einen sündenbock? Gewalt und erlösung in den biblischen schriften (Do we need a scapegoat? Violence and salvation in the biblical writings), 2nd edition. Munich: Kösel.

Smith, C., and Lundquist, M. (2005). *Soul searching. The religious and spiritual life of American teenagers.* New York: Oxford University Press.

Westhof, J. and Birkenstock, A. K. (2006). Die 3-minuten-kinderbibel (The three-minute children's Bible), Neukirchen-Vluyn, Germany: Aussaat.

Weth, I. (1994). Wenn euch kinder fragen: Biblisches erzählen heute (If children ask you: Biblical telling nowadays), 2nd edition. Neukirchen-Vluyn, Germany: Aussaat.

———. (2003). Die dunklen seiten des Alten Testaments: Zumutung nicht nur für kinder (The dark sides of the Old Testament—Not only an unreasonable demand for children). In G. Adam, R. Lachmann, and R. Schindler (Eds.), *Das AT in Kinderbibeln (The OT in children's Bibles)* (äpp. 153–70). Zurich: TVZ Theologischer.

Contributors

Christa Adams is currently serving in children's ministry at Fellowship Bible Church in Rogers, Arkansas. She also edits and formats curriculum for World Vision. Christa plans to start graduate school in Fall 2011 to pursue a Master's Degree in counseling with an emphasis in play therapy.

Holly Catterton Allen (PhD, Talbot School of Theology, Biola University) serves as Professor of Christian Ministries and Director of the Child and Family Studies Program at John Brown University, in Siloam Springs, Arkansas. She edited *Nurturing Children's Spirituality: Christian Perspectives and Best Practices*, the collection of papers from the 2006 Children's Spirituality Conference: Christian Perspectives (Cascade, 2008). E-mail: hallen@jbu.edu

Donald L. Batisky, MD, is Associate Professor of Pediatrics at the Emory University School of Medicine and a board-certified pediatric nephrologist at Children's Healthcare of Atlanta. He can be reached via e-mail at dbatisk@emory.edu.

Jennifer Beste (PhD, Yale University) is Associate Professor of Theological Ethics at Xavier University. E-mail: bestej@xavier.edu

Duane R. Bidwell, PhD, is Associate Professor of Practical Theology, Spiritual Care and Counseling at Claremont School of Theology. He also serves as Senior Staff Clinician and Supervisor at The Clinebell Institute for Pastoral Counseling and Psychotherapy in Claremont. He can be reached via e-mail at dbidwell@cst.edu

Melodie Bissell (MDiv, Tyndale Seminary, Toronto) is President and Founder of Winning Kids Inc., and the National Children's Facilitator for The Christian and Missionary Alliance in Canada. E-mail: mbis-sell@winningkidsinc.ca

Dean G. Blevins (PhD, Claremont School of Theology) serves as Professor of Christian Education at Nazarene Theological Seminary. E-mail: dgblevins@nts.edu.

William P. Brown (PhD, Emory University) serves as Professor of Old Testament at Columbia Theological Seminary. This chapter is based on his plenary session presentation at the 2009 conference. E-mail: BrownB@ctsnet.edu

Marcia J. Bunge is the W.C. Dickmeyer Professor and Director of The Child in Religion and Ethics Project at Valparaiso University. Email: Marcia.Bunge@valpo.edu

Grant Burns (MA, Christian Formation and Ministry, Wheaton College) serves as youth pastor at Immanuel Presbyterian Church in Warrenville, Illinois.

David M. Csinos is a doctoral student in practical theology at Emmanuel College of Victoria University in the University of Toronto. In addition to his book, *Children's Ministry that Fits*, he has written a chapter for *Shaped by God* and articles for several journals, including *Religious Education, International Journal of Children's Spirituality*, and *Journal of Childhood and Religion*. E-mail: davecsinos@yahoo.com

Elizabeth Dodd is a PhD Candidate in Theology, Faculty of DivinitySelwyn College, University of Cambridge. E-mail: esd26@cam.ac.uk

James Riley Estep, Jr. (PhD, Trinity Evangelical Divinity School) serves as Professor of Christian Education at Lincoln Christian University, in Lincoln, Illinois. E-mail: jestep@lincolnchristian.edu.

Kelly S. Flanagan (PhD, Pennsylvania State University) serves as Assistant Professor and Program Director for the Psy.D. Clinical Psychology Program at Wheaton College. E-mail: Kelly.Flanagan@wheaton.edu.

Kara Jenkins graduated with her bachelor's degree in Children and Family Ministries from John Brown University in 2009. She currently works as a nanny and writes curriculum for Ministry-to-Children. com in Louisville, Kentucky.

Eva Jenny Korneck, Dipl. Theol. geb. 1973 in Germany, has studied theology at Frankfurt University and Heidelberg University. She has worked with children in German Primary schools for several years and is presently teaching theology at Karlsruhe University of Education. Her dissertation project focuses on research on the subject of the Book of Job and children. E-mail: jennykorneck@gmx.de

Kevin E. Lawson earned an MA in Christian education at Trinity Evangelical Divinity School and an EdD in educational administration from the University of Maine. He serves as Director of PhD and EdD programs in Educational Studies and Professor of Christian Education at Talbot School of Theology, Biola University, in La Mirada, CA, and the editor of the *Christian Education Journal*. E-mail: kevin.lawson@ biola.edu

Rebecca L. Loveall (MA, Wheaton College) is a missionary in Guatemala and Project Manager of Escuela Integrada schools. E-mail: Rebecca.laces@gmail.com.

Scottie May (PhD, Trinity Evangelical Divinity School, Deerfield, IL) serves as Associate Professor of Christian Formation and Ministry at Wheaton College, Wheaton, IL. E-mail: Scottie.may@wheaton.edu.

Jill Meek graduated from John Brown University in 2009 with a degree in Children and Family Ministries. She now lives in Washington DC with her husband Craig, and is the Director of Children's Ministries at the National Presbyterian Church.

Jennifer Haddad Mosher holds a ThM from St. Vladimir's Orthodox Theological Seminary and is an independent scholar. E-mail: jenny mosher@mac.com

Catherine Posey earned her PhD in Curriculum and Instruction with a specialization in Children's Literature, from The Pennsylvannia State University. She currently teaches adjunct for Shasta College, Redding, California. E-mail: kate.posey@gmail.com

Eugene C. Roehlkepartain is executive vice president at Search Institute, Minneapolis, Minnesota, a nonprofit organization dedicated to discovering what kids need to succeed in their families, schools, and communities (www.search-institute.org). He is currently pursuing his PhD in Education, Curriculum, and Instruction from the University of Minnesota. E-mail: gener@search-institute.org

Sharon Warkentin Short (PhD, Talbot School of Theology, Biola University) has served as an educational ministry staff member in three different churches, an adjunct instructor in a Christian college, and a consultant for a Christian curriculum publisher. Currently she is pursuing a career as an online college professor and is working on various freelance writing projects. E-mail: sharonwshort@aol.com

Katie Stemp (MA, Christian Formation and Ministry, Wheaton College) is currently pursuing a masters degree in counseling.

La Verne Tolbert (PhD, Talbot School of Theology) is Director of the Society for Children's Spirituality: Christian Perspectives, and President of Teaching Like Jesus Ministries, Inc. An adjunct professor in the graduate school at Azusa Pacific University, she assists the Department of children and Family Services and the mentoring program KidSave to provide mentors and ultimately place children into permanent adoptive families. E-mail: ltolbert@earthlink.net.

Ann M. Trousdale (EdD, The University of Georgia) serves as Associate Professor at Louisiana State University, and Deacon at First United Metholdist Church in Baton Rouge, Louisiana. E-mail: atrous@lsu.edu

Karen Marie Yust (ThD, Harvard Divinity School) serves as Associate Professor of Christian Education at Union Presbyterian Seminary. E-mail: kmyust@upsem.edu